AF517174

Historians and Historiography of Northeast India

Historians and Historiography of Northeast India

Professor H.K. Barpujari Centenary Publication

Edited by
J. B. Bhattacharjee

AKANSHA PUBLISHING HOUSE
NEW DELHI • GUWAHATI • VISAKHAPATNAM

AKANSHA PUBLISHING HOUSE
4649-B/21, Ansari Road
Darya Ganj, New Delhi - 110 002
Ph.: 23263193 / 9811582579 / 09435116718
Fax: 011-23263193
Email: ektabooks@yahoo.com
www.akanshapublishinghouse.com

Historians and Historiography of Northeast India

First Published 2012
ISBN 978-81-8370-320-8

PRINTED IN INDIA

Published by Akansha Publishing House, New Delhi and Printed at Harmain Offset, Delhi.

HERAMBA KANTA BARPUJARI
Born : 31st August 1912
Died : 16th April 2002

Contents

Preface

The Birth Centenary of Professor H.K. Barpujari is an appropriate occasion to pay homage not only to the memory of that 'Doyen of Historians of Northeast India' but also to the entire galaxy of historians whose works earned a legitimate place for Northeast in the field of Indian historiography. That history had through the ages enjoyed a place close to the heart of the creative literary talents of the Northeast is amply borne out not only by the works like *Kâlikâ Purâna*, *Jogini Tantra* and *Brahmavaivartya Purâna* or the royal chronicles like *Râjamâlâ* of Tripura, *Cheithârol Kumbâbâ* of Manipur, *Darangrâj Vamsâvali* of Assam and *Sivavamsâvali* of Coach Behar but also by the large number of *Buranji* in Ahom and Assamese, *Puthi* in Assamese and Bengali, *Panchali* in Bengali and *Puyâ* in Manipuri, which were authored both by official and non-official writers and the host of songs and ballads on important events or the feelings, hopes and aspirations of the people composed by unknown poets and bards (e.g. *Sonâdhaner Geet* of Jayantia or *Gosâinimangal* of Cooch Behar) preserving facts that essentially belong to history. The pre-literate communities in the region also had various traditional methods of orally preserving data for history through folklore and ritual practices. A sense of pride in own history is common to the communities in the region, and history is their strongest tool in the contemporary quest for identity.

The modern historiography of the Northeast could not immediately snap its linkage to the long tradition of history writing, primarily because of the popular bond of that tradition with the communities. The slow and gradual modernization of the early chronicler tradition is noticed in the continuity of the earlier format of presentation for a long time even in the modern vernacular historiography. Assam was annexed by the British in 1826 and within three years of Assam's annexation came out Haliram Dhekial Phukan's *Âsâm Buranji Bâ Âsâm Desher Kathâ* (Calcutta, 1829) in Bengali. This was the beginning, but a good number of modern historical works, besides that of Haliram Dhekial Phukan, had already been published in Assamese, Bengali and other local languages before Sir Edward Gait's *A History of Assam* (London, 1906) in English that was indeed a landmark in modern historiography of Northeast India. Kashiram Tamuli Phukan's *Asam Buranji* updated till 1833 (Calcutta, 1844) was possibly the first modern *Buranji* in Assamese. On the other hand, Gunabhiram Barua's *Asam Buranji* (Calcutta, 1884) was a great modern work in the standard of Nineteenth Century Indian vernacular historiography. Beginning with geographical description and the land and people, the treatment between the chapters was chronological and thematic. Besides the Ahom kings, it also gave brief accounts of other dynasties who formerly ruled in Assam. Like Dhekial Phukan's *Buranji*, it too had an expanded title, *Asam Buranji Arthât Asam Deshar Itihâs,* perhaps to differentiate history from chronicle. This was followed by Padmanath Gohain Barua's *Asomar Buranji* (North Lakhimpur, 1899) which, though primarily written as a textbook for schools, began with a brief chapter on the pre-Ahom period, including the Baro Bhuyans, then dealt with the Ahom period in several chapters, and thereafter, covered the neighouring kingdoms like Koch, Chutiya, Kachari, Jaintia, Srihatta and Manipur, and finally, the rise of British power and the hill tribes who were brought within British Assam. A close look at Gait's work will show that the broad outline of his book had already emerged between the works of Gunabhiram Barua and Padmanath Gohain Barua.

Umesh Chandra Ray's *Sikimer Itihâs* (Calcutta, 1875), Kailash Chandra Singha's *Râjmâlâ Bâ Tripurâr Itibritta* (Calcutta, 1876), Tarini Prasad Sen's *Bijni Râjvamsa* (Goalpara, 1878), Maulavi Mohammad Ahmmad's *Srihatta Darpan* (Calcutta, 1886) and Mohini Mohan Das Gupta's *Srihatter Itihâs* (Calcutta, 1903) in Bengali and Haodeijam Chaitanya Singh's *Manipur Itihâs* (Imphal, 1890) in Manipuri were also published before Gait's *A History of Assam* (1906). The historiography in vernacular languages continued its youthful stride of the renaissance era for rediscovery of the region's past even after the publication of Gait's book. The remarkable works published before India's independence included Suryya Kumar Bhuyan's *Ahomar Din* (Jorhat, 1918) and Hiteswar Barbarua's *Ahomar Din* (1925) in Assamese, Upendra Chandra Guha's *Kâchhârer Itibritta* (Dhaka, 1910), Achyutcharan Choudhury Tattvanidhi's *Srihatter Itibritta* (Calcutta, 1910), Samarendra Chandra Debbarma's *Tripurâr Smriti* (Agartala, 1927), Jogendra Chandra Gupta's *Âsâmer Itihâs* (Calcutta, 1929), Kali Prasanna Sen's *Sri Râjmâlâ* (Agartala, 1930) and Khan Saheb Amanatulla Ahmad's *Kuchbehârer Itihâs* (Coach Behar, 1936) in Bengali, P. Parijat Singh's *Manipur Purâbritta* (Imphal, 1917), K. Kaomacha's *Manipur Itibritti* (Imphal, 1938), M. Jhulan Singh's *Manipur Itihâs* (Imphal, 1939), Atombapu Sharma's *Manipur Itihâs* (Imphal, 1940), W. Wumjao Singh's *Manipur Itihâs* (Imphal, 1946) and R.K. Sanahal's *Manipur Itihâs* (Imphal, 1947) in Manipuri, B.K. Sarma Roy's *Ka Histori Jong Ka Ri Khasi* (Shillong, 1914), Joel Gatphoh's *Ka Histori Ki Syiem Synteng Ha Ka Jingshisha* (Shillong, 1923) and Homiwell Lyngdoh's *Ki Syiem Khasi Bad Synteng* (Shillong, 1938) in Khasi, and Jobang D. Marak's *A'chik Kata* (Tura, 1930) in Garo.

The foundation of Kâmarupa Aunusandhân Samiti (KAS) at Guwahati (1912) and publication of Padmanath Bhattacharyya Vidyavinod's *Kâmarupa Sâsanâvali* (Rangpur, 1931), in the meantime, are important milestones in the progress of historical research in the Northeast. Kâmarupa Aunusandhân Samiti launched the publication of *Journal of Assam Research Society* (*JARS*), the first ever historical research journal of the region, in 1933, providing a window to the scholars to publish their studies. The Department of Historical and Antiquarian Studies (DHAS), Govt. of Assam, under the stewardship of S.K. Bhuyan, played a historic role in bringing the region into focus by collecting, preserving and publishing the pre-colonial historical works. The literary organizations like Asam Sâhitya Sabhâ (1917) and Srihatta Sâhitya Parishat (1920) also immensely contributed to the historical studies through literature and by publishing articles on aspects of history in their respective journals.

Gait's work in English was followed by the publication of E.F. Sandys' *History of Tripura* (Calcutta, 1915), N.N. Vasu's *Social History of Kamarupa* (Calcutta, 1922-1928), S.K. Bhuyan's *Early British Relations with Assam* (Shillong, 1928), K.L. Barua's *Early History of Kamarupa* (Shillong, 1933), S.C. Ghosal's *History of Cooch Behar* (an English version of *Kuchbehârer Itihâs*; Cooch Behar, 1942) and A.C. Banerjee's *Eastern Frontier of British India* (Calcutta, 1943) to take historiography of the Northeast to the dawn of India's independence. The post-independence era is remarkable for proliferation of publications, particularly after the establishment of the Gauhati University. The department of Assamese in the new University, with Banikanta Kakati and Birinchi Kumar Barua as senior faculty, both of whom had distinguished themselves as historians by their significant contributions in history of Assam, besides in Assamese language and literature, took keen interest in historical research and the first three doctorates of the University from that department, namely, Maheswar Neog, Satyendranath Sarma and Prafulladatta Goswami, worked on subjects that were of immense relevance to history. The department of history shoot into prominence after H.K. Barpujari joined as Professor in 1963. In the meantime, the publication of Banikanta Kakati's *The Mother Goddess Kamakhya* (Gauhati, 1948), Rajmohan Nath's *The Background of Assamese Culture* (Gauhati, 1948), S.K. Bhuyan's *The Anglo-Assamese Relations* (Gauhati, 1949), Suniti Kumar Chatterji's *Kirata-Jana-Kriti* (Calcutta, 1951), B.K. Barua's *A Cultural History of Assam* (Gauhati, 1951), R.M. Lahiri's *The Annexations of Assam* (Calcutta, 1954), and P.C. Choudhury's *History of Civilisation of the People of Assam* (Gauhati, 1959), amongst others, had laid the foundation for further research, while Barpujari's *Assam : In the Days of the Company* (1963) dawned a new era of scientific methodology in modern historiography.

Edward Albert Gait (1863-1950) was undoubtedly the first great modern historian of Northeast India, and the twentieth century historiography in the region dawned in his hands. Besides the pioneering *A History of Assam* (London, 1906), his *Report on the Progress of Historical Research in Assam* (Shillong, 1897) laid the foundation of modern source-based history writing by surveying the sources of history. The compilation of *The Assam Land Revenue Manual* (1896) was also an important work of Gait which involved a great deal of research. He was the first historian of the region not only to use literary, epigraphic, numismatic and archaeological sources to the extent these were recovered till that point of time but also to discuss the sources used in the work. The historical notes and comments contributed by him in the Census of India Report, 1891 as Superintendent of Census, Assam, and later on, as Census Commissioner of India in Report for 1911(Pt. I, Assam) emerged out of his critical study of the empirical evidence and his sound knowledge of the region and sources of its history. His articles published in the *Journal of the Asiatic Society of Bengal* are indeed products of source-based sustained research. Gait also introduced a scientific academic temper in historical research in the Northeast by acknowledgingly taking into account the critical reviews of the first edition of his work by A.W. Botham, H.E. Stapleton and Padmanath Bhattacharyya before bringing out the revised edition of *A History of Assam* (Calcutta, 1926). However, Gait's book is mainly on the Ahom period and his treatment of the early period till twelfth century as well as the modern period is very sketchy.

The historian who single handedly opened up the region for scientific reconstruction of its past and critical history writing by his voluminous works in English and Assamese was Suryya Kumar Bhuyan (1894-1964). The chief architect of the Department of Historical and Antiquarian Studies (DHAS), Assam, and an executive of the Kamarupa Anusandhan Samiti (KAS) for many years, Bhuyan drew the attention of historians and historical research organizations in rest of India and the world by collecting, editing and publishing the historical manuscripts of pre-colonial Assam, namely, *Buranjis* and *Puthis*, not only with introductions in both Assamese and English but also by translating some of those into English and publishing and circulating the catalogues of the materials nationally and internationally. His extensive original works in English and Assamese, in the form of books, pamphlets, and articles, gave a strong foundation to the studies in pre-colonial history of Assam, particularly of the Ahom period, besides popularizing history among the common literati of Assam. The biographies of a large number of great men and women belonging to medieval and modern periods written by Bhuyan made the beginning of a rich tradition of historical biographies in Assamese. The writing of a booklet *Early British Relations with Assam* (1928), perhaps for official use of the government, for which he studied the records preserved in Assam Secretariat Records Department, Shillong, including those transferred from the erstwhile Bengal Government and the Board of Revenue, Dacca, inspired his interest in modern archival sources and this was carried further while in the London University for a formal degree in history, namely, Doctor of Philosophy, for which he virtually ransacked Assam records at the India Office Library & Records, London. His *Anglo-Assamese Relations, 1772-1826* (Guwahati, 1949), growing out of his doctoral dissertation and covering the years of transition from medieval to modern, is a work that conformed to the norms and practices in modern history writing. S.K. Bhuyan thus opened up the modern period, although his main contribution was on the medieval period.

The history of the modern period as well as the modern age of methodological standardization in history writing in Northeast India bloomed in the hands of Heramba Kanta Barpujari (1912-2002) who, while doing his doctoral research at the London University in modern history, had undergone a regular course in historical methodology under the stalwarts of modern Indian history of the time, like H.H. Dodwell, C.H. Philips and D.G.E. Hall, from whom he mastered the science of using and interpreting the archival records. Besides strictly adhering to the standard methods and global conventions in writing modern history in his own works, he made a course in methodology compulsory for all his research students at the Gauhati University, though it was not an essential requirement under rules of the University at that point of time. The authentication of information through 'rigorous documentation for each statement of fact' was a hallmark of the format that Barpujari used in his works. Like the format of presentation, his concept of history was also clear and loud. Accepting the felicitation volume presented to him by the Northeast India History Association (NEIHA) at its seventh session at Pasighat (Arunachal Pradesh) in 1986, Barpujari in the opening sentence of his speech had said that his 'Gurudev' R.C. Majumdar taught him that 'history is a search for truth in which emotion, sentiment, pride and prejudice, fear and favour have no place' and that he has always tried to follow the lesson he received from his illustrious teacher. In fact, the impact of Dodwell School and R.C. Majumdar on Barpujari is clear in what he said and wrote. He articulated his approach to history in various speeches and writings, including his presidential address at the first session of NEIHA in which he virtually worked out a guideline for historical research in Northeast India. Finally, he wrote *Itihâs : Rachanâ Bidhi Âru Cromobikâsh* (a book on historiography in Assamese). Barpujari as a historian and his approach in history writing are thus before the generations to come. 'Truth, whole truth and nothing but the truth' is the maxim that Barpujari uncompromisingly stood for in all his works.

Barpujari made voluminous contributions by his original research in history of Northeast India. *Assam : In the Days of the Company* (1963), *Problem of Hill Tribes : North East Frontier* in three volumes (1970, 1976 and 1981), *The American Missionaries and North-East India, 1836-1900* (1986), *Francis Jenkins : Report on the North East Frontier of India*, 1831-32 (1988) and *India's North-East : Problems, Policies and Prospects* (1998), and *The Political History of Assam*, vol. I (1977) that was edited by him, in English, and *American Misonerisakal aru Unavimsa Satikar Asom* (1981) and *Asamar Nava-Jagaran : Ana-Asamiyar Bhumika* (1987) in Assamese, are on the modern period. *An Account of Assam and Her Administration, 1603-1822* (1988) is on the medieval period, while *The Comprehensive History of Assam* in five volumes (1990-1991), edited by Barpujari, covered the period from pre-historic times to 1919. Although the chapters in the monumental *The Comprehensive History of Assam* were contributed by the specialists in respective fields, the evidence of his effective editing is imprinted in the literary style and format, documentation, bibliography, glossary and indexing uniformly followed in all the volumes. Some of the chapters in the volumes on modern period were authored by the editor himself. Barpujari also contributed in English and Assamese a good number of research papers and articles in journals and proceedings, besides presidential and keynote addresses and a chapter in *Comprehensive History of India* (vol. XXII) of the Indian History Congress. Between these works, he covered almost the whole of Northeast and all major aspects of history, namely, political, social and economic. He developed his doctoral thesis of London University 'The British Administration in Assam (1826-45)' into his first book, *Assam : In the Days of the Company* (1963), almost as a comprehensive history for the period 1826 to 1858 covering all aspects of history. His incomplete autobiographical work published posthumously, *Kuri Satikar Kahini* in Assamese (Calcutta, 2010), is indeed a source book on Twentieth Century Northeast India. The originality of Barpujari's contributions, the areas he explored for further research by other historians and the standardized methodology made him a phenomenon in the historiography of Northeast India.

Basically a historian of the British period of Indian history (called modern India) and trained in the London School in 1940s when historiography in Europe was dominated by Rankean tradition, the archival records constituted the primary source for the works of Barpujari. He made complete use of all archives in India, UK and USA wherever there are records on Northeast India and it is held by many that Barpujari did not leave any file relevant to his work unseen in those archives. The stories of his working in the research rooms from 'nine to nine' are known to many in the historians' circle, and even in his eighties whenever he visited Delhi and Calcutta for a seminar or a meeting he would stay at least a day extra to visit the archives. His association with the Indian Historical Records Commission for the scientific preservation and management of historical records in India is almost proverbial, and the upgradation of state records department to the Assam Archives required him to run from pillar to post for many years. However, Barpujari made it clear again and again that the official records provide only 'the official point of view' and, therefore, the historians should verify the contents from non-official sources. He emphasized the use of archaeological, numismatic and literary sources, particularly private papers, and he himself always used multiple of alternatives, wherever available, of course, after due verification, criticism and content analysis. In 1978, he visited the Cambridge South Asia Archives of Private Papers to consult the private papers of some of the British officers posted in the Northeast before publication of his later works, and earlier, while in Gauhati University, he directed a UGC funded project on survey and collection of private papers in Assam. He also played his role as a historian in the transfer of private papers of eminent national leaders to Nehru Memorial Museum and Library, Teen Murti Bhavan, New Delhi. Barpujari's emphasis on the use of archives was also for the fact that the provincial and district records in Assam included some pre-British records collected by the early British officers from private hands, including the members of former royalty and aristocracy and the ordinary land holders. The 'verification of information from all possible angles' was the key word in his research.

Barpujari's contribution to the historiography of Northeast India needs to be assessed not only by the quantum and the quality of his own research publications but also for the deep impact he made on historical studies in the region in various ways. Immediately after he joined Gauhati University as Professor and head of the department of history in 1963, the post-graduate syllabus in history was revised, and the revised syllabus included a paper on 'methods and concepts in history' with E.H. Carr's *What is History?* as the main book, though at optional level, and shortly afterwards, the department organized a UGC funded workshop on revision of undergraduate syllabus involving the teachers in affiliated colleges. In early 1970s the UGC initiated a programme for curriculum development in history; Barpujari was a member of the national core group and the convenor for the eastern region (viz. Northeast, West Bengal, Bihar and Orissa). In the five-day workshop for eastern region held at Gauhati University in March 1976, Barpujari strongly argued for a thorough orientation of the post-graduate syllabi towards research. He was in the history chair at Gauhati University in 1960s and 70s when higher education network in the region was undergoing expansion with establishment of new universities and new colleges and there was a renewed interest in research degrees not only in the process of academic enlightenment but also by the institutional requirement of doctoral degree, preceded by M. Phil or Pre-Ph.D involving course work or formal training in methodology, under UGC regulations of early 1970s. Methodology became a much talked about integral component of research and Barpujari, in any case, was an old advocate of this requirement. It was also the time that Barpujari's students were joining new universities and colleges and a large section of the new generation of researchers was either his direct students or the students of his students. A common forum for interaction among researchers of the region also became available with the formation of North East India History Association (NEIHA) with Barpujari as its first President and the membership of the organization opened to all researchers on Northeast irrespective of the disciplines. The multidisciplinary study of history that NEIHA emphasizes is beyond any doubt a laudable strategy to continuously reinforce, revitalize and update the discipline and to keep it socially relevant. Barpujari was the most charismatic personality in the field of history during the years of those changes in the Northeast. In fact, Edward Gait, S.K. Bhuyan and H.K. Barpujari mathematically shared between them the twentieth century historiography of Northeast India, and there is no doubt that the impact of Barpujari continues in the twenty-first century as well.

Institute of Northeast India Studies, Kolkata, decided to prepare a volume on 'historians and historiography of Northeast India' to recall the works of those historians (i) who made substantive contributions to history of the Northeast, but (ii) who are no more in this world, and (iii) to publish the volume in August 2012 to commemorate the birth centenary of Professor H.K. Barpujari (1912-2002). A list of such historians was tentatively prepared in March 2010 and the format that was developed for the contributors to the volume provided for at least three common areas, namely, (a) biographical sketch, (b) survey and assessment of contributions, and (c) an estimate as a historian. As it must be a common experience in such wishful academic endeavours, we are sorry that some of the historians originally identified by us could not be included in the volume as the contributors could not help us despite our long awaiting due to unavoidable difficulties coming on their way and we also could not wait longer as we had to bring out the volume within the centenary year. The historians included in the volume are not necessarily professional historians or those institutionally educated and trained in the discipline of history. In fact, majority of them belonged to other disciplines and other professions. Nonetheless, they are historians by their outstanding contributions in history of Northeast India through studies and publications. However, the volume does not claim that those included here were the only historians of significance in the Northeast. There might have been many more historians, even with greater justification for inclusion in the volume, whose contributions we must always gratefully remember. We have said that there were already some more historians in our own list and explained as to why we had to rush for publication without waiting longer for the papers. We are indeed sorry that we could not include papers on all the historians who deserved a place in the volume. We pay our homage to the memory of all of them on the occasion of the birth centenary of Professor H.K. Barpujari. We also expect that this volume will run into editions and there will be more volumes to celebrate the birth centenaries of the historians of Northeast India, and we will get more chances to recall the contributions of our historians who are in the great beyond.

We need not tell our readers that the volume has been prepared with all possible care and affection with a pious objective of commemorating the birth centenary of a great historian whose contribution in studying the history of Northeast India is phenomenal. The editor of the volume craves indulgence for all the lapses and omissions that might have crept in despite the best efforts to eliminate as many errors as possible keeping in mind that we are writing about those who are in the great beyond and fervently appeals to the readers to kindly bring to our notice such lapses and omissions so that these may be rectified in the next edition or, if necessary, even by bringing out a supplementary publication. We are aware that correctness and precision is among the ideals that Professor H.K. Barpujari had always emphasized in historian's craft and we would like to stand by those ideals of the great historian. 'To err is human' and to accept and correct the errors is a manifestation of the scholarly temper.

I am thankful to the authors for helping the Institute of Northeast India Studies in bringing out the volume by contributing papers on the historians individually assigned to them. It would never be possible for us to succeed in an effort of this nature without their voluntary support and cooperation. The contributors were indeed so enthusiastic about the proposal and so supportive to the editor that most of the papers were received within the originally proposed date and those who needed more time due to unforeseen detractions coming on the way also eventually obliged us by completing the task. The authors also extended excellent cooperation to the editor by readily providing additional information or clarification, wherever required, in course of editing the volume. My personal relation with all the contributors is only one of love and affection and this has been deepened further by working together in preparing the volume to commemorate the birth centenary of the historian who is loved and respected by all historians and lovers of history in the region. I am also thankful to my colleagues in the Board Trustees of the Institute of Northeast India Studies for deciding to bring out a volume on the occasion of the birth centenary of my revered mentor and giving me a free hand in planning and executing the volume. Finally, my thanks are due to Shri M.P. Misra of Akansha Publishing House, New Delhi, for bringing out the book in time.

(J.B. Bhattacharjee)

Institute of Northeast India Studies, Kolkata
15 January 2012

1

Kailash Chandra Singha (1851-1914)

—*Mahadev Chakravarti*

Biographical Sketch

Kailash Chandra Singha (1851–1914), historian, archaeologist, epigraphist, folklorist, author of the renowned book *Rajamala ba Tripurar Itihas* and many other history-related publications, was born in the Singha family of Comilla in 1851. He is least known outside Tripura, though his research articles were mainly published in leading contemporary Bengali journals and periodicals of Kolkata. We come to know from the introduction of his book on *Rajamala,* how for long three generations, the Singha family of Comilla (known during the British period as 'Plains Tipperah') rendered service to the Tripura royal family in various capacities. His paternal grandfather Rama Prasad Singha was in royal service of Tripura since the last decade of the eighteenth century and spent his entire life at Jahangir Nagar (Dhaka) as *am-mukhtar* or representative of the Manikyas of Tripura. His father Golok Chandra Singha, though primarily a *serishtadar*, had to shoulder many other responsibilities during his more than thirty-two years' royal service, particularly to assist Maharaja Ishan Chandra Manikya (1850-1862) to face the complicated, stormy and tumultuous days during the Great Revolt of 1857, popularly known as the 'First War of Indian Independence', when the British authorities constantly threatened the Tripura king with dire consequences for being allegedly sympathetic to the cause of the mutineers. However, following the advice of Golok Chandra, Ishan Chandra Manikya assured the British officials that he was taking all possible measures to round up the mutineers. After the death of his father Golok Chandra Singha in 1273 *Bangabda*,[1] Kailash Chandra also joined the administration of Tripura at the age of only 15 and after serving the Manikya family for only four years he left the job for a 'particular reason' which he was unwilling to mention. The reason might be due to his direct involvement in the controversy regarding the real claimant to the throne of Tripura and his opposition to king Birchandra Manikya (*b*. Agartala, 1838) who ruled Tripura from 1862 to 1896 AD. It is likely that Kailash Chandra resigned from the royal service on ethical reason.

For about two decades Kailash Chandra Singha worked in the Archaeological Survey of India and as a result of that training, he could easily verify the authenticity of the prevalent literary documents with the available archaeological source materials, particularly coins and inscriptions of Tripura. Some archaeological investigators, like Kailash Chandra who sought more information, raised some interesting questions and thus due to that juxtaposition, the extremely intriguing and complex history of Tripura, so long based on literary sources like the *Rajamala,* got a new dimension and a new lease of life. In 1283 *Bangabda* (i.e. 1876 AD) Kailash Chandra had published an outline of a book entitled *Rajamala ba Tripurar Itibritta* or the royal chronicle of Tripura, and he was overwhelmed by the response of the intelligentsia. After a lapse of twenty years, he had enlarged that sketchy edition and published from Kolkata in 1896 A.D. that controversial book *Rajamala ba Tripurar Itihas* about which most of the contemporary scholars virtually remained muted. However, after going through Kailash Chandra's first book, i.e. *Tripurar Itibritta* (1876), Rabindranath Tagore (1861-1941) became so fascinated about Tripura that in his maiden letter to King Birchandra Manikya dated May 6, 1886, the poet had sought some more ingredients of Tripura's history and on the basis of the inputs from the king, the poet later created his celebrated novel *'Rajarshi'* and the dramas like *'Visarjan'* and *'Mukut'*. In fact, Kailash Chandra in his book highlighted how the age-old practice of human sacrifice in Tripura underwent some changes since the time of Dhanya Manikya, in the fifteenth century, who had imposed some restrictions on the practice.[2] But the custom of other types of sacrifices and bloodshed went on as usual. According to Kailash Chandra Singha, Deva Manikya was killed because of the severe opposition of the *chantais* (royal priests) to the attempts of the Manikyas to draw a curtain to bloodshed in the temples, and Govinda Manikya (1660-75 AD) was ultimately dethroned and humiliated due to the conspiracies hatched by the royal priests in collaboration with others in the palace.[3] Tagore's immortal creation *'Rajarshi'* and *'Visarjan'* virtually echoed the voice of Govinda Manikya at the Bhubeneswari temple (built by the king) on the southern bank of river Gomati at Udaipur (the then capital of Tripura) against bloodshed in the temple.[4] Thus, though the sacrifices and killings in the name of religion for the purpose of ritual in Tripura came to light through the historical work of Kailash Chandra Singha, he remained unknown to many, despite the fact that the names of the Bhubeneswari temple, Govinda Manikya etc. got idolatrized or canonized through the timeless creations of the Nobel-laureate in his *'Rajarshi'* and *'Visarjan'*.

Kailash Chandra passed away in 1914. Till the last days of his life, he loudly proclaimed: *Always stand on principle, even if you stand alone.* World history has many records of crimes against humanity, which were also justified by the ruling class and very few contemporary historians dared to raise their heads against these anti-humanitarian acts of the rulers. Criticism, as it was first instituted by the ancient Greek classical philosopher Aristotle (384 BC-322 BC), a worthy student of Plato (428/427 BC-348/347 BC), was meant as a standard of judging well; but that honest criticism was hard to take and digest by the dominant class everywhere – especially, in the case of Tripura - when it came from a former employee of the Manikyas and an acquaintance like Kailash Chandra Singha.

Sometimes it so appears that if a historian was to relate truthfully the weaknesses, disorders and the crimes of the ruling class, his readers would take his work for satire rather than for history.[5] For that reason, Kailash Chandra's scholarly work on *Rajamala* was virtually a forbidden book within the boundaries of princely Tripura till 15 October, 1949.[6] The book *Rajamala ba Tripurar Itibritta*, although of striking merit, did not seem to have received either the critical recognition or the general appreciation that his work deserved.[7] In fact, Singha's knowledge was encyclopedic, his enthusiasm for the forgotten past irrepressible and his commitment to the cause of truth steadfast. In spite of his creative work of a very high merit, one can see that Kailash Chandra Singha remained as an 'unsung historian' of Northeast India during his lifetime.*

About the *Rajamala*

The royal chronicle *Rajamala* (literally meaning the 'Garland of Kings') passed down orally through the *Chantai*, the royal tribal priest of Tripura, like the *Vedas* used to be memorized *(sruti / smriti)* and passed down from generation to generation. The early history of the kingdom of Tripura is a complex blend of history with mythology. It is said that the *Rajamala* was first composed during the reign of Dharma Manikya in the fifteenth century

---

* Kailash Chandra Singha's *Rajamala ba Tripurar Itibritta* (1890) was indeed a great modern historical work in Bengali. It also demonstrates the fact that the quality of nineteenth century vernacular historiography in Northeast India was comparable with all-India standard and practices. In this context, it may also be noted that the pioneer in modern historiography in Bengali in Northeast India was Haliram Dhekial Phookan of Assam, whose *Asam Buranji ba Asam Desher Katha*, in Bengali, was published in 1829. Born in the well known *Duaria Barua* family which regulated the Assam-Bengal trade on behalf of the local government for generations, Haliram Dhekial Phookan (1802-1832) succeeded his father as customs officer of the Ahom Govt. at Bangalhat (Hadiracaki) in Goalpara and later on, served the administration of the East India Company after the British annexation of Assam as a Sheristadar at Guwahati. He was an enlightened and scholarly person who wrote series of articles and letters to editors in newspapers like *Samachar Darpan* and *Samachar Chandrika* of Calcutta on aspects of revenue, fiscal and business to keep the business circles in Calcutta informed about the economic condition of Assam. He wrote at least two books, viz. *Asam Buranji* (1829) in Bengali and *Kamrup-Jatra-Paddhati* (1833) in Sanskrit. His *Asam Buranji* is the first work in history written immediately after British penetration in the Northeast. Dr. Sukumar Sen considered this book as the only independent historical work of that period in Bengali. Published in four parts, printed in Samachar Chandrika Press, Calcutta, and distributed at 'gratis', the first part of the book dealt with political history of Assam from earliest times to the British annexation (1826); the second part threw light on governance, revenue administration, judiciary, status of the ruling Ahoms in society and the classes of people exempted from poll-tax; the third part dealt with physical geography, population, land settlement, revenue system, coinage and currency, administrative divisions under British, and the Kamakhya shrine; and the fourth part discussed caste divisions in the society, manners and customs, modes of worship, Brahmanical and Mahapurusiya sects, indigenous methods of treatment of various diseases, festivals, products, apparels, architecture, dresses, ornaments, weapons, flora and fauna. *The India Gazette* (27 March, 1832) highly praised the work as encyclopaedic in scope and a very valuable historical and sociological document. A combined volume of all four parts of Haliram Dhekial Phookan's *Asam Buranji* was republished in 1962 by Mokshada Pustakalay, Guwahati, with an introduction by Jatindra Mohan Bhattacharyya and an appendix containing Haliram's letters to the editors published in Calcutta newspapers and some comments on his *Asam Buranji*. Haliram's son, Anandaram Dhekial Phukan (1829-1859) was a great literary genius and leader of the renaissance era, who is remembered as 'Father of Assamese prose' and for his article '*Ingraj Jatir Bibaran*' in *Orunodoi* and his memorandum to A.J.M. Moffat Mills entitled 'Observations on the Administration of the Province of Assam', while his grand nephew Gunabhiram Barua (1837-1894) was a well known Assamese writer and a historian. [*Editor's Addendum]

which contained descriptions and legends of the kings of Tripura, origin of the royal family and their reigns, etc. It was originally recited in Tripuri language by *Chantai* Durlabhendra, which was translated into Sanskrit and Bengali *kavya* style as *Rajaratnakara* (ocean of kings) by two noted *pandits* - Sukreswar (c. 1403-1487) and Baneswar (c. 1400-1480). The *Rajaratnakara* is analogous with the *Rajatarangini* (river of kings), a metrical chronicle of the kings of Kashmir from earliest time, written in Sanskrit by another reputed *pundit* Kalhana in c. 12th century AD. The *Rajamala* of Tripura, supposed to have been written in Bengali verse in the 15th century, is considered an ancient book of Bengali language and literature. There are different editions of *Rajamala* composed in different times, but the original manuscript of *Rajaratnakara* is not traceable.[8] Kailash Chandra Singha in the introduction of his book had acknowledged how for the early history of Tripura he got material from the manuscripts of : (i) *Prachin* (ancient) *Rajamala, (ii)* Sanskrit *Rajamala*, and (iii) *Saṇkhipta* (abridged) *Rajamala* (by James Long which is virtually *Krishnamala* as written during the time of Maharaja Krishna Manikya). After Kailash Chandra Singha's *Rajamala* in prose, Chandrodaya Vidyavinod's (1858-1945) edition of *Rajamala* and *Silalipi Samgraha* were published in 1901 and 1904 respectively. But, above all, there is the widely famed *Sri Rajamala* under royal patronage edited by Kali Prasanna Sen in Bengali verse in four volumes (*lahars*) which were printed and published from the 'Rajmala Press', Agartala, between 1926 and 1931.[9] In Kali Prasanna's *Sri Rajamala,* the first *lahar* (the early legendary period up to Ratna Manikya), the second (from Dharma Manikya to Jaya Manikya), the third (from Amar Manikya to Kalyan Manikya) and the fourth volume (up to Krishna Manikya) were narrated by Senapati Ranachaturanan, Siddhantabagish, Ujir Durgamani respectively on the basis of the *Prachin Rajamala*. From the point of view of authenticity, whatever its shortcomings, the *Sri Rajamala* in metrical verse as edited by Kali Prasanna Sen, still remains unrivalled and artistically more imposing to the general readers than the prose research work of Kailash Chandra Singha. Again, from a transcription of the only available manuscript preserved in the Bangiya Sahitya Parishad, Kolkata, another *Rajamala* was published by the Education Directorate, Government of Tripura, Agartala, in 1967.[10]

Thus, we have lot of *Rajamalas* and it becomes evident from the above that the different copies of the *Rajamala* sometimes record conflicting traditions. But Kailash Chandra Singha's *Rajamala* is totally different from the rest. The question naturally comes, if Kailash Chandra's approach was so different, then why the name of his book was *Rajamala?* Kailash Chandra himself had answered that question in the preface of his book. His great concern was that the fifteenth century original version in Tripuri language as recited by *Chantai* Durlabhendra, which was recorded in manuscript into *kavya* style as *Rajaratnakara* by Sukreswar and Baneswar, the only first literary source of Tripura's past, might have been misconstrued or distorted later by someone to serve his petty ends. So, beginning from the achievements of the great king Dharma Manikya (c.1431-1462), whatever was there in the manuscript (in spite of its legendary character and overestimation of some heroes), should be faithfully preserved and to that end, he kept in tact both the theme and name of that great book *Rajamala*.

It is well established in historiography that century after century the 'court historians' have dominated academia in our country, and Tripura is no exception to this general rule. Naturally, the *Rajamala* and the other literary and epigraphic sources of Tripura are mostly eulogies or *prasastis* that were usually composed by the court poets or members of the royal family (or *Thakurs / Kartas*). But, excepting some legendary achievements of the rulers of Tripura in the past, Kailash Chandra Singha's *Rajamala* was not a *prasasti* of any kind. Kailash Chandra sincerely believed that history ought never to be confused with nostalgia as it is written not to revere the dead, but to inspire the living. Like many others, he was not a believer of the theory of 'Divine right of kingship'; hence, his approach was totally different from the rest. That was perhaps enough for the Manikya rulers to make his book a forbidden one in princely Tripura. For example, towards the beginning of the British Raj in India, zamindari oppression had made the life of the peasants and farmers miserable everywhere, particularly in the Chakla Roshnabad zamindari of the Manikyas of Tripura. Shamsher Gazi, born in an ordinary peasant family, took the cause of the peasants; he first became the ruler of the entire Chakla Roshnabad and ultimately seized political control of Tripura. There was thus a violent interlude (1748-1760) of the long Manikya rule drawn by Shamsher Gazi, a maverick who rose and fell like a meteor. In other versions of *Rajamala* this chapter is conspicuously absent; but Kailash Chandra, after reading the manuscript of *Gazinama,* authored by Sheikh Manohar, accepted that as a primary source of information on Shamsher Gazi and incorporated the episode in his book.

It is true that the name 'Tripura' has a halo of mystery around it and signifies different aspects to different people. Being a linguist of great merit, Kailash Chandra Singha dismissed the theories as advanced by colonial scholars, and tried to prove in a scientific way that the name of Tripura was formed from the two Tipra words: viz. *tui* and *pra* (`*tui'* meaning water, *'pra'* meaning near); the people 'near the water'. The word *tui-pra>tipra* in its Sanskritised form ultimately became 'Tripura',[11] with the implication that in ancient times the boundaries of Tripura might have extended up to the Sea or the Bay of Bengal and the people might have come from that region. Indeed, the early history of the kingdom of Tripura is a complex blend of history with mythology. According to the court poets, the kings of India had descended either from the legendary 'lunar' or 'solar' dynasties of epic fame. Thus, following the footsteps of their counterparts in the royal houses of the country, the *'Rajamala'* speaks the story of a mythological prince Druhya, third son of king Yayati of *'Mahabharata'*, who moved eastward before reaching the lower course of the Ganges and the Sagar island and Tripura's royalty trace their origin to that celebrated 'lunar' dynasty. Kailash Chandra Singha, however, gives a different opinion about the origin of the Tripura dynasty. He mentioned that the Tripuras are a Tibeto-Burman race, akin to the Shan, one of the tribes included by Friederich Muller (1705-1783) and other German ethnologists under the generic term 'Lohitic' or *Lauhitya* implying connection with Lohit or Brahmaputra river. According to Singha, the Tripuri people are of Mongoloid stock and the common reference to the Mongoloid people was *'Kirata'* in the early Sanskrit texts.[12] Kailadsh Chandra opined that Cachar was the place from where the ancient Tripura dynasty spread and in course of time, the Tripuris, due to various reasons, were compelled to shift their kingdom to the northern part of Cachar. He had also used some documents as cited by Aitchison in his book on *Treaties* etc.[13] Granting that regarding the exact location of 'Tribeg', the so-called capital of the ancient kingdom of Tripura, though there is still now a big debate among scholars, it was Kailash Chandra who could emphatically point out that it was nowhere other than in Cachar.[14]

Birchandra Manikya's succession to the throne after the death of Ishan Chandra Manikya in 1862 was marred by controversy and the matter had to be ultimately settled by judicial intervention of the British government. Nabadwip Chandra Dev Burman (1854-1931), the sole surviving son of the deceased king Ishan Chandra Manikya, was deprived by his paternal uncle Birchandra who ascended the throne in 1862 on the strength of a so-called death-bed *robkari* (dated 4 August, 1862) of Ishan Chandra Manikya, the validity of which was doubtful and rightly challenged as a 'forged document' by other claimants to the throne, who moved the British court in Comilla. Kailash Chandra sincerely believed that the succession episode of Birchandra (a younger half-brother of Ishan Chandra Manikya) would ever remain as a black chapter of the history of Tripura and on his advice, Navadwip Chandra Dev Burman filed a suit in 1874 claiming Chakla Roshnabad zemindari. Notwithstanding the long legal battle in the court, Birchandra was accepted as *de facto* ruler of Tripura by the British government. Finally, matters reached the Privy Council in London and, in its verdict pronounced on March 15 1869, the Council upheld Birchandra Manikya's claim and he was formally coroneted as the king of Tripura on 9 March 1870 with prior approval of the British Indian government. Though Birchandra is painted as the 'first modernizer' and by some as the 'Vikramaditya' of Tripura, his maltreatment of the rival claimants to the throne, particularly his torture and oppression on Nabadwip Chandra who was compelled to take shelter in Comilla, had shocked and convulsed Kailash Chandra so much that he became the prime mover in the British court for justice on behalf of Nabadwip Chandra for his legitimate claim on Chakla Roshanabad zemindari.[15]

Kailash Chandra Singha appears to have been the only scholar who dared to write in his book about the controversial issues like legitimate and illegitimate sons of the royal family - an important issue in that case - (as previously some of the contenders for the throne were disqualified by the British Resident on grounds of illegitimacy) and, like an expert ethnologist, sociologist or social anthropologist, dealt in detail about three types marriage system as was prevalent in the royal family of Tripura and the real meaning and implications of the *kachua* (usually known as the maid-servant of the palace in various capacities) and *hiknanani* marriage system of the kings, which the western administrators and judges could not practically comprehend.[16] Singha criticized the westerners for their ignorance in that context and delivering judgment at the same time. Kailash Chandra gave a long list of Tripura kings whose mothers were practically *Kachuas* and boldly asserted that the marriage system of the Tripuri people was so simple that the birth of an illegitimate child was both an impracticability and impossibility. Nabadwip Chandra, the only surviving son of the deceased king Ishan Chandra Manikya and the real claimant to the throne, in his autobiography '*Abarjanar Jhuri*' in Bengali stated that his father Ishan Chandra Manikya had four queens, one of whom was a Bengali and the other three (including his own mother) were Manipuri women.

Other Source Materials

It becomes evident from the works of Kailash Chandra that the scholar had subscribed regularly the *Indian Law Reports* as published by various State governments (according to Section 3 of the Indian Law Reports Act 1875) because these *Reports* were considered as the most authentic and binding authority to be referred to and relied upon by the British Courts. Thus, Kailash Chandra, for the cause of Nabadwip Chandra, also became a legal expert at that time, though his client had lost his suit. Regarding travellers' accounts about Tripura, Kailash Chandra quoted Ralph Fitch (1550-1611),[17] Tavernier (1605-1689),[18] Bernier (1625–1688),[19] Ratna Kandali Sarma and Arjun Das Bairagi's accounts written in 1724.[20] Again, though Kailash Chandra organised his book on the model of the colonial writers and exhaustively used the primary source materials in English as found in the gazetteers, census reports, letters and reports of the colonial administrators, and particularly *The Statistical Account of Bengal*, vol. VI (which was first published in 1876 and which dealt with five districts — Chittagong Hill Tracts, Chittagong, Noakhali, Tipperah and Hill Tipperah); he did not always subscribe colonial interpretations of the history of Tripura and with the use of logic and convincing arguments, he sometime refuted their conclusions. Here lies the novelty of Kailash Chandra's works. In this connection, it should be mentioned that after half a century of the Battle of Plassey (1757) the East India Company saw the need to learn about the land it had acquired and in 1815 the Company began publishing a series of gazetteers (Imperial Gazetteers, Provincial Series and the District Gazetteers) designed to further the knowledge of its territories and the practice continued even after Indian independence. These series of gazetteers, being the treasure house of data and bearing the stamp of authenticity, which have been very valuable for colonial officials from the administrative point of view, have also proven of immense value to Indian scholars and particularly to the social scientists. One aspect of colonial historiography was compilation of local history. At the same time, as there is a little debate about the role played by history in the articulation of nationhood, the gazetteer genre of Indian historiography and the census reports earned tremendous importance particularly among the Bengali intellectuals who evaluated these gazetteers and reports both favourably and critically from the national angle. Kailash Chandra exhaustively used the works of the following contemporary pioneers, e.g. Sir William Wilson Hunter (1840-1900), Father of the Gazetteers of India, who brought out his *Imperial Gazetteer of India* in 1881 in nine volumes and Herbert Risley,[21] W.S. Meyer, Richard Burn[22] and J.S. Cotton[23] who jointly compiled the monumental twenty-six volumes *Imperial Gazetteer of India* after Hunter's death in 1900. W.W. Hunter himself edited *The Statistical Account of Bengal* in 20 volumes and *The Statistical Account of Assam* in 2 volumes. The gazetteer tradition with the aim of understanding the localities of the empire was further strengthened by other civilian scholars such as Henry Beveridge (1837-1929), L.S.S. O'Malley (1874-1941), B.C. Allen, James Taylor, J.C. Jack and others.

Kailash Chandra in his book on *Rajamala* also quoted from the writings of Charles Stewart,[24] and Sir Alexander Mackenzie's book[25] which made a general survey of the political relations of the then British government of India with the rulers of Tripura and the hill tribes of Assam, Cachar and Chittagong which no historian or even no ethno-historian interested in the region can afford to ignore even today. Kailash Chandra had also quoted James Long,[26] Capt. Lewin,[27] Sir Grierson,[28] Sutherland Cotton's 'Tipperah', and from the *Annual Administration Reports of the Political Agency of Hill Tipperah,* particularly the letters and reports of A.W.B. Power[29] and many other British administrators and academicians. He had also consulted some contemporary important research journals in English either to vindicate or disapprove their opinions and commentaries.[30]

Twin position of the Manikyas

Kailash Chandra highlighted how the Manikya rulers enjoyed the twin positions, i.e. on one hand, as the king of 'Hill Tipperah' (present Tripura) and on the other, as the zamindar of the British district of Tipperah, called Chakla Roshnabad.[31] The Chakla Roshnabad zamindari of the Manikyas once played a vital role in pushing forward the process of state formation and economic strength and power of Tripura. In fact, the financial foundation of the Tripura *Raj* was largely due to the Chakla zamindary and Kailash Chandra Singha, by quoting *Annual Administration Report* of 1890-91,[32] had shown this in the fourth chapter of the first part of his book on *Rajamala*. In order to have more land revenue (the prime source of income of princely Tripura), the Manikya rulers had also openly invited the non-tribal peasants of the zemindary through *jangal-avadi* and other systems to settle permanently in Tripura. Singha had also shown how in a land-abundant but labour-scarce economy, there were very few land disputes at first. However, the entire scenario changed with the march of time. Thus, the genesis of the present-day burning issues like land alienation of the tribal people of Tripura and emerging ethnic issues and tensions are to be understood in that historical context as outlined by Kailash Chandra Singha during his time. It is interesting to note that the important report of J.G. Cummings on Chakla Roshnabad zemindari of the Manikyas[33] was published three years after the publication of Kailash Chandra Singha's *Rajamala*, and *E.F. Sandys' History of Tripura* was published in Calcutta in 1915, i.e. one year after the demise of Kailash Chandra Singha.[34] Hence, Kailash Chandra could not pass any comment about these books.

Each age tries to form its own conception of the past and writes the history of the past anew with reference to the conditions uppermost in its own time and the historiography should be made relevant and meaningful to those who live today. Hobsbawm[35] remarked, "nations without pasts are contradictions in terms. What makes a nation is the past." In fact, Kailash Chandra truly wanted to unravel the past and his *Rajamala* reflects an urge to rethink the place of history to understand the present. To quote E. H. Carr :[36] "The function of the historian is neither to love the past nor to emancipate himself from the past, but to master and understand it as the key to the understanding of the present." Or again, to quote Pearl Buck, who used to say: "If you want to understand today, you have to search yesterday."[37] Like any military historian who serves his/her country by collecting and preserving valuable information and documents of the opponent, Kailash Chandra Singh was also actually a 'Field Historian in Action'. Arnold J. Toynbee, who is usually considered as the greatest western modern historian-philosopher, once remarked : "A life which does not go into action is a failure. History not used is nothing, for all intellectual life is action, like practical life, and if you don't use the stuff well, it might as well be dead."[38]

Kailash Chandra Singha knew the ins and outs of Birchandra Manikya's individuality,[39] but as Singha censured coarse invectives and character-assassination campaign against anyone, he did not speak or record his mind in harsh language against any particular individual, far to speak of Birchandra Manikya, his main antagonist. As a true social scientist, though he had a deep sense of fairness and justice for the victims, he usually kept covered his emotion as long as possible by the 'trousers of decorum'. Though being a critic of Birchandra Manikya, he painted in his *Rajamala* the following qualities of Birchandra in glowing terms:

> The Maharaja possesses a handsome physique with bright and beautiful features. He is very well-versed in the Bengali language and is a poet of high order…also well-versed in Urdu and Manipuri… possesses some knowledge of Sanskrit and English. He is an expert artist and a good photographer. He possesses extraordinary abilities as a musician. He is temperate in habit and never touches liquor. He is extremely intelligent, shrewd and an attractive conversationalist. He is so fascinating in conversation that a talk with him for a few minutes would disarm even his worst enemies.[40]

True, Kailash Chandra was not the only critical historian; even James Long in his book *An analysis of Rajmala or Chronicles of Tripura* also commented about the court-sponsored *Rajmala* in the following way:

> There are a few points omitted in this history which are rather singular- no mention is made of Dacca though it carried on a trade with the Romans…. No reference is made to Buddhism, though it was at one period the predominant religion in Bengal, and extended its sway from the Indian Ocean to the frontiers of China: this may be accounted for, perhaps, on the ground that those chronicles were composed by Brahmans who may have adopted in them their usual policy of taking little notice of their religious opponents, passing over their history in contemptuous silence.[41]

But compared to Kailash Chandra's critical history, the above comments of James Long are of little significance. At the same time, it should also be pointed out that though iron sharpens iron and a critical historian has the responsibility of creating other critical historians; Kailash Chandra unfortunately could not do that. As a result, after him Tripura historiography remained more or less uncritical and dull for decades. Supposing that the term 'interdisciplinary approach' (which sometimes arise from a shared conviction that the traditional disciplines are unable or unwilling to address an important problem) is a twentieth century term (as frequently viewed), nevertheless the concept had historical antecedents, and in the case of history writing, Kailash Chandra Singha was perhaps the first example in Tripura in that respect. His had a holistic approach of history and by promoting such new approach, history was brought into contact with a wide range of disciplines like archaeology, anthropology, sociology, ethnology, geography, economics, linguistics etc. which it conventionally ignored. Kailash Chandra sincerely believed that such a holistic approach would serve to augment, rather than a fragment researcher's understanding and imagination of the past and to make it relevant to the present.[42] From Kailash Chandra Singha's *Rajamala,* one could easily conclude that he was the pioneer in this region to uphold such interdisciplinary approach in the case of history writing.

Contemporary historians

Regarding the search and use of source material for history writing, Kailash Chandra Singha had been enlightened by the conversations and correspondences of some illustrious scholars of contemporary Bengal. To name a few, they were: (i) Rajendralal Mitra (1823-1891) who was the first modern Indologist of Indian origin, the first Indian President of The Asiatic Society of Bengal and one of the pioneers of the 'Bengal Renaissance'. (ii) Among the contemporary archaeologists, numismatists, epigraphists, antiquarians who threw some new light on medieval Bengal, Tripura and its neighbours was Nalini Kanta Bhattasali (1888-1947), whose contributions have gone a long way in clarifying many obscurities. Like Kailash Chandra Singha, Bhattasali was also a stout controversialist and his powerful pen never yielded from any conclusion he had arrived at. (iii) Ramaprasad Chanda (1873–1942) was a reputed historian and archaeologist from Rajshahi in East Bengal. Chanda wrote, in his celebrated *Gaudarajamala*,[43] that the most useful piece of learning for the uses of life is to unlearn what is untrue and the two most important methodological steps in historical research were (a) a meticulous search for 'sources' and (b) the sources must be checked for authenticity by the use of the right kind of scrutiny. (iv) Akshay Kumar Maitra (1861-1930) asserted that historians needed to maintain professional objectivity and detached impartiality from the subjects of their research and there could be no room for feelings and emotions in the process of historical analysis. Both Maitra and Ramaprasad Chanda came together for their common interest in research and antiquarian studies and they established the Varendra Research Society for the promotion of higher studies and research on the glorious past of Bengal. In *Gaudalekhamala*, published in 1912, Maitra included a few Pala copper-plates and inscriptions, and provided their Bengali translation which opened up new avenues of historical research. (v) Rakhaldas Bandyopadhyaya's (also known as R. D. Banerjee 1885-1930)[44] two-volume *Bangalar Itihas* (1914 and 1917) was one of the first attempts of writing a scientific history of Bengal and its neighbours. (vi) Romesh Chunder Dutt (1848-1909), with his charismatic personality, was a nationalist historian, economist, linguist, civil servant and politician of repute.[45] R.C. Dutt was indeed a source of inspiration to many scholars, including Kailash Chandra. (vii) The great scholar, Dinesh Chandra Sen (1866–1939),[46] also encouraged Kailash Chandra in various ways.

On areas bordering Tripura

Although the name of Kailash Chandra Singha's monumental work was *Rajamala ba Tripurar Itibritta,* the third part of this book was devoted to the history of Manipur,

Sylhet, Chittagong (including CHT), Bhulua/Noakhali, Kuki tribe (particularly the episode relating to Rutton Poiya), etc. Kailash Chandra had also given a detailed picture of the Jamatia Uprising of 1863 under Parikshit and its fall-out when Tripura was totally darkened by that *dreadful revolt.* Despite his very limited means, Singha made strenuous efforts to visit some inaccessible parts of the region, to gather more information about the inside people and to ascertain the identity of place names and also verify various historical information recorded in the ancient scripts and inscriptions. Regarding the limitations of Kailash Chandra Singha it is to be remembered that when he wrote about Sylhet and Cachar, Achyutacharan Chaudhuri's monumental work *Srihatter Itibritta* was not yet published.[47] The same is true regarding the history of Manipur, Chittagong, Noakhali, Kuki tribe etc. True, Kailash Chandra could not fully utilize the advantage of some recent archaeological excavations in Northeast India which virtually altered or remodeled some of our traditional concepts about the past. As a result, some of the conclusions that Kailash Chandra arrived at, may not stand with the test of time and like other scholars, his opinions are not always infallible. For example, Pilak in Belonia subdivision of South Tripura, drew the attention of researchers long after the death of Kailash Chandra, when Samarendra Chandra Debbarma, a scion of Tripura's royal family, gave first in 1927 a description of archaeological specimens contained underground the place in his book *Tripurar Smriti* and the German scholar H. B. Beshart opined that the sculptural and architectural remains of Pilak closely resemble those found in the Maynamoti-Paharpur area in Comilla district (present-day Bangladesh), *where the influence of Buddhism was apparent in the excavated art. Similarly, recent* archaeological excavations at Boxanagar in Sonamura subdivision of West Tripura have unearthed a large Buddhist complex, including relics of a *stupa*, teaching centre, a bronze image of Buddha and seals in Brahmi script etc., triggering a controversy over the exact history of the state. Several archeological wonders have also recently been excavated from Kalacherra village near Dharmanagar in North Tripura district, not very far from famous Unakoti rock cuts, the biggest bas-relief sculpture in Northeast India (belonging to the 8th or 9th century AD, if not, earlier). Thus, new and newer source materials are now becoming available to rewrite the history of Tripura. In fact, in the words of R. G. Collingwood (1889–1943), "Every new generation must rewrite history in its own way" as history is always an argument without an end.

Other publications

Among other publications of Kailash Chandra it should be mentioned that he had also edited *Shrimad Bhagabadgita*,[48] and contributed *Lichhabi Rajagan*[49] in *Bharati,* 1297 B.S., *Jajnagar Raja,*[50] in *Bharati,*[51] 1297 BS., *Kabindra Parameshwar O Srikar Nandir Mahabharat,*[52] and Kailash Chandra again mentioned about Parameshwar and Srikar Nandi in the third part of his *Rajamala,* (pp. 309ff). Kailash Chandra Singha was also in the editorial board of the *Tattyabodhini Patrika,* which was first published in 1843 from Calcutta not only to propagate the Brahmo faith and but also to enable regular contact among members of *Tattyabodhini Sabha*. Most of the luminaries of the 'Bengal Renaissance' were associated with that *Patrika*. In fact, Kailash Chandra Singha was a product of the nineteenth century 'Bengal Renaissance', though his main concern was Tripura and its adjacent areas.

As a historian

Although Kailash Chandra had never ever received a Ph.D. degree from any institution of higher learning, his major academic achievements in the field of history of Northeast India should not be underestimated. It can not be forgotten that *Rajamala ba Tripurar Itihas* is one of the few truly lasting books written for the general readers during the nineteenth century by a man of great scientific stature, a book, which though of striking merit, did not seem to have received either the critical recognition or the general audience that his work deserved. Even in *Sansad Bangali Charitabhidhan* ,[53] Kailash Chandra Singha's name did find only casual mention.

In the conclusive note of his great historical work, Kailash Chandra Singha quoted that ancient catholic priest St. Jerome (c. 347–420), who produced a number of globally acclaimed commentaries on Christian scriptures and who used to say : "It is always the best policy to speak the truth - unless, of course, you are an exceptionally good liar." In the seventeenth chapter of the second part of his *Rajamala,* Kailash Chandra Singha quoted the following remarks of Jerome regarding writing of history :[54] "If an offence comes out of the truth, better it is that offence comes, than the truth be conceited." That shows Kailash Chandra Singha's scholarly temperament. The renowned German philosopher Arthur Schopenhauer (1788–1860), best known for his pessimism, once remarked that "All truth passes through three stages. First, it is ridiculed. Second, it is violently opposed. Third, it is accepted as being self-evident."[55] In fact, the greatest friend of truth is time and in case of the estimable historical works of Kailash Chandra Singha, who tirelessly explored and investigated Tripura's forgotten past all through his life, Schopenhauer's remarks proved prophetic. Kailas Chandra was indeed an unsung historian of Northeast India.

Notes & References

1. The solar based Bengali Calendar year *Bangabda* is always 593 less than the year in the Gregorian Calendar. Thus 1273 *Bangabda* corresponds to 1866 AD.
2. Kailash Chandra Singha, *Rajamala ba Tripurar Itihas,* Kolkata, 1896, pp. 45-46.
3. The rivalry between the kings and priests for supremacy was nothing new in this context. In medieval history of the West, the papal-imperial conflict led to the weakening of the Western (Holy Roman) Empire, and gave birth to a series of proto-"nation" states [France, England, Spain, Portugal and eventually set the "nation-state" rather than the "imperial" standard for all European states. The conflict between church and state, in European history, unlike many other countries of the East, firmly established that **church** and **state** were distinct entities. T. F. Tout's famous book *The Empire and the Papacy, 9I8-I273,* is an eye-opener in this respect.
4. Rev. James Long in his 'An analysis of Rajmala Or Chronicles Of Tripura', [as published first in the *Journal Asiatic Society of Bengal,(JASB),* V0L. XIX, 1850, Calcutta] also mentioned:- *Human sacrifices prevailed at an early period in Tripura, and even of the late years strong suspicions have been entertained of the practice being occasionally observed at the Shrine of*

Kamakhya in Assam, and at the Kalighat at Calcutta. But in no part of India were more human victims offered than in Tripura which appears to have been one of the strongest holds of Hinduism.

5. Pierre Bayle (1647–1706), *Historical and Critical Dictionary*, published in 1695; Selections in English: Pierre Bayle (Richard H. Popkin transl.), *Historical and Critical Dictionary-Selections*, Hackett Publishing Company Inc, 1991.

6. On 15 October, 1949, Princely Tripura, after bidding farewell to the age-old kingship, was merged with the Indian Union and the administration of the state was actually taken over by the Govt. of India.

7. In 1983 and 1984 'Barnamala Prakashani' of Agartala reprinted in two volumes Kailash Chandra's *Rajamala ba Tripurar Itibritta* respectively as edited by Mahadev Chakravarti *et.al.* Again, in 1997, 'Akshar Publication' of Agartala reprinted *Rajamala ba Tripurar Itihas* with an introduction by Amalendu De.

8. Some *Kokborok*-speaking people claim that the Kokborok language had its *koloma* scripts, but lost in the ocean of times. They point out that a significant hint for the antiquity of the Kokborok language can be found in the following lines of Kali Prasanna Sen's *Sri Rajamala (SRM)* written in Bengali, which mentions that the *"Rajamala"* was first written in *Kokborok:- " Purbe Rajmala chhilo Tripur bhashate / Payar gathila sab sakale bujhite..,"—SRM,* I, p.6. But such thinking is rightly challenged as Tipra/Tuipra language in fifteenth century may not have been as developed to have a script of its own. It was Doulot Ahmed who first published only in 1897 AD from Comilla his Kokborok grammar book "*Kokbokma*". In 1900 AD Radhamohan Thakur of Agartala had written Kokborok grammar book namely, *Kokborokma,* and then *Troipur Kathamala* (learning book) and *Troipur Bhashabidhan* (dictionary) in 1906 and 1907 respectively. According to pioneer Linguists like Haraprasad Shastri (1853–1931) or Suniti Kumar Chatterji (1890-1977), even Bengali language in the fifteenth century was in its infant stage.

9. Reprint by Tripura State Tribal Cultural Research Institute & Museum, Govt. of Tripura, Agartala, 2005.

10. See also: Dinesh Chandra Bhattacharya, *SwadhinTripurarRajamala*, in *Prabasi,Falgoon*, 1345 BS.

11. Tipra/Tuipra/Tripuri language [now known as *'Kokborok'*] belongs to the Tibeto-Burman group of languages, and its roots can be traced to the Sino-Tibetan family of speeches. Some *Kokborok*–speaking people, however, think that it was actually *'twi-bupra'* (*twi* = water and *bupra* = confluence) meaning "confluence of water".

12. It is to be mentioned that Suniti Kumar Chatterji in his monumental work *Kirata-Jana-krti,* has analysed the entire story and its implications in such a way that the book, in the words of Sir Jadunath Sarkar, served "as a road-chart for future workers on the cultural history of these peoples." But Kailash Chandra Singha without taking any benefit from that great work of S.K. Chatterji [as it was first published only in 1951 by the Asiatic Society, Calcutta] could show before him the 'road-chart'.

13. See C. U. Aitchison, *A Collection Of Treaties, Engagements, And Sunnuds Relating To India And Neighbouring Countries*, London, 1862, p.213, where Aitchison mentions : *The early history of Cachar or Hadimba as it was anciently called, is obscure. It would appear that it formerly belonged to the kingdom of Tripura. It is, however, certain that the last native king of Cachar was the descendant of a line of princes who originally came from the Assam Valley. The Cachar Kings were forced, by the aggressions of the Ahoms on the north and to the Angami Nagas on the south, to remove and take up their abode on the Mahar river. While settled there, about the beginning or*

middle of the 17th century, the Cachari king married a daughter of the Tripura Raja and received the valley of Cachar as her dowry, and the capital was transferred to Kaspur between 1700 and 1750. Govinda Chandra, the last Rajah of Cachar, was assassinated in 1830 and, as he left no heir natural or adopted, the country was annexed by the British Government on the 14th August 1832.

14. Kailash Chandra Singha, *op.cit.*, second chapter, pp. 13 ff.
15. Nabadwip Chandra was the father of the famous music maestro Sachin Debbarman (S.D. Barman) who was born in Comilla on 1 October 1906 and died on 31 October 1975 in Mumbai.
16. The ancient Indian mythology says that there are eight different types of marriages. But according to the customary law and traditional marriage practices followed by the common tribal people of Tripura, a young man has to serve his prospective bride's family if he wants to marry her and the custom is called *Jamai-khata / Jamai Utha* or *kaijagnani*. On the other hand, non-ritualised *hiknanani* form of marriage was similar to the *Gandharva* marriage or simple love marriage of ancient Indian mythology, without any document or ritual. The *hiknanani,* in a modified form, was also known as the *Kachua* marriage system.
17. England's one of the earliest and pioneer traders to India and Burma. At first Fitch was no chronicler but did eventually write descriptions of the south east Asia as he saw in 1583-1591, upon his return to England in 1591.
18. Jean-Baptiste *Tavernier* was a French traveller and pioneer of western trade with India.
19. François Bernier was a French physician and traveller who treated the Mughal emperor Aurangzeb for around 12 years during his stay in India.
20. Sarma and Bairagi were the two Assamese envoys to Tripura sent by the Ahom king Rudra Singha (1696-1714) of Assam. Their accounts written in 1724 were later on edited and published by Surya Kumar Bhuyan, as *Tripura Buranji* or *A Chronicle of Tipperah*, Department of Historical and Antiquarian Studies, Government of Assam, Gauhati, 1938.
21. Sir Herbert Hope Risley (1851–1911) did extensive work on the tribes and castes of Bengal. Risley is, however, remembered most importantly for the formal application of the theoretical *Varna* (caste) system to the entire Hindu population of India in the decennial 1901 Census, of which he was in charge. Risley's famous book on *Castes and Tribes of Bengal* was published in 1891.
22. The Numismatic Society of India was founded in 1910 at Allahabad by a group of six persons among whom Sir Richard Burn was the most prominent.
23. James Sutherland Cotton (1847-1918), Editor of the *Academy* (a weekly literary magazine) in London and writer of *Colonies And Dependencies,* Part I (India), London, 1883 and writer of many books and publications on Indian life and history.
24. In Bengal historiography, Charles Stewart (1764-1837) is taken as a pioneer historian. Stewart's *History of Bengal: From the First Muhammadan Invasion until the Virtual Conquest of that Country by the English AD 1757*, London, 1813, is, in fact, the first rigorously researched and interpretative work.
25. Sir Alexander Mackenzie (1842- 1902) a civilian and Lieutenant Governor of Bengal from December 1895 to April 1898 published his book *The North-East Frontier of India.* The book has its genesis in his Memorandum on the North-East Frontier of Bengal [Alexander Mackenzie. *History of the Relations of the Government with the Hill Tribes of the North-East Frontier of Bengal*. Calcutta, 1884.]

26. Rev. James Long (1814-87), "An analysis of Rajmala Or Chronicles Of Tripura", in the*Journal of the Asiatic Society of Bengal,(JASB),* xix, 1850, Calcutta.
27. T.H. Lewin, *Hill Tracts of Chittagong and Dwellers Therein,*Calcutta, 1869.
28. The multi-volume *magnum opus, Linguistic Survey of India,* often referred to as the *LSI* - a monumental and comprehensive survey of the languages of British India, describing 364 languages and dialects - was a project conducted between 1894 and 1928, under the direction of Sir George Abraham Grierson [1851-_1941], an ICS officer.
29. The British Political agents of Tripura state in between 1871 and 1890 were A.W.B. Power, Captain E.G. Lillington, Captain W.L. Samuels, T.E. Cox head, C.W. Bolton etc. As a result of the clash of power between Birchandra Manikya and the British Agents, the Political Agency system was abolished in 1890.
30. Kailash Chandra had also consulted English journals like the *Asiatic Researches, comprising history, antiquities etc. as* published by the Asiatic Society, Calcutta, from 1788 to1839, *JASB, Calcutta Gazette, Calcutta Review,* etc.
31. Chakla Roshnabad area, a zemindari of Tripura kings, spread over present Comilla, Brahmanbaria districts and parts of Habiganj sub-division of Sylhet and Noakhali districts in present Bangladesh with headquarters in Comilla, which was far the most valuable of their possessions. The zemindari land once belonged to the Raja of Tripura until 1733 when Shuja-ud-Din Muhammad Khan (1727-1739) of Bengal invaded and seized the territory that later formed the district (and part of Noakhali). With the grant of the *Diwani* in1765 administration of the territory fell to the British East India Company, and the Manikyas first paid mainly a tribute of ivory and elephant.
32. The system of an annual report embodying the main events and performances of all the tiers of the administration was introduced since 1786. *Annual Report on the Administration of Bengal* is a record serial on the activities and achievements of the Government of Bengal, comprising the so-called Chakla zemindary of the Manikyas. Thus the Report on the Administration of Bengal and the *Annual Administration Reports of the Political Agency of Hill Tipperah,* provide extraordinary insight into the state of the colonial governance.
33. J.G. Cummings, *Survey and settlement of the Chakla Roshnabad Estate in the districts of Tippera and Noakhali, 1892-99,* Calcutta: Bengal Secretariat Press, 1899.
34. *E.F. Sandys, History of Tripura*. The Star Printing Works, Calcutta, January 1915; Reprint by Tripura State Tribal Cultural Research Institute & Museum, Govt. of Tripura, Agartala, 1997.
35. Eric J. Hobsbawm, "Ethnicity and Nationalism in Europe," in Gopal Balakrishnan, ed., *Mapping the Nation*, London, 1996, p. 255.
36. Edward Hallett "Ted" Carr (1892– 1982) was a liberal realist and later left-wing British historian, best known for his 14-volume history of the Soviet Union,and for his remarkable little classic *What is History?,* in which he laid out historiographical principles rejecting traditional historical methods and practices.
37. Pearl S. Buck (1892-1973), also known by her Chinese name Sai Zhenzhu, was most popular American writer of her day, who spent most of her time until 1934 in China. Her novel *The*

Good Earth was the best-selling fiction book in the U.S. and she was awarded the Nobel Prize for Literature in 1938.

38. Arnold Joseph Toynbee (1889–1975) was a British historian whose twelve-volume analysis of the rise and fall of civilizations in his *magnum opus, A Study of History*, 1934–1961 as published by Oxford University, examined history from a global perspective. See, *A Study of History,* volume V, entitled *The Disintegration of Civilizations (Part One)*, Oxford University, 1939.

39. For example, because of the influence of queen Bhanumati, the king nominated his fourth son Samarendrachandra (son of Bhanumati) as *Barthakur,* setting aside the claims of other senior sons belonging to other queens.

40. English translation of this portion of Kailash Chandra Singha's *Rajamala* [second part, seventeenth chapter, pp.244-246] by Apurba Chandra Bhattacharyya, *Progressive Tripura.* Calcutta, 1930, p. 40.

41. James Long (1814-1887), 'An analysis of Rajmala Or Chronicles Of Tripura', in the *Journal of the Asiatic Society of Bengal, (JASB),* xix, 1850, Calcutta; Reprint by Isan Press, Dacca, 1911; Reprint by Tripura State Tribal Cultural Research Institute & Museum, Govt. of Tripura, Agartala, 1995; Revised. ed. by S. Chaudhuri. (Alternate Title : *Ananalysis of the chronicles of the kings of Tripura*), Firma KLM, Calcutta, 1978.

42. Even in today's medical science, an increasing number of physicians are advocating a holistic approach to health care, emphasizing prevention as well as treatment. It may be mentioned that since the late 1990's the term 'holistic' evolved into the term 'wholistic' in order to clarify the concept even further in the field of every discipline as a holistic approach is a recognition of the homogeneity and wholeness of life.

43. *Gaudarajamala* was published by 'Varendra Research Society', Rajshahi, in 1912.

44. Rakhaldas Bandyopadhyaya is best known for his work *Eastern Indian Medieval School of Sculpture,* and is famous for the discovery of Mohenjodaro, dating from 3000 BC.

45. R.C. Dutt's first book on the economic problems of the cultivators was *'Peasantry of Bengal'*, written in 1875; *'Famines in India,'* published in 1900, containing his strongly-argued thesis about the over-assessment of land revenue, was a treasure to many nationalist historians. But his greatest works were *India under Early British Rule, 1757-1837* published in 1901, and the *Economic History of India in the Victorian Age* in 1902. His thesis on land revenue was reiterated in the famous 'Open Letters', to which Lord Curzon's Government gave an official reply in the Resolution of 1902.

46. Dinesh Chandra Sen wrote and edited about 55 books in Bengali (including *Bangabhasha o shahitya* and *Brihat Banga*) and twelve books in English in addition to a large number of research articles published in various learned journals.

47. Achyutacharan Chaudhuri, *Srihatter Itibritta,* Kolkata and Silchar, 1317-1324/ 1920-27, 2 vols.

48. Kailash Chandra Singha's edited *Shrimad Bhagabadgita* was published by Victoria Press, Kolkata, in 1885 and dedicated to Maharshi Debendra Nath Tagore, father of Rabindranath Tagore, and a copy of the book is to be found in Jayakrishna Public Library, Uttarpara, Hooghly, West Bengal. This book is comparable with Kali Prasanna Singha's (1840–1870) famous translation from Sanskrit *Mahabharat-Adi Parba,* as published from Kolkata in 1859.

49. The *Lichhabis* are said to have migrated into Nepal from north India around 250 AD. The *Lichhabi* rule spanned over a period of about 830 years. S. K. Chatterji declares that *Lichhabis* are from *kirata* origin. *'Lichhabi'* itself is a *kirata* word meaning children of *Li* family (*chhabi* = children). They themselves claimed Indo-Mangoloid or *kirata* nationality. However, they adopted Hinduism and preferred to be called as *'Kshetri'* meaning ruling family.

50. *Jajnagar, i.e.* the former Jajatinagar (modern Jagati on the *Mahanadi* river) in present Odisha, previously known as Kalinga, Utkal, Orissa etc.

51. From 1877 to 1915, the headquarters of the literary magazine *Bharati* was at the Tagore House, Jorasanko, Kolkata and Kailash Chandra, being associated with *Bharati,* was deeply influenced by the cultural traditions of the Tagore family.

52. *Kabindra Parameshwar O Srikar Nandir Mahabharat* was published in *Sahitya patrika,* 5th year, pp. 800 ff. The poet Srikar Nandi rendered Bengali translation of the Sanskrit *Mahabharata* for his patron, Chhuti Khan (c 1520 AD) of Chittagong, and the poem is generally known as *Chhutikhani Mahabharat,* composed in *payar* and *tripadi* rhyme, which was very popular in Bengal during the 16th century.

53. *Sansad Bangali Charitabhidhan* is the biographical dictionary in Bengali about the noted Bengalees, as edited by Subodh Chandra Sengupta and Anjali Bose, *Sahitya Sansad*, Kolkata, 1976/1998.

54. See, Kailash Chandra Singha, *op.cit.,* Seventeenth chapter, fn. 32.

55. Robert I Fitzhenry (ed.), *The Harper Book of Quotations*, Collins, New York, 3rd edition, 1993, p. 451.

2

Achyutcharan Choudhury (1865-1953)

—*Subir Kar*

Biographical Sketch

A traditional scholar and one of the pioneer historians of early twentieth century Northeast India, Achyutcharan Choudhury was born on 23rd *Magh*, 1272 BS (1865) in the village Maina in a decaying zamindar family of Pratapgarh in the Sylhet district (now in district of Karimganj) of Assam. He breathed his last on 10th Aswin, 1360 BS (1953). His father Adyaitacharan Choudhury was a devout Vaishnava, while his great grandfather Kanuram Choudhury was a powerful land lord of Pratagarh-Jaffargarh *parganas* and said to have been a loyal follower of the East India Company's administration in Bengal. Since the rebellion of Nawab Radharam against the Company (1786) up to the revolt of Kuki tribes (1871) this Choudhury family helped the British in consolidation of their rule in southern Barak-Surma valley in many ways. Even at the time of 'Sepoy Mutiny' they acted against the braves of 'the first war of independence' and tried to harvest their fortune.[1] Appreciating their services to the British at the time of Lushai expedition, then Collector of Sylhet Mr. H. S. Sutherland wrote in a letter to the Assistant Secretary to the Government of Bengal that "Madhabcharan Choudhuri is one of the most tractable and obliging Mirasdars in the district. During the Lushai expedition he was most useful. In the Lushai survey, when a stampede of the coolies, early in 1873, might have brought the whole of the survey operation to an end Madhabcharan Choudhuri was again useful. I started him off at a moment's notice to meet Assistant Collector who was out in the district, and who received great assistance from Madhabcharan Choudhury", etc.[2] Achyutcharan Choudhury himself unhesitatingly admitted this fact in his book *Srihatter Itibritta*.[3]

After completion of his early education in his village school Achyutcharan was admitted in Sylhet Government High School. He stayed in the house of Piyaricharan Das, who was imprisoned for three months for an assault on William Circes in Calcutta in 1875 and after his release left the government job, returned to Sylhet and launched the publication of a Bengali weekly *Srihatta Prakash* which played a significant role in nationalist fervour in the Barak-Surma valley.[4] A patriot and a poet, Pyaricharan was among those who were critical about the transfer of Sylhet-Cachar from Bengal to Assam in 1874.[5] The stay in such an environment of patriotic and literary firmament impacted the young mind of Achyutcharan. However, after completion of his high school education he returned to his village and continued traditional Sanskrit learning at home. He joined as a school teacher in their family school, named Banga Vidyalaya, which was founded by Krishna Prasad, an ancestor of Achyutcharan. He also built-up a museum-cum-archive and a library in his own house and developed a collection of antics, archaeological specimens, rare manuscripts, documents and other historical objects collected from different parts of the valley. In 1904 he joined Girish Banga Vidyalaya, as a Second Pandit, on a monthly salary for Rs. 20. He also served for sometimes in the Tahsil Office of Patherkandi-Ratabari revenue circle. A branch of the Post Office was opened in the Kutcherry (Zamindar's office) of the family, before it was shifted to the nearby market area at Kanaibazar, and Achyutcharan voluntarily served as honorary Branch Postmaster for a long time in the interest of local people.[6]

The Choudhury family of Maina was well known for their devotion to Vaisnavism and Achyutcharan's philosophy of life was guided by this religious inspiration and spirit. He inherited his faith and belief from his father Advaitacharan who was a devotee of *Sri Sri Madhava Sampradaya* of the Adyaita School. Achyutcharan regularly contributed articles in the Vaishnavite journals like *Sri Patrika, Sri Sri Vishnupriya Patrika, Sri Sri Vishnupriya-Gauranga Patrika, Brahma Vidya Patrika*, etc. and the number of such articles contributed by him numbered more than two hundred. Some of his articles were research oriented, particularly those on Vaishnavism in Assam and Sylhet. He wrote as many as twenty-eight books on Vaisnavism and related literary and cultural subjects, including historical biographies of the Vaishnava saints like *Vidyapati, Advaita Prabhu,* and *Jagadish Pandit*. Some of his works are still unpublished.[7] His works on Vaisnavite literature was highly appreciated by the *Vaisnava Mahamandala* and they honored him with the title *'Tattvanidhi'*. The great littérateur and historian Dinesh Chandra Sen called him *'Gaudabhusana'* and expressed his indebtedness to Achyutcharan saying, "I sought the help of my friend Babu Achyut Charan Choudhury of Maina, Kanaibazar, Sylhet, for the solution of many problems. He is now the greatest living authority on all questions regarding the old history of Sylhet."[8] Nagendranath Basu also expressed his gratitude to Achyutcharan in his monumental historical work *Banger Jatiya Itihas*.[9] In fact, Achyutcharan Choudhury Tattvanidhi was recognized as a researcher and littérateur of merit in Bengal and Assam well before the publication of his *Srihatter Itibritta*.

Achyutcharan's inquisitiveness about the myths, tales and fables since his early boyhood developed into a historical consciousness and his search for historical objects in own surroundings drew his attention to the ruins of the palace of Pratapgarh. He then wrote a book in Bengali entitled *Pratapgarher Rajbarir Bibaran*, which is a historical narrative of the palace of the kings of Pratapgarh (Sylhet).[10] The association with literary organizations and periodicals provided him the outlet to share his research findings with contemporary literati in Assam and Bengal. In 1920, a branch of the Bangiya Sahitya Praishad was established in Sylhet and Achyutcharan Choudhury, Padmanath Vidyavinode and many other local scholars were associated with it.[11] In the first session of the Parishad in 1920 Achyutcharan presented a research article on the Bhatera Inscriptions of Sylhet which was published in the *Sahitya Parisad Patrika*.[12] He had earlier presented another article on the same inscriptions in 'Surma Upatyaka Literary Conference' held at Maulavi Bazar in 1916.[13] Achyutcharan Choudhury was Vice-President of the Shrihatta Sahitya Parisat, of which Padmanath Vidyabinode was the President, and the organization published for many years its mouth piece *Shrihatta Sahitya Parisat Patrika*. He was also the associate editor of a Bengali literary magazine, *Kamala*, and editor of the monthly *Srihatta Darpan*. He contributed several articles on aspects of history and culture of Sylhet in those publications.[14]

Achyutcharan's personal life was full of turmoil and tragedies but he never surrendered to the fate. The tragic events of his life included the death of his two wives, three children and a younger brother. While he was busy for the publication of *Srihatter Itibritta* his second wife died of cholera at the age of 25. After a few days his one and a half year old son Kusumanga died. The last tragedy occurred in the year of publication of the first part (*Purbangsha*) of his *magnum opus*, called *Srihatter Itibritta*. The year of publication of the second part (*Uttarangsa*) of the same book saw the death of his daughter Nilima. The tragic death of Kusumanga caused a sense of guilt in his mind as he was then more involved in *Srihatter Itibritta* than attention to the family and to console his bereaved heart he composed a poem in memoriam of his dear departed son. He also renamed his personal library as 'Kusum Library'. This library, which Achyutcharan had developed bit by bit for many years with more than two thousand valuable books and rare manuscripts, was opened to the public. Finally, this library was donated to Srihatta Sahitya Parisat.[15]

Contributions to history

Achyutcharan Choudhury's hunger to unfold the history of Srihatta (modern Sylhet), which in early times included the entire Barak-Surma valley (now divided between India and Bangladesh), grew in his childhood and immediately after his high school education he started collecting manuscripts, documents, books and archaeological and numismatic objects and artifacts to develop a personal library-cum-museum in his own house. A literary persona by nature, he took interest in collecting oral literature of the valley in the form of myths and legends, tales and fables, folksongs, hymns, riddles and couplets and looked for historical contents in those creative but timeless literary pieces. He visited all the historical sites and places of worship in the valley over the years. He also visited important persons, families and local scholars and collected their family histories and whatever documents, *puthis* and other materials were in their possessions. He also studied a vast range of mainstream Indian literature, particularly those of Bengal and Assam, and surveyed them from the period of *Veda*, *Purana* and *Mahabharata* up to the latest historical books, journals, official reports, records and other available documents on Bengal and Assam. In fact, Tattvanidhi's crowning effort and industrious zeal in the field of historical research is well understood when we go through his bibliographical notes, index and anecdotes etc. which show how successfully he attempted to adopt a scientific methodology to construct a true history of Srihatta in real terms. The bibliography includes almost all the books written and published till then in history of India, Bengal and Assam, gazetteers, administrative and census reports, accounts, travelogues, etc. in English and Bengali.[16]

Achyutcharan Choudhury Tattvanidhi is still a living legend for his outstanding work, *Srihatter Itibritta* (or history of Sylhet), in Bengali. The first volume (*Purbangsha*) of this book was published by Shri Upendranath Paulchoudhury from Calcutta in 1317 BS (1910), with an introductory note of Shri Padmanath Devasarmah (Mahamohapadhyaya Pandmanath Bhattacharyya Vidyavinod), and volume II (*Uttarangsha*) was jointly published by Shri Achyutcharan Choudhury Tattvanidhi and Shri Baidyanath Dey from Saraswati Library, Silchar, in 1323 BS (1916). Volume I covered the history of Sylhet in general from the prehistoric times to the close of nineteenth century in 606 pages, with several impressive visuals of monuments, art objects and coins and the facsimiles of rare documents, both private and official, while volume II dealt the life-history of well known personalities and important families in 360 pages.[17] His treatment is indeed very detailed on the basis of whatever sources had come to notice till writing of the volumes. Beginning with geographical and sociological description of the region, he dealt with all major aspects of history, namely, political, social and economic, in a chronological order, covering all major events and developments. As stated already, the book has been organized by the author in two volumes, namely, *Purbangsha* or Volume I and *Uttarangsha* or Volume II. Volume I is divided into two parts - geographical accounts and historical accounts, while Volume II is also divided into two parts - genealogical accounts and biographical accounts. The narratives in Volume I are detailed in 42 chapters and those in Volume II in 32 chapters, besides the appendices.[18]

The purpose behind writing the book seems to have been twofold for Achyutcharan. Firstly, the Indian renaissance in the nineteenth century, which inspired the recovery of cultural heritage of the people of India, had significantly impacted the minds of the people in Bengal, including the Barak-Surma valley. Bankimchandra Chattopadhyaya, one of the harbingers of renaissance and nationalism in India, in particular, had called upon the Bengali intelligentsia to write the history of Bengal and he himself penned several essays on the subject.[19] A large number of books on history of Bengal and Bengalis, including micro-level history of the districts, subdivisions, *parganas*, estates, etc., covering the major themes of life and culture, and historical biographies, were written and published in Bengali in the nineteenth and early-twentieth century. In Sylhet also, several such books, particularly on erstwhile local kingdoms, genealogies and biographies, were published before *Srihatter Itibritta*. Among the earlier books on history of Sylhet were *Srihatta Darpan* by Maulavi Mohammad Ahmad[20] and *Srihatter Itihas* by Mohinimohan Dasgupta.[21] Achyutcharan used those publications, including the essays of Bankimchandra, in his work.[22] Secondly, the Sylhet-Cachar region, or ancient Srihatta, suffered apprehensions of a crisis of identity ever since these two districts were transferred from the Dacca Division of Bengal to Assam in 1874 and the local intelligentsia were loud in their protests against this separation from Bengal. Achyutcharan also mentioned about the dissatisfaction of the people on this point of separation. He was critical of the land revenue system that was imposed on Sylhet under Assam Land Revenue Regulation, 1886 and emphatically opined that such an imposition was contrary to the decision and the assurance which was given by Lord Northbrook, the then Governor-General of India.[23] The first volume of *Srihatter Itibritta* came out in 1910 when Sylhet was in the 'Province of Eastern Bengal and Assam' and the second volume in 1916 when it was again in Assam. However, as regards his inspiration in writing *Srihatter Itibritta*, Achyutcharan said in his Preface,

> In my school days in Sylhet, I stayed in the house of Pyaricharan Das (the editor of the newspaper *Srihatta Prakash*). One day at home while the then renowned Deputy Inspector of School Rai Sahib Navakishore Sen and Piyaricharan were discussing about the glorious history of Sylhet, with dazzling eyes I witnessed and listened parts of their conversations and felt the sigh of their lamentation for the absence of any authentic history. That day I also came to know that Pyaricharan prepared a note on the historical events of Sylhet and both of them agreed to publish that note incorporating some more details. But that book could not see the light of the day. The deep concern and love for the land of those two great friends and their absorbing voice followed me all the time. Gradually, I felt that we are not ordinary creatures, we have a great heritage of socio-religious and cultural traditions. Sylhet is a sacred land of Sri Chaitanya and other great saints and intellectuals. ... Afterwards I decided to collect the materials to know and to inform others of the glory of our ancestors."[24]

Achyutcharan further informed that when he was editor of the monthly magazine, *Srihatta Darpan*, he collected some materials from different places and compiled them for publication as a book, '*Srihatta Deepika*'. He had sent his manuscript to the press, though he was not sure whether he would be able to bear the cost of publication. In the mean time, Padmanath Vidyabinode, then Deputy Inspector of Schools, Sylhet, came to know about it and he himself offered to meet all the expenses for publication of the book. In fact, Padmanath was himself planning to write a history of Sylhet and for this purpose he was collecting materials for many years. He handed over all the materials he had already collected to Achyutcharan and asked the latter to make the work more comprehensive. It transpired from the discussions between the two that the manuscript that was sent to press and a part of which was already printed, required some changes. The manuscript of '*Srihatta Deepika*' was thereafter withdrawn from the press and a circular appeal was made to the enlightened members of public through local newspapers and periodicals to share with Achyutcharan whatever documents or information they possessed to make the proposed work a comprehensive history of Sylhet. The response was spontaneous and the source materials poured in from all quarters. The result was that '*Srihatta Deepika*' developed into the massive *Srihatter Itibritta*.[25]

The publication of first volume (*Purbangsha*) of *Srihatter Itibritta* was immediately hailed by the enlightened and responsible quarters in Bengal and Assam as a great work in history. The Eastern Bengal and Assam Text Book Committee, Dacca, recommended this monumental work of history for libraries and prize books in schools and colleges in Dacca, Chittagong and Rajshahi Divisions. The Director of Public Instructions, Govt. of Eastern Bengal and Assam, accepted the recommendation and notification to the effect were promptly issued.[26] The newspapers and literary magazines, both English and Bengali, in Calcutta, Dacca, Silchar and Sylhet highly appreciated the book and carried laudable comments of the historians on the illustrious work of Achyutcharan Choudhury. Sir Jadunath Sarkar said : "In writing the history of Sylhet the systematic study and the method he (Achyutcharan) applied is a rare example and may be an ideal for the other historians of Bengal. Firstly, the materials collected for this book is a product of collective enterprise. To collect the related data leaflets were distributed and appeal made to the people through different newspapers. After that, information was collected from the village school teachers in every locality of the district. Lastly, the necessary records and documents were collected from various archives. All the available materials were then examined and scrutinized. As a result, the methodology and discipline and collective efforts which are applied in writing history in modern Europe, the author of this book has also followed the same procedure and technique. ... 'The History of Sylhet' is the only instance of such an ideal historical work.... In writing social history of Bengal this book may be accepted as a primary source." [27] *The Empire* wrote : " It is with very great satisfaction, therefore , that we announce the publication of a 'History of Sylhet' by Mr. Achyut Charan Choudhury Tattvanidhi written in a way in which a history should be written. ... We can say without hesitation that it will make the work of future Historians of Bengal easier in many ways."[28] The same newspaper again commented in another review : "If Bengali writers will follow in his steps they will be able to produce many excellent historical works in due course."[29] *The Amrita Bazar Patrika*, in a leaded news item under caption, 'The Geographical and Historical works of Sylhet', said : "We are glad to notice that Srijut Achyut Charan Choudhury Tattvanidhi of Sylhet, who some years ago, undertook to write a History of the District he lives in, has at last brought out a big volume containing the Geographical and Historical accounts of the District of Sylhet. This of course, is the first volume, with a promise to complete the work in another volume similar to this size. [This work] when complete, will undoubtedly add to the store of our vernacular literature, which is going to be enriched almost every day with valuable production and will prove useful to the reading public. The author of this work is already well known for his steady pursuit to collate and collect information - historical, biographical and geographical. In these pages his merit has been displayed quite in keeping with the reputation he has already acquired in the field of researches. It is pleasing to find that the author has taken great pains in gathering information about religious sects and sentiments which are calculated to be factors of cardinal importance to mould the character of the people and to form a basis of the History of a Nation. The author is to be congratulated for the fair performance of the arduous task he has undertaken. The work has been decorated with several pictures, and facsimiles of some documents he happened to find in the mass of neglected papers both private and official. The author richly deserves encouragement at the hands of the public for the production of this valuable work which we doubt not throws a flood of light on the materials which served to constitute the basis of History of the District of Sylhet and which were hitherto unknown even to those who had curiosity to peep into the past regarding the important District of Sylhet. The enterprise of the author is most laudable, which if undertaken by patriotic and learned residents of other Districts, would, we are sure, positively tend to give us much more important information regarding the history of the nation than what we are now obtaining from the official Gazetteers." [30] *The Indian Messenger* wrote : "Babu Achyut Charan Choudhury is already known to the Bengali reading public as a writer of some importance. His crowning effort in the field of research has been this volume of history. .. The amount of industry and research he has brought to bear upon this work of love does Mr. Choudhuri no small credit. ....In the opinion of the author, Sylhet, in the remote past, formed a part of the Aryan kingdom of Pragjyotishpur and the country of 'Shi-li-tsa-to-lo' that Huen Tsang described as situated to the north-east of the kingdom of Samatata was no other than Sylhet. The long line of eminent men that it produced would be unaccountable. To mention only a few, Shri Chaitanya though born in Nabadwip, belonged to Sylhet by his father's and mother's side. Sylhet claims as its own Advaita, the great Raghunath Siromani, subtlest logician that Bengal ever produced. Mahesh Nyayalankar, who like Raghunandan wrote 28 books on old Smriti, called 'Pradeepas', Baninath Vidyasagar whose commentary is one of the best ever written in Sanskrit, Shah Rehanuddin who for the excellence of his composition was given the title of 'the Bulbul-I-Bangala' by the Emperor of Delhi, of whose sons he was a tutor. Copious references and useful appendixes have enhanced the value of the book. We recommend it to the public and congratulate the author on the success he has attained." [31] Kailaschandra Singha, author of *Rajmala ba Tripurar Itibritta* (1876), remarked : "National history is the foundation of a glorious nation. The time has come to write the national history of Bengal; but if the history of the regions is not collected the writing of the history of Bengal will not be possible. .. It is now our duty to come forward to write the history of our own districts following the model of *Srihatter Itibritta*."[32] As a matter of fact, almost all the leading Bengali newspapers of the time, like *Anandabazar Patrika*, *Bangabasi*, *Bangla Masik Patra*, etc. came forward with positive comments in appreciating the wonderful work that was done by writing the real history of Sylhet.[33]

As a historian

Achyutcharan Choudhury Tattvanidhi was not a historian, either by education, training or profession. A scion of a Zamindar family, he served as a teacher of a junior school and a postmaster by choice in the spirit of social work. He had no formal higher education either. On the other hand, he was widely read, self-educated, and born with skill and passion for scholarship that guided him to write a large number of books and articles. History was his passion and revealing the real history of Sylhet to the people of Bengal was his mission. In this, he was inspired by the spirit of the renaissance era to rediscover own heritage in every region of India and the threat to the cultural identity of his own people in the Barak-Surma valley due to the redrawing of provincial boundary artificially by the British colonial rulers of India. He read a large number of books in history which were written by well known historians of India and the world. He was a pioneer in the region in developing a private library-cum-museum and archives by collecting and preserving source materials and live objects of history. The books and articles he wrote on the history of

Sylhet were source-based and he used footnotes and references like modern historians. For writing *Srihatter Itibritta* he used not only the mainstream (Indian), regional (Bengal and Assam) and local (Sylhet-Cachar) literary sources but also official and non-official documents as well as the archaeological, epigraphic and numismatic evidences to the extent these were recovered till the time he wrote his work. He also used oral sources like myths, legends and genealogies, but only after due verifications in light of conventional sources. As stated already, the great historians of his time appreciated *Srihatter Itibritta* as a great work in history. The contemporary historians of Barak-Surma valley, like J.B. Bhattacharjee[34] and Sujit Choudhury,[35] have also extensively used *Srihatter Itibritta* in their works. Hence, Achyutcharan Choudhury Tattvanidhi was a historian by his contributions to history.

Besides unfolding the history of Sylhet to all lovers of history, *Srihatter Itibritta* served a great purpose of history in establishing the historical identity of the people of Barak-Surma valley at a time when an apprehension loomed large that the real identity of the people of the valley might be overshadowed someday due to its political separation from Bengal. Achyutcharan responded to the call of the time and his work re-discovered the region and the territorial and cultural identity of its people with political, cultural and anthropological uniqueness from ancient times to the height of British colonial rule in India. This explains why the millions of people of Sylhet origin all over the world look upon *Srihatter Itibritta* as a deed of their identity and the original book is required to be reprinted again and again even after hundred years of its publication.[36]

Notes & References

1. Subir Kar, *1857 in North East – A reconstruction from folk and oral sources*, Akansha Publishing House, New Delhi, 2008, p. 76; J.B. Bhattacharjee, *Cachar Under British Rule in Northeast India*, Radiant Publishers, New Delhi, 1977, pp. 287-91.
2. Extract of a letter from H.C. Sutherland, Collector of Sylhet, to the Assistant Secretary to the Government of Bengal, No. 971 dated Sylhet, the 30th August 1874.
3. Achyutcharan Choudhury, *Srihatter Itibritta*, *Purbangsa* (Volume I), p.46-65, Calcutta, 1317 BS (1910), pp. 46-65.
4. Narendra Kumar Guptachoudhury, *Srihatta Pratibha*, Sylhet 1368 BS (1961), pp. 91-92.
5. Mohiuddin Shiru, *Sylheter Shatabarser Sangbadikata* (Hundred Years of Journalism in Sylhet), Utsa Prakashan, Dhaka, 1998, p. 25.
6. Narendrakumar Guptachoudhury, *op.cit*.
7. The published books of Achyutcharan Choudhury include *Bhakti Niryyan* (1299,BS), *Srimat Gopal Bhatta Goswamir Jiban Charita* (1302 BS), *Srimat Haridasthakurer Jiban Charita* (1302 BS), *Prem Prasanga [Madhavendra Katha]* (1304 BS), *AbhiramCharita* (1306 BS), *Srimat Shyamananda Charita* (1307 BS), *Sripad Iswarpuri* (1309 BS), *Sabas Chhabi [Sachitra Sisupath]* (1311 BS), *Srimat Rup-Sanatan* (1312 BS), *Sri Chaitanyacharita [Sachitra Sisupath]* (1312 BS), *Srihatter Itiĥas pranayankalpe Samgrihita Bibaranabalir Suchipatra* (1314 BS), *Srihatter Itibritta [Purbamsa]* (1317 BS), *Nitai Leelalahari* (1319

BS), *Sadhu Charit* (1319 BS), *Shantilata* (1320 BS), *Sri Balyaleelasutramer padyanubad* (1322 BS), *Srihatter Itibritta* [*Uttaramsa*] (1324 BS), *Rajbhakti O Mahajuddha* (1324 BS), *Sri Gauranger Purbanchal bhraman ba Assam O Dhakadakshin Leelaprasanga* (1328 BS), *Jagadish Pandit*, *Raghunathdas Goswamir Jibancharita*, *Sitacharita* [*Adwayita Acharyyer grihini*] (1333 BS), *Bishadita*, *Charucharitra*, *Chand Sadagar*, *Vishnupriyar bibaha*, *Ashrukana*, *Prarthana* [*Sri Sri Thakurmahasayer*] (1339 BS). His unpublished books are *Adwayitaprakash Sammandhe Baktabya*, *Amudrita Kabita*, *Mangalgita* (1298 BS), *Atma Kahani* (1313 BS), *Atmakatha* (1329 BS), *Atmasmriti*, *Dinalipi* (1319 BS), *Dharma Ki?* (1348 BS), *Padakalpatarur Suchipatra* [4 Volumes], *Parikarparichay* (1318 BS), *Pratapgarher Bishes bibaran* (1318 BS), *Bayasadutam* (1345 BS), *Vichitrakatha*, *Mainar Choudhury Vamsatalika*, *Srihatta Zilar Gramyashabda*, *Srihatter Itibritter grahak talika*, *Swabarta* (1346 BS), *Swakiya sambad*, Vol. I, (1348 BS), *Swakiya sambad*, Vol. II, (1348 BS), *Jibankatha*, etc. It is to be noted that a good number of the published and unpublished books written by Achyutcharan are historical biographies and some his unpublished manuscripts are also works in history.

8. Dineshchandra Sen, *Purbabanga Githika* (Eastern Bengal Ballads), vol.II, pt. I, Calcutta, 1919, p. 380.

9. Nagendranath Basu, *Banger Jatiya Itihas*, Calcutta, 1916. It may be noted that same Nagendranath Basu (N.N. Vasu) is the author of *Social History of Kamarupa*, 3 vols, Calcutta, 1922-1928.

10. Subir Kar, *Achyutcharan Tattvanidhi – Jibani O Sahitya*, Arijit Technoprint, Calcutta, 1991, p. 59.

11. *Ibid*, see Appendix.

12. *Bangiya Sahitya Parisad Patrika*, 28th year, 4th issue, Calcutta, 1921.

13. *Shribhumi* (Bengali monthly), *Baishakh* 1323 BS.

14. *Srihatta Sahitya Parisat Patrika*, 1st year, 1st issue, cited in Usharanjan Bhattacharya, *Srihatta Sahitya Parisat O Patrika*, Akshar Publications, Agartala, 2006, p. 19.

15. For the details of life and works of Achyutcharan Choudhury see *Achyutcharan Tattvanidhi – Jibani O Sahitya*, Arijit Technoprint,Calcutta, 1991.

16. *Ibid.*, see Appendix. The primary and secondary sources used by Achyutcharan Chhoudhury in *Srihatter Itibritta* in Sanskrit, Persian, Urdu, Bengali and Assamese included *Atharva Samhita*; *Adyaita Prakash*; *Adyaita prerita Prahelika*; *Adyaita mangal*; *Anuragballi*; *Abhay Khatir Jama*; *Abhaypatra*; *Amiya Nimai Charita*; *Aloukik Rahasya Patrika*; *Ain-i-Akbari*; *Agam Samhita*; *Ajnapatra* (sealed by the King of Tripura); *Ananda Bazar Patrika*; *Apastamba*; *Afel-I- Mahefil*; *Aryyabarta* /1319 BS; *Arati Patrika*; *Ali Amzad khaner Jibancharit*; *Assam Pradesher bishesh bibaran*; *Assam Bandhav Patrika / 1320 BS*; *Asam Buranji*; *Itihas Punyakatha*; *Udvaha tattwam*; *Unakuti Tirtha Mahatya*; *Rig Veda Samhita*; *Ekbal-name-Jahangiri*; *Aitihasik Chitra*/1318 BS; *Kabita*/Pyaricharan Das; *Kamakhya Tantra*; *Kalika Purana*; *Kukider Puja-mantra*; *Kul Pratibha*; *Kulanjali*; *Gaurpada Tarangini*/ Jagadbandhu Bhadra; *Gauranga Leela*/Ramsaday Bagchi; *Gauranga Sanyas* (Manuscript by Dhupraj); *Gramya Giti*; *Chandi Tika*; *Charitra Chinta Ratna*; *Chaitanya Charit*/Purandar; *Chaitanya Charitam*; *Chaitanya Charitamritam*/Krishnadas Kabiraj Goswami;*Chaitanyer Panchali*/Jagannath Baidya; *Chaitanya Bilash*; *Chaitanya Bhagabat*/Brindaban Das; *Chaitanya Mangal*/Jayananda; *Chaitanya Ratnabali*/Ramratna Bhattacharyya; *Hakikatnama*/1054 BS; *Herambarajyer Dandabidhir Bhumika*/Padmanath Bhattacharyya; *Jgadish Charitra*; *Jgannathpurer Itihas*; *Jaganmohan Bhagavat*/Labani Das; *Jatitattwa*

Baridhi; *Jiban Brittanta*/Ramesh Chandra Datta; *Jaimini Bharat*; *Jyoti Pradip*/Harihar Acharya; *Dhakar Itihas*/ Jatindramohan Roy; *Tantra Chudamani*; *Tarafer Itihas*; *Tripurar Itihas*/Kailashchandra Singha; *Tirtha Chintamani*; *Toarikhe Jalali*; *Datta Bangshabali* (manuscript); Deeds of gift: 1103, 1107, 1164 BS; Deeds: 1048, 1120, 1125, 1150, 1166, 1171 and 1194 BS; Deeds: Sales and Purchase of man/ 1029 BS; Deeds: Home Department; *Durgabhakti Tarangini*/Vidyapati; *Dwijabangchi Das*; *Deshpradip* (Sanskrit)/ Maheswar Nyayalankar; *Deshbarta*; *Narayan Dev*; *Narayani Padmapuran*; *Nariratnamala*/ Baikunthanath Das; *Nitaileela Lahari*/Achyut Choudhury; *Nimai Sanyas*/Matilal Roy; *Nitya Mangalchandir Panchali*/Krishnadeb Bhattacharyya;*Padakalpataru*; *Padmapuran*/ Hridayananda; *Parashuram Samhita*; *Paridarshak Patrika*; *Pradip Patrika* / 1311 BS;*Prabashi*/1315 BS; *Prabhat Patra* / 1318 BS (published from Karimganj); *Piyaricharan Das: 'Padyapustak' praneta*; *Pujak Bamser Katha*; *Purnananda Giri O Kamakhya Mahapith*/ Padmanath Vidyabinode; *Prithivir Itihas*; *Prem Bilash*; *Fakir Shah Jalal*/Padmanath Vidyabinode; *Banga Darshan*/Bankimchandra Chattopadhyaya; *Banga Bhasa O Sahitya*/ Dineshchandra Sen; *Bangakshare Manipuri Lipi*; *Bangiya-Sahitya-Parishat- Patrika*; *Bangiya Sahitya Sevak*/Shivratan Mitra; *Banger Jatiya Itihas*/Nagendranath Basu; *Bange Brahmanadhikar*/Bankimchandra Chattopadhyaya; *Banchitcharit Grantha*/Gangaram Ghosh; *Ballalcharit*; *Brahmabaibarta Puran*; *Bangalar Itihaser Bhagnamsa*/ Bankimchandra Chattopadhyaya; *Bangalar Itihas*/Kaliprasanna Bandopadhyaya; *Babambarer Panchali*; *Barahi Samhita*; *Balyalila Sutram*; *Vayu Purana*; *Vijaya Patrika*/1320 BS; *Vidyapati*; *Vidyasagari Tika*/Baninath Vidyasagar; *Viswakosh*; *Visnupuran*; *Bishnupriya Patrika*/1313 BS; *Bishnupriya O Anandabazar Patrika*/1308 BS; *Vishnu Samhita*; *Brihaddharmapuran*; *Brihatparasar*; *Vaidiknirnay grantha*/ Kashichandra Vidyasagar; *Vaidiksambadini*; *Vaishnabachar Darpan*; *Vaishnab Bandana*; *Byom Samhita*; *Bhaktiratnakar*; *Bhabaniprasad Datter lipi*; *Bharatvarsher Itihas*/Rameshchandra Datta; *Bharatbarshiya Upasak Sampradaya*/Akshaykumar Datta; *Manosantoshini*; *Manusamhita*; *Maymansingher Itihas*/ Kedarnath Majumdar;*Masnadalir Itihas*; *Mahabharata* (Sanskrit); *Mahabharat* (Bengali, published by Bangabasi Press); *Mahalingeswar Tantra*; *Murshidabader Itihas*/Nikhilnath Roy; *Maulabi Ali Amzadkhar Jibani*; *Raghunath Lilamrita*; *Rasatattwa Bilas*; *Raghav Pandavia*; *Rajtarangini*; *Raj Nirghanta*; *Rajbangsabali Talika*/1261 BS; *Rajmala*; *Radhanath Charit*/Umeshchandra Dev; *Ramayaner Itihas*; *Shabdakalpadruma*; *Shah Jalal*/ Rajanikanta Dev; *Shyamal Varama Charit*/Balabhadra Bhattacharyya /1039 Saka; *Shrimat Madhukar Mishrer Bamsabali*; *Srihatta Gaurab Chitrabali*; *Srihattadarpan Patrika*; *Srihattabasi Patrika*; *Srihatte Shah Jalal*; *Shastibar Datta* (author of *Padma Puran*); *Sajjantoshini Patrika*; *Sanjibani Patrika*; *Sat-Sampradayar Katha* (Assamese)/Bhattadev Kabiratna; Sanads (27 Sanads written in Persian); Samrat Firoze Shah's letters/1850 AC; *Samkshipta Assam Buranji*/Padmanath Vidyabinode; *Sahitya Parichay Patrika*; *Subarnagramer Itihas*/ Swarupchandra Roy; *Suhen-I- Eman*; *Yogini Tantra*; while those in English included *A Collection of Treaties, Engagements & c.*/Aitchinson; *A Critical Study of Mr. Gait's History of Assam*/Padmanath Vidyabinode; *Analysis of the Finances of Bengal*/ Harrington; Annual Report of the Archaeological Survey, Bengal Circle (1903)/T. Bloch; *Annual Report on the Work of the Geological Survey of India* (1901); *A Short History of the Purkayastha Family*; *Asiatic Society of Bengal, Proceedings*/Aug.1880; *Assam District Gazetteers* (Sylhet; Vol.II)/Allen; *Assam Gazette* (1897); *Bengal*/Barton; *Brief History of Indian People*/ Hunter; *Buddhist Records of the East Countries*, Vol.II/S.Beal; *Civilisation in Ancient India*/ R.C. Dutt; *Dacca Blue Book*; *East Indian Gazetteer*, Vol. II/Hamilton; *Fifth Report of the Select Committee on the affairs of the East India Company*, Vol. I; *Friend of India* (1837); General Administration Report for 1880-81; *Geography and History of Bengal*/Blochman; *Himalayan Journal*/Sir Josheph D. Hooper; *History and Statistics of the Dacca Division*/ Hunter; *History of Assam*/Gait; *History of Bengal*/Marshman; *History of Bengal*/Stewart; *Imperial Gazetteer of India*; *Report on the progress of the Historical Researches in Assam*,

1897/Gait; *Report on the Re-Settlement of the Jaintia Parganas*, 1880; *Journals of Asiatic Society of Bengal*; *Land Tenures*/Philip; *Lives of Lindsey*; *Majumder Family of Sylhet*; *Megasthenes*/Frag; *Modern History of the Indian Chiefs Rajah &c*/L.M.Ghose; *North-East Frontier of Bengal*/Mackenzie; *Observer* (1871); *Outline of the History of Bengal*/Marshman; Pemberton's *Report on North-East Frontier* (1835); *Principal Heads of the History and Statistics of the Dacca Division*; *Principles of Geology*/Sir Charles Lyell; *Proceedings of the Asiatic Society of Bengal*; Report of Mr. Robert Lindsey; Report on the Census of Assam,1901; *Sanad* related to the establishment of Madrasas; *Statistical Accounts of Assam*, Vol. II/ Hunter; *Tales from Indian History*/Wheeler; *Tribes and Castes of North-Western Province*/ Crooke; *Report on Tea Gardens in the Province of Assam*, 1902.

17. Achyutcharan Choudhury, *Srihatter Itibritta*, *Purbangsha* (Vol. I), Calcutta, 1317 BS and *Uttanrangsha* (Vol. II), Silchar, 1323 BS.
18. *Ibid*, see Contents in both volumes.
19. For example, *'Bangalar Itihas'*, *Bankim Rachanabali*, Vol. II, Sahitya Samsad, Calcutta, 1961, pp. 331-35.
20. Maulavi Mahammad Ahmad, *Srihatta Darpan*, 1st edn. Calcutta, 1886, reprint Utsa Prakashan, Dhaka, 2004.
21. Mohinimohan Dasgupta, *Srihatter Itihas*, 1st edn. Calcutta, 1903, reprint Utsa Prakashan, Dhaka, 2004.
22. See Achyutcharan's bibliography in n. 16 above.
23. *Srihatter Itibritta*, vol. I, p. 413.
24. *Ibid*, vol. II, see Preface (trans. mine).
25. 'Preface' to *Srihatter Itibritta*, *Uttarangsa* (Vol. II).
26. Notification No. 59k., dated the 23rd September, 1912., signed by W.W. Hornell, Director of Public Instruction, Bengal; *The Empire*, 1st July 1911.
27. *Prabashi* (monthly, Calcutta), *Aswin* issue, 1318 BS (trans. from Bengali, mine).
28. *The Empire*, 1st July 1911.
29. *The Empire*, 2oth November 1911.
30. *The Amrita Bazar Patrika*, 16th September 1911.
31. *The Indian Messenger*, 30th May 1912.
32. *Dhaka Review O Sammelan* (Bengali monthly, Dacca), 11th issue, *Falgun* 1318 BS.
33. For details see Subir Kar, *Achyutcharan Tattvanidhi – Jibani O Sahitya*, Arijit Technoprint,Calcutta, 1991.
34. J.B. Bhattacharjee, "The Ancient Political Structure of the Barak Valley", *The North-Eastern Hill University Journal of Social Sciences and Humanities*, vol. X, No. 2; *Social and Polity Formations in Pre-Colonial North EastIndia*, Har-Anand Publications, New Delhi, 1991; *State and Wealth : Early States in Northeast India*, DVS Publishers, Guwahati, 2010.
35. Sujit Chhoudhury, *Srihatta-Cacharer Prachin Itihas*, 1st edn. Calcutta, 1992, 3rd revised edn. Dinkal Press Ltd., Silchar, 2006.
36. Among the recent reprints of *Srihatter Itibritta* are those by Purva Prantik, Guwahati, 1995; Utsa Prakashan, Dhaka, 2005; Katha Prakashan, Calcutta, 2010.

3

Padmanath Bhattacharyya (1868-1938)

—*Nishipad Dev Choudhury*

Biographical Sketch

A great Sanskrit scholar and Indologist of Assam, Padmanath Bhattacharyya was born on 6 September, 1868 in village Vidyabhusanpara of Baniachang in the Sylhet district of Assam. He had his schooling in the Primary and Middle English schools in his own village and, thereafter, in the Sylhet Government High School. In 1886, he passed the Entrance Examination of the Calcutta University securing highest position among the successful candidates from Assam and was awarded a gold medal and a monthly scholarship for his meritorious performance. He studied in Dacca College for F.A. Course and passed F.A. of Calcutta University securing a senior scholarship. A brilliant student all throughout his career, he was allowed to take Honours in three subjects in the degree course, viz. English, Philosophy and Sanskrit. In 1890, he passed B.A. with Honours in all three subjects, securing first class in Sanskrit and second class in English and Philosophy, from the University of Calcutta. Padmanath was the first and last student who was allowed to study three subjects in Honours at the same time. He was also a brilliant student in History which was an elective subject in his B.A. and for his proficiency in that subject; he received the Doneli Medal, Lav's Medal and a merit prize. He was also awarded the Abhay Kumar Das Award and a scholarship of Rs. 22/- per month. In the mean time, the Dacca Saraswata Samaja conferred on him the title of *Vidyavinoda* in recognition of his brilliant performance in the *Kavya* examination. Padmanath passed M.A. in English in 1892.

Padmanath Bhattacharyya started his career in 1893 as a Lecturer in Murarichand College, Sylhet, where he was required to teach English, Sanskrit, Logic and History, but after a year, he joined Assam Secretariat Service in Shillong and continued there for three years. In 1897, he was appointed as Deputy Inspector of Schools, Surma Valley, at Sylhet and in 1900, he was transferred to Guwahati as Deputy Inspector of Schools, Assam Valley. In 1901, he was appointed as Assistant Superintendent of Census Operations of Assam, and in 1902, transferred to Sylhet as Deputy Inspector of Schools. In 1903, he was appointed as Officer on Special Duty in the Office of the Director of Public Instructions, Govt. of Assam, Shillong. In June 1905, he was appointed as a Professor in Cotton College, Guwahati, to teach English, Sanskrit and History and he continued in that position till his retirement in I923. In Cotton College, he proved himself as a very successful teacher by his scholarship and teaching methods in Sanskrit and History. He also earned many laurels in life. On the eve of his retirement, the Governor of Assam conferred on him the honour of *Mahamohopadhyaya* with a citation which said, "Your enthusiasm for the promotion of Sanskrit learning continues unabated although you are now approaching the close of your service.... Your well merited honour will be welcomed by all those who are interested in Sanskrit learning in Assam." He was awarded the honorific title of *Dharmadhiropadhyaya* by an assembly of the Sanskrit scholars of Assam. After his retirement from Cotton College in 1923, he left for Benares where he lived for few years before he returned to his ancestral village in Sylhet in 1935. Vidyavinoda passed away on 30th October, 1938, in his ancestral home in Baniachang.[1] The sad news of his demise was immediately flashed in a large number of newspapers like *The Statesman*, *Hindustan Standard*, *Ananda Bazar Patrika*, *Basumati*, *Sylhet Chronicle*, *Janashakti*, *Pratibha*, etc.[2] An 'Obituary Notice' in the *Journal of the Assam Research Society* paid eloquent tributes recalling his contributions to the historiography of Assam.[3] A book, entitled *Shokasindhu* (Ocean of Sadness) was published from Sylhet to pay homage to the departed scholar.[4]

A great scholar, researcher and archaeological explorer of Assam, Mahamohopadhyaya Padmanath Bhattacharyya Vidyavinoda collected significant historical and archaeological evidences and immensely contributed in the field of historical studies in Assam. He laid the strong foundation for research in ancient history of Assam by collecting most valuable archaeological and epigraphic materials and publishing his research findings in journals, magazines and newspapers throughout the country. He was actively associated with Uttar Bangiya Sahitya Sanmilan, Rajshahi Sahitya Sanmilan, Surma Upatyaka Sahitya Sanmilan, Bhagalpur Sahitya Sanmilan, Medinipur Sahitya Sanmilan, Kashidham Ayurveda Sanmilan, Bangiya Sahitya Parisad, Srihatta Sahitya Parisad and many other organizations. He was one of the founders of the Kamarupa Anusandhana Samiti, the oldest research organization in Northeast India, which is currently celebrating the centenary of its foundation.[5]

Foundation of Kamarupa Anusandhana Samiti

Padmanath Bhattacharyya was associated with the foundation of the Kamarupa Anusandhana Samiti (known in English as 'Assam Research Society'), the oldest research organization of Northeast India, in 1912. The idea of the Samiti owes its origin to the 'Banga Anusilani Sabha', founded by Padmanath at Guwahati in 1908 with the limited objective of introducing the history of Assam to the learned societies in neighbouring Bengal by writing articles in Bengali. The activities of the Sabha could attract the attention of the European officers interested in historical pursuits and it could enlist the cooperation of local scholars like Pandit Hem Chandra Goswami, Mm. Dhireswar Acharya and others. However, it soon transformed into the Guwahati Branch of the Bengali Literary Association

(Bangiya Sahitya Parishad) and eventually merged with the North Bengal Literary Society (Uttar Bangiya Sahitya Parishad) incorporating the whole of Assam into the sphere of its activities. In 1912, the annual session of the Uttar Banga Sahitya Parishad was held at Kamakhya (Guwahati) at the initiative of a host of intellectuals of Assam led by Padmanath Vidyavinoda, Kalicharan Sen, Mm. Dhireswar Acharya and others. The Kamakhya session discussed at length the possibility of undertaking research in history and culture of Assam, during which Vidyavinoda pleaded for the formation of a Society under the name and style of 'Kamarupa Anusandhana Samiti' (hereinafter KAS). A committee was formed on 7th April, 1912 to look into matter, and on behalf of the committee Khan Choudhury Amanatullah Ahmed of Cooch Behar formally proposed before the general body the formation of KAS and his proposal was seconded by Rai Mritunjay Choudhury Bahadur of Rangpur. The proposal was adopted unanimously. Babu Shasadhar Ray, a Vakil of the Calcutta High Court, who presided over the conference, made a donation of Rs.25/- on the spot for developing a corpus fund for the KAS.[6] The oldest research organization of Northeast India thus came into existence due to the initiative taken by Padmanath Vidyavinoda.

The Kamarupa Anusandhana Samiti was thus established by a decision in the annual session of the Uttar Bangiya Sahitya Parishad at Kamakhya session to investigate into the antiquities of Assam and to throw light on the history, culture and civilization of ancient Assam and to disseminate research findings throughout India. It was also decided that the Samiti would undertake the publication of the inscriptions of Assam with translations and prefaces in Bengali. It was resolved in the meeting that Vidyavinoda would initiate, on behalf of the Kamarupa Anusandhana Samiti, a series of discussions on the inscriptions of Kamarupa so far discovered and would serially publish those in different journals with Bengali translations and ultimately compile a volume entitled *Kamarupa Sasanavali*. Padmanath duly completed the task within few years and the *Kamarupa Sasanavali* was published by the Rangpur Sahitya Parishad in 1931.[7] The book laid the foundation for scientific research in history of Northeast India. The literati in Northeast India still remember Vidyavinoda with gratitude for his pioneering role in the promotion of historical studies in the region by way of publishing the most authentic sources of ancient history and in foundation of the Kamarupa Anisandhana Samiti. In last one hundred years, KAS has grown manifold maintaining the objective and purpose with which the idea of the organization was conceived by its illustrious founders in the Kamakhya session of the Uttar Banga Sahitya Parishad and the people of the Northeast will always remember the initiative of Mahamohopadhyaya Padmanath Bhattacharyya Vidyavinoda in founding the organization.

The KAS was founded to carry out researches on the area formerly included in the 'sacred and ancient province of Kamarupa, now comprised within Assam, Eastern Bengal, North Bengal and Koch Behar' and the society originally consisted of Mm. Dhireswar Acharya Kabiratna, Mm. Padmanath Bhattacharyya Vidyavinoda, Ananda Chandra Vedantabagisha, Sibanath Smrititirtha, Uttam Chandra Barooah, Govinda Chandra Sarma, Taranath Kavyabinoda, Pratap Chandra Goswami, Rajani Kumar Das, Gopal

Chandra Dey, Suresh Chandra Bondopadhyaya and Umesh Chandra Dey as members. The number soon began to increase, and the office-bearers were elected to manage the affairs of the society. Thus, Chandra Nath Sarma was elected as Secretary and Babu Gopal Krishna Dey as Assistant Secretary. Professor Padmanath Bhattacharyya Vidyavinoda undertook to help the Secretary in all matters, including the correspondences. The Government of Assam was approached for financial help. The KAS received a grant of Rs.250/- in 1915 and from the next year an annual grant of Rs. 1000/-. It also received the patronage of eminent personalities like Sir Archdale Earle, His Highness the Maharaja Sir Jitendra Narayan Bhup Bahadur of Koch Behar, Sir Edward Gait, Lt. Col. P.R.T. Gordon and Raja Prabhat Chandra Barua Bahadur of Gauripur. A prospectus of the Samiti was published on 5th December, 1914 and widely circulated among European and Indian gentlemen asking for cooperation in research works of the Samiti. The research papers on different subjects used to be read in the Samiti from time to time, amongst which a very interesting paper on the Copper-plate of Bhaskaravarmana was read by Padmanath in the first academic meeting. This plate was discovered in a village called Nidhanpur in Sylhet and it was deciphered by Padmanath himself. The paper was later on published in *Epigraphica Indica* and other journals.

The involvement of Padmanath in the KAS can be appreciated from the fact that he did not stand for election to the Executive Committee in 1916 as he had decided to move to Benares after his retirement from service within few years, but he continued his support and cooperation to the Samiti in all its activities and also in editing the inscriptions of Kamarupa that was already assigned to him. In 1920, the KAS published a collection of its annual reports and some articles of historical interest contributed by Lt. Col. P.R.T. Gordon, Sarat Chandra Goswami, Mm. Padmanath Bhattacharyya Vidyavinoda, Hem Chandra Goswami, Sarbeswar Kataki and Professor S.K. Bhuyan. This and the subsequent annual reports of the KAS (1927, 1931, 1937) mentioned Mm. Padmanath Bhattacharyya Vidyavinoda, formerly Senior Professor of Sanskrit in the Cotton College, Guwahati, as a Honorary Member of the Samiti and stated that he has left Assam after his retirement and settled in Banaras, and also mentioned his address in Benares (45 House Katara, Benares City). These documents are testimonies to what Padmanath meant to KAS and how much the scholars in Assam loved and respected him.[8] While in Benares he completed his commitment to KAS by publishing *Kamarupa Sasanavali* (1931). Despite the fact that he had decided to stay in Benares, Vidyavinoda maintained regular contacts with KAS. When the KAS launched the publication of its journal, *Journal of Assam Research Society* (*JARS*), in 1933, Vidyavinoda contributed a paper in the first issue and till his death in 1938, he had contributed as many as eight papers in that journal. His last two papers appeared in nos. 1 and 2 of 1938.[9] Thus, Padmanath continued his research in the history of ancient Assam and maintained connections with KAS till his death. Padmanath's following papers were published in the *Journal of Assam Research Society* :

1. "The sign 'S' in ancient Copper Plate Inscriptions of Kamarupa", Vol. I, No. 1, 1933, pp. 9-11.

2. "Extent of Vaidyadeva's Kingdom", Vol. III, No. 1, 1934, pp. 21-23.
3. "Buddhism in Assam", Vol. III, No. 4, 1936, pp. 115-118.
4. "Ruins in Laur", Vol. IV. No. 1, 1936, pp. 24-27.
5. "A Stray Cannon at Baniachang", Vol. IV, No. 2, 1936, pp. 52-53.
6. "Location of Nidhanpur Grant of Bhaskar Varma of Kamarupa", Vol. IV, No. 3, pp. 58-66.
7. "Dates of the Bhatera Copper Plates", Vol. VI, No. 1, pp. 18-21.
8. "Sir Edward Gait on Human Sacrifice in Assam", Vol. VI, No. 2, pp. 53-55.

Research Contributions

The most significant and path-breaking contribution of Mahamohopadhyaya Padmanath Bhattacharyya Vidyavinoda to the historiography of Northeast India was the publication of the *Kamarupa Sasanavali* (writs of land grants issued by the kings of Kamarupa), which was edited by him and published by the Rangpur Sahitya Parishad, a monumental work which laid the foundation for the use of authentic historical materials for reconstruction of history of Assam for the ancient period.[10] The volume (entitled *Kamarupa Sasanavali*) included the original texts and Bengali translations of ten copper-plates and two rock inscriptions (in total twelve inscriptions) of ancient Assam, viz. (i) *the Nidhanpur Copper Plate of Bhaskaravarman*, (ii) *the Copper Plate Inscription of Harjara Varma* (known as the Hyanthal Grant), (iii) *the Tezpur Rock inscription of Harjaravarmana*, (iv) *the Copper Plate Inscription of Vanamalavarmadeva* (the Tezpur Plate), (v) *the Copper Plates Grant of Balavarma* (Nowgong Plates), (vi) *the first Copper Plate Inscription of Ratnapala* (Bargaon Grant), (vii) *the Second Copper Plate Inscription of Ratnapala* (Sualkuchi Grant), (viii) *the first Copper Plate Inscription of Indrapala* (Guwahati Grant), (ix) *the Second Copper Plate of Indrapala* (Guakuchi plates), (x) *the first Copper Plate Grant of Dharmapala* (Subhankarapataka plate), (xi) *the Second Copper Plate Grant of Dharmapala* (Puspabhadra plates), and (xii) *the Kanaibarasi Rock Inscription*. The volume included all the twelve inscriptions that were discovered till that time. Some of these inscriptions were deciphered by Padmanath Bhattacharyya himself, while the remaining inscriptions by other scholars and published by the respective decipherers, with translations and discussions in learned journals. However, the Bengali translations and discussions on all the twelve inscriptions in his *Kamarupa Sasanavali* were single handedly done by Padmanath. He was well aware of the culture and civilization of Northeast India and had felt that the literati in rest of the country should be made acquainted with the achievements of the ancient people of this part of India. As he said, "Though the province of Assam is very close to Bengal and many Bengalis have settled here, still the real story of Assam is not properly known to the Bengali people outside the province. Contrary to it, they have many wrong notions about Assam and innumerable fantastic stories about the beliefs and customs of the Assamese people and about Assam as a land of sorcery and magic came to be widely prevalent."[11]

As a matter of fact, the *Kamarupa Sasanavali* was an outstanding contribution of Padmanath, the idea of which was conceived by him to give a scientific foundation to historical research in Assam. The book contains 215 pages and a very scholarly introduction of eight pages by its illustrious editor. It gave a fillip to modern research in the history of ancient Assam. Sir Jadhunath Sarkar wrote a long review of the book in *Indian Historical Quarterly* in which he predicted that Assam's place shall henceforth be duly recognized in ancient Indian history.[12] B. K. Barua paid tribute to Padmanath Vidyavinoda by saying, "My indebtedness is indeed very great to Mahamohopadhyaya Padmanath Bhattacharya's *Kamarupa Sasanavali*. Since the publication of the *Kamarupa Sasanavali* researches in the early history of Assam have taken a new turn."[13] C. P. Saikia wrote in the Preface of the *Kamarupa Sasanavali*, edited by Dimbeswar Sarma : "The vital importance of archaeological evidence like epigraphy in the proper study and authentic reconstruction of our country's hoary past can hardly be over emphasized. In the absence of any system of keeping written records of important events in the dim past, it is on such evidence that historical scholars rely while trying to rediscover the ancient history of a country. The title *Kamarupa Sasanavali* immediately brings to our mind the pioneering work done by Mm. Padmanath Bhattacharya Vidyavinoda (1868-1938) in this particular field. It is he who first compiled and edited some twelve writs of land grants issued by the Kamarupa kings from Bhaskara Varman to Dharmapala under the title of *Kamarupa Sasanavali*. Of course, the first edition of *Kamarupa Sasanavali* contained the texts of only twelve inscriptions together with their Prefaces in Bengali."[14] No wonder, the people of this part of India still remember Vidyavinoda with gratitude for the splendid contribution he made for the cause of historical studies in Assam. As Dimbeswar Sarma says in 'Introduction' to *Kamarupa Sasanavali* edited by him, "The new edition which we have brought out is a fully different volume from that of the Vidyavinoda because it contains fifteen new inscriptions both copper plates and rock cut together with the twelve inscriptions included in the *Kamarupa Sasanavali* of the late P.N. Vidyavinoda. Even then we have retained its name as *Kamarupa Sasanavali* after Vidyavinoda because it has already attained a well established celebrity and the two names, the *Kamarupa Sasanavali* and Vidyavinoda, have almost become inseparable in Assam."[15] Rethinking on Padmanath occur as one of the pioneering authorities on the textual criticism (a very modern branch of study of literature) as one goes through the recent studies on epigraphy in Assam. In fact, Padmanath's pioneering work became a source of inspiration for the series of works like *Inscriptions of Assam* by Mukunda Madhava Sharma (1978),[16] *Prachya Sasanavali* by Maheswar Neog (1978),[17] *Kamarupa Sasanavali* by Dimbeswar Sarma (1981)[18] and many others.

Although *Kamarupa Sasanavali* remains to be the most celebrated work of Padmanath Bhattacharyya for last eighty years, he had written a large number of books and research articles in journals, magazines and newspapers of his time on history and culture of Northeast India. He made his mark as a historian by writing critical reviews of *A History of Assam*[19] by Sir Edward Gait* soon after the book was published in London (1906) and became available in India. His reviews were published in leading journals and newspapers in India[20] and later on compiled into a booklet published from Guwahati.[21] Sir Edward Gait acknowledged and accepted some of Padmanath's criticisms and made changes in the second edition of his book.[22] Padmanath's major works in history and culture included *Pravandhastak, Hedamba Rajyer Danda Bidhi, The Penal Code of the last king of Cachar, Hedamba Rajyer Rindan Bidhi, Hindu Vivaha Samskara, Baijnaniker Bhranti Vilas, Parasuram Kunda O Vadarikasram Paribhraman, Ramkumar Charit, Alochana Chatustay, Ramkrishna Vivekananda Prasanga, Mahacapatam, Sir Gurudas Prasanga* and, of course, *Kamarupa Sasanavali*. He wrote *Asam Buranji* in Bengali (1922) to introduce the history of Assam to people of Surma Valley. He wrote more than eighty research papers in English in the frontline research journals of his time, like *Journal of the Asiatic Society of Bengal, Journal of the Royal Asiatic Society of London, Journal of the Orissa and Bihar Research Society, Dacca Review, East and West, Epigraphia Indica, Indian Antiquary, Indian Historical Quarterly, Mahashakti, Malabar Quarterly Review, Man in India* and *Journal of the Assam Research Society*, and also in leading newspapers like

---

* Edward Albert Gait (1863-1950), an English gentleman of the ICS, KCSI and KE, who served in British Assam for many years in the last quarter of the nineteenth century in different capacities such as Sub-Divisional Officer at Mangaldai in the Darrang district to the Chief Secretary of the Chief Commissioner's Province of Assam, deserves to be considered as first great modern historian of Northeast India. On his transfer from Assam, he served as the Census Commissioner till 1915 and thereafter, as Lieutenant Governor of Bihar and Orissa from 1915 to 1920. In fact, he was the Lieutenant Governor of Bihar during Mahatma Gandhi's historic 'Champaran Satyagraha' in Bihar in 1917 and there was some exchange of letters between the two. M.K. Gandhi's letters to Sir Edward Gait, dated 4 October, 10 October, 15 November 1917, etc. are preserved in National Archives of India, New Delhi and India Office Library, London. Gandhi's autobiographical work *The Story of My Experiments with Truth* (part V/ xix) also contains a section, entitled 'When a Governor is Good', in which Gandhi praised Gait for humanly handling the Champaran issue and ensuring relief for the long exploited plantation workers. Although a British administrator of high rank in Colonial India, Gait's approach to Indian history was substantially different from what is generally called 'colonial historiography' contributed by the officer-historians of British India. Besides the pioneering *A History of Assam* (London, 1906), his *Report on the Progress of Historical Research in Assam* (Shillong, 1897) laid the foundation of modern source-based history writing by surveying the sources. His compilation of *The Assam Land Revenue Manual* (1896) was also an important work which involved a great deal of research. He was the first historian in the Northeast not only to use literary, epigraphic, numismatic and archaeological sources to the extent these were recovered till that point of time but also to discuss the scope and quality of the sources in his *A History of Assam*. The historical notes and comments contributed by him in the Census of India Report, 1891 (Pt. I, Assam) as Superintendent of Census, Assam, and later on, in the Assam volumes of the same reports for 1901 and 1911 as Census Commissioner of India, emerged out of his critical study of the empirical evidence and his sound knowledge of the region and sources of its history. His articles on Northeast published in the *Journal of the Asiatic Society of Bengal* included "The Koch Kings of Kamarupa" (vol. LXII, NO. 1, 1893), "Abstract of the contents of one of the Ahom *Puthis*"(vol. LXIII, no. 1, 1894), "Some notes on Jaintia history" (vol. LXIV, no. 1, 1895), etc. The *Proceedings of the Asiatic Society* also included his "The Koch Kings of Kamrup – An Abstract" (1893) and "Historical research in Assam" (1895). Gait also introduced a scientific academic temper in historical research by taking into account A.W. Botham, H.E. Stapleton and Padmanath Bhattacharyya's critical reviews of the first edition of his work before bringing out the revised edition of *A History of Assam* (Calcutta, 1926). The revised edition included

(Contd...)

Amrita Bazar Patrika, *Hindu Review*, *Hindustan Review*, *Monthly Review*, *New Monthly Review* and *Sylhet Chronicle*. In addition to these, he wrote innumerable poems, stories and essays in English, Assamese, Bengali and Sanskrit.[23]

As a historian

Maahmohopadhyaya Padmanath Bhattacharyya Vidyavinoda was an outstanding scholar who immensely contributed as a pioneer in the field of epigraphic, archaeological and historical studies in Assam. But for him, the ancient history of Assam would have remained in the dark for more time to come. His name will remain ever enshrined in the heart of all lovers history as far as the study of the ancient culture and civilization of Assam is concerned. Prior to the establishment of the Kamarupa Anusandana Samiti (KAS) primarily due to the efforts of Padmanath Vidyavinoda, there was no such academic forum in Assam or Northeast India to carry out historical research. Although the Cotton College was established in 1901 for higher education, the conditions were very poor for undertaking any meaningful research programme though the same was indispensable for college teachers. Suryya Kumar Bhuyan, who happened to be a student of Cotton College

---

references to some newly identified sources like the inscription of Bhaskaravarman found in Nadhanpur village of Sylhet and translated by Professor Padmanath Bhattacharyya, Bana's *Harsha Charita* translated by Cowell and Thomas, *Baharistan-i-Ghaibi* and *Fathiyya-i-Ibriyya* translated by Professor Jadunath Sarkar, the translations of some *Buranjis* made by Dr. J.P. Wade in 1792-93 and preserved in India Office Library, an account of some Jaintia kings in Loch's *Jaintia Settlement Report of 1839* and Babu Chandra Kanta Sen's *Jaintia Settlement Report of 1897*. It seems that Gait maintained personal contacts with some Indian historians even after he had left India on his retirement from the service, as he says in Preface to second edition (while explaining the additional sources used in that edition) : "The *Baharistan-i-Ghaibi* is a contemporary account of events in the reign of Jahangir. This has recently been translated by Professor Jadunath Sarkar, who has kindly sent me advance extracts of the passages relating to certain Mohammedan invasions of Assam." As regards Sarkar's translation of *Fathiyya-i-Ibriyya*, Gait says, "Professor Sarkar's translation of the description of Assam at the time of Mir Jumlah's invasion contained in the *Fathiyya-i-Ibriyya* is more complete and accurate than Blochmann's analysis of the same work which was utilized in the first edition." (see Gait's Preface to Second Edition, Calcutta, 1926) These facts show how critical and careful was Edward Gait in using the sources in writing history. As a matter of fact, Edward Gait was the first historian to highlight the importance of *Buranjis* as sources of history, a work that was later on vigorously taken forward by S.K. Bhuyan. Gait informed us in Preface to the first edition of his book *A History of Assam* that it was in 1894 that Sir Charles Lyall, the then Chief Commissioner of Assam, decided for a sustained and systematic endeavour to arrest the process of destruction of the extant historical manuscripts and wanted Gait to draw up a scheme for the prosecution of historical research in the province. Gait's proposal to make a survey of materials was accepted and a small grant was also made available to cover the necessary expenses. In course of the survey, a rock inscription at Tezpur, five copper-plates and the manuscripts of *Kalika Purana*, *Jogini Tantra*, *Mahabharata*, *Dipika Chanda*, *Darangraj Vamsavali*, writings of Sankaradeva and his followers, and a large number of *Buranjis* and *Puthis* in Ahom and Assamese languages came to his notice. Gait selected Babu Golap Chandra Barua, then a young clerk in the office of the Deputy Commissioner, Lakhimpur, and attached to him five *Deodhais* to teach him Ahom language and to assist him in translating the manuscripts into English. Gait tested Barua's knowledge in Ahom and the accuracy of his translations in various ways, like comparing one *Buranji* with another, before using those in *A History of Assam*. (see Preface to first edition, London 1906). The activities that started with Charles Lyall, Edward Gait and Golap Chandra Barua thus seem to have formed nucleus of the organization that eventually developed into the Department of Historical and Antiquarian Studies (DHAS), Assam. [*Editor's Addendum]

during 1909-11 and later on a colleague of Padmanath in the same college, paid his tribute later on for the grand contributions of Padmanath Vidyavinoda towards original research in the field of Assam history, saying, "We all respected him for his scholarly pursuits and vigour with which he was working for dissemination of information on Assam. He was the first to discover the Copper Plate grant of Kumar Bhaskara Barman issued from his camp at Karnasuvarna, now generally known as Nidhanpur Copper Plate."[24] Kanaklal Baruah, who was possibly the first scholar to use the epigraphic findings of Padmanath for writing a full-length book on ancient history of Assam, entitled *Early History of Kamarupa* (1933), said : "Pandit Padmanath Bhattacharya Vidyavinoda recovered the oldest and most valuable of all the Copper Plate inscriptions, i.e., that of Bhaskaravarman as well as the stray plate of Harjaravarman. He has also published for the first time the text of Guakuchi grant of Indrapala and that of Dharmapala grants, the perseverance with which he searched for and recovered nearly all the lost plates of Bhaskaravarman's grant is indeed beyond all praise."[25] As a matter of fact, the greatness of Mahamohopadhyaya Padmanath Bhattacharyya Vidyavinoda as a historian is so imprinted in all his works that the stresses and strains of times and circumstances will never be able to obliterate his name from the heart of the academia in the soil of Assam.

Notes & References

1. Jatindramohan Bhattacharya, *Padmanath Bhattacharya*, *Sahitya-Sadhak-Caritamala*, Vol. XI, Bangiya-Sahitya-Parishat, Kalikata, 1378 BS (1971), pp. 5-18; Tarinicharan Das, "Porolokey Dharmadhiropadhyaya Pandit Padmanath Bhattacharyya", *Shiksha Sevak*, Kartik, 1345 BS (1938), pp. 66-76; Narendra Kumar Gupta Choudhury, *Srihatta Pratibha*, Kalikata, 1368 BS (1961), pp. 92-95; Nandita Bhattacharya, "Mm. Padmanath Bhattacharya Vidyavinoda", in B. Sarma (ed.), *Kamarupa Anusandhana Samiti Through the Ages,* Kamrupa Anusandhana Samiti, Guwahati, 2011.

2. Jatindramohan Bhattacharya, *Padmanath Bhattacharya*, *Sahitya-Sadhak-Caritamala*, Vol. XI, *op. cit.*, p. 47.

3. *Journal of the Assam Research Society*, Vol. VI, No. II, October 1938.

4. Shrischandra Bhattacharyya (ed), *Shokasindhu*, Sylhet, 25 February, 1939, cited in Jatindramohan Bhattacharya, *Padmanath Bhattacharya*, *Sahitya-Sadhak-Caritamala*, Vol. XI, *op. cit.* pp. 9-12, 47.

5. *Report and Conspectus of KAS*, compiled by S.K. Bhuyan, Kamarupa Anusandhana Samiti, Guwahati, 1927.

6. Chandra Nath Sarma (ed.), *The work of the KAS*, Kamarupa Anusandhana Samiti, Guwahati, 1920.

7. *Reports and Conspectus of the* KAS, compiled by Chandra Nath Sarma B.L.,1920.

8. Padmanath Bhattacharyya (ed.), *Kamarupa Sâsanavali*, Rangpur Sahitya Parishad, Rangpur, 1338 BS (1931). Also see *Reports and Conspectus of the* KAS, compiled by Chandra Nath Sarma. B.L.,1920; *Reports and Conspectus of the* KAS, compiled by S. K. Bhuyan, 1927; *Reports and Conspectus of the* KAS, compiled by D. Goswami, 1931; *Reports and Conspectus of the* KAS, compiled by S. Kataki, 1937.

9. See relevant volumes of the *Journal of Assam Research Society*.

10. Padmanath Bhattacharyya (ed.), *Kamarupa Sasanavali*, Rangpur Sahitya Parishad, Rangpur, 1338 BS (1931).

11. *Ibid*, see '*Mukhabandha*', p. 1 (trans. ours).

12. *Indian Historical Quarterly*, Vol. X, No. 2, 1933.

13. B. K. Barua, *A Cultural History of Assam*, Kitap Ghar, Guwahati, 1951, see Preface, p. iv.

14. Dimbeswar Sharma (ed.), *Kamarupa Sasanavali*, Asom Prakashan Parishad, Guwahati, 1981, see Preface, p. vi.

15. *Ibid*, p. 1.

16. Mukunda Madhava Sharma, *Inscriptions of Ancient Assam*, Gauhati University, Gauhati, 1978.

17. Maheswar Neog, *Prachya Sasanavali*, Asom Prakashan Parishad, Guwahati, 1978.

18. Dimbeswar Sharma (ed.), *op.cit.*

19. Edward Gait, *A History of Assam*, London, 1906.

20. For example, *The Hindustan Review* (1908), *The Indian Press* (1908).

21. Padmanath Bhattacharyya Vidyavinod, *Mr. Gait's History of Assam*, Gauhati, 1908.

22. Edward Gait, *A History of Assam*, second revised edition, Thacker Sprink & Co., Calcutta, 1926.

23. For a complete bibliography of the publications of Mahamohopadhyaya Padmanath Bhattacharyya Vidyavinod, see Jatindramohan Bhattacharya, *Padmanath Bhattacharya, Sahitya-Sadhak-Caritamala*, Vol. XI, Bangiya-Sahitya-Parishat, Kalikata, 1378 BS (1971), pp. 18-46.

24. S. K. Bhuyan, *Men I Met*, LBS, Guwahati, 1962, p. 17.

25. K. L. Barua, *Early History of Kamarupa*, (1s edn. Shillong, 1933) Reprinted LBS, Guwahati, 1988, Preface, vii.

4

Jobang Dajel Marak (1870-1963)

—Milton S. Sangma

Biographical Sketch

At the south-eastern ranges of the Garo hills (Meghalaya) overlooking the plains of Eastern Bengal (now Bangladesh), there exists an A'beng Garo village (A'beng, a sub-division of the Garo tribe), called Halwa, located in the midst of the A'tong villages (A'tong, another Garo sub-tribe). In this solitary and remote village, a boy was born in about 1870 to Singjan Gagra Sangma and Noche Dajel Marak, whom they named Jobang Dajel Marak. There was no school in that village at that time, not even within 30 kms. The nearest village where there was a Bengali medium L.P. School was Baghmara, more than 30 kilometers from his native village. Baghmara village was founded by Rev. Rangku W. Momin, third Garo Christian convert and an ex-policeman who took part in suppressing the uprising in the area during the Sepoy Mutiny (1857). On his appointment as the first Garo Mauzadar in 1878 and deputed to the south-eastern *mauza* of the Garo hills district, Rangku and another Garo, named Balman A. Sangma (popularly known as Bong Lasker), founded the Baghmara village in 1879. The name of the village Baghmara has been derived from the utterances of the neighbouring plains people of Bengal (Bangladesh) when they came and saw the tiger killed by Bong Lasker after a fierce face to face fight.

Jobang studied in the Baghmara Bengali Medium L.P. School from 1885 to 1890, staying with his elder sister Rakje D. Marak who had married Harimohan Sarkar, an estate manager of Bong Lasker. In 1891, his mother brought him to Tura for further studies in the Tura Mission M.E. School where he studied from 1891 to 1895 under the care and supervision of the American Baptist missionaries. While Jobang was studying in Tura Mission M.E. School, the missionaries found him possessing intellectual capability and leadership qualities. They decided to train him up for leadership among the Garos in the field of religion and education. In December 1905, Dr. M. C. Mason, one of the pioneer missionaries of Garo field, took Jobang to America for further studies and got him admitted to the Howard Denison University at Granville, Ohio, USA. Jobang was so happy to go to

USA that he paid his own journey expenses out of the money he had saved by working in the Mission office for more than ten years. He studied Latin, English Grammar, Geometry and Algebra at the level of Senior Cambridge course from 1905 to 1911 in Howard Denison University.

On his return from USA in 1911, Jobang D. Marak served as the Sub-Inspector of Schools in Garo hills. During the absence of U Alexander, a Khasi gentleman, he also officiated as Deputy Inspector of Schools in Garo hills (1912-1913). However, Alexander was shortly replaced by Nissor Singh, another Khasi gentleman, who became the Deputy Inspector of Schools of Garo hills and served till his death at Tura in 1918. In 1913, Jobang was appointed as Assistant Head Master of Tura Mission M.E. School where he worked till 1918. After the death of Nissor Singh in 1918, Jobang again officiated as the Deputy Inspector of Schools of Garo hills until 1928, when he resigned his job. The reason for the resignation is perhaps, as it is commonly said, that while he was working as the Assistant Headmaster of Tura Mission M.E. School, Jobang's relationship with the American Baptist missionaries became strained as he did not enjoy taking orders from them and considered them as equals. This ultimately resulted in his expulsion from the membership of the Baptist Church, after which he joined the Roman Catholic Church. As a member of the Roman Catholic Church, he helped the Mission to acquire a large plot of land where the present house of the Bishop is located.

On his family side, after his return from America in 1911, Jobang D. Marak married Alice W. Momin, the eldest daughter of Bakal K. Sangma, an Assistant to the Baptist missionaries, and Dobaki W. Momin, the first Garo female teacher and sister of Ramke W. Momin and niece of Omed W. Momin, the first two Garo Christian converts. After their marriage, they settled down at Chandmary locality of Tura town where they owned a large hillock with imposing building and a large compound. They had two sons and three daughters, of whom; the eldest son was Howard Denison W. Momin, named after the University where Jobang had studied in America. Howard Denison was the first Garo to have passed M.A. (English) from Calcutta University in 1936 and become a Professor of English in Cotton College, Guwahati. Jobang's second son was Godwin Clinton W. Momin, an engineer, who was the first Garo to become the Superintending Engineer in Assam and the first Chairman of the Meghalaya Public Service Commission. His two daughters, named Henrietta and Adeline, died when they were studying in schools in Calcutta, while their youngest daughter Margareth Ruth W. Momin retired as an Assistant Teacher in the Tura Government Higher Secondary School.

Jobang D. Marak is remembered in the Garo hills for his contributions to the development of the Garo society. One of his contributions in social sector was his help in recruiting many Garo volunteers for the Garo Labour Corps during the First World War, who were sent to France. Due to the efforts of Jobang and other Garo leaders, more than one thousand Garos were recruited in the 69th Garo Labour Corps and dispatched to different parts of France during the most critical period of the war. He had his share of contribution in uplifting the standard of education as an Assistant Headmaster and Deputy Inspector of

Schools. He also rendered valuable services to the Roman Catholic Church to have a permanent establishment at Tura by acquiring land for the mission. His social services and his educational qualifications enabled Jobang to gain ascendancy to a leadership role in the Garo society. In the general elections in 1937, two representatives from Garo hills, Jobang D. Marak and Benjamin Ch. Momin were elected to the Assam Legislative Assembly. They were elected not by adult suffrage but by the Nokmas (Garo traditional clan chiefs). Jobang continued to be a member of the Assam Assembly till 1946 as the term of the Assembly was extended due to the war conditions.

Jobang D. Marak was one of the important Garo leaders during the crucial years of the transfer of power and partition of India. In the early 1940s, the Garo leaders were aware that the British were going to leave the country and India will be partitioned into two sovereign states – India and Pakistan. They were concerned as to what would be their position in an independent but divided India, especially in the context of M.A. Jinnah's demand for the Garo hills to be included in Pakistan and his followers campaigning openly in support of the demand. To consider this issue and the protection of their religion, custom and culture, Emonsing M. Sangma, another Garo leader, summoned a general conference of the Garos (known as the first Garo National Conference) at Tura in 1946. In that conference, Mody K. Marak and Jobang D. Marak were elected as President and Vice-President respectively of the Garo National Conference, which was formed in the conference as an organization. However, in the subsequent years, Mody K. Marak, Emonsing M. Sangma and Williamson A. Sangma played major role in the Garo politics and in the undivided state of Assam as leaders from Garo hills. Jobang D. Marak suffered from illnesses due to old age and he was almost bedridden for a long time before he died on 22 July, 1963.[1]

Contributions to history

Jobang D. Marak was born in a humble family in a remote village in the Garo hills, but by his caliber and hard work for the development of his tribe he ascended to a significant position in the Garo society, particularly in the fields of education, politics and literature. Despite his multifarious activities, he found time and energy to study the traditions and culture of the Garos and to write and publish books and magazines in Garo and English. He and a Khasi gentleman, named Macdonald, who was the Head Master of the Teachers' Training School at Tura, jointly launched the publication of a monthly journal in Garo language, called *Phring Phrang* (or 'Morning Star'), in 1912. However, as the Garo spellings in the magazine were not in conformity with the spellings adopted for Garo Primers and Readers and other text books in the schools there were exchanges of letters between Jobang and the Baptist missionaries who authored and published the text books for all Garo schools. The *Phring Phrang* was in circulation only for two years and its publication was discontinued since 1914. Jobang also published a number of books, and some of those books are considered as significant contributions in history, culture and education of the Garos. Among his books are, (i) *Deshi Kasrat* (1916); (ii) *A'chik Aganani* or Garo folklores (1927); (iii) *A'chik Kata, Bak I & II* or Garo history, Part 1 & 11 (1930); (iv) *Garo Law* (in English)

(1932), (v) *Odek Education* or the origin and development of education (1955); (vi) *Chengoni A.gilsak aro chengoni Mande, Bak 1* (Ancient Man and Ancient World, Book I) (1955).[2] His books on Garo folklore, Garo laws and Garo history are invaluable contributions to history and culture of the Garos, while his 'Ancient Man and Ancient World' bears the testimony that he was also well read in early history of the mankind.

As a matter of fact, Jobang D. Marak was one of those early Garo writers who prepared the ground for future development in the disciplines of history, customary laws and other secular branches of literature in Garo language. The missionaries as well as the educated Garos began to recognize him as a good writer when he used to send letters from America about progress in his studies, his University as well as America and her people which were published in different issues of *A.chikni Ripeng* ('Garo's Friend'), a monthly magazine run by the Baptist missionaries. Jobang himself seem to have some interest in journalism. The monthly journal, *Phring Phrang* ('Morning Star'), was started by Jobang jointly with Macdonald, with a view to promote secular Garo literature. But it had run into rough weather for using the spellings of some Garo words which Jobang wanted to spell differently from how those words were spelled already in the school text books by the missionaries. The spelling controversy reached such a stage that Jobang ultimately decided to suspend the publication of *Phring Phrang*. It had lasted only for two years. However, Jobang started writing and publishing books on the subjects he considered useful for the Garos, particularly for the students. His first publication was a small book, called *Deshi Kasrat* (1916).[3] It was a booklet on numerals. His second book was on Garo folklore, entitled *A.chik Aganani Bak 1*(1927).[4] It contained 15 common Garo folk stories told and re-told for generations. It has stories such as an orphan, a crab and a water wagtail, Rinna and Rinje sisters, a hog and a dog, a frog and a monkey, a man called Gangbo, a monkey and a wild fowl, a monkey and a tortoise, etc. This book on folklore is the first of its kind in Garo literature. Some of these folklores are found common in D. K. Sangma's book on Garo folklores (*A.chik Golporang*) published later on in three volumes containing 180 stories.[5] In 1927, jointly with Simison Marak, Jobang wrote another book *A'chik Aganani Baksa*.[6] His interest in folklore inspired other scholars to study the subject. Harendra W. Marak's *A'chik Aganbewalrang* (1959) is an important work that drew on oral literature.[7] Dewansing Rongmuthu also published in Garo a book called *Apasong Agana* ('Our Fathers Tell Us'),[8] which covered several aspects of Garo folklore, such as, origin of the universe, its living and non-living beings, origin of rice, rice beer, Wangala festival, iron, poison, ancestry of Garo deities, human beings, etc. Many of these topics are also included in Rongmuthu's *Folk Tales of the Garos* in English, which was published by the Guahati University in 1960 and is considered as an important book on the folklores of Northeast India.[9] Rongmuthu's another significant contribution to folklore studies is *Epic Lores of the Garos* (1967).[10] However, it may be important to recall that the beginning in studying the folklores of the Garos was made by Jobang D. Marak and he wrote in Garo language.

The insight Jobang gained from his study of the folklore and oral traditions of the Garos enabled him to write his third book, *Garo Kata, Bak I & II*, or Garo History, Parts

1 and 2 (1930).[11] This book is a documentation of the common and a traditional narrative of the migration story of the Garos from Tibet to the Garo hills. Part1 narrates the story of migration from Tibet to North Bengal, and then from Jogighopa up to Kamakhya and the retracing of their steps to Habraghat Pargana (in the modern Goalpara district of Assam), and finally, the settlement of a section of them in the Garo hills. Part 2 documented the traditional narrative of how under the leadership of one Abong Noga, a section of the Garos migrated from Habraghat Pargana to the Nokrek Peak, the highest peak in Garo hills, and how Abong Noga became rich and powerful in that place by undertaking *Jhum* cultivation and how he sent out his own people to different parts of Garo hills assigning them different professions. For example, he assigned the job of cutting trees and hewing them smooth for use as posts for construction of houses to the A'wes (northern Garos), the A'bengs (west) were assigned the task to grow cotton, the Garas (middle south) to make boats, the Atongs (southeast) to smelt iron, and the Kotchus (Koch) to prepare dry fish, etc. Jobang's book seems to be the first attempt to write down the oral tradition of the Garos in the form of a book of history. Till that time, the stories of migrations and settlements of the Garos were very briefly mentioned only in two books, namely, A. Playfair's *The Garos* (1909)[12] and William Carey's *The Garo Jungle Book* (1919).[13] Many years after Jobang's work came out another book in traditional history of the Garos, namely, *A'chikni Gimin Aganani* (history of the Garos) by Levisoned N. Sangma (1965).[14]

The study of customary laws is another field in which Jobang D. Marak made pioneering contributions and for which also he had to delve into the oral history materials like rites, ritual practices, beliefs, traditions, tales and fables, etc. Thus, his fourth book is *The Garo Law* (1932) which he wrote in English.[15] This is the first publication of its kind either in English or Garo and it was written much before the need for codification of the tribal customary laws came to be talked about in the sixth schedule areas. The book contains the Garo customary laws on marriage, divorce, inheritance, criminal, moral and religious laws, Nokma system, etc. The work Jobang silently did came to be appreciated in course of time and the study of customary laws became a popular academic field for useful social and legal purposes. Father G. Costa's *The Garo Code of Law* first appeared in International Anthropological Magazine, *Anthropos*, in 1954 and it was published in English by the author himself in the same year at Gauhati.[16] It deals with the same topics of Garo customary laws which were covered by Jobang, but Costa's work was more systematic and his approaches were different and academically higher in refinement. More books on customary laws came out later on. For example, *The Principles of Garo Law* by Jangsan Sangma (1963)[17] and *The Garo Customary Laws and Usages* by K. R. Marak (1964)[18] to name only a few, while Julius L. R. Marak's *Garo Customary Laws and Practices* (2000)[19] is one of the latest in the field. Nonetheless, Jobang's work is still remembered as pioneering in the field.

Jobang D. Marak's fifth book *Chengoni A.gilsak aro chengoni Mande, Bak 1* or 'The Ancient World and the Ancient Man, Book 1',[20] gives a picture of the earth in its origin and describes it as full of dense jungles with sparsely human habitations. Then he talks of man as food-gatherer and hunter, then domesticator of animals like cow, horse, goat, donkey, sheep, etc., and then taking up of some cultivations, discovery of iron, settled agriculture and trade. The themes and organization of the book show that the author had read some books on early history of the mankind. The same knowledge is reflected in his sixth book *Odek Education*, Book 2 (or the origin and beginning of education and civilization).[21] He describes how man instinctively drew pictures of animals, aquatic beings, birds, etc. on clays, rocks, dead leaves and then about the invention of letters in the Arab World, called the Roman Script, and how these letters were first written on dead wild reeds, skins of animals, clays and finally, on papers. Although written for the school children, this book finds a place in the history of Garo literature for its pleasant literary style and choice of vocabulary.[22] Jobang thus left a permanent mark among the Garos as an educator and a good writer.[23] His two volumes on Garo history is considered as an invaluable work both from literary presentation and oral history points of view and these were, therefore, prescribed as text books for undergraduate and post-graduate classes in Garo literature. His book on Garo law is consulted by the lawyers and his two volumes on education and civilizations reflect his wide readings.

As a historian

Jobang D. Marak was not a historian by training or profession, but he made a place for himself in modern history and culture of the Garos as an educator and a writer. He painstakingly collected the oral traditions popular among the Garos about their own past, their original home and their ancestors, and faithfully recorded those in the form of writing history. He wrote what the Garo people believed to be their own history. Interestingly, his book on Garo history found wide acceptability among the people. Those who write on the history and culture of the Garos, particularly the traditional period and early migrations, do refer to his works.[24] He explored the myths, traditions, customs and practices of the Garos while writing on folklore and customary laws. In the process, he discovered the historical contents of the oral traditions, the belief systems and world view of the Garos. In fact, what Jobang found about the Garos is true of all the tribal communities in Northeast India who did not have written historical records till the modern period and whose early histories were preserved in traditions, myths and legends. Jobang recorded those oral traditions in his book on Garo history and in this way he wrote the first book in early history of the Garos. The history he wrote can be called traditional history as it is based on documentation of oral traditions, and Jobang D. Marak was thus a traditional historian. However, the materials he painstakingly collected are invaluable source materials for writing the Garo history for the early periods and the institutional historians are able to use them in their modern works. Moreover, it is being more and more appreciated that the history of the pre-literate societies, like the tribal communities in the Northeast in pre-colonial period, can be reconstructed only on the basis of non-conventional sources, like the oral traditions, since other categories of sources are almost unavailable in the hill tribal region. In this sense, Jobang D. Marak was one of the pioneers in the field of oral history in Northeast India.

Notes & References

1. The biographical sketch of Jobang D. Marak has been compiled by the author of this paper by collecting information from the elders in Tura and Baghmara, including the youngest daughter of Jobang D. Marak, Shrimati Margareth Ruth W. Momin who is the only surviving member of Jobang's immediate family.
2. The books written by Jobang D. Marak were mostly printed in Calcutta and published by the author himself. The years of publication are indicated in the text after each title.
3. Jobang D. Marak , *Deshi Kasrat*, Calcutta, 1916.
4. Jobang D. Marak, *A.chik Aganani Bak 1*,Calcutta, 1927.
5. D. K. Sangma, *A'chik Golparang, Bak I* (1960), *Bak II* (1963), *Bak III* (1963), Tura Book Room, Tura.
6. Jobang D. Marak and Simison Marak, *A'chik Aganani Baksa* (Garo), American Baptist Mission, Gauhati, 1927,
7. Harendra W. Marak, *A'chik Aganbewalrang* (Garo), (First edition, 1959) reprint NEHU Publications, Shillong, 1983.
8. Dewansing Rongmuthu, *Apasong Agana* (Garo), Calcutta, 1970.
9. Dewansing Rongmuthu, *The Folk Tales of the Garos*, Gauhati University, 1960.
10. Dewansing Shangma Rongmuthu, *Epic Lore of the Garos*, Department of Tribal Culture and Folklore Research, Gauhati University, 1967.
11. Jobang D. Marak, *Garo Kata, Bak I & II*, Calcutta, 1930.
12. A. Playfair, *The Garos*, Trubner & Co., London, 1909.
13. William Carey, *The Garo Jungle Book*, The Juden Press, Philadelphia, 1919.
14. Levisoned N. Sangma, *A'chikni Gimin Aganani* (History of the Garos), Tura, 1965.
15. Jobang D. Marak, *The Garo Law*, Calcutta, 1952.
16. Rev. G. Costa, "The Garo Code of Law", *Anthropos*, Vol. IL, 1954, reprinted as a book *The Garo Code of Law*, Gauhati, 1954; edited with an introduction by P. C. Kar, Tura Book Room, Tura, 1975.
17. Jangsan Sangma, *The Principles of Garo Law,* Tura, 1963.
18. K. R. Marak, *The Garo Customary Laws and Usages*, Tura, 1964.
19. Julius L. R. Marak, *Garo Customary Laws and Practices*, Akansha Publishing House, New Delhi, 2000.
20. Jobang D. Marak, *Chengoni A.gilsak aro chengoni Mande,Bak1,* Narayan Industrial Press, Tura, 1955.
21. Jobang D. Marak, *Odek Education*, Book 2, Narayan Industrial Press, Tura, 1955.
22. Milton S. Sangma, *History of Garo Literature*, NEHU Publication, Shillong, 1983, p. 75.
23. Milton S. Sangma, *History of Education in Garo Hills*, Spectrum Publications, Guwahati, 1985.
24. See, for example, Milton S. Sangma, *History and Culture of the Garos*, Books Today, New Delhi, 1981.

5

Kanaklal Barua (1872-1940)

—Gajendra Adhikary

Biographical Sketch

An officer-historian *par excellence*, Kanaklal Barua remains immortal in the minds of the scholars and students of Assam history in particular and among the students of Indian history in general for his invaluable and pioneering contributions in reconstructing the early history of Northeast India. He was born at Guwahati on 25th *Agrahayana* 1794 *Saka*, equivalent to 11th December, 1872 AD. His father Lakshilal Barua was a Judicial Superintendent at the office of the Deputy Commissioner at Guwahati. In 1874, getting nomination to the civil service Lakshilal went to Goalpara to assume the office of the Extra Assistant Commissioner. Thereafter, he was transfered to Barpeta with the same rank. Kanaklal was admitted in a school at Barpeta where he completed his middle school standard. All of a sudden his father Lakshilal fell ill and during a journey to upper Assam died near Tezpurghat while he was on board of a steamer cargo. Their kiths and kin then advised the little boy Kanaklal and his mother to go back to their ancestral home in Namti Kakati gaon in Sivsagar district .His mother, however, decided to stay at Guwahati and Kanaklal was admitted to the upper section of Guwahati High School. He was, moreover, taught at home by his father's friend Hemchandra Barua.

Kanaklal Barua, in his later life, attempted to know details of his ancestors. He collected several *purusanama* in manuscript form from different parts of upper Assam. It was found that his first ancestor in Assam, named Pitambar Ghose, belonged to a Bengali Kayastha family that had migrated to Assam from Bengal in the seventeen century A.D. Most probably, he was sent to Assam by one of the Mughal Commanders, Satrajit, who once developed a diplomatic friendship with the Ahom king in 1615 AD. Pratapsimha, the Ahom king (1603-1641 AD), appointed him as a land surveyor.[1] After a careful scrutiny of these *purusanama* Kanaklal Barua drew his genealogy as follows:[2]

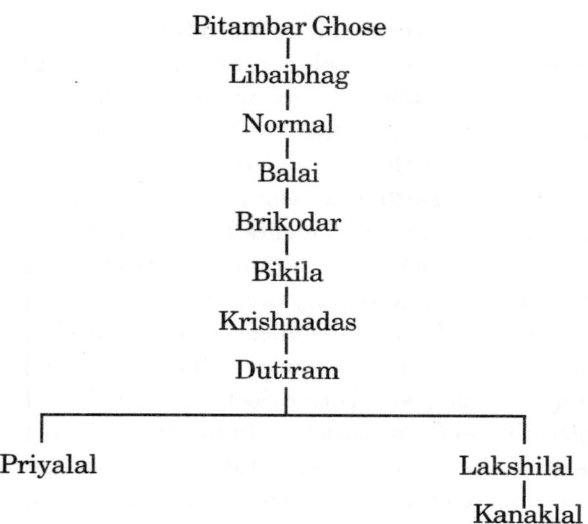

Kanaklal passed the entrance examination of the Calcutta University from Guwahati High School in 1888 and secured one of the fourteen government scholarships of rupees twenty reserved for the students of the Brahmaputra valley. He then proceeded to Calcutta to study in General Education Institution for his B.A. degree. It was a remarkable year for Assamese language and literature for the launching of the epoch making Assamese monthly *Jonaki* from Calcutta, mainly at the initiative of Chandra Kumar Agarwala. Kanaklal Barua was associated with the magazine from the very beginning and when he was in the third year class, he took the responsibility of editing the magazine. In 1893, another Assamese monthly, *Bijuli*, also started to be published from Calcutta. The publication of *Jonaki* was stopped in 1893, for which Kanaklal began to contribute regularly in the *Bijuli*. Some of these contributions were later on included in a book entitled *Sahitya Samgraha*, which was edited by Padmanath Gohain Barua. Kanaklal passed the B.A. examination in 1894, and he took the B.L. degree of Calcutta University in 1896. To meet the expenditure of his studies in Calcutta, he had to work hard by writing for an English newspaper. He also compiled a text book, named *Bhugol Siksha*, in Assamese. In addition, he earned some money by becoming a private tutor of Nabin Chandra Bardoloi, later on the most pronounced nationalist leader (popularly acclaimed as *Karmaveer*) of Assam. In Calcutta, Kanaklal was very active in public and literary fields. Jointly with Ramakanta Barkakati, he became the Secretary of the *Asamiya Bhasar Unnati Sadhini Sabha* (in all probability during 5th to 7th sessions of the *Sabha*). In 1895, they also jointly compiled a catalogue of 740 books in Assamese, entitled *Asamiya puthir talika*.

In 1898, Kanaklal returned to Guwahati to join the Bar. He married Bhubaneswari Devi. In 1900, he was appointed Extra Assistant Commissioner and joined his office at Sivasagar. This was the turning point in the career of Kanaklal Barua as a historian for he got an opportunity to visit different places of Assam in the capacity of a government officer. During this period he developed his interest in unearthing the sources of Assam history. In 1904, he was transferred to Sylhet as a Sub-Divisional Officer and thereafter to Barpeta, the most pronounced seat of Vaisnavisim in Assam. Barpeta was also the place of

Kanaklal's early school days. It was but natural that he was influenced by the Vaisnavisim of Assam and made an intensive study of the religion and philosophy of Sankardeva, resulting in a series of writings on the subject which were published in Lakshminath Bezbarua's *Bahi*, another important Assamese monthly of the time. Later on, those articles were published in a book form under the title *Mahapurusia Sampradayar dharmamata*. These essays were also incorporated in Bezbarua's compilation, called *Mahapurusa Sri Sankaradeva aru Sri Madhavadeva* (1916). Co-incidentally, Kanaklal Barua in that year was awarded the title of *Rai Bahadur* for his meritorious services as a civilian. He was then appointed as the Deputy Megistrate and Deputy Collector of Jorhat and next year, he was transferred to Goalpara as the Sub-Divisional Officer. In 1918, he was appointed as a member of the Thomas Holland Industrial Commission. In the same year, he became the Director of Industries and Registrar of Co-operative Societies of Assam. He had also to serve as a member of the Agricultural Commission of India. In 1923, in addition to his normal duties, Kanaklal was made the Director of Agriculture, Govt. of Assam. He played an active role in establishing the present-day Assam Textile Institute (Guwahati), Technical and Industrial Schools at Titabar, the Haflong Sericultural Farms, Sylhet School of Handicrafts, and the Khanapara Diary Farm (Guwahati). For his sincerity in discharging the duties, Kanaklal was promoted to ICS grade and was appointed as Deputy Commissioner of the United and Jaintia Hills District, at Shillong, in 1922. On 1st January 1928, he attained his superannuation. Next year, he was elected to the Assam Legislative Assembly and became the Minister for Local Self-- Government. In 1937, he was conferred the title of CIE. Barua passed away on 8th January 1940 at Calcutta where he had gone to attend the annual session of the Indian History Congress (held in December 1939) but fell ill in course of the session.[3]

Contributions to history

Kanaklal Barua cherished his interest in historical studies since his boyhood. In the 'preface' of his celebrated work *Early History of Kamarupa*,[4] he said :

> While a school boy, I noticed the digging up of the foundations of an old fortification in the eastern part of Gauhati town and the breaking of the carved and chiseled stones for road metal. Though a boy, I then wondered why such nicely carved stones dug out were ruthlessly broken into fragments. I now realize that the remains of the fortification then exposed probably belonged to the citadel named 'Sri Durjaya' or the 'impregnable' by Ratnapala in the eleventh century A.D. No one in the authority then intervened to stop the destruction. Again when the great earthquake in 1897 destroyed the Silsako, 'an ancient stone bridge' as recorded by Sir Edward Gait himself, no one in authority then raised his little finger to prevent the people of Barpeta and other places from taking away the stones of the pires and the platform, though at that time the Deputy Commissioner of Kamrup was Col. Gurdon an officer having keen interest in historical research and preservation of ancient monuments and chief secretary to the Government of Assam was Sir Edward Gait, the author of the history of Assam.[5]

As a retired government officer as well as the Minister for Local Self-Government, Kanaklal Barua made up his mind to devote his time and energy in studying the ancient history of Assam. The opportunity became bountiful as he was to be involved in some of the leading research organizations in the country and abroad. He became the President of the *Kamarupa Anusandhan Samiti* (KAS), otherwise known as the *Assam Research Society* (ARS), and the founder editor of its Journal – *Journal of Assam Research Society* (*JARS*). He edited the journal from 1933 till he breathed his last in 1940.The Viceroy and Governor-General of India appointed him as one of the members of the *Indian Historical Records Commission*. He was also a member of the *Asiatic Society of Bengal*, a Fellow of the *Royal Economic Society of London*, member of the *Royal Asiatic Society of Great Britain and Ireland* and of the *Council of the Indian Anthropological Institute.* As a foreman of the '*Jonaki* Age' in Assamese literature, Barua was invited to adorn the chair of the Asam Sahitya Sabha session at Dibrugarh in 1924. In 1937, he again presided over the history session of the Sabha's annual conference at Guwahati.[6]

Kanaklal Barua is remembered mostly for the investigations he made in the field of ancient history and culture of Assam in particular and that of India in general. *Kamarupa Anusandhan Samiti* (KAS) was the prime vehicle through which he mainly operated in his academic pursuits. Under his leadership the KAS also moved from strength to strength. From its very inception in 1912, the KAS began to collect the old manuscripts, inscriptions and coins and to study the remains of the old temples, buildings, sculptures, etc found in and around Guwahati and also in other parts of Assam. In fact, Kanaklal was one of the general members of KAS till he visited its office in 1928. He became so impressed upon the activities of the Samiti that by exercising his discretionary power as Minister of Local Self-Government he granted a sum of rupees three hundred for publication of a research journal which was " to publish the results of their labours and to bring their contributions to the notice of the orientalists throughout India and abroad."[7] Thus, the *Journal of Assam Research Society (JARS)* came out in 1933, obviously under the editorship of K.L. Barua. It is, therefore, acknowledged in the Annual Reports of the KAS for the years 1932-33 and 1933-34 that "we (the members of the KAS) are deeply grateful to him (K.L. Barua) for his giving a good and effective start to the journal which is expected to further the cause of research work in Assam." From the Annual Report of the KAS for the year 1935-36 it is known that Kanaklal Barua enhanced the financial grant up to rupees eight hundred "to meet the cost of publication of the journal during the first three years." Kanaklal Barua, thus, became the patron, editor and the publisher of the *JARS.* His involvement in this way with the research organization even created a murmur that the Minister spent more time for the growth and development of the KAS than for Local Self-Government.[8]

The idea of establishing the Assam State Museum was first conceived by the KAS under the stewardship of K.L. Barua. A movement took place in 1934 to collect donations from the public for establishing a museum at Guwahati. A sum of rupees 9,750/- was thus collected. It was mainly at K.L. Barua's instrumentality that the then Education Minister of Assam, Maulana Wahid, was persuaded to sanction a grant of rupees 10,000/- for this noble purpose. In 1939, the Government of Assam constituted a Board of Trustees of the proposed Assam Provincial Museum with Rai Bahadur K.L. Barua as its President. In an executive committee's meeting held on 26th June, 1939, the KAS unanimously resolved to handover all "such articles now in the custody of the Samiti as may be considered... suitable as exhibits in the museum." Thus the dream child of K.L. Barua, i.e. the Assam Provincial Museum, was all set to its birth when the Governor of Assam formally declared that the Museum would be opened on 21st April, 1940. However, the destiny directed otherwise. Kanaklal Barua was not allowed by the cruelty of time to see his dream child born. He breathed his last in Calcutta on 8th January 1940. Kaliram Medhi, who succeeded to the chair on the death of K.L. Barua, rightly acknowledged in his speech delivered in the inaugural ceremony of the museum : " This museum is a monument of the Rai Bahadur's love for the motherland and fruit of his indomitable energy and selfless activities."[9]

K.L. Barua's contribution to ancient history of Assam was voluminous. However, even if he did not write anything else, he would have been remembered for his *magnum opus*, namely, *Early History of Kamarupa* (1933). He got his stimulation to trace out the polity, society, economy and culture of the old Kamarupa kingdom for the lacunae he found in Sir Edward Gait's *A History of Assam* (1906). In the words of Barua, Gait tells so little of the early period of Assam's history that " only 14 pages have been devoted in that book for the history of the period from fourth to twelfth century A.D."[10] Two other scholarly works, viz, *Kamarupa Sasanavali*, edited by Padmanath Bhattacharyya, and *Social History of Kamarupa*, 2 vols., by N.N.Vasu, were also published in 1931 and 1922-28 respectively. Barua found these works "with large mass of unassorted and critically unexamined materials."[11] Padmanath Bhattacharya did not attempt to present a detailed history of the period which was covered by the inscriptions published in the book.[12] On the other hand, in his *Social History of Kamarupa* N.N. Vasu "...tried to piece together a history of this period from the records of several well known Kayastha families of Kamarupa, but his otherwise praiseworthy attempt has been vitiated by his eagerness to prove the Bengali origin of the Kayastha Bhuyans of Assam. He seems to have overlooked the fact that the inscription of Bhaskaravarman proves the existence of Kayasthas in Kamarupa in the beginning of the seventh century..."[13] Barua, therefore, came forward to shoulder the responsibility "...to treat the early history of the province systematically" in his *Early History of Kamarupa*.[14] He utilized the inscriptions and other literary sources included in the above works as well as the observations and notes on these sources made by A.F.R. Hoernole, K.N. Dikshit. H.P. Sastri and other historians of repute in such a scientific way that after going through the pages of the *Early History of Kamarupa*, the renowned Indologist A.L. Basham was convinced that "From about the beginning of the Chirstian era, and indeed from much earlier date... the land of Kamarupa, the valley of the Brahmaputra river around Gauhati was the eastern most outpost of Hindu culture, maintaining a vigorous and independent political and social life and... At least once, under the great king Bhaskaravarman, Kamarupa became a decisive factor in the politics of India as a whole."[15] J.P. Mills said, "It is a book we have been longing for".[16] Another profound scholar of ancient Indian history and archaeology K.N. Dikshit paid high compliments to K.L. Barua for this book and opined that Barua had done "really yeoman's service to the neglected cause of Assam's history."[17]

As a matter of fact, K.L. Barua's *Early History of Kamarupa* was the first book on the history of ancient Assam. As Pragjyotisha-Kamarupa at times included within its geographical limits not only the most of present Northeast but also the adjoining areas of northern and eastern Bengal, Barua's work deserves to be considered as the first book on ancient Northeast India. Divided into fifteen chapters, the book covered 'Pragjyotisa', 'Pre-historic period', 'Kamarupa in the Gupta period', 'Kamarupa of Bhaskaravarman', 'Dynasty of Salastambha', 'Dynasty of Brahmapala', 'Cultural and Material Progress', 'Later Kamarupa Kings', 'Muhammadan Invasions', 'Kings of Kamata', 'Chutia Kingdom', 'Rule of the Bhuyans', 'Koch Kingdom', 'Vaisnava Reformation' and 'Growth of Literature'. Though focused on the ancient period, the narrative continued fairly deep into the medieval period. The texts of four inscriptions of ancient Kamarupa in English translations are given in the appendices, and the photographs of as many as twenty-five art objects, archaeological sites, covers of literary texts etc. have been provided in the book as illustrations. More epigraphic and archeological evidences, including literary sources, have come to notice after publication of the work of K.L. Barua, but it is indeed incredible that most of the formulations in this first book on the history of ancient Assam are considered valid till today. Barua worked out genealogy of the ruling dynasties of Kamarupa on the basis of evidences that were available to him. Besides political history, he also discussed social, cultural and economic life of the people of Kamarupa, including external trade and commerce. Although not a professional historian, he used the standard format of history writing of his time; used notes and references, and took account of the contributions of other historians in his discussions.

Apart from the *Early History of Kamarupa*, K.L. Barua contributed a large number of research articles in *Journal of Assam Research Society (JARS)* including "Some notes on Assam coins" (*JARS*, vol. I, no. 2, 1933), "Stray notes on Buchanon's Account of Purnea" (*JARS*, vol. I, no. 2, 1933), "Kamarupa in the sixth century A.D." (*JARS*, vol. I, no. 4, 1934), "Dr. Hutton on the races and religions in India" (*JARS*, vol. I, no. 4, 1934), "The Kamarupa era" (*JARS*, vol. II, no 1, 1934), "The Hatimuria temple in Nowgong" (*JARS*, vol II, no. 1, 1934), "Kamarupa in the eighth century" (*JARS*, vol. II, no. 1, 1934), "Was there a Buddhist temple at Hajo ?" (*JARS*, vol. II, no. 2, 1934), "Kamarupa and Vajrayana" (*JARS*, vol. II, no. 2, 1934), "A manuscript of the sixteenth century" (*JARS*, vol. II, no. 2, 1934), "Prasioi and Gangaridai" (*JARS*, vol. II, no. 2, 1934), "The date of Saraha" (*JARS*, vol. II, no. 3, 1934), "Note on some ancient ruins" (*JARS*, vol. II, no. 4, 1935), "Origin of the Bhauma kings of Orissa", (JARS, vol. II, no. 4, 1935), "Kamarupa in the ninth century A.D." (*JARS*, vol. III, no. 1, 1935), "Kausika or Kausiki" (*JARS*, vol. III, no. 1, 1935), "Purusattama Vidyavagisa" (*JARS*, vol. III, no. 1, 1935), "Stemming of the tide of Muslim conquest in Eastern India" (*JARS*, vol. III, no. 2, 1935), "The name of Assam, an explanation" (*JARS*, vol. III, no. 2, 1935), "Some more Kamarupa seals in Nalanda" (*JARS*, vol. III, no. 2, 1935), "The ancient Tripuri kingdom in the Kapili valley" (*JARS*, vol. III, no. 3, 1935), "A Koch hero of the seventeenth century A.D." (*JARS*, vol. III, no. 3, 1935), "Amherst's collection of Assamese coins" (*JARS*, vol. III, no. 4, 1936), "A rejoinder" (*JARS*, vol. IV, no. 1, 1936), "An Assamese source of Mughal history" (*JARS*, vol. IV, no. 1, 1936), "The

Maharaja of Koch Behar" (*JARS*, vol. IV, no. 2, 1936), "Another rejoinder" (*JARS*, vol. IV, no. 3, 1936), "Clay seals of Bhaskaravarman" (*JARS*, vol. IV, no. 4, 1937), "Kamarupa in the *Markandeya-purana*" (*JARS*, vol. V, nos. 1-2, 1937), "Mirza Nathan's narrative" (*JARS*, vol. V, no. 3, 1937), "Seventeenth century Portuguese travellers in Assam" (*JARS*, vol. V, no. 3, 1937), "Uttarakuladesa" (*JARS*, vol. V, no. 4, 1938), "An unjust accusation" (*JARS*, vol. V, no. 4, 1938), "Human sacrifice in Assam" (*JARS*, vol. VI, no. 1, 1938), "Genealogical lists of the Pragjyotisha dynasties" (*JARS*, vol. VI, no. 1, 1938), "Iran and Eastern India" (*JARS*, vol. VI, no. 2, 1938), "Metallic icons found in Alinagar" (*JARS*, vol. IV, no. 2, 1938), "History behind a phonetic difficulty" (*JARS*, vol. V, nos. 3-4, 1938), "Some noted mediaeval Kamarupi authors and their works" (*JARS*, vol. VI, nos. 3-4, 1938-1939), "Pre-historic culture in Assam" (*JARS*, vol. VII, no. 1 and no. 2, 1939), "Kamarupa and Kautilya : Addendum" (*JARS*, vol. VII, no. 1, 1939), "Were there colonists from Assam in Indo-China ?" (*JARS*, vol. VII, no. 2, 1939), "Two newly discovered ancient inscriptions in Assam" (*JARS*, vol. VII, no. 3, 1939), "Ksauma, dukula and patrorna" (*JARS*, vol. VII, no. 3, 1939) and "Was Kautilya an Easterner ?" (*JARS*, vol. VII, no. 3, 1939). At least seven of his research articles were published in *Indian Culture*, Calcutta, viz. "Kausika and Kusiara" (vol. I, No. 3, January 1935), "Nagar Brahmanas and Sylhet: A Rejoinder" (vol.1, no.4, April 1935), 'Kausika or Kausiki" (vol.1I, no.1, July 1935), "Kausiki and Kusiara : A Rejoinder" (vol.II, no.I, July,1935), "Alpines in Eastern India" (vol. III, no.1, July 1936), "The Pala kings of Kamarupa" (vol.VIII, no.2, October 1937) and 'The Gupta era" (vol. V, no.I, July 1938). Barua also critically reviewed several books and many articles with bearings on ancient Kamarupa that appeared in various journals and periodicals.[18]

K.L. Barua was also a prolific writer in Assamese. He played a historic role in the development of modern Assamese language and literature by his association with the renowned periodicals of his time like *Jonaki*, *Bijuli* and *Bahi* and his organizational involvement in *Asamiya Bhasar Unnati Sadhini Sabha* in Calcutta. His writings in Assamese covering his poetical compositions to serious essays on historical and cultural themes, besides some of the contemporary political as well as natural events and calamities, appeared in leading weekly and monthly magazines of his time.[19]

As a historian

Kanaklal Barua was an administrator-turned-historian who was driven by a desire to unearth the history and culture of the people within the bounds of ancient Pragjotisha-Kamarupa-Kamata kingdoms from 4th century to the 16th century AD and worked whole heartedly till he breathed his last at the age of 68. By his untiring zeal for the cause of reconstructing the history of Assam, Barua has cut a niche in the hearts of the people for which he is still remembered whenever the history of Assam and Northeast India comes up for discussion. There are many in Assam who feels that Kanaklal died for the cause of history because he had gone to present a paper at the annual session of the Indian History Congress at Calcutta where he was taken ill and never returned home. Though he was not a historian by profession, he was actively involved in the academic bodies promoting historical research in India and he was in personal contact with the leading historians of his time. He was the first historian to attempt a full length study in the ancient history of Assam and the Northeast in the form of his *Early History of Kamarupa*. He also contributed a large number of articles in learned journals on ancient and early medieval history of Northeast India and reviewed the works of other scholars in his field in those journals. As a matter of fact, Kanaklal Barua's works laid the foundation for systematically studying the ancient history of Assam and the Northeast and the historians who worked in that field after Barua have extensively used *Early History of Kamarupa* to go beyond the book and to develop this research field further.[20] Anundaram Barooah+'s *Ancient Geography of India* (1877), which was published more than half century before K.L. Barua's work, very briefly referred to Pragjyotisha-Kamarupa and its neighbourhood as the book covered the entire subcontinent.[21] Many years after the publication of *Early History of Kamarupa* came out *The History of Civilization of the People of Assam to the Twelfth Century AD* (1959) by P.C. Choudhury,* a seminal research work in ancient history of Northeast India, which emerged out of author's doctoral thesis at the London University.[22] Choudhury's work is in the nature of a comprehensive history of ancient Assam. Choudhury, later on, published another major work on Assam-Bengal Relations in the ancient period.[23] In between

---

+ An internationally acclaimed Sanskrit scholar and the first Assamese in ICS, Anundaram Barooah (1850-1889), who studied in Calcutta in the years of Bengal renaissance and rediscovery of India's ancient heritage and came in contact with Frederick Max Muller in England, had authored *A Practical English-Sanskrit Dictionary* (3 vols; 1877, 1878 & 1980), *Bhababhuti's Mahabiracaritam* (1877), *Bhababhuti and his place in Sanskrit Literature* (1878), *A Comprehensive Grammar of the Sanskrit Language* (1882 & 1884), *Vaman Sutra-Vritti*, *Vagbhatalankara*, *Saraswati Kanthabharana* (1883), among his other works, besides *Ancient Geography of India* (1877). His *Ancient Geography of India* is a pioneering work in historical geography of ancient India which included Pragjyotisa-Kamarupa. [+Editor's Addendum]

* A distinguished historian trained in the true tradition of ancient Indian history and Indology, P.C. Choudhury (*ne* Pratap Chandra Choudhury) obtained his M A in history from the Banares Hindu University, Varanasi, in 1944, and did his Ph. D. at the School of Oriental and African Studies, London University, in 1953. He taught history at various colleges in Assam and Gauhati University, and thereafter, joined the Department of Historical and Antiquarian Studies (DHAS), Govt. of Assam, as its Director, in 1956. On his retirement after 18 years of distinguished service at the DHAS, he joined the Dibrugarh University as Professor and Head of the Department of History, in 1974, and served that University for three years. As a Senior Fellow of the Indian Council of Historical Research, New Delhi, he worked on an important research project entitled 'Studies in Source Materials of the History of Medieval Assam' for another three years. Choudhury's major publications on ancient Assam are *The History of Civilization of the People of Assam to the Twelfth Century AD* (DHAS, Guwahati, 1959) and *Assam-Bengal Relations : From the earliest times to the twelfth century A.D.* (Spectrum Publication, Guwahati, 1988). As Director of the DHAS, he wrote, edited and published a number of seminal works, including *Vittamanjani*, *Vaidyakasaroddhara*, *Smriti-Jyotisa-Sarasamgraha* and *A Catalogue of Sanskrit Manuscripts*. He also translated and edited *Hastividyarnava* (a profusely illustrated work), published by the Publication Board, Assam, and *Ananda Lahari*, published by Kamarupa Anusandhana Samiti, Guwahati. Associated with Visveshvaranand Rig Vedic Institute (Hoshiarpur), Kamarupa Anusandhana Samiti (Guwahati), and the International Congress of Sanskrit and Orientalists, P.C. Choudhury has been regularly contributing research papers and book reviews in various journals, including *Journal of Indian History* (Tiruvanthapuram), *Visveshvaranand Indological Journal* (Hoshiarpur) and *Journal of Assam Research Society* (Guwahati). He also edited the *Journal of Assam Research Society* for many years. A nonagenarian historian at Guwahati, Choudhury's *The History of Civilization of the People of Assam to the Twelfth Century AD* has already gone into fourth edition. [*Editor's Addendum]

Barua's *Early History of Kamarupa* and Choudhury's *The History of Civilization of the People of Assam to the Twelfth Century AD* two scholars, namely, Banikanta Kakati[24] and Birinchi Kumar Barua,[25] made substantive topical contributions in aspects of ancient history of the region. In the meantime, Suniti Kumar Chatterji's *Kirata-Jana-Kriti : The Indo-Mongoloids, Their Contributions to History and Culture of India* (1951)[26] and *The Place of Assam in the History and Civilisation of India* (Gauhati, 1955)[27] opened up the early history of the tribal communities in Northeast India. However, it has to be admitted that the ancient history of the region, other than the Assam proper, is still a less researched field.

As a historian, Kanaklal Barua used the conventional sources, like literary, archaeological and epigraphic records, and combined the insights he personally gained while in employment as an officer in different districts of undivided Assam while interpreting those sources. Though generally very strong in his own views about the cultural heritage of Assam, Barua always kept his mind open to revise his views and opinions whenever new information and interpretation became available. As an example of his openness to corrections one may recall that while preparing the chronology of the kings of Kamata, who left no epigraphic or numismatic records behind, he had categorically said that "some of my conjecture may be unfounded and if any one can present a more reliable history of this period, I shall be the first to congratulate him."[28] We may, therefore, share the opinion of S.K. Barpujari when he remarks that "the impetus which Kanaklal Barrua gave to historical research in Assam will be enshrined for all times to come in the minds of every lover of Assam."[29]

Notes & References

1. Kanaklal Barua , "My reminiscence", in Maheswar Neog (ed.) , *Studies in the Early History of Assam,* Asom Sahitya Sabha, Jorhat/Guwahati, 1973, p.312.
2. *Ibid*, pp. 311-312.
3. *Ibid*, see Introduction, p. ii.
4. K.L. Barua, *Early History of Kamarupa*, 1st edn. 1933; reprint 1966, Lawyers Book Stall, Gauhati. The book has since been reprinted several times.
5. *Ibid*, see Preface, p. 2.
6. Maheswar Neog (ed.), *Studies in the Early History of Assam, op.cit*, Introduction, p. iii.
7. *Journal of Assam Research Society (JARS),* vol. I, Guwahati, 1933.
8. *Annual Reports of the KAS* for relevant years.
9. *Ibid*.
10. K.L. Barua, *Early History of Kamarupa, op.cit*, Preface, p. 7.
11. Maheswar Neog (ed.), *Studies in the Early History of Assam, op.cit.*, Introduction, pp. iv-v.
12. K.L. Barua, *op.cit.*, p. 8.
13. *Ibid*, p. 9.

14. B.K. Barua, *A Cultural History of Assam*, 1st edn. Nowgong, 1951, reprint Guwahati, 1986, Preface to the first edition, p. 3.

15. Quoted in Maheswar. Neog (ed.), *Studies in the Early History of Assam*, *op.cit.*, p. xi.

16. J.P Mills, "Assam as a Field of Research" in *JARS* , vol. 1, no. I, 1933.

17. *JARS*, vol. 1, 1933.

18. For a detailed list of the articles of K.L. Barua and his reviews of books and articles published in various research journals and periodicals in English see Maheswar Neog (ed.), *Studies in the Early History of Assam*, *op.cit.*, pp. 9-14.

19. The following is a tentative bibliography of Kanaklal.Barua's publications in Assamese:

Sl.	*Content*		*Title*	*Published in*
1.	Poems	(i)	*Stotra*	*Asam Bandhu*, vol. II, nos. 1-2, 1886
		(ii)	*Brahmaputra*	*Jonaki* (monthly), vol.II, 1890
		(iii)	*Vasanta-vidya*	-do- vol. III, 1891
2.	Drama	(i)	*Sabitri-Satyaban*	-do-
3.	School text book :	(i)	*Bhugol-siksha*	(Kalikata, 1893)
4.	Essays and notes :	(i)	*amar silpa* I	*Jonaki*, vol. II, 1890
		(ii)	-do- II	-do- vol. III, 1891
		(iii)	*Asamat utpanna vaniya vastu*	-do— vol. III, 1891
		(iv)	*siksha*	-do- vol. III, 1891
		(v)	*bhukapar upakarita*	-do- vol. v, no 2
		(vi)	*paritattva*	-do- vol.v, nos. 3-4
		(vii)	*manav jatir sabhyata*	-do-
		(viii)	*samsarat sukh ne dukh*	-do-
		(ix)	*sahanubhuti*	-do-
		(x)	*hemchandra barua*	*Usha*, vol. III, 1909
		(xi)	*buranjir vividh toka*	*Bahi*, vol.v, 1928-29
5.	Essay notes :	(i)	*maha purusia sampradayar dhammamata*	*Bahi*, v. iii, 1926 (reproduced in Laksminath Bezbarua's *Mahapurusa Sri Sri Sankardev aru Sri Sri Madhabdev*, Calcutta, 1914
		(ii)	*Kautiliyar samayat Pragjyotishpura*	*Bahi*, vol.xxv, no. 1
		(iii)	*Hemchandra Baruar smriti*	*Bahi*, vol. xxvii

(Contd...)

Sl.	*Content*		*Title*	*Published in*
		(iv)	*Bondhuvara goswam*	*Milan*, 1928
		(v)	*Kamrupa samrajya*	*Avahan*, 1929
6.	Reports etc.	(i)	*Asamiya bhashar unnati sadhani sabha*	*Jonaki*, vol. v, 1895
		(ii)	*a bha,u, sa sabhar karya vivarani* (1895)	
		(iii)	*Sampadanar katha*	*Jonaki*, vol. v. 1895
		(iv)	*kobalagiya katha* (preface to *asamiya puthir talika* (1895)	
7.	Addresses	(i)	*Sabhapatir abhibhasana* (presidential Address)	Asom Sahitya Sabha, Dibrugarh, 1924
		(ii)	*Sabhapatir abhibhasana* (presidential address, History section)	Asom Sahitya Sabha, Guwahati,1937

20. For example, P.C. Choudhury, *The History of Civilization of the People of Assam to the Twelfth Century AD*, DHAS, Guwahati,1959; H.K. Barpujari (ed.), *The Comprehensive History of Assam*, vol. I, Publication Board Assam, Guwahat, 1990; Nayanjot Lahiri, *Pre-Ahom Assam :Studies in the Inscriptions of Assam between the Fifth and the Thirteenth Centuries AD*, Munshiram Manoharlal, New Delhi, 1991; Nirode Boruah, *Early Assam*, Spectrum Publication, Guwahati, 2007.
21. Anundaram Barooah, *Ancient Geography of India*, 1st edn. Calcutta, 1877; reprint Publication Board, Assam, Gauhati, 1971, pp. 68-72..
22. P.C. Choudhury, *The History of Civilization of the People of Assam to the Twelfth Century AD*, DHAS, Guwahati, 1959.
23. P.C. Choudhury, *Assam-Bengal Relations : From the earliest times to the twelfth century A.D.* Spectrum Publication, Guwahati, 1988.
24. Banikanta Kakati, *The Mother Goddess Kamakhya*, Gauhati, 1948.
25. B.K. Barua, *A Cultural History of Assam*, Gauhati, 1951
26. Suniti Kumar Chatterji, *Kirata-Jana-Kriti : The Indo-Mongoloids, Their Contributions to History and Culture of India*, The Asiatic Society, Calcutta, 1951.
27. Suniti Kumar Chatterji, *The Place of Assam in the History and Civilization of India*, Gauhati University, 1955.
28. K.L. Barua, *op.cit.*, p. 9.
29. S.K .Barpujari, "Rai Bahadur Kanaklal Barua", in B. Sarma (ed.), *Kamarupa Anusandhana Samiti Through the Ages,* Kamarupa Anusandhana Samiti, Guwahati, 2011, p. 370.

6

Amanatulla Ahmed (1873-1957)

—*Ananda Gopal Ghosh*

Biographical Sketch

An extraordinary vernacular historian of the princely state of Cooch Behar, an illustrious public figure, erudite scholar and a connoisseur of Bengali language and literature, Khan Choudhury Amanatulla Ahmed was born of a respectable family of Bara Maricha in the Mathabhanga Subdivision of the erstwhile princely state of Cooch Behar in 1873. His father Munshi Amirulla Patoary was a prosperous *Jotedar* (landlord) and influential person of the locality. It is not clearly known whether the family was indigenous Muslim in Bengal or their ancestors migrated from somewhere else. However, it appears from some historical sources of the northernmost part of Bengal that during the declining phase of the Khen Dynasty of Kamatapur kingdom, a good number of Muslims had settled in Goraghat, Sitai and Sitalkuchi region of the Mathabhanga subdivision of the present-day Cooch Behar district and the Munshi family of Mathabhanga to which the Khan Choudhury was born seems to be one of those families. Be that as it may, the Munshi family had not only adopted the local language and culture of Bengal but they also became the champions of it. It is a well known fact that *Mir*, *Mufti*, *Munshi*, etc honorific Muslim titles were synonymous with the learned and intellectual Muslim world. On the other hand, the *Patoary* title is indigenous one in the North Bengal-Assam region. The local people in Cooch Behar as well as Koch-Rajbanshi people of Lower Assam (*Namoni Asom*) used this surname in the suffix of their names. The adoption of local *Patoary* title by an ancestor of Khan Choudhury Amanatulla Ahmed is an example of assimilation of the family with the local language and culture of that part of Bengal where it was a common surname for the landed gentry in the medieval period. It is, of course, definitely known that the forefathers of the Khan Choudhury acted as Vakil (agent/representative) of the Cooch Behar kings in the Darbar (court) of the Nawab of Murshidabad. Moreover, the Khan Choudhury title used by Amanatulla was bestowed upon him by Maharaja Raj Rajendra Narayan Bhup Bahadur of Cooch Behar by an official notification in 1911 for his contributions in the field of social and humanitarian works.[1]

Amanatulla had his early education in *pathshala* and *maktab* in his own village and received regular attention of his father in matters of education. He was then sent to Cooch Behar town for further education. But we could get any information about his collegiate or higher education, although it is believed that he was a highly educated person because of the positions he held and his writings and speeches in Bengali and English. He did not mention any educational degree or academic title after author's name in his book, which was almost a common practice on the part of authors in those days. He simply wrote – 'Khan Choudhury Amanatulla Ahmad'. It is to be noted that a search of the old records of the Victoria College, Cooch Behar, did not yield his name as a student of that oldest college in Northeast India and former princely state of Cooch Behar. Whatever might be his institutional education, it is an acknowledged fact that he had keen interest in archaeology, history, language and literature of the princely state of Cooch Behar as well as the neighbouring areas of Assam and Bengal. It also appears from his writings, speeches and the positions he held in the Raj Darbar (royal court) of Cooch Behar that he was well versed in English, Bengali, Parsee, Arabic, Urdu, Sanskrit, Rajbanshi and Assamese. A member of the royal court of Cooch Behar for a long time, Amanatulla Ahmed was also a member of the Cooch Behar Legislative Council constituted by the Maharaja of Cooch Behar in the model of the administrative reforms of the British Indian Government. In 1946, he successfully contested the elections in Cooch Behar, and he was appointed by Maharaja Jagaddipendra Narayan Bhup as the Revenue Minister of the State. He had earlier represented the Mohammedan community in Maharaja's cabinet.

Amanatulla Ahmed was one of the architects of the Uttar Banga Sahitya Sanmelan, founded in 1907 at Rangpur. This literary organization had received liberal patronage of Maharaja Raj Rajendra Narayan Bhup of Cooch Behar. Amanatulla not only attended almost all the sessions of Uttar Banga Sahitya Sanmelan but also regularly presented articles for discussions in various sessions of the Sanmelan on history, archaeology and literature of Cooch Behar and Lower Assam. He was also instrumental in founding the Kamarupa Anusandhan.Samiti at Guwahati. It was in the annual session of the Uttar Banga Sahitya Sanmelan held at Kamakhya, Guwahati, in 1912, that Amanatulla Ahmed formally moved a resolution for formation of the Samiti and the said resolution was unanimously accepted. The primary objective of Kamarupa Anusandhan.Samiti was to be the study of history, archaeology, language and literature of ancient Pragjyotisa-Kamarupa, which included modern Assam and North Bengal (besides Cooch Behar).[2] He also felt that a similar organization of the like of Uttar Banga Sahitya Sanmelan and the Kamarupa Anusandhan Samiti was necessary for exploring the past of the Koch kingdom. As he had close connections with the royal family of Cooch Behar, he urged upon the royal court for founding an organization in the state. The result was the birth of the Cooch Behar Sahitya Sabha, in 1915, of which he was the founder-Secretary. All these organizational initiatives of Amanatulla Ahmed created a popular ground in North Bengal-Assam region for the development of vernacular historiography in the region.

Khan Choudhury Amanatulla Ahmed was a staunch advocate of composite culture. He edited *Damodar Charitamrita* of Govinda Dev Goswami with a note on the royal dynasty of Cooch Behar. As Secretary of the Cooch Behar Sahitya Sabha, he had promoted the compilations and publications of several books written in Cooch Behar. It is indeed unbelievable that such an extraordinary personality of the princely state of Cooch Behar was suspected to be involved in an anti-Indian conspiracy on the eve of India's independence to prevent the merger of Cooch Behar with the Union of India. A prominent founder-member of the Cooch Behar Hitasadhini Sabha, he is said to have espoused the merger of Cooch Behar with Pakistan. This had resulted in his expulsion from the Cooch Behar state in 1950. He took shelter at Rangpur in East Pakistan (now Bangladesh) and died there in 1957.[3]

Contributions to history

Khan Choudhury Amanatulla Ahmed's most significant contribution to history of Northeast India is his *Cooch Beharer Itihas* which is a huge book on the history of Cooch Behar in Bengali and it was published in 1936. In fact, there was a glorious tradition of vernacular history writing in Bengali in Cooch Behar. A good number of historical works had been published in the princely state before Amantulla's book. Among those, Jaynath Ghose's *Rajopakhyan* is well acclaimed as a path-finding modern work in Bengali on the regional history of Bengal. As a matter of fact, the tradition of history writing in Cooch Behar is very old. Even in the medieval period, the scholars in the court of the Koch kings had a celebrated tradition of maintaining *vamsavali* in an impressive poetical literary style. Several such *Vamsavalis* have come to notice of the historians and among these the *Shiva Vamsavali* (Bengali) by poet Dvija Birupaksha is very important as a source book for history because this beautiful poetic literary piece describes the history of the Koch kingdom since the reign of the founder of the dynasty, namely, Biswa Simha, and traces the lineage of the founding king Biswasimha from Lord *Shiva* (i.e. *Mahadeva*) down to the founder of the Bijni branch of the family.[4] Similarly, *Rajakhanda, Visvasinhacaritam, Harabhaktitaranga* and *Gosainimangal* are valuable literary works in Cooch Behar which also captured history in a significant way. While *Rajakhanda* and *Visvasinhacaritam* are purely historical works in Sanskrit, *Harabhaktitaranga* and *Gosainimangal* are locally composed literary pieces in the tradition of the *mangal kavyas* of medieval Bengal. There are many other literary works in and outside the royal court in Cooch Behar which are indeed important sources for the history of Cooch Behar.[5] The *Rajakhanda* was composed in Sanskrit in the seventeenth century by one Kaviratna who was one of the ministers of Maharaja Prannarayan of Cooch Behar. The original text is no longer available, but it has been referred to in Jaynath Ghose's *Rajopakhyan* and in an article entitled '*Kochviharer Itihas*' by Anandachandra Ghose published in 1865.[6] The *Visvasinhacharitam* was also composed in Sanskrit in the seventeenth century in the court of Maharaja Prannarayan by the young poet Sreenath, who was the son of a Brahmin, named, Ramesvara and grandson of Bhavananda.[7] *Harabhaktitaranga* was composed in Bengali verse by poet Durgadas in the court of Maharaja Shibendranarayan in the eighteenth century, while *Sangitsankar*, also in Bengali verse, was composed by Jagatdurlabh Biswas in the court of Maharaja Harendranarayan in the beginning of the nineteenth century.[8] The *Darangraj*

Vamsavali (Assamese) by Suryakari Daibajna, a chronicle of the eastern branch of the Koch kingdom, is a historical account of the Koch royal family since the foundation of the kingdom with some details of the reigns of early kings, including wars and conquests,[9] and thereby, a very important eighteenth century document on the history of Assam and Cooch Behar. However, Jaynath Ghose's *Rajopakhyan* is a modern work in Bengali on the history of northernmost corner of Bengal, namely, Cooch Behar and its neighbouring areas. Ghose began his career as a *Munshi* (writer) and rose to be a *Tahsildar*, holding the positions of *Nazir* and *Sheristadar* in between, in the princely state of Cooch Behar, during 1202 to 1265 BS (1795-1858 AD). He wrote *Rajopakhyan* between 1230 and 1240 BS (1823-1833 AD) during the reign of Maharaja Shibendranarayan of Cooch Behar. The book was translated into English by Rev. R. Robinson, Superintendent of Education, Cooch Behar State, and it was printed at the Baptist Mission Press, Calcutta, in 1874.[10] Similarly, Tariniprasad Sen's *Bijni Rajvamsa*, a modern history of the Bijni branch of the Koch royal family, in Bengali prose, was published as early as in 1876.[11] However, the mainstream historians of Bengal were not fully aware of the nineteenth century vernacular historiography of the princely state of Cooch Behar. As a result, in various discourses on the vernacular historiography of Bengal (or, in other words, modern historiography in Bengali) the contribution of Cooch Behar has not been properly assessed. On the other hand, a good number of books and monographs were published on history, archaeology, language and literature of Cooch Behar and the neighbouring areas by the scholars in the princely state of Cooch Behar. Thus, it may be said without any hesitation that Amanatulla Ahmed had inherited a glorious legacy of history writing in Bengali in Cooch Behar.

In assessing the contribution of Khan Choudhury Amanatulla Ahmed in the historiography of Cooch Behar it is important to appreciate that he not only carried the legacy further by producing almost a comprehensive history of Cooch Behar in the norms and practices of modern history writing in his *Cooch Beharer Itihas* but also added new splendours by studying archaeology, language, literature and culture of a larger geographical area in and around the princely state of Cooch Behar which had historical connections with the Koch kings. His interest in history and archaeology of Cooch Behar was indeed keen and this was reflected in his participation in the annual session of Uttar Banga Sahitya Sanmelan held in the premises of the Gauripur Raj State (Gauripur, Goalpara, Assam) in 1910. This conference was attended by eight representatives of the Cooch Behar State, including Rai Saheb Panchanan Barma (Sarkar), Maulavi Abdul Halim, Banshidhar Kanjee, Amanatulla Ahmed and others. Khan Choudhury Amanatulla Ahmed presented a paper on 'Koch-Rajbanshi Bhasatattva'.[12] The paper received wide acclamation of the well known scholarly participants. He also held for long twenty-five years the position of the Secretary of the Cooch Behar State Sahitya Sabha which regularly organized its annual conferences in Cooch Behar exploring history and culture, art and archaeology, language and literature, etc.[13]

A great lover of Bengali language and literature, Amanatulla Ahmed wielded his pen in writing the history of Cooch Behar, Kamatapur and Kamarupa region and regularly contributed articles in the periodicals like Suresh Chandra Samajpati's *Sahitya*, Rani Nirupama Devi's *Paricharika*, Sarat Chandra Ghosal's *Cooch Behar Darpan*, etc and in the annual conferences of Uttar Banga Sahitya Sammelan, Rangpur Sahitya Parishad, and Cooch Behar Sahitya Sabha.[14] It was in this background that Khan Choudhury Amanatulla Ahmed was making preparations for writing a comprehensive history of Cooch Behar. A golden opportunity came for him on 31st March 1920 when the Cooch Behar Raj Darbar (royal court) issued an order for writing a history of Cooch Behar and the same order bestowed the responsibility of writing the book upon Khan Choudhury Amanatulla Ahmed who was considered to be the most competent person then available for the assignment. The Darbar also sanctioned a sum of rupees three thousand five hundred only for the publication of five hundred copies of the book. It was a golden opportunity for Amanatulla Ahmed to write a book on history of Cooch Behar as he was already making preparations for the task and he commenced the work immediately.[15] His keen interest in the national history of India, even after publication of *Cooch Beharer Itihas*, is also established by his participation in the annual session of the Indian Historical Records Commission held at Peshwar (now in Pakistan) in 1945 where he presented two papers on Cooch Behar - one on 'military history : arms and ammunitions' and another on 'archaeology' of the region.[16]

Amanatulla Ahmed's *Cooch Beharer Itihas* is a great work in history which filled in a spectacular void in the historiography of Northeast India as the Koch kings ruled not only in modern Cooch Behar but also in large parts of the valleys of Brahmaputra and Barak and for sometime during the reign of Naranarayana subjugated the Ahom, Jayantia, Dimasa-Kachari, Tripuri, Meitei and few other kingdoms and principalities in the region. The organization of the book was planned to cover all the areas that were at times under rule of the different branches of the Koch royal family and to chronologically discuss the reigns of various kings from beginning of the Cooch Behar dynasty and its branches. The book opens with a large section discussing the sources under 'bibliography' and thereafter organized into eighteen chapters, covering name of the country and its situation; popular history; Kamatapur; Kamatesvar; condition of the country; religious reformers; Haihaya dynasty; Maharaja Bisvasinha; Naranarayan; Lakshminarayan, Birnarayan, Prannarayan; Modnarayan, Basudevnarayan, Mahindranarayan, Rupnarayan, Upendranarayan, Devendranarayan; Dhairyendranarayan, Rajendranarayan, Dharendranarayan, Dhairyendranarayan (2nd reign); Branches of the royal family – Raikat Raj, Panga Raj, Kachhar Raj, Darang Raj, Bijni Raj, Beltala Raj; Mohammedan relations; Narayani coins; Nazir-Gosvami conflicts; Bhutan Duars; Treaty with the British (Pincely State). The book ends with a chronological discussion on the reigns of all the kings from the founding king Biswasimha to the contemporary Khagendranarayan and a chronology of events in the history of the region since ancient times. The documents produced in the appendices are historically significant and there are five maps and fifteen illustrations in the book.[17]

An English version of the book was published in 1942, under the title *A History of Cooch Behar*, at the initiative of Maharaja Jagaddipendra Narayan.[18] It was translated by

Sarat Chandra Ghosal, MA BL and a Sanskrit scholar (Kavyatirtha, etc.), who earlier taught English and Sanskrit at Hindu College, Calcutta and Edward College, Patna and later on became a Civil and Sessions Judge at Cooch Behar.[19] While translating the book, he was a Member of the Cooch Behar State Legislative Council. The English version was edited by L.G. Wallis ICS, Vice-President, State Council of Cooch Behar, who also wrote a 'Foreword' for the book, while the principles adopted for translation are explained in the Translator's Note. The beauty of this translated English version is that maximum care was taken by the translator and the editor to avoid any interference with the contents of the original text of Amanatulla Ahmed so that the originality of the work is maintained for use of the future researchers. The appendices, maps, photographs and others illustrations are also the same as in original version by Khan Choudhury Amanatulla Ahmed in Bengali. As regards the purpose of translated version, the translator said, "A Bengali work being however of limited circulation, the present English Edition was taken up to meet the demand of the readers in different provinces and Native States in India for a knowledge of the history of Cooch Behar and its rulers traced as far back as the 7th century A.D."[20] And the editor said, "The present translation which has been undertaken, at His Highness' personal wish, by Mr. S.C. Ghosal, could not have been committed to more able hands. The form in which the original was cast, and the original text, have been adhered to closely and literally. The few interpolations, for which the Editor is responsible, have been denoted by the symbol '(Ed.)."[21] It was indeed a salutary decision of the Maharaja to bring out a translated English version of the book to make it available for the non-Bengali reading public at large. This also explains the quality of the work of Amanatulla Ahmed. The translated version of 1942 has recently been reprinted.[22]

As a historian

Khan Choudhury Amanatulla Choudhury was not a professional or institutional historian, but his *Cooch Beharer Itihas* is a modern work on the history of Cooch Behar for which he followed the modern methodology and literary style of history writing. His study is absolutely source based and he used footnotes in the contemporary style. He not only used the sources but also discussed their availability, quality and reliability. The bibliography, appendices, maps and sketches and the visual reproduction of coins, monuments and other artifacts are supportive of the narrative and statements of facts made by the author.

In writing *Cooch Beharer Itihas*, Amanatulla Ahmed not only extensively consulted the archival records of the Cooch Behar State and British India (Calcutta, Delhi, Shimla, Jaipur and Peshwar), British Museum, London and the Nepal Royal Court, Kathmundu but also used the literary, archaeological and numismatic sources, including the mythologies and oral traditions. He collected records from the Khuda Box Library, Patna, Imperial Library (now National Library), Calcutta, Bangiya Sahitya Parishad, Calcutta and used almost all available secondary works, including the articles published in various journals and proceedings of literary conferences. The sources used by him included documents, chronicles and literary works in Sanskrit, Bengali, Arabic, Persian, Urdu and Assamese, besides English, and the archaeological and numismatic sources. He personally interacted with the scholars in Kamarupa Anusandhan Samiti and obtained their views in interpreting various issues. In fact, while writing the book he had been constantly consulting the giants of Indian history and Indology of the time like Sir Jadunath Sarkar and Mahamohopadhyay Pandit Padmanath Vidyavinod.[23]

An analysis of the nature of the sources used by Amanatulla Ahmed reveals that he had written the history of Cooch Behar like the acclaimed historians of the twentieth century. It may be said without any reservation that he had written history in a modern way by conforming to the standard methodology followed by the institutional historians of his time. In this connection, it is also worth observing that a devout Muslim like Amanatulla Ahmed wrote the history of a Brahmanical Hindu kingdom, namely, Cooch Behar, and in doing so, he had used the Hindu myths and mythologies related to the origin of the kings and places of worship in the kingdom. As a matter of fact, he displayed his dispassionate and unorthodox academic temperament of a secular and scientific historian in writing the history of a Hindu kingdom. No wonder, while reviewing the book, *Prabasi*, a leading contemporary Bengali periodical of Calcutta, found the secular approach of a Muslim historian in writing the history of a Hindu kingdom in Bengal as most commendable part in the work.[24]

Notes & References

1. *The Cooch Behar Gazette*, Extraordinary, vol. 13, November, 1911, p. 3.
2. Chandra Nath Sarma (ed.), *The work of the KAS*, Kamarupa Anusandhana Samiti, Guwahati, 1920.
3. The biographical sketch of Khan Choudhury Amanatulla Ahmed has been compiled on the basis of information gathered from his relations in Mathabhanga and by using the sources like S.C. Ghosal (trans.), *A History of Cooch Behar*, Cooch Behar State Press, Cooch Behar, 1942, see Editor's Foreword and Translator's Note; Anindya Bhattacharya & Rajarshi Biswas (ed.), *Mansai – 2008*, Mathabhanga, 2008; Biswanath Das, *Anchalik Itihas Charcha*, Cooch Behar, 1998.
4. For the text of *Shiva Vamsavali*, see Prasun Barman (ed.), *Bijni Rajvamsa* by Tariniprasad Sen, Banga Bhasa-Sahitya-Sanskriti Parishad, Guwahati, 2007, see Appendix, pp. 62-79.
5. S.C. Ghosal (trans.), *A History of Cooch Behar*, Cooch Behar State Press, Cooch Behar, 1942, pp. xx-xxv.
6. *Ibid*, p. xxviii.
7. *Ibid*.
8. *Ibid*.
9. Nabin Chandra Sarmah (ed.), *Darangraj Vamsavali*, Baniprakash, Patshala, 1973.
10. S.C. Ghosal (trans.), *op.cit.*, pp. xxix-xxxi.
11. Tariniprasad Sen, *Bijni Rajvamsa*, Goalpara Hitavidhayini Yantra, Goalpara, 1876. Also see Prasun Barman (ed.), *Bijni Rajvamsa* by Tariniprasad Sen, Banga Bhasa-Sahitya-

Sanskriti Parishad, Guwahati, 2007. For an analytical review of the edited volume with emphasis on historiographical issues see Jayati Bhattacharjee, "Book Review - *Bijni Rajvamsa* by Tariniprasad Sen", *Northeast Researches*, Vol. I, no. 1, March 2010, pp.123-125.

12. *Uttar Banga Sahitya Sammelan, Tritiya Barsik Adhibeshan, Karyabibarani*, Gauripur, 1910.

13. Biswanath Das, *Anchalik Itihas Charcha*, Cooch Behar, 1998.

14. See, for example, *Uttar Banga Sahitya Sammelan, Tritiya Barsik Adhibeshan, Karyabibarani*, Gauripur, 1910; *Rangpur Sahitya Parishad Patrika, Dasham Sambatsarik Karyabibaran*, 1321 BS; *Cooch Behar Sahitya Sabha, Chaturtha Barsa Karyabibarani Pustak*, 1326 BS, p. 11.

15. Khan Choudhury Amanatulla Ahmed, *Cooch Beharer Itihas*, Cooch Behar State Press, Cooch Behar, 1936 (1343 BS), see Preface.

16. *Proceedings of Indian Historical Records Commission*, 22nd session, Peshwar, 1945, p. 11.

17. For details see the book Khan Choudhury Amanatulla Ahmed, *Cooch Beharer Itihas*, 1st edn. Cooch Behar, 1936 (1343 BS), reprint Modern Book Agency, Calcutta, 1990.

18. S.C. Ghosal (trans.), *A History of Cooch Behar*, Cooch Behar State Press, Cooch Behar, 1942.

19. In the title page of the English version of the book (1942), it is stated as follows : "Translated from Original Bengali by Sarat Chandra Ghosal, M.A., B.L., Sarasvati, Kavyatirtha, Vidyabhusan, Bharati, Jubilee Post-Graduate Scholar, Bankimchandra Gold Medalist & Jyotishchandra Medalist (University of Calcutta), Ewart Prizeman, Scottish Charge College; Sometime Professor of English & Philosophy - Hindu College, Professor of English & Sanskrit – Edward College, Patna; Member, Legislative Council, Civil & Sessions Judge, Cooch Behar". This impressive citation on the educational qualifications of the translator and the positions professionally held by him was possibly intended to inform the readers of the educational and professional abilities of the translator. In fact, it was a common practice in those days to mention academic degrees and professional designations of the authors in the books. However, in contrast, for Khan Choudhury Amanatulla Ahmad as author of the original Bengali version of the book only his name was mentioned. His educational qualifications are still unknown, though some of the positions held by him are known only from other sources.

20. S.C. Ghosal (trans.), *A History of Cooch Behar*, Cooch Behar State Press, Cooch Behar, 1942, p. xiii.

21. *Ibid*, p. xi.

22. S.C. Ghosal (trans.), *A History of Cooch Behar*, 1st edn. Cooch Behar, 1942, reprinted N.L. Publishers, Siliguri, 2005. This latest edition has further been edited by Hiten Nag.

23. See Preface and discussion on Bibliography in Khan Choudhury Amanatulla Ahmed, *Cooch Beharer Itihas*, Cooch Behar State Press, Cooch Behar, 1936 (1343 BS).

24. *Prabasi, Paus Sankhya*, 1345 BS, p. 445.

7

Homiwell Lyngdoh (1877-1958)

—D. R. Syiemlieh

Biographical Sketch

Homiwell Lyngdoh, as he was generally referred to, came from the Nonglait clan of Mawklot village close to upper Shillong. His mother was Thangdamon Nonglait. His father Bir Singh Nongkhlaw was a *Myntri* of Mylliem *hima*. Born on 26 February 1877,[1] he was among the first generation of Khasis to have received an education. After his schooling in the mission school in Shillong he proceeded to Calcutta where after a year pursuing the first arts class, he joined the Calcutta Medical College. He passed the Licentiate in Medicine and Surgery in 1903. Homiwell Lyngdoh had an illustrious career in medical service that took him to Gauhati, Dhubri, Chittagong, Imphal, Nowgong and Silchar. He was posted as Civil Surgeon in Shillong for five years during which time it is said he got involved in activities which were to make his name remembered as a writer. He also served for several years on a temporary commission in the Indian Medical Service. The Government awarded Dr Lyngdoh the medal of the 'Order of the British Empire'. In his retirement from government service, Homiwell Lyngdoh involved himself in the political activities in the Khasi hills with the revival of the Federation of Khasi States, the formation of the Khasi-Jaintia Political Association and the concerns in these hills with the transfer of power from Britain to independent India. Homiwell Lyngdoh passed away on 22 April 1958.[2]

Early Researches in Khasi history

In the select bibliography in English and Khasi of references used in Hamlet Bareh's[*] *The History and Culture of the Khasi People*, the author notes that until 1967-68, "nothing

* Retired as Professor at the Centre of Creative Arts, North-Eastern Hill University, Shillong, Hamlet Bareh is a distinguished historian. An M.A. and D. Phil in History of Gauhati University, he taught History in Union Christian College, Barapani and St Edmund's College, Shillong, served as editor of gazetteers in Arunachal Pradesh and Nagaland, and thereafter, was a Fellow at the Indian Institute of Advance Studies, Shimla, before joining North-Eastern Hill University in 1974. His *The History and Culture of the Khasi People* (Nava Mudran Pvt. Ld., Calcutta, 1967), which emerged out of his doctoral

(Contd...)

on the history and culture of the Khasis came out. Thereupon my effort to produce it".[3] It may be true that nothing substantial and comprehensive had been written in English before Bareh's *History*, though his interpretation of events had to depend on existing published histories many of which were in the Khasi language including the publications of Homiwell Lyngdoh. A close look at his Khasi sources and a search for what had preceded and came after this first comprehensive history of the Khasis reveals a fair interest among the Khasis in their history, the nation and even world events. That the Khasis had a sense of history is reflected in their oral tradition and folklore. That today these traditions are being lost out with the many influences on the society and the lack of appreciation of how the Khasis came to be till the present, is sadly reflected in their lack of interest in the past.

Thomas Jones, the first Welsh missionary to the Khasis started the use in 1842 of Roman Script for the Khasi language. In the first flush of literary works a combination of primers, Christian literature and translations were published. Beginning with a translation of *Rhodd Mamm* (1842), a popular Welsh story, Jones worked on *Ca Citap Nyngkong Ban Hicai Poole Ci Citin Cassi* (*First Khasi Reader*, 1842), *Oo Nonghicai* (*The Instructor*, 1843), and *Ca Gospel Jong OO Mathiaos* (1847). By the time Rev. William Lewis who came after Thomas Jones, tried his hand in the new expression some standardization had taken place. He added a small catechism, a hymn book (1850) and a translation of the Four Gospels and the Acts of the Apostles (1856).[4] In 1855, Rev William Pryse's *Khasi Grammar* was published. In the Prefatory Note to the vocabulary, Pryse takes a stand that the Khasis, "a small and uninfluential tribe will not be able to retain characters different from those of the larger natives of the plains which surround their hills." He continued:[5]

> Should the Khasia tribe be ever brought under the influence of education, civilization, and commercial intercourse, the Bengali character must supplant the Roman at a not very distant day.

Pryse may have been influenced in this opinion as he had started work among the Bengalis of Sylhet before going up into the hills. Perhaps a not too encouraging start was made with the setting up of three schools at Mawmluh, Mawsmai and Cherrapunji where Khasi was taught with the British official policy of encouraging the use of the Bengali script.[6] The debate of which script to use was not a long one. By the 1860's-1870's the decision of the Welsh Mission to use the Roman Script prevailed.[7] It was followed by an outpouring of literature that stimulated literary creativity in prose, poetry and drama; the establishment of Ri Khasi Press (1896) and monthly journals *U Khasi Mynta* (1896),

dissertation, is a comprehensive history of the Khasis. *The Khasi Democracy* (Shillong, 1963), *History of Khasi Literature* (Shillong, 1965), *Khasi Fables and Folk-Tales* (Firma K.L. Mukhopadhyay, Calcutta, 1971) and *Language and Literature of Meghalaya* (IIAS, Shimla, 1975) are among his other major works. He also contributed large number of articles in English and Khasi in various periodicals and collections. After his retirement, he dedicated himself to research more vigorously and published a series on all the states in Northeast India covering history, ethnography, economy and culture. He also directed and produced Khasi films that made him immensely popular in the region. A 'Padmasree', Professor Bareh is still engrossed in his research, writing and publishing. [Editor's Addendum]

U Nongphira (1903), *Nongkit Khubor* (1889), replaced in 1902 by *U Nongialam Kristan*. It was not long before Calcutta University, where many Khasis first went for higher education, gave recognition to the development of the language in its many expressions when it decided in 1902 that Khasi could be included in the use of subjects for the Entrance Examination.[8]

Before and by the turn of the century fragments of Khasi history were appearing in Alexander Mackenzie, *History of the Relations of the Government with the Hill Tribes of the North East Frontier of Bengal* (1884); W.W. Hunter, *A Statistical Account of Assam* (1879); C.U. Aitchison, *A Collection of Treatise, Engagements and Sanads* (1892), (1909); J.H. Morris, *The History of the Welsh Calvinistic Methodists' Foreign Mission* (1910); and D. Herbert, *Report on Succession to Siemships in the Khasi Hills* (1902). These and other material in the *Journal of the Asiatic Society of Bengal*, reprints of A.J.M. Mills *Report on the Khasi and Jaintia Hills 1853* (1901), and W.J. Allen, *Report on the Administration on Cossyah and Jynteah Hill Territory, 1858* (reprinted 1903), would have enabled B.K. Sarma Roy to write *Ka Histori Jong Ka Ri Khasi* (Shillong, 1914). The book of 104 pages has chapters on the Khasi states, a chapter on neighbouring Manipur and one on the Syiemlieh clan.[9] From the title of this first history in Khasi, its subject was the Khasi people. As an observer of the society B.K. Sarma Roy's work becomes important as a start and reference point.

Contributions of Homiwell Lyngdoh : First Detailed History

Those who wrote on the early history of the Khasis were not trained historians. They were largely administrators and missionaries and the first of the educated Khasis, many of whom had attended school and college in Calcutta. Homiwell Lyngdoh's first effort in writing history was *Ka Pom Blang bad Thang Syiem Sohra* (1928). Early in 1925 he had closely observed the elaborate ceremonies related with the cremation of Syiem Roba Singh[10] of Sohra and his succession by Join Manik Syiem. In May that same year he recorded the religious ritual of the Khyrim state. The death rituals and process of the embalming of the Sohra *Syiems* is described in detail. Similarly his notes on the ceremonies at Smit in Khyrim *hima* were the most detailed description of this significant tradition in the Khasi order of state and religion. This was followed by *A Short Account of Cherrapunji* (1933) which was published on the occasion of the visit of the Governor-General Lord Willington to Sohra in October 1933.

Lyngdoh's connection with the Presbyterian Church of which he was an elder did not deter him from appreciating his roots in the traditional Khasi religion and its practices and ceremonies. To the Khasi society's understanding of their religion authored several years earlier by Jeebon Roy in his *Ka Niam jong Ki Khasi* (1897) and *Ka Kitab Ba Batai Pynshynna Shaphang U Wei U Blei* (1900), Homiwell Lyngdon added *Ka Niam Khasi* (1937). In this he detailed the ideas of the Khasi religion, its religious performances and the chanting of incantations connected with different ceremonies in the life of the Khasis. A fairly detailed book of 271 pages, *Ka Niam Khasi* also makes reference to the cremation of the *Syiems* of Sohra, the monoliths and the origins of the Syiem and Lyngdoh clans.

Homiwell Lyngdoh followed this marvelous book with his *magnum opus, Ki Syiem Khasi Bad Synteng*, (Shillong, 1938). Interestingly he does not refer to the history mentioned above. He has as a reference Joel Gatphoh's *Ka Histori Ki Syiem Synteng Ha Ka Jingshisha* (1923-1926!) which unfortunately is not located. Lyngdoh's book was a trend setter for historical studies in Khasi. The book examined the Khasi-Jaintia political history providing details of each of the Khasi *himas*. He goes into a long introduction of the origin of *Syiemship,* its variations, powers and functions of *Syiems,* the role of the founding clans, the *Bakhraw*, and the linkage of Khasi religion with the Khasi *himas.* He starts with an account of the founding of the Khasi polity with the establishment of the first of the Khasi *himas,* the *Syiemships* of Madur Maskat, Jaintia and Shillong. The reprinted edition of the book (1964) brings up the introduction to the national movement, the establishment of the federation of Khasi States, the Constituent Assembly of India, the integration of the Khasi States into the Indian Union and the establishment of the District Councils.[11] Then follows in much more detail nineteen chapters in which accounts are given of the 18 *Syiemships.* Each of the shorter histories of the *himas* under *Syiemships* concluded with a genealogy of the *Syiems.*[12]

Homiwell Lyngdoh did not examine the effects of British paramountcy over the Khasi *himas* and their connection, if any, with the Federation of Indian States which had emerged in the early part of the 1920s and was strengthened just before the transfer of power from Britain to India. While providing a history of the Khasi *Syiemships* the author does not make much reference to the other Khasi *Himas* under *Lyngdohs*, *Sirdars* and *Wahadadars*. What is appreciated, however, is that this was the first and elaborate political history of the Khasi and Jaintia states. Its contribution to literature may be assessed from the numerous references other writers have made to this significant publication. A recent review of this book says:[13]

> Though this book continues to serve as a basic text in the study of Khasi-Jaintia political history, its tendency in the retention of the divided nomenclature like Khasi and Synteng did not simply show lack of local exposure especially with the Pnars but displayed far significant colonial influence.

Other histories

Homiwell Lyngdoh's works significantly impacted the Khasi minds. Though Rev. J.J.M. Nichols-Roy, a church elder and politician and perhaps the most prominent Khasi of his times, did not write history, many of his writings with their political bend made use of history. We may here cite just one of his pamphlets: *Ka Ri Khasi Bad Jaintia: Shabar Bad Hapoh Ka Reform*. The lecture was distributed in October 1936 to educate the Khasis of their position in the reformed constitution of 1935. He continued to write till the 1950s both in Khasi and English on a variety of subjects.[14]

With independence came the freedom to interpret the history of Khasi-Jaintia. In this new approach L.L.D. Basan very early published a bilingual pamphlet *The Khasi States under the Indian Union* (1948), which questioned the position of the Khasis under the Indian Union and the process by which the Khasi states and British villages had come into an Assam administration. Many years were to pass before L.G. Shullai took up where L.L.D. Basan left. Shullai campaigned for a relook into the status of the Khasi *Syiems*, the integration of the Khasi-Jaintia Hills into the Indian Union and kindred other topics. His *Ki Hima Khasi* (1975) draws much from the references noted above and from the author's perseverance in collecting every scrap of information on the subject of the Khasi *Syiems*. The importance of this small book is that it updates the issue to the present times and has become a ready reference on the Khasi *Syiems*. A variation of this appeared not long after in *Ka Ri Shnong Pdeng Pyrthei* (1989), the introduction of which is addressed to the youth as an inspiration for them to see their society as distinct despite their small numbers. Other writings of L.G. Shullai that have a historical approach are *Ki Symboh History Bad Ka Ri Hynniewtrep* (1989), a collection of essays on aspects of British rule in India; the Assam Legislature 1912-1950, the Constituent Assembly of India, and the administration of the Khasi-Jaintia Hills after 1950 and till 1974.

Rather disappointing as a work of history is I. Nongbri's *Ka History Ka Ri Hynniewtrep* (1992). A close look at the cover clears that the history he writes does not go back to the early past but starts in 1952. His is a repetition of what Shullai and Basan had earlier published; more particularly in the appendices that form a large part of the paperback. To his credit are the appendices of interesting letters of Wickliffe, *Syiem* of Nongstoin, who challenged the Government of India's integration of *hima* Nongstoin into the Indian Union in 1947.

Before we again bring the history down to our times it would be convenient to go back to the early part of the century and again build up the literature on other aspects of history. With the spread of Christianity in the hills and the establishment of the Seng Khasi (1899) a literature which may be termed revivalist emerged. In this category are the writings of Jeebon Roy in his *Ka Niam Jong Ki Khasi* (1897) and *Ka Kitab Ba Batai Pynshynna Shaphang U Wei U Blei* (1900); Radhon Singh Berry published *Ka Jingsneng Tymmen Shaphang Ka Akor Khasi* (1902) and Rabon Singh Kharsuka's *Ka Kitab Jingphawar* (1905). These stalwarts of Khasi religion and culture are especially noted for they gave the Khasi society a strong influence to remain in the traditional faith.

Just how concerned Homiwell Lyngdonh and his contemporaries were about the past is illustrated in the studies by two Salesian priests. J. Bachhiarello could identify himself with the people sufficiently to author *Ki Dienjat Ki Longshuwa* (1930). Another of his confreres G. Costa endeared himself to the Khasis with his *Ka Riti Jong Ki Laiphew Syiem* (1936). These writings in Khasi have become invaluable texts for scholars wishing to pursue a search into the Khasi past. While at this stage of Khasi religion, it would not be inappropriate to note the histories of Christianity. *Centenary History Ka Balang Presbyterian* was published in 1941. Though many small tracts had been brought out by that time it was only in 1966 that Rev. G. Angell Jones translated and updated J.H. Morris' *History of the Welsh Calvinistic Methodists Foreign Mission* (1910). The Catholic mission history was put in simple language and style by Fr. O. Paviotti in *Ka Matti Jong U* (1989). Fr. H. Elias', *Ka Histori Jong Ka Balang Catholic* (1965) and Francis Diengdoh's *Ka History Jong Ka Balang* (1980) give a general picture of the Catholic Church's history.

It is not intended to exclude the history of Khasi poetry, prose and drama from this account for these genre of literature were as important in the transformation of the Khasis as were other factors such as education, British administration and urbanization. As much has already been done on this by the members of the Khasi Author's Society it may suffice to note that the Khasi literature has grown sufficiently to be reflective of a society's wish that their language and literature receive the recognition of the Sahitya Academy.

Today a trend is clearly emerging in Khasi history of biographical sketches and monographs. Tirot Sing and Kiang Nangbah, two resistance leaders have received a fair amount of adulation and if the present position is any indication, the lives of these patriots will continue to inspire writers.[15] Thomas Jones is beginning to find a more befitting place in Khasi history.[16] J.J.M. Nichols Roy has found his biographer in O.L. Snaitang.[17] John Roberts, a medical missionary, is given a sketch by L.G. Shullai.[18] Other Khasis such as Jeebon Roy, Mavis Dunn Lyngdoh already have accounts of them in English and it may be not before long that Khasi readers are made familiar with their lives.

In the absence of comprehensive histories one has to be on the watch for small pamphlets, booklets and paperbacks such as V.B. Ryngnga's *Na Them Riwar* (1992), a collection of 20 short notices in the *War* area. Short histories of the Khasi *himas* are not many. One such is E.W. Chyne's, *Ka History Jong Ka Hima Mawlong* (1977) which is useful little booklet. Another small publication is Jor Manick Syiem's *Ka Jingiathuh Khana Shaphang Ki Syiem Jong Ka Hima Mylliem 1830-1960* (1984). Spiton Kharakor's, *Ki Khun Ki Ksiew U Hynniew Trep* (1981) makes very interesting reading, particularly the chapters 'Ki Kur U Hynniew Trep' and 'Ki Jait U Hynniew Trep' which enumerates 3363 Khasi clans. Other essays are on a variety of subjects relating to culture, Kiang Nangbah, Tirot Sing and the Khasi National Dorbar.

As a historian

One reason why history in Khasi has not acquired interest as much as literature has, is due to the absence of history in the vernacular in the school syllabus. An earlier generation of Khasi school goers had to go through texts in Khasi.[19] This made them familiar with the history of India and the world. For young students not familiar with English, this medium would have enabled them to better understand their histories. Today in the change of school syllabus, history has taken a back seat. Whatever incentive was there to write history school texts is gone and so has the base for an appreciation of the past. Homiwell Lyngdoh's *Ki Syiem Khasi Bad Synteng*, though not taught in schools, is read by most of the educated Khasis who take interest to know about their own past, traditions and heritage.

Another point to note is that the histories in the Khasi vernacular may have been written with the intention of portraying the past but many of the authors are not trained in the art of collecting, interpreting and presenting their findings. This has made the better written history rare. Homiwell Lyngdoh's *Ki Syiem Khasi Bad Synteng* was the exception. The book remains a classic for its language, spread of history and the details provided on the Khasi *himas.* Khasi historians, if we may make a categorization, have preferred the English medium for a number of reasons of which the principal would be that English would have a larger number of readers. Before long it is hoped, the Khasis who are becoming increasingly conscious of their roots and culture will find histories relevant to this time and age. To them, among many writers, the contribution of Homiwell Lyngdoh to Khasi history would remain outstanding.

Notes & References

1. For details on the life of Dr Homiwell Lyngdon, see Maurice G Lynngdoh, *Life and Works of Dr. Homiwell Lyngdoh*, reprinted Shillong, 2009. A brief biographical sketch is also provided in O. L. Snaitang, *A Dictionary of Khasi Literature*, Shillong, 2011, pp.107-111.
2. *Ibid*, pp.43-47.49.
3. H. Bareh, *The History and Culture of the Khasi People*, first published Shillong 1967, revised and enlarged edition, Shillong, 1985, p. 400.
4. Anon, "The Role of the Presbyterian Church in the Development of Khasi Language and Literature 1841-1902', *Khasi Author's Society Souvenir 1842-1992*, pp.12-13.
5. Cited by I .M. Simon, " Tribute to the Rev. Thomas Jones", *Ibid.*, pp. 25-26.
6. D. R Syiemlieh, "Education, Elite and Politicisation in the Khasi Jaintia Hills", in Ashish Bose (ed.), *Tribal Demography and Development in North East India*, New Delhi, 1990, p. 178.
7. D. R. Syiemlieh, *British Administration in Meghalaya*, Heritage Publishers, New Delhi, 1989, pp. 103-106.
8. *Assam Administration Report 1902-1903*, p. 44.
9. Cited by L. S. Gassah "Don Katno Tylli Ki Elaka ha Ri Jaintia", *Hynniew Trep Endeavour Society*, September 1989, p. 33, and Suniti Kumar Chatterji, *Kirata Jana Krti*, The Asiatic Society, Calcutta, 1954, p. 172.
10. See a related article on the Sohra Syiemship in D. R. Syiemlieh, "Colonialism and Syiemship Succession : a Study of Cherra State (1901-1902)," *Proceedings of the North East India History Association* ,Third session, Imphal. pp. 147-157.
11. "Jinglamphrang," pp. i-xvii and "Ka Juk Thymmai," pp. i-vii.
12. Homiwell Lyngdoh must have drawn heavily from D. Herbert's *Report on Succession to Siemships in the Khasi Hills* (1902) which oddly is not listed in the references of book used to write this history.
13. O. L. Snaitang, *op. cit.*, p. 110.
14. For a collection of the writings of J. J. M. Nichols-Roy, read O. L. Snaitang, *Memoirs of the Life and Political Writings of the Hon'ble J. J. M. Nichols- Roy,* Shillong. 1998.
15. Hamlet Bareh, "Ka Thma Synteng Bad U Kiang Nongbah," (1961); Hamlet Bareh, *U Syiem Tirot Singh bad Kiwei Pad Ki Para Syiem Ki Hima Khasi* (1977); Hamlet Bareh,

Shishpah Sanphew Snem Mynshwa: U Tirot Singh bad Ka Mynnor ba Iphuh Ipheng (1984); Quotient Sumer, *U Kiang Nongbah* (1978) are only several of the many articles that have been published in Khasi in souvenirs/tracts remembering these two Khasi and Jaintia leaders who struggled against the British. The literature in English on this subject is large and better researched.

16. Refer to the many articles in the *Khasi Author's Society Souvenir 1842-1992*, and S.S. Majaw, *U Kpa Ka Thoh Ka Tar Khasi*, Shillong ,1992.Very recently was published S. S. Majaw, *U Thomas Jones Bad Ka Pyrthei Saitpohpen*, Khasi Book Stall, Shillong, 2011.
17. O. L. Snaitang, *Ka Biography U J.J. M. Nichols -Roy*, Shillong, 1993.
18. L G. Shullai, *U Dr. John Roberts DD,* Shillong, 1975.
19. Prescribed for schools at one time were Frank Pugh, *Ka Histori Jong Ka Khasi Jaintia Bad Assam*, Shillong (n.d.) and Tngensi Rynjah, *Ka History Ka Ri Khasi Jaintia*, Shillong, 1991.

8

Suryya Kumar Bhuyan (1894-1964)

—*Shiela Bora*

Biographical Sketch

Suryya Kumar Bhuyan, whose contribution towards the promotion of historical research in Assam had raised him to the position of a legendary figure in India during his lifetime, reigned supreme in the field of historical research in Northeast India during the entire period of his professional career and profoundly influenced history-writing in the region. His interest in history had developed during the period of political turmoil in Assam when the economy of the state had been shattered by the Burmese invasions and British colonial exploitations wiping out the memories of past glories. At a time when the desire for intellectual pursuit among the people of Assam had reached a low ebb, Bhuyan, through his historical and literary writings, attempted to exploit the adverse socio-political and economic situation of the state into Assam's strength for nation-building. In his attempt to reconstruct what he believed to be the glorious pre-colonial past of Assam, he professionalized the discipline of historical research in Assam. It is probably Bhuyan's childhood experiences at the threshold of the colonial and pre-colonial regimes that inspired him in developing a different form and style of telling history.

The ancestry of Suryya Kumar can be traced to the Zamindars of the Purnia district in Bihar. His great-great grandfather, Kaunar Singh, happened to be one of the fourteen leading zamindars whose annual revenue ranged between two to nine lakhs, even during the period of turmoil and disorder in the country in eighteenth century. Kaunar Singh had entered into an armed confederacy against the tyrannical Moghul Fauzadar of Keori or Katori (in Bhagalpur) in order to curb his growing exactions but was forced to surrender in the conflict that followed, consequently losing the Zamindari that was in possession of the family for more than two hundred years. The family being reduced in circumstances, Mangal Singh Chettri, the only surviving offspring of Kaunar Singh, was compelled to seek employment in the East India Company's army in Bihar. He accompanied Captain Thomas Welsh during his expedition to Assam in 1792-94 and was one of the soldiers who were left behind at the instance of the Raja of Assam to train up the Assam forces on the Company's lines. Posted as a Subedar of the British East India Company, his training camp was situated in Kandhulimari Chapari on the bank of the river Dikhow. It was here that Mangal Singh was married to Saniani Ai, a girl from the Sani Bhuyan family of Sibsagar, thus becoming a son-in-law of Assam. To them was born a son, named Sibcharan, and a daughter, named Duroli. Following the death of Mangal Singh, his widow and her two children continued to live under the protection of the members of Sani Bhuyan family with whom they fled from Sibsagar during the Burmese disturbances of 1817-25. The family then settled at Kaliabar in Nowgong.[1] Sibcharan, who served in the Police Department for thirty-four years and had played an active role in the establishment of the district headquarters at Khagarijan, the present site of Nowgong town, finally settled at Fauzdari Patti. Sibcharan was married to two sisters and to his second wife was born Robilal, the father of Suryya Kumar Bhuyan.[2]

Suryya Kumar was born on 27 January 1894. He lost his mother to an attack of *kala-azar* at the age of three. Bhuyan's wife, Bhubaneswari, hailed from Roha. He had his early education in Nowgong Middle Vernacular School (1900-1901), Nowgong Government High School (1901-1904), and Shillong Government High School (1904-1909), and thereafter, in Cotton College, Guwahati, (1909-1911), and Presidency College, Calcutta, (1911-1915). He completed his Master degree in English literature from Calcutta University in 1916 and law examination from the Calcutta University Law College the same year. Bhuyan joined as a Professor of English in Cotton College in March 1918. He was at first tempted to specialise in some branch of English studies and write books relating to literature. However, his association with the *Kamarupa Anusandhan Samiti* as its Honorary Secretary, in 1921-22 and again in 1926-29, was an expression of his in-born interest and natural talent in history writing. The association with the Department of Historical Antiquarian Studies (DHAS) of the Government of Assam in honorary capacity, as Assistant Director (since 1928) and Director (since 1933), in addition to his regular job in Cotton College, was an opportunity for him to lay the foundation of historical research in Assam. The year 1936 was indeed a hallmark of the historian's career when he proceeded to England on two years' study leave from the Cotton College (1936-38) to work for his Ph. D degree in history at the School of Oriental and African Studies under the supervision of Professor H.H. Dodwell, one of the greatest authorities at the time on the British period of Indian History. Meanwhile, he had also been elected as a Fellow to the Royal Asiatic Society of Great Britain and Ireland (1936). During the two years that Bhuyan spent in London working in some of the best libraries of the world like the British Library and the India Office Library, he was attracted to newer aspects of Assamese history that diverted his attention, for a period, away from the *buranji* sources of which he had already acquired a rich knowledge. He returned to India in July 1938 with the degree of the Doctor of Philosophy from London University. His thesis later on published under the title of *Anglo-Assamese Relations* (1949) offered a giant leap in the progress of historical research in Assam. On his return from England, Bhuyan rejoined Cotton College as a Professor of English and continued to serve in this position till his appointment as Principal of the College in 1946. On January

6, 1947, he was appointed as the whole time Director of Historical and Antiquarian Studies in Assam. He was the Director of Public Instructions (DPI), Assam, in 1948-49. Even after his retirement from the Government service in 1949, he was twice re-employed as whole time Director of the DHAS (between April 1 to March 10, 1952 and May 1, 1954 to February 21, 1957). He had a stint as a Member of the Parliament during 1952-54. Finally, he served as the Vice-Chancellor of Gauhati University from 1957 to 1960. Bhuyan passed away on 5 July 1964 at Guwahati leaving behind glories of the magnificent career of an academic administrator and a historian.[3]

Beginning and progress of historical research in Assam

In early 20th century, when Bhuyan's interest in Assam's pre-colonial past had taken a definite shape, historical writings on Assam had gained considerable significance and scholarship. He himself corroborated the existence of an abundance of historical literature in his work entitled *Buranjimulak Prabandhar Talika* (1955), wherein he enlisted the historical articles published in Assamese magazines since the days of *Orunodoi* (1846). The *buranji* literature, written in Tai and Assamese languages, which had emerged from the thirteenth century onwards, was the first to initiate historical consciousness amongst the people of Assam. Compiled primarily at the behest of the royal house, the *buranji* manuscripts were mainly written on oblong strips of the bark of *Sanchi* tree. The *buranjis*, or state chronicles, maintained by the Ahom monarchs, contained records not only of every event that happened within the kingdom but even outside it. The content of the *buranjis* depended much on the direction given by the royalty and were finalised only after consulting official communications and letters of ambassadors or spy reports. Since *buranjis* provided the Ahom state with a basis for deciding their diplomacy, the Ahom bureaucracy had complete control over production and circulation of these *buranjis*. In fact, "The famous *Buranji* literature of the Ahom period falls into the medieval tradition of Annals and chronicles which were external records of the historical consciousness of the time."[4] Considered valuable for the study of early and later medieval history of Northeast India, the *buranjis* have been compared to the *bakhars* and the *khayats* in Maharastra and Rajasthan.[5] They also bore a marked similarity with the Southeast Asian tradition of historical chronicles.[6] George Grierson had remarked that,

> The chain of historical events, for the last six hundred years, has been carefully preserved, and their authenticity can be relied upon. These historical works, or buranjis as they are styled in Assam, are numerous and voluminous. According to the custom of the country, knowledge was an indispensable qualification to an Assamese gentleman; every family of distinction, as well as the Government and the public officers, kept the minute records of contemporary events.[7]

The British annexation of Assam in 1826 brought to an end the isolation of the region and coincided with the beginning of modern era in the Northeast. The gradual but purposeful introduction of new elements in the political, economic, social and cultural composition of the region brought about transformation of the society in a way that would serve the British vested interests.[8] Following the gradual extension of British rule in Northeast

India and their contact with the hill-tribes, an era of historical writing by the British civil and military officials was inaugurated. Those English officers were not professional historians, but their knowledge of the region and its people proved invaluable for compilation of numerous historical literatures. The beginning was made by J.P. Wade who originally came to Assam as a doctor along with Captain Welsh's army in 1792 and compiled his translated version of Assamese *buranji* captioned *An Account of Assam* together with a geographical account entitled A *Geographical Sketch of Assam.* With the establishment of a department of ethnography intended to delve into the archaeological and historical resources that were lying unattended in the province, investigation into the past was given firm institutional shape. Thereafter followed a host of valuable works like Francis Hamilton's *An Account of Assam* (1820), R.B. Pemberton's *Report on the Eastern Frontier of British India* (1835), John M' Cosh's *Topography of Assam* (1837), William Robinson's A *Descriptive Account of Assam* (1840), John Butler's A *Sketch of Assam* (1847) and *Travels and Adventures in the Province of Assam* (1854), E.T. Dalton's *Descriptive Ethnology of Bengal* (1872) and William Hunter's *Statistical Account Assam,* vols. i-ii, (1879). By far one of the most authentic and comprehensive works of merit of the period was A.J.M. Mills' *Report on the Province of Assam* (1854). It is with gratitude that the scholars of the region remember the contributions made by these European officers towards advancement of historical studies. The publication of scores of books and accounts on the frontier tribes is also a redeeming feature of nineteenth century historiography. One of the greatest scholars of this school was J.H. Hutton who wrote monographs on various Naga tribes. The American Baptist Mission Society too showed keen interest in the study of history and culture of the people amongst whom they lived and worked and published several ethnographical works relating to various tribes living in the region.

Though the writings of the British administrators-cum-historian-anthropologists and the missionaries gave a solid beginning to the writing of history of the Northeast, it must be borne in mind that many of them who served and wrote on the north-eastern hills in the early modern period belonged to the 19th and early 20th century school of anthropology and were basically administrators, military officers or missionaries. The heroic resistance of the small tribal groups like the Khasis, Nagas or Lushais against the might of the modern military power of the British found no appreciation in the original official imperialist documents prepared by Mackenzie,[9] Pemberton,[10] Butler, Mills,[11] Woodthrope,[12] Needham[13] or Robert Reid.[14] "Instead the emphasis was on how the tribes created problems for the British by committing raids, plunders and kidnapping in the British territory."[15] Thus the growing interest of colonial scholars in the history of the region resulted in laying the foundation of understanding Assam's past through models of Western historical tradition.

In the century that followed the publication of John Peter Wade's works, the study of history in the region underwent spectacular changes towards a more systematic understanding of the past. With the publication of Edward Gait's *A History of Assam* in 1906, considered a standard book on Assam even today, historical research in Northeast India entered a new age. Edward Gait who had evinced keen interest in the study of the history of the region by first compiling The *Assam Land Revenue Manual* (1896) and then preparing a monumental report entitled *Report on the Progress of Historical Research in Assam* (1897), may be credited for having set the trend of writing comprehensive histories of the region, on modern historiographical lines. Truly speaking, Gait's was the first full-length and scientific history of the province. "The book, though not based on original materials, was free from the colonial bias for which it is freely used by the scholars as an authentic source material."[16]

In an attempt to reconstruct Assam's past a number of Assamese chroniclers also did not lag behind. Spearheaded by Haliram Dhekial Phukan who wrote a history of Assam in Bengali in 1829, this group of scholars made considerable contribution to the progress of historical study in 19th century Assam. Since knowledge of the region's history elevated an educated man's status in society, a section of the Assamese intelligentsia often strove to achieve this status by writing a history of his country or his region. In doing so he chose from amongst two dominant trends of writing history which had developed parallel to each other in the early part of the 19th century. The first group, directly encouraged by the British administrators, continued to write in the pre-colonial literary tradition or the *buranji* tradition, a notable example of this tradition being Maniram Dewan's *Buranji-Bibekaratna*. Meanwhile, there emerged a class of followers of a 'modern' tradition of Assamese historical engagement based on the Western notion of the positivist-rationalist historical tradition. This group of Assamese scholars, though nurtured in a powerful pre-colonial tradition of historical engagement, had also been exposed to Western modernity and its various forms of engagement with the past as a distinct scholarly pursuit and began to manifest itself in the writings of Haliram Dhekial Phukan's *Assam Buranji* (1829) written in four parts in the Bengali language mainly intended for Bengali pilgrims and traders. While several writers emulated this style, Dhekial Phukan's style was perfected and matured towards the end of the 19th century by the scholar-administrator, Gunabhiram Barua who actually wrote the first comprehensive history of Assam entitled *Assam Buranji* (1884). In his *Assam Buranji*, Gunabhiram made a critical departure from pre-colonial Ahom historical investigation on several accounts.

> His intervention in the field of historical study can be briefly identified by the fact that his history was a secular project, it had a pan-Indian perspective; and he intelligently employed tools like the caste division and a larger pan-Indian narrative to give a perspective on the region's past. More important was his style of description, which not only secularised the process of telling and its engagement with the readers, but also created a sharp break with the pre-colonial style of narration. More importantly, however, Gunabhiram tried to arrive at his truth where logic played the central role.[17]

Contributions to history

Suryya Kumar Bhuyan, who entered the field of writing and researching history by the early decades of the 20th century, admitted that Carlyle's insistence on finding the 'inner reality of things' as embodied in his *Heroes and Hero-worship* and *Sartar Resartus*, had a strong appeal for him.[18] He also mentioned that the effort of M. I. Bora in translating the Persian version of the *Baharistan-i-Ghayabi* into English was instrumental in helping him to get over his temptation of pursuing English literature and direct his attention to the past history of Assam. In his preface to Bora's English translation of *Baharistan-i-Ghaybi*, Bhuyan wrote,

> It is a matter of special gratification that the present translator, an Assamese by birth, has employed his Persian scholarship in translating this valuable source-book of his country's history; for, there will be men all over the world to expound the mysticism of the Sufi poets, or delineate the scholarly zeal of the Abbasids, but who will exert in the past history of Assam except her own children ?[19]

Convinced of the need to study Assam's past, Bhuyan's mind was further swayed in this direction by Gait's contribution to the study of Assam history. Impressed by this work, Bhuyan decided to devote his life in the pursuit of Assam's historical legacy. Explaining the diversion from his literary career as a poet, Bhuyan admitted that,

> ....The supreme importance of Assam's legacy first dawned on me about the year 1906 when I was a student of the Shillong Government High School. Sir Edward Gait's *History of Assam* was just published. As he had to cover the whole story from the earliest times to the present within the compass of a single volume the narrative necessarily depicted only the dry-bones of Assam History. Many an episode, forming an inseparable part of the traditional lore of the Assamese people and brimming with human touches, did not find any place in that otherwise monumental work.[20]

Bhuyan's decision to take to history writing came at a time when India's economic and intellectual dependence on the British colonial regime had brought erstwhile Assam face to face not just with political, economic and cultural marginalisation, but also with historiographical marginalisation. Thus "historical research in the region which had fallen a victim to this trend, particularly in its interpretative and analytical aspects, required a great deal of development."[21] In his attempt to professionalize the discipline of history writing Bhuyan had to face several odds. It was to his credit that though he "... stood at the threshold of the colonial and pre-colonial historical practices, [he] succeeded in shaping a different form and style of telling history. His predecessors failed to solve the conflict between pre-colonial practices and the colonial parameters of engagement with the past. He successfully professionalized the discipline."[22] In his effort to give a new direction to the history of the region, his attention was first drawn to the necessity of building a repository of sources for Assam history. The idea of archive based research was not new in the twentieth century and mention may be made of the efforts of the Indian Historical Records Commission in this direction. The foundation of the *Kamarupa Anusandhan Samiti*, or Assam Research Society, as an institution for historical research, in 1912, by a handful of enlightened scholars to assemble evidences and source materials of history was an important step towards the progress of historical research in the region. J. H. Hutton, in his Presidential address on the occasion of the inauguration of the Society, had stressed on the virtue of asceticism and said : "I put before you the idea of scientific research as a form of intellectual asceticism...and I maintain that the ascetic ideal is not necessary to intellectual achievement."[23] While serving the *Kamarupa Anusandhan Samiti* as its Honorary Secretary in 1921-22 and again in 1926-29, Bhuyan directed his attention not only in systemising the management of the Society but also in collecting a number of relics and manuscripts for its library. In his Report for 1925-26 he wrote,

> I see before my eyes students of the future University of Assam aspiring after academic laurels poring over books and manuscripts in the library of the Kamarupa Anusandhan Samiti, the epigraphist deciphering the illegible characters of the inscriptions, and the numismatist trying to read undiscovered annals in the coins preserved in the museum.[24]

By this time, a man of 27 years of age, Bhuyan had already published six books and several articles in Assamese, indicating his sustained interest in history. Some of Bhuyan's earlier historical studies are *Ahomar Din* (1918), providing an account of the Ahom system of administration, and *Early British Relations with Assam* (1928). However, by 1926 Bhuyan was beginning to express his discomfort with the set-up of the *Kamarupa Anusandhan Samiti* and began to advocate the cause of setting up an *Asiatic Society* for Assam so that the vast historical resources lying unused could be harnessed. Emphasising on the need for 'scientific reconstruction' and 'critical history writing', he reiterated his idea of building up an institution in Assam for providing facilities to students and scholars to study the life, manners and customs of the people of the region even later in life. His effort in this direction continued as late as in 1952 when while delivering the inaugural address at the general session of the Manipuri Sahitya Parishad at Imphal in October that year, he suggested that, "The institution may be called Purba-Bharati as its primary object will be diffusion of knowledge about Eastern Assam."[25]

The institution that provided Bhuyan's main channel of activities in the field of history writing was the Department of Historical and Antiquarian Studies (DHAS), established by the Government of Assam in June 1928. Set up to assume most of the responsibilities of the Department of Ethnography, Bhuyan had no hesitation in joining this institution as its Assistant Director (Honorary). It was from here that Bhuyan spearheaded the new movement for professional and scientific history. In his effort to produce a type of history which differed from the "romancings, inventions and exaggerations of uncritical history writers", he admitted that he continued with the work of original research with his comrades in spite of the fact that the public in Assam were not trained to appreciate the laborious and scientific reconstructions of academic work.[26] Life and soul of the DHAS, Bhuyan spared no efforts to ensure permanency for this department for the benefit of future scholars. Following the retirement of W. Bentinck, the Honorary Director of this institution in 1933, the Government of Assam appointed Bhuyan as its Provincial Director providing him the scope to promote the Department's objectives. Whatever scanty leisure was available to Bhuyan, then serving as a college teacher, he utilised for the benefit of the Department. As early as in 1932, J. R. Cunningham, the then Director of Public Instructions in Assam, had observed : "The fact is that had it not been for one S.K. Bhuyan the Department would never have come into being, and were it not for the abilities and devotion of the same S. K. Bhuyan it would have had but little to record in the way of accomplishment."[27] The first bulletin, published in 1932, contained both its objective and its activities and was circulated amongst scholars in India and Europe. The establishment of the DHAS was hailed by personalities like Sir Laurie Hammond, Sir Edward Gait, Col. P.R.T. Gordon and Sir Jadunath Sarkar.

As favourable reviews of the first bulletin were published in a number of periodicals and journals, Bhuyan was encouraged to collect all manuscripts, transcripts and rare books that he could lay his hands on. It was from here that he made available to researchers many *buranjis* by compiling, editing and translating them. Bhuyan's effort to make the DHAS a huge repository of sources for future historians was a painstaking job and even involved foreign travel. The sources made available from the India Office Library came as a major relief for Assamese scholars and local historians. As the activities of the DHAS became known, links were established with other national and world bodies of historical research providing ample scope for intellectual exchanges between Assam and the world outside.[28] The laborious work undertaken by Bhuyan won him recognition not only from his peers but also from various national and international bodies. As opined by Banikanta Kakati, S.K. Bhuyan henceforth became a valued name in the noted centres of historical studies in India.[29]

S.K. Bhuyan did not hesitate to defy both the Assamese tradition and the modern Western tradition of studying the past. His works range over a period of over four decades and fall mainly into three categories: historical, biographical, original and miscellaneous. A close look at the bibliography[30] of Bhuyan's works in English and Assamese would reveal that his initial publications are mostly biographical with only occasional attempts to write what appeared to him to be interesting periods of history. His extraordinary contribution to the development of historical studies in Assam stems from several advantages over his contemporaries. Trained both in literature and historical studies he was well aware of the necessity of addressing the needs not only of his peers and scholars but also of the Assamese public at large. Hence literature played an important part in his attempt to delve into Assam's past legacy. His literary pursuits were in the form of poems, short biographical sketches and short stories and his first book *Gopal Krishna Gokhale* was published in 1916. This was followed by the publication of a series of biographical sketches known as *Ratnamala Granthavali*. However, his chief literary preoccupation was the collection of materials for a full-length biography of Anundoram Borooah for which he ransacked old book-shops in Calcutta. He believed that 'Great men without biographers are soon forgotten', and true to his conviction he may be credited with the distinction of writing Anundoram Borooah's biography. In a conversation with Bijoy Bhuyan, son of S. K. Bhuyan, Guruprashad Barua had observed that,

> On Saturdays, Sundays and holidays we would invariably be in the playgrounds playing games, but your father [S.K. Bhuyan] would cross the mighty Brahmaputra, monsoon or no monsoon, either by steamer ferry or by country boat, and visit North Gauhati regularly to collect materials for Anundoram Barooah's biography. If it was not for your father that great scholar and the first Assamese ICS officer, who died at a young age, would not have been remembered today.[31]

Bhuyan was proficient in several languages like Assamese, Bengali, English, Khasi and Sanskrit and wrote in all the languages. While he spared no efforts to make available to the scholars of Assam a modern archival repository of sources, he simultaneously published professional and popular history, both in English and in Assamese. An examination of his bibliography will indicate how he made combined use of the medium of Assamese and English for his literary and historical works. Comparing himself to an emaciated mother suckling her twin babies he explained the use of two mediums in the following words,

> This practice has sprung from my conviction that my own countrymen must be enlightened about their heritage and culture, and also that outsiders should be acquainted with the redeeming features of our history and civilisation. While writing in Assamese, my mother-tongue, I therefore feel that the contents should be placed before the people who do not know the language; and similar thoughts arise in me when I write in English, specially because the contents relate primarily to Assamese history and literature.[32]

Bhuyan could reach out to a large section of the Assamese society due to his skill in composing and writing in simple and easily comprehensible language, both in Assamese and in English. True to his sentiments he has not only edited and published several Assamese chronicles in their original Assamese form, but has also provided their translated version in English as far as possible, or at least an introduction in English to the Assamese works for convenience of his English readers. Besides writing in Assamese and English, Bhuyan had even won a prize as a student of Presidency College for writing a sonnet in Bengali in the Eden Hindu Hostel Sonnet Competition. The incident was cherished by Bhuyan throughout his life as it brought him into direct contact with Sir Gurudas Banerji, the then Vice-Chancellor of Calcutta University. Overwhelmed by Bhuyan's rendering of the sonnet, Gurudas Banerji honoured the budding poet by bestowing on Bhuyan the garland that was hanging round his neck.[33]. Bhuyan also contributed to different Bengali journals and periodicals on the history and culture of Assam. On the other hand, while a student of the Shillong Government High School, he had acquired a reasonably sound knowledge of the Khasi language. With the help of materials obtained from old Assamese chronicles, he wrote a series of articles on Assam-Khasi relations which were published in the Khasi journal *U'Lurshai* in 1926. During his student days at Calcutta, Bhuyan made valuable contacts among whom were Bengali, Bihari and Oriya friends.[34] Here he also had the opportunity to meet and hear some of the architects of modern India like Ambika Charan Mazumdar, Bipin Chandra Pal, N. G. Chandravarkar, Annie Besant, Ashutosh Mukherjee, Gopal Krishna Gokhale, Gurudas Banerjee, Madanmohan Malaviya, Muhammad Ali, Rabindranath Tagore, Rash Behari Ghose, Surendra Nath Banerjee, Sankaran Nair, and Mahatma Gandhi. Amongst his Professors at Gauhati and Calcutta whose achievements in the field of poetry, literature or history created a deep impression upon his youthful mind were Padmanath Bhattacharyya Vidyavinode, Vanamali Chakravarti Vedantatirtha, Manmohan Ghose, H. R. James, J. W. Holme, Prafulla Chandra Ghose, S. Khuda Buksh, Henry Stephen, and Asutosh Sastri.[35]

While serving the *Kamarupa Anusandhan Samiti*,. Bhuyan came in personal contact with eminent personalities like Kasinath Dikshit of the Archaeological Survey of India,

Professor D. R. Bhandarkar of Calcutta University, Professor Gieuseppe Tucci of the University of Rome, Sir Devaprasad Sarvadhikari, Sir Hari Sing Gaur and Rakhaldas Banerji. Having accompanied them in their visits to the temples and ruins in the vicinity of Gauhati, he was provided with the opportunity of talking and emulating from the experiences of these renowned personalities. The period of study at the London School of Oriental and African Studies (1936-38) was another rewarding period for him since this provided him the opportunity to get acquainted with a galaxy of intellectuals and scholars of the world with whom he could share his experience. C.H. Phillips was his close associate at the School of Oriental and African Studies with whom he continued to maintain regular correspondence even in later years regarding the study of history. In doing so he interacted widely with other national and world bodies engaged in historical studies. Bhuyan sent his innumerable works on the history of Assam to the stalwarts of Indian History like Sir Jadunath Sarkar, Nihar Ranjan Ray, Neelkanta Sastri, Pratul Chandra Gupta, Surendranath Sen and others who appreciated his achievements. His well known work entitled *Studies in the Literature of Assam* was even sent to Dr. Rajendra Prasad, Pandit Jawaharlal Nehru, Abul Kalam Azad and Dr. S. Raddhakrishnan with a view to bringing Assam into prominence in the national forums. In 1937, Bhuyan was invited to Rome by Giuseppe Tucci to deliver a lecture at the Oriental Institute. His lecture on the Assamese political history, social life, literature, music, paintings, sculpture and architecture was published in the Italian daily, *Popolo D'Italia*.

Bhuyan struggled throughout his life to unfold the hidden history of Assam from the pages of ruined manuscripts, documents and other antique sources. His love for the nation and his fellow-countrymen transcended his life to a mission of historical investigation. Convinced about the fact that Indian historical studies and Indian historiography was dominated by the study of the Gangetic valley, he struggled to bring into prominence the history of Assam in the context of the broader issues of Indian history, always keeping in mind the well-being of both the national and the regional interests. To quote his own words, his mission formulated as early as his school days in Shillong was to "acquaint the world with the good and beautiful things of Assam, and to make [his] countrymen conscious of their strength."[36] Thus, very early in life he had realized that Assam was never outside the momentous developments in India, but it was only due to lack of dissemination of Assam history that very little was known about the historical events in the province. He believed that the lost glory of Assam and the Assamese nationality vis-à-vis the British rule could only be retrieved by a renewed emphasis on the unique features and the secular character of the Ahom monarchy. Lamenting the ignorance amongst his countrymen and the world at large about Assam's past, he believed that a knowledge of Assam's history and literature, if properly disseminated, would not only be a source of inspiration for the people of the state and the rest of the country, but would also exercise a vitalising influence upon the cultural and political progress of India. His views on Assam were aptly summed up at the end of a paper read at the All-India Oriental Conference held at Lahore in 1928:

> Assam suffers by being curiously reticent about her past achievements. She is not vocal, and there is not that atmosphere here which leads to cultural intercourse with other

> countries. The antiquity of Assamese prose literature was unheard of even in Bengal till 1919, when Sir P.C. Roy, after returning from a tour in Assam, introduced the fact to his countrymen. Who ever heard of the martyred princess Jaimati before it was broadcast throughout the length and breadth of India from the pavilion at Pandavnagar in December 1926? Kamarupa played an important part in the history of Northern India. The emperor Harshavardhana felt gratified at the friendship of Kumara Bhaskaravarman. According to Yuan-Chwang the colleges of Kamarupa attracted students from all quarters, and the Kumara king was himself a man of learning. A special school of *Smritis* had developed here fostered by the penetrating genius of Kamarupa Brahmans. The *Tantras* are believed to have first originated in Assam as a result of the reconciliation between the demands of the preliterate tribes and the gentle concessions of their Brahmanical neighbours. Assam was one of the few provinces in India which could successfully stem the tide of Moghul invasions. All this is not a mere matter of chance. There was at its foundation a culture which permeated the life of the people and which raised the average man to a superior level endowed with a consciousness of patriotism which would never desert him even under the severest temptations. But the glories of Kamarupa remain buried because no vigorous investigations have been launched to discover the treasures and reveal them to the rest of India which may as well be proud of them.[37]

While making a conscious effort to disseminate the history of Assam, Bhuyan often touched upon the amicable relations that had once existed amongst the different races and communities in Assam, to the fusion of the Aryan and non-Aryan influences and to the consequent evolution of a culture which is highly realistic, dynamic, liberal and versatile.[38] He highlighted the fact that the hills-plains contact maintained from time immemorial, had entered "the texture of Assam's religious developments, into Assam's music and dancing, into Assamese vocabulary and into the liberalisation of the Assamese society."[39] This intimacy, he believed, was advantageous both for the plains people and the hillsmen and brought the two elements so close that even the independence and solidarity of Assam depended on the measure of success that was attained in maintaining a closer understanding and a spirit of mutual dependence between the two. It is surprising however, that notwithstanding the fact that Bhuyan was one of the top-ranking historians of his time, having the honour of chairing even the Modern History Section of the Indian History Congress in 1952, he remains to be ranked in 'the historiographical recapitulations on South Asia.'[40] Though the reason for this glaring omission is difficult to explain, there is no doubt that Bhuyan's reconstruction of Assam's pre-colonial past was Ahom-centric and consequently, his historical works were heavily dependent on the *buranji* literature. In attempting to look at Assam's past greatness, he constantly analysed the place of the Ahom State in the context of the Mughul Empire and its historical connection to the Indian subcontinent. The untiring efforts of Bhuyan had succeeded in legitimizing the use of *buranjis* for the reconstruction of the pre-colonial history of Assam to such an extent that by the beginning of the 20th century *buranjis* almost became an indispensable tool for the historians of the region.

Since the *buranji* manuscripts conserved the language, customs, institutes, official and judicial procedures, social and religious usages, and the intricate details of the state, 'The Ahom State' was the new theatre that emerged in the history written by Bhuyan.

The details of the State machinery which were completely missing in the Sanskrit sources for the history of Kamarupa, came to be looked upon by Bhuyan as of primary importance. According to him, knowledge about the people it governs is of primary concern to the state and he pointed out that,

> Full detailed knowledge of the institutions of a country is indispensable for its good government; for no political measure, however assiduously conceived and constructed will fall in the natural stage of evolution unless it is based on the corresponding indigenous system which is already in existence. The mentality of the people must be realised, their expectations thoroughly studied, and precedents under the old regime must clearly be sifted in order to eliminate the risk of committing catastrophic political blunders.[41]

Bhuyan's strong conviction about the strategic connection between the discipline of history and the art of government was further confirmed between the years 1930 and 1938, during which period at least nine *buranjis* were published by Bhuyan from the DHAS. While the Ahom State and its machinery became the central theme of his works, his choice of sources was arbitrary and centered round the Ahom State. He chose to retain dialogues or diplomatic conversations that appealed to the masses and succeeded in creating national heroes in the face of a crisis. As Bhuyan explicitly said, "the Buranjis are our strengthening tie to bind us with the past, and maintain the solidarity of the Assamese people, and protect us from any threatened erosion of our nationalism." In his introduction to the *Tungkhungia Buranji*, Bhuyan categorically said that "the history of the Ahoms of the 17th century was the history of the Ahom-Mughul conflict." Proud of the Ahom state structure that could hold its own against the mighty Mughul invasion, Bhuyan's attempt was to fold the Ahom period into the mainstream history of India, an attempt that could be successful only by placing the Ahom realm in the context of the Mughul Empire and the Indian subcontinent. Thus with utmost care he tried to trace Assam's link with Punjab, Dravida, Orissa, Maharashtra and Kashmir and had no hesitation in comparing the Ahom General, Lachit Barhukan to Shivaji, or Mula Gabharu to Lakshmi Bai, Queen Phuleswari Konwari to Nur Jahan or even to term the Moamaria revolt as the North-Eastern Sikh Revolt. Thus local heroes and heroines or even events were exalted to the status of already existing national heroes or national events.

While reminding his readers about Assam's glorious culture and her past in an attempt to arouse Assamese passion for the nation, Bhuyan had no hesitation in using various icons that suited the contemporary social dynamics and raising his heroes and heroines to a level equivalent to contemporary world figures. Thus in the Third Bulletin of the DHAS, published in 1936, Bhuyan created similar models from world history and had no hesitation in declaring Bhaskaravarman as Assam's Alexander; Momai-Tamuli Barua as Assam's Solon; Atan Buragohain as Assam's Pericles; Pratap Singha as Assam's Charlemagne; Rudra Singha as Assam's Frederick the Great; Joymati as Assam's Griselda; Assamese Vaisnavism as Assam's European Protestanism; the Battle of Saraighat as Assam's Battle of Blenheim; the Battle of Itakhuli as Assam's Battle of Trafalgar; the Battle of Mohgarh as Assam's Battle of Waterloo; the Syiemships of the Khasis and the Jaintias as Assam's democracies of Athens and Sparta; and the Boros as Assam's Macedonians. However,

Bhuyan was so engrossed in retrieving the lost autonomy of the Assamese history through specific events and its distinctive sources that his attention was not equally directed to the fact that Assam had maintained cultural and political relations with the northern regions of the south Asian sub-continent since ancient times and that there existed regular exchanges between the inhabitants of the hills and the plains in the social and traditional life of the people. His works, while extolling various aspects of the Ahom dynasty, remained by and large political in nature. Much remained to be investigated in themes like agrarian structures, peasant societies, trade and commerce and other such problems connected with material aspects of people's life during various periods of their history. Thus, consequent to the attempts made by Bhuyan to glorify the Ahom state vis-à-vis its relation with the Moghul Empire, the Ahom kingdom's "Yunnan trade, its Ava obligations, its cultural transactions with Southeast Asia were all attending trifles." [42] The tribal kingdoms which either had diplomatic relations or had a strong presence in the Ahom kingdom were marginalized in Bhuyan's *buranjis*. The important role which these kingdoms played in the making of the Ahom Empire was hardly brought to focus, thereby reducing the position of the kingdoms to petty structures that played only an inconsequential role in matters of Ahom diplomacy and statecraft.

Historians are also not so comfortable with Bhuyan's complete reliance on the *buranjis* for reconstructing the history of pre-colonial Assam. Despite Bhuyan's awareness of the limitations of *buranjis* that they recorded only those events which were crucial to the royal polity, Bhuyan believed that they could play an important role in reconstructing the past. He never doubted the authenticity of the *buranjis* and hence never hesitated to use them as the key tool in structuring the history of the pre-colonial past even though he was well aware that not only had these *buranjis* been updated over the years by successive generations of rulers, but that often folios had also been added to supplement them with additional narrative, resulting in a change in content, language and calligraphy. The first *buranjis* that appeared in print form from the mid-nineteenth century were mere reproductions without any editorial interference and were published by the American Baptist Missionaries in their journal, *Orunodoi*. Though the new *buranjis* written by members of the Ahom nobility in the colonial period did not contain much editorial work, Kashinath Tamuli Phukan explains that the new additions to his *Asom Buranji* was necessary because, "...the previous edition had left out many crucial dimensions of Ahom polity."[43] However, it is important to bear in mind that not all later *buranjis* followed this practice. It is also important to bear in mind that *buranjis* were written not only by official chroniclers, but also by general scholars. It is surprising that modern historians rarely hesitate to accept the legitimacy of these manuscripts as important historical evidence in spite of the fact that they rarely mention the name of the author. As Bhuyan worked hard to make the *buranjis* available in print, he used various editorial methods. The editorial work to which he devoted a large part of his time and energy was not only enormous but also laborious. The period classified as the medieval period in Assam could only be reconstructed by a scholar whose determination was willing to even overlook the inconsistencies in the *buranjis*. The task was a difficult one and he elaborated the difficulties encountered by him in this job in the first Bulletin of the DHAS thus:

> The trend of narratives in old chronicles cannot be followed by uninitiated readers on account of the multiplicity of facts of a similar character, viz. wars, intrigues, and diplomatic negotiations, etc. Considerable difficulties also arise from the archaic character of the language, from the strings of toponomous and patronymic appellations to indicate the identity of historical personages, generally aggravated by the mixing up of words and sentences, when there are no signs separating them. The reduction of the chaotic mass of materials full of unfamiliar names and expressions to a presentable form, without at the same time making any alteration in the text, is obviously a matter of delay, and requires long practice, discretion and judgement which can be attained only by close and intimate knowledge of the minutiae of Assam history.[44]

Eager to bring home to his readers the salient features of the Ahom statecraft, Bhuyan himself did not hesitate to manoeuvre his ability to edit the numerous *buranjis* in a way to prove his point. It is important to bear in mind that as the original *buranjis* gradually became inaccessible for most scholars, it was Bhuyan's edited volumes that were used by most and came to be considered as the standard *buranjis*. It was indeed a matter of great privilege for the Assamese intelligentsia that *buranji* manuscripts were now readily available to the society for a glimpse and was hardly a matter of concern to the scholars that only a few *buranjis* had been printed in their original forms. Even British scholars engaged in a study of Assam's past history showed no hesitation in using the *buranjis* as historical sources in spite of the fact that a majority of European scholars tried to negate the existence of any historical consciousness in pre-British India. Even the invaluable *Tungkhungia Buranji* (1933) was compiled by Bhuyan from numerous contemporary *buranjis* and hence in spite of providing a complete history of the early rulers of the Tungkhungia dynasty in a manner and language that resembled the old chronicles, "the whole method of mobilizing discrete and widely spaced texts into one historical narrative might appear disquieting to the professional historians today."[45] Though Bhuyan did not frame any new sentence but simply picked up sentences or passages from older chronicles, he inserted them in a manner to fill in the missing links in evolving the reign of a monarch. Similarly, while editing the *Satsari buranji,* a compilation of several *buranjis,* Bhuyan did not hesitate to confess about having borrowed from other *buranjis.* He explained the necessity of having to do so since a single manuscript often missed or lost vital information.

Like his reliance on the *buranjis* for the reconstruction of Assam's pre-colonial history, Bhuyan relied heavily on colonial historiography for writing the history of Assam during the colonial regime. The historians who followed in his footsteps in the pre-1947 period and the years that closely followed were also heavily influenced by western liberal ideas of empiricism and documentation with very little attempts at critical interpretative analysis. Though these historians have done yeoman service as pioneers in untrodden fields and their works are valuable for bringing to light many source materials that had hitherto been unknown, history writing continued to follow the trend that had been set by colonial historiography with the publication of the original official imperialist documents of Alexander Mackenzie, Pemberton, Butler, Mills, Woodthrope, Needham or Robert Reid. The publication of Bhuyan's *Anglo-Assamese Relations* roused tremendous interest in studying the British relations with the various tribes and communities of the Northeast. Some such notable works include H.K. Barpujari's study on Anglo-tribal relations, S.K. Barpujari's work on Anglo-Naga relations, J.B. Bhattacharjee's contribution on Anglo-Garo relations, S. Chatterjee's study on Anglo-Lushai relations, Helen Giri and Hamlet Bareh's work on Anglo-Khasi relations, Lakshmi Devi's contribution on Ahom-tribal relations and Milton Sangma's writings on Anglo-Garo relations.

Bhuyan's untiring effort at professionalizing the discipline of history did not go in vain and in the post-Independence period Gauhati University, established in 1948, became the centre from where historical research continued in right earnest. His personal contributions apart, many renowned scholars of his time and of later generations were benefited by his guidance. Bhuyan's path was followed by a band of dedicated historians like B.K. Barua who wrote A *Cultural History of Assam* (1951), P.C. Choudhury who wrote *The History of Civilisation of the People of Assam* (1959), Maheswar Neog who wrote on *Sankaradeva and His Times* (1965), *Prachya Sasanavali* (1974) and *Pavitra Asom* (1969), S.N. Sarma who studied the *Neo-Vaishnavite Movement and the Satra Institution of Assam* (1966) and R.M. Lahiri who wrote on the *Annexations of Assam* (1954). However, it was H. K. Barpujari who dominated historical writing in Assam in the post-1960s period, despite the fact that his method and style of writing history was not similar to that of S.K. Bhuyan. Unlike Bhuyan, Barpujari's writings in Assamese are very few and his primary interest appeared to be focussed on the making of the colonial empire, not withstanding the fact that towards the end of his career he also deliberated on certain contemporary political issues and edited the monumental *The Comprehensive History of Assam*, in five volumes, covering the period from pre-historic times to 1919. Barpujari was firm in his opinion that the historical truth can be arrived at by documenting the hard core of historical facts that exist and he strongly believed that such facts are independent of the interpretation of the historian.[46] Some of Barpujari's important works include *Assam : In the Days of the Company* (1963); *Problem of Hill Tribes : North-East Frontier* (3 vols, 1970-81), *An Account of Assam* and *Her Administration* (1987); *Itihas Rachana Bidhi Aru Cromobikash* (in Assamese, 1988); *Political History of Assam,* vol.1 ed., (1977); *The Comprehensive History of Assam,* vols. I-V ed. (1990-93). A stalwart of Barpujari's stature promoted research in history not merely by confining his energies to writing but also by teaching and supervising research in the Gauhati University. Like S.K. Bhuyan, Barpujari was also well connected with his contemporary historians in India and abroad.

As a historian

Suryya Kumar Bhuyan was the first Assamese intellectual who had a wider vision of history and who tried to link the history of Assam with the greater domain of history. He was more deeply interested in the medieval period since he firmly believed that the knowledge about the greatness of the Ahom monarchs and their statecraft could retrieve Assam's lost prestige and glory vis-à-vis the British rule in Assam. His sense of duty towards society was instrumental in inspiring him to shoulder several responsibilities both in national and regional contexts. Similar to Emile Durkheim's sociology, his constructive idea of trying to secure a better scientific, regional and national harmony was a way to attainment of peace and harmonious intercultural integration."[47] However, the most important aspect of a historian's approach which includes the richness of source material, extensive investigation and an awareness of the historical setting appeared to be missing in Bhuyan's works because of his heavy reliance on the *buranjis*. The information gleaned from these *buranjis* have neither been examined in the light of Persian and other sources of the period nor subjected to new sets of questions posed by scientific historical research. However, in spite of his limitations, Bhuyan's contribution towards crafting the discipline of history writing in 20th Century Assam is unparalleled. He not only created an interest in the history of Assam amongst the scholars and the masses of the state but also worked assiduously towards disseminating information about Assam's past to the rest of the country and abroad. He was the first to project Assam as a geographical unit with a distinct linguistic and cultural heritage within India. It is indeed creditable that he could exploit the adverse socio-politico-economic situation in the state caused by colonial rule to the advantage of the Assamese (*jati*) and the nation, by converting Assam's weakness into her strength. He instilled pride in Assam's past glory and restored an atmosphere favourable for intellectual pursuits. In spite of all the limitations under which he worked, Bhuyan could rouse interests in Assam's history and her civilisation among eminent scholars both in India and abroad. As Banikanta Kakati said, "Dissemination of knowledge about the Assamese people and creation of interest in their past history and civilisation, far and wide, has been a welcome offshoot of Dr. Bhuyan's life-long devotion for the cause of Assamese historical research."[48]

Notes & References

1. S.K. Bhuyan, "Recollections and Reflections", *The patriarchs of our family*, Guwahati, 2010, pp. 101-102.
2. *Ibid*.
3. *Ibid*; Nanda Talukdar, *Suryya Kumar Bhuyan*, Guwahati, 1984, p. 308.
4. Manorama Sharma, "Theoretical Trends in History writing and Status of Historical Research in North East India", *Proceedings of North East India History Association*, Fourteenth Session, Jorhat, 1993, p. 382.
5. S. D. Goswami, "Progress of Historical Research in North East India, A Survey", *Proceedings of North East India History Association*, Fourteenth Session, Jorhat, 1993, p. 355.
6. Srinath Barbarua's 'foreword/introduction' to *Tungkhungia Buranji.*
7. George A. Grierson, *Linguistic Survey of India*, Calcutta, 1862, SI, Vol. 5, Part, 1, p. 396.
8. B. B. Goswami, "The Tribes of Assam: A Few Comments on their Social and Cultural Ties with the Non-Tribes" in K. Suresh Singh (ed.), *Tribal Situation in India*, Vol. I, IIAS, Shimla, 1982.
9. Alexander Mackenzie, *Memorandum on the North East Frontier,* Bengal Government Press, Calcutta, 1869.
10. R.B. Pemberton, *Report on the Eastern Frontier of British India*, Bengal Government Press, Calcutta, 1835.

11. J. M. Butler,, *Travels and Adventures in the Province of Assam*, London, 1855; A. J.M. Mills, *Report on the Khasi and Jaintia Hills*, Calcutta, 1854.
12. Woodthrope, *Lushai Expedition 1871-72,* London, 1873.
13. Needham, *Report on the Trip into Abor Hills*, Shillong, 1885.
14. Robert Reid, *History of the Frontier Areas Bordering on Assam*, Assam Secretariat, Shillong, 1942.
15. Sajal Nag, "Aspects of Historiography of North East India", *Proceedings of North East India History Association*, Seventeenth session, Aizawl, 1996, p. 67.
16. S. D. Goswami, *op. cit.*, p.357
17. Arupjyoti Saikia, "History, buranjis and nation: Suryya Kumar Bhuyan's histories in twentieth century- Assam", *The Indian Economic and Social History Review,* 45, 4 (New Delhi, 2008), pp. 473-507.
18. S. K. Bhuyan, *Some Literary Reminiscences*, Guwahati, 2010, p.10.
19. *Ibid.*, p.12.
20. *Ibid.*, p. 9.
21. Manorama Sharma, *op. cit.,* p.381
22. Arupjyoti Saikia, *op. cit.*
23. S. K. Bhuyan's inaugural speech at the 7th annual meeting of the Anthropological Society of Assam held on March 16, 1952, Courtesy his personal library at Guwahati.
24. *Ibid.*, p.13
25. S. K. Bhuyan, 'Relationship between the Hills and Plains of Assam', A collection of extracts on the subject from the writings and speeches of Dr. S. K. Bhuyan. Courtesy his personal library at Guwahati.
26. S. K. Bhuyan, 'Review of the second D.H.A.S. Bulletin', Courtesy his personal library at Guwahati.
27. Quoted in Bani Kanta Kakati, "Dr. Bhuyan's Literary and Historical Output", reprinted in *Professor Suryya Kumar Bhuyan Commemoration Volume*. Gauhati University, 1965, pp. 1-6.
28. S. K. Bhuyan, 'Preface' to *Bulletin V,* Department of Historical and Antiquarian Studies (DHAS), Gauhati, 1943.
29. Bani Kanta Kakati, *op.cit*, p. 5.
30. See Annexure.
31. S.K. Bhuyan, *Quintessence of Experience*, Pub. P.K. Bhuyan & B. C. Das, Guwahati, 198, reprinted Guwahati, 2010, p. xvii..
32. Bhuyan, *Some Literary Reminiscences*, Guwahati, 2010, p.32
33. Arupjyoti Saikia, *op. cit.*, p10I
34. *Ibid.*, p.8

35. S. K. Bhuyan, *Some Literary Reminiscences*, Guwahati, 2010, pp. 8-9.
36. *Ibid.*, 'Foreword'.
37. *Ibid.*, pp.4-5
38. S. K. Bhuyan's speech at St. Stephen's College, Delhi, July 26, 1952, File No. A/1 Vol.22.
39. S. K. Bhuyan's speech delivered at the 'Hills and Plains Week', Shillong, November 5, 1947, Courtesy Dr. Bhuyan's personal library.
40. Cited from Boddhisattva Kar, "The Tragedy of Suryya Bhuyan", *History, Biblio*, May-June, 2008, p. 26.
41. *Ibid.*
42. *Ibid.*
43. Arupjyoti Saikia, *op. cit.*, p. 10
44. *Ibid.*
45. *Ibid*
46. Manorama Sharma, *op. cit.*, p. 382
47. J. A. Berlie, Centre for Asian Studies, University of Hong Kong, Letters to the Editor, *The Assam Tribune*, dated 5 June 2010.
48. Bani Kanta Kakati, *op. cit.*, p. 3.

Annexure

Published Works of Dr. S. K. Bhuyan

A. English

(i) Original Works

1. *An Assamese Nur Jahan*, Gauhati, December 1926.
2. *Early British Relations with Assam*, Assam Govt. Press, Shillong, 1928.
3. *Tungkhungiya Buranji* (comp.), DHAS, Gauhati, 1933.
4. *Preliminary Report on the old Records of the Assam Government 1823-74*, Govt. of Assam, Shillong, 1931.
5. *Assamese Literature : Ancient and Modern*, Govt. of Assam, Shillong, 1936.
7. *Lachit Barphukan and His Times*, DHAS, Gauhati, 1947.
8. *Annals of the Delhi Badshahate* (a translation of the old Assamese chronicle '*Padshah-Buranji*'), DHAS, Gauhati, 1947.
9. *Anglo-Assamese Relations*, DHAS, Gauhati, 1949.
10. *Atan Buragohain and His Times*, DHAS, Gauhati, 1931.
11. "A Note on Assamese Language and Literature", prefixed to Hemchandra Goswami's *Typical Selections from Assamese Literature*, Calcutta University, 1929.

12. *The Military System of the Assamese People*, being the fourth Pratibha Devi Memorial Lectures delivered at Gauhati in February 1941, KAS, Gauhati, 2010.
13. *Mir Jumla's Invasion of Assam*, DHAS, Gauhati, 1956.
14. *Some Literary Reminiscences*, with a foreword by Dr. Radha Kumud Mookerjee, New Delhi, 1954.
15. *Quintessence of Experience*, Pub. P.K. Bhuyan & B. C. Das, Guwahati,1986.
16. *Studies in the History of Assam*, Pub. Lakshewari Bhuyan, Gauhati, 1986.
17. *Studies in the Literature of Assam*, with Foreword by Shri Prakasa, Gauhati, 1956.
18. *London Memories (1936-36)*, Publication Board, Assam, 1979.
19. *Recollections and Reflections*, Publication Board, Assam, 2010.
20. *Men I Have Met* (sketches of 152 contemporaries), Gauhati, 1962.
21. *Seven Hindrances*, Gauhati, 1953.
22. *My Years in Parliament* (speeches), Publication Board, Assam, 2010.
23. *Copper-Plate and Stone Inscriptions of Ancient and Medieval Assam*, Guwahati, 2010.
24. "Assamese Historical Literature", *Proceedings of the Fifth All India Oriental Conference*, Lahore, 1928; *Indian Historical Quarterly*, Calcutta, September, 1929.

(ii) Reports and Bulletins

1. *Report and Conspectus of the Kamarupa Anusandhan Samiti* (Assam Research Society) for 1925-26 and a part of 1926-27, with a statement of its aims and objects and of its activities since 1912, Gauhati, 1927.
2. *Bulletin I of the D.H.A.S.*, With an Introduction by His Excellency Sir Laurie Hammond, Governor of Assam, containing a hand-list of manuscript and transcripts collected by the DHAS, Gauhati, 1932.
3. *Bulletin II of the D.H.A.S.*, With an Introduction by His Excellency Sir Michael Keane, Governor of Assam, and containing list of manuscripts newly collected, DHAS, Gauhati 1934.
4. *Bulletin III of the D.H.A.S.*, A souvenir of the opening ceremony of Narayani Handiqui Historical Institute, on April 4, 1936, containing the speeches of H.E. Sir Michael Keane and the Honorary Provincial Director of the DHAS. etc., Gauhati, 1936.
5. *Bulletin V of the D.H.A.S.*, Gauhati, 1951

B. Assamese

(i) Original Works

1. *Gopal Krishna Gokhale*, Calcutta.
2. *Nirmali* (Collection of poems), Jorhat, 1918.

3. *Ahomar Din*, Jorhat, 1918.
4. *Rabindra Nath Thakur*, Nowgong, 1920.
5. *Jaimati Upakhyan*, Gauhati, 1920.
6. *Anundoram Borooah*, Gauhati, 1920.
7. *Barphukanar Git*, Gauhati, 1924.
8. *Panchami* (Collection of short stories), Calcultta, 1927.
9. *Jonaki* (Life-sketches of eminent men), Jorhat, 1928.
10. *Chaneki* (Life-sketches of eminent women), Jorhat 1928.
11. *Asam-Jiyari* (Women of old Assam), Gauhati, 1935.
12. *Kowanr-Bidroh* (Revolt of princes), Gauhati, 1948.
13. *Ramani Gabharu* (Life-sketch of Princess Ramani Gabharu), Gauhati, 1951.
14. *Buranjir Vani* (message of history), Gauhati, 1951.
15. *Rajeswar Singha, 1751-1769*, Publication Board, Assam, Gauhati, 1975.
16. *Tripadi* (three essays on literature, history and culture). Gauhati, 1959.
17. *Bibidh Prabandha* (thirty-eight articles of historical and literary interest, written between 1908 and 1962), Lawyer's Book Stall, Guwahati, 2005.
18. *Kavita-Sangraha* (Collection of poems in Assamese, Bengali and English, edited by Bireswar Barua), Gauhati, 1994.
19. *Mirjumlar Asom Akraman* (Moghul invasion of Assam in under Nawab Mir Jumla), Gauhati, 1956.
20. *Asom Buranjir Katha* (25 historical essays on Assam), Bani Mandir, Guwahati, 2010.
21. *Buranjimulak Prabandhar Talika* (List of historical articles published in Assamese magazines), Gauhati, 1955.
22. *Lachit Barphukan*, Publication Board, Assam, Gauhati, 1979.
23. *Saraighatar Subachani* (Patriotic utterances of Saraighat), Gauhati, 1963.
24. *Jiwani Sahitya* (biographical literature), Guwahati, 2007.
25. *Harihar Ata* (Life-sketch of a Vaisnava saint of Assam), Gauhati, 1960.

(ii) Assamese Buranji** or **Chronicles: edited with Introduction

1. *Asam Buranji* (by Kashinath Tamuli Phukan and Radhanath Barbarua), DHAS, Gauhati, 1930.
2. *Kamrupar Buranji*, DHAS, Gauhati, 1930.
3. *Tungkhungia Buranji*, DHAS, Gauhati, 1933.
4. *Deodhai Asam Buranji*, DHAS, Gauhati, 1932.
5. *Asamar Padya-Buranji*, DHAS, Gauhati, 1933.

6. *Padshah-Buranji*, Kamrupa Anusandhan Samiti, Gauhati, 1935.
7. *Kachari Buranji*, DHAS, Gauhati 1936.
8. *Jayantia Buranji*, DHAS, Gauhati, 1937.
9. *Tripura Buranji*, DHAS, Gauhati, 1938.
10. *Asam Buranji* (Mss. obtained from the family of Sukumar Mahanta), DHAS, Gauhati, 1945.
11. *Satsari Asom Buranji*, Gauhati University, 1960.

9

Banikanta Kakati (1894-1952)

—*J.B. Bhattacharjee*

Biographical Sketch

A great scholar in the fields of language, literature, culture and history and one of the finest academic minds of twentieth century Assam, Banikanta Kakati was born to Lalitram Kakati and Lahobala Devi in village Batikuriha in Barpeta, Assam, on 15 November 1894. Beginning his primary education in own village school, he passed the Matriculation Examination of the Calcutta University in 1911 from Barpeta High School in first division securing first position among the successful candidates from British Assam which then included the present-day states of Meghalaya, Nagaland and Mizoram in India and the Sylhet Division of Bangladesh, besides Assam today. A highly meritorious student, it was in Barpeta High School that Banikanta began to cultivate his talents as a scholar of the future. Inspired by his elder brother Paramananda Kakati, a teacher in the same school, he read some of the best available classics of the time while a student in the senior classes and is said to have been greatly influenced to Indology by reading a biography of Max Muller. He passed the Intermediate of Arts Examination of Calcutta University in 1913 from Cotton College, Guwahati, standing first in the University, and B.A. Examination of the same University in 1915 from Presidency College, Calcutta, winning the Tawney Memorial Prize as topper among the candidates from the Presidency College. He did his M.A. in English in Group A (Literature) from Calcutta University in 1918 and in November same year, he was appointed Assistant Lecturer in English at Cotton College, Guwahati. In 1922, he did M.A. in English in Group B (Language), securing first position in first class from Calcutta University and was awarded the Kshetra Mohan Chatterji Gold Medal for securing highest marks among all successful candidates in Groups A and B put together. He was awarded the Degree of Doctor of Philosophy by the Calcutta University in 1935 for his thesis on 'Origin and Development of the Assamese Language'. In 1945, Kakati was appointed Professor of English at Cotton College, and in 1947 he became Principal of the College. A great call came to him in 1948 when the first University in Northeast India, namely, Gauhati University, was established. Same year, he joined the new University as

Professor and Head, Department of Assamese. In fact, Banikanta Kakati was the first Professor in Gauhati University, of which another great scholar and Indologist from the Northeast, namely, Krishna Kanta Handiqui,[1] was the first Vice-Chancellor. In 1949, Kakati was elected first Dean, Faculty of Arts, Gauhati University. Indeed, the University was fortunate to experience the academic leadership of the duo in its formative years and, no wonder; it proved to be a great starter among the Indian Universities. Unfortunately for the academia of the region and the country, Banikanta Kakati passed away on 15 November 1952 at a rather young age of 58 when he was in the prime of his career as a scholar of extraordinary skill and promises.[2]

Immediately after the demise of Kakati, the department of Assamese, Gauhati University, under the leadership of Birinchi Kumar Barua,[3] another great scholar and historian, instituted the Banikanta Kakati Memorial Biennial Lecture Series, for which Barua is said to have raised funds from the public, to perpetuate Kakati's memory. The inaugural lecture of the series was delivered in 1954 by Suniti Kumar Chatterji, the renowned linguist and then National Professor of India. The text of the lecture was later on published by the University as *The Place of Assam in the History and Civilization of India*.[4] What Chatterji said in the opening section of the lecture was indeed a eulogy of the scholarship and academic stature of Banikanta Kakati by a mentor and an elder scholar in the same field whose eminence as a linguist was then acknowledged among the peers throughout the world. In words of Chatterji,

> Banikanta Kakati, whose sudden and untimely passing away at the comparatively early age of 58 in November 1952 we all mourn, was a scholar and educationist of whom not only Assam but the whole of India is proud, and he has a place in the front rank of linguisticians and investigators of history and culture who have added luster to Indian scholarship of the present day. Because of his significant contributions, his name will always be held in respect along with his works wherever people take an interest in the languages and culture and religion in India. He did not attain to a hoary old age, and if he had joined the majority in the fullness of his years and after greater achievements which were promised by the works he has left, it would not have been a matter of such keen regret among his relations, friends, fellow-workers and admirers as this taking him away from the very useful sphere of work in which he was manifesting the full maturity of his mind and his powers, leaving hardly any one as distinguished as himself, to carry on the work he had commenced, at least for sometime to come, until capable successors come forward.[5]

Contributions to history

Banikanta Kakati's major scholarly publications include *Life and Teachings of Sankara Deva* (1923), *Assamese: Its Formation and Development* (1941), *The Mother Goddess Kamakhya* (1948) and *Visnuite Myths and Legends* (1952). Among his books in Assamese *Purani Asomiya Sahitya* (1940), *Kalita Jatir Itibritta* (1941) and *Purani Kamrupar Dharmar Dhara* (1955) are research works in different branches of history in vernacular language. His two other major works in Assamese are *Sahitya aru Prem* (1943) and *Pokhila* (1951). He also published several research papers and articles in English and Assamese in various journals and periodicals and edited some early Assamese texts.[6] Some of his essays in historical themes are reprinted in *Banikanta Rachanavali* (2003), edited by Maheswar Neog.[7]

The survey of the works of Banikanta Kakati would reveal that he was basically a scholar of immense depth and insight in the field of language and literature, but his contribution to historiography of Northeast India was also equally significant. The fact that he attended the 22nd session of the Indian Historical Records Commission at Peshwar in 1945 is an indication of the recognition of his interests in history by the Government of Assam which he represented in the conference. He attended the 26th session of the All India Oriental Conference at Lucknow in 1947 and presented a paper on the cult of Jagannatha. The department of Assamese, Gauhati University, of which Kakati was the founder Professor and Head, emerged as a potentially strong centre of research in history and culture of Assam, besides Assamese language and literature. Birinchi Kumar Barua was next to Kakati in the same department and among their first doctoral students were Maheswar Neog, Satyendranath Sarma and Prafulladatta Goswami, all of whom became legends in their own life time as scholars in history, literature and culture of Assam. Kakati was also associated with Kamarupa Ausasandhan Samiti, Guwahati, and was its President in 1951-52.

Kakati's first major work at a comparatively young age, namely, *Life and Teachings of Sankara Deva* (1923),[8] is a historical biography of the great saint of Assam, who was the voice of the Bhakti movement of medieval India in the Northeast. The work is based primarily on literary sources, and the analysis so contextual that it reflects a deep insight of the author into life and conditions in the region during the life-time of Sankaradeva. As a matter of fact, he situated Sankara Deva in time and space and analyzed the teachings of the saint in that context. The format he followed was essentially of a historical study. The life-history of the Sankara Deva from birth to death is followed by a section on 'historical background' and thereafter, the author proceeds to explain the teachings of the saint. More importantly, 'Sankaradeva of Assam' became 'Sankara Deva of India' in Kakati's hands, not only by the inclusion of his work in the 'Saints of India' series but also by his analysis of the different schools of Vaisnavism and Vaisnavite traditions in the subcontinent. His *Visnuite Myths and Legends* (1952) is a collection of ten essays on different forms of Vaisnavism in India and the author discussed the origin and development of each of those forms historically. The most celebrated *Assamese : Its Formation and Development* (1941),[9] which actually emerged out of his doctoral dissertation at the Calcutta University (1935), is indeed a scientific treatise on the history and philology of the Assamese language. *The Mother Goddess Kamakhya* (1948), *Kalita Jatir Itibritta* (1941) and *Purani Kamrupar Dharmar Dhara* (1955) are in any case directly in the realm of history. He also contributed scholarly researched papers in reputed Indological journals and collections on historical themes. For example, he contributed at least four papers in *The New Indian Antiquary* (Bombay), viz. "Austric Substratum in the Assamese Language" (vol. I, no. 4, July 1938, pp. 259-264), "Place and personal names in the early land-grants of Assam" (vol. IV, No. 11, February 1942, pp. 388-394), "Certain Austric-Sanskrit Correspondence" (vol. VI, no.

3, June 1943, pp. 49-51), and "A note on the word Prag-jyotisa" (vol. VII, nos. 7-8, October-November 1944, pp. 134-135) which, besides being contributions in linguistics, probed into the Indo-Mongoloid roots of the cultural traits in Assam and its neighbouring areas by using linguistics as a tool for historical research. Similarly, "The Cult of Jagannatha" (*Journal of the University of Gauhati*, vol. I, 1952, pp. 65-77), which he originally presented at the 26th session of the All India Oriental Conference at Lucknow in 1947, "Vaisnavism in Assam and Southern India : certain points of correspondence" (*A Volume of Studies in Indology*, Presented to Professor P.V. Kane, Poona, 1941) and "The boar in mythology and folk-lore" (*Mm. Potdar Commemorative Volume*, Poona, 1952, pp. 38-44) are also important contributions in history for the same methodology. His article entitled "Assam through the ages" was published in *The Assam Tribune* (Independence Day Number, 1949). Finally, he wrote two articles on historian S.K. Bhuyan, first, a scholarly 'introduction' to *Bibliography of the Works of Dr. S.K. Bhuyan* (Gauhati, 1951) and the second, an article entitled "Dr. Bhuyan's Literary and Historical Output". The second article was reprinted in *Suryya Kumar Bhuyan Commemoration Volume* (1965) edited by H.K. Barpujari and Maheswar Neog.[10] These two articles on works of S. K. Bhuyan are important for understanding Banikanta Kakati's concept of history, historian and historiography.

Banikanta Kakati's *magnum opus* in the field of history is, of course, his *The Mother Goddess Kamakhya* (1948),[11] which is an in-depth study of the Brahmanical transformation of a pre-Aryan deity and its cult-site and through this transformation the author reflected analytically on the fusion of the Aryan and extra-Aryan religious beliefs and practices and the cultural processes in the Northeast. The author spelt out in the 'preface' of the book : "In the present political set up of India, Assam is fast shedding her character of a mere geographical expression in the map of India. And yet she has not yet told the story of her growth and a development as a meeting ground of the Aryans and the Mongols."[12] He regretted that the early period of Assam's cultural history had not till then been properly studied excepting some gazetteers of the British regime, Edward Gait's *A History of Assam* (1906), K.L. Barua's *Early History of Kamarupa* (1933), B.K. Barua's *Assamese Literature* (1941) and Kakati's own *Life and Teachings of Sankara Deva* (1923) which, according to him, are "the sketches that give in outline the purely Aryan aspect of Assamese thoughts and activities."[13] As regards his study of the Kamakhya, he said, "The present publication is a mere introduction towards the study of the fusion of the Aryan and extra-Aryan religious beliefs and practices in Assam in the light of the comparative method of modern sociological studies. The beliefs and practices have been tracked as far as possible to their sources."[14] A dip into the pages of the book, however, will convince one that he studied almost all the available literary sources, including the *Tantras* and *Puranas*, as well as the inscriptions of ancient Assam and laboured hard to find meanings for certain terms and terminologies used in different sources. In terms of contents, it covered land and people, Siva worship, Naraka of Mithila, Mother Goddesses, and Visnu worship.[15] Shortly after publication of the *The Mother Goddess Kamakhya* (1948) he contributed two papers under the same title ("The Mother Goddess Kamakhya"), one in *Triveni Quarterly* (Bangalore)[16] and another in Siddheswar Varma Presentation Volume (Hoshiarpur), reporting his major findings in the book.[17] His *Purani Kamrupar Dharmar Dhara* (religious tradition of ancient Kamarupa)[18] covered almost the same contents as in *The Mother Goddess Kamakhya* (1948). As a matter of fact, in an earlier work, *Kalita Jatir Itibritta* (history of the Kalitas)[19] also Kakati had taken the position that the basic framework of culture in the region was Mongolian, the Brahmanical culture being a fact of life at the supper structure and at the grassroots it was Mongoloid. It was the courage of conviction of a historian in Banikanta Kakati to put squarely that the Kalitas have been living in Assam for a long time and they had once a kingdom in the region, but they are not autochthonous in Assam and, like the Brahmins, they also might have migrated from the west (Mithila, Kanauj etc.). In a long essay entitled "The Kalita Caste of Assam",[20] Kakati also did not rule out the possibility of the Kalitas migrating to Assam from South India, and he took that position only after a detailed comparative analysis of linguistic and archaeological data from the two regions. In his words,

> The presence of *Kalitas* in Sambalpur coupled with probable instances of linguistic and other archaeological parallelisms between Assam and South India noticed in the foregoing sections would seem to make the suspicion about their migration from the south not wholly unfounded. More than half the inhabitants of Assam is made up of Tibeto-Burman people. They are indigenous to the province. Genuine Kayasthas constitute a handful and their ancestors migrated into Assam in historical times. Other castes like *Kewats*, *Kumars*, *Suris* etc. have pan-Indian denominations and might as well belong here as come from elsewhere. It cannot be said that they were brought over by king Narakasura to Aryanise the kingdom. The topmost position of the *Kalitas* amongst the fully Ayanised population seems to lend itself to the interpretation that they came in with the earliest Brahmins. But nothing definitely can be said till more materials are available. But as there are *Kalitas* also in other parts of India, it is hoped that better informed scholars will throw greater light upon this subject.[21]

In the context of racial composition of the population of modern Assam, Banikanta Kakati and Suniti Kumar Chatterji held similar views, the latter having observed that Assam and the neighbouring areas, including northern Bengal, was a Kirata or Indo-Mongoloid region in early times.[22] No wonder, while writing 'foreword' to Chatterji's First Banikanta Kakati Memoral Lectures, K.K. Handiqui had remarked that on the subject of the lecture, namely, the contributions of Assam to history and culture of India, both Chatterji and Kakati 'could speak with authority'.[23] The renowned physical Anthropologist of Assam, B.M. Das while commenting on Kakati's *Kalita Jatir Itibritta* says,

> When Kakati published this book in 1943, there was no full-fledged account of the socio-cultural life of the Kalitas (and, I am afraid, even now there is none). At that time the concept and implication of biological distinctiveness was yet to be properly developed. There was no record relating to ethno-biological aspects of caste. (In recent years attempts have been made by some to collect such information, but the records now available are still insufficient for utilization in such an approach). Therefore, Kakati could not take help of any data collected from the anthropological (socio-cultural and biological) point of view. But whatever scanty information was there, he did not fail to harness that. This clearly indicates what broad perspective he had.[24]

Nonetheless, every one in the intelligentsia of Assam might not have spontaneously shared Kakati's views on the primacy of Mongolian element in the culture of the region.

Thus, while covering a lecture delivered by Kakati, in July 1947, at the Narayani Handiqui Institute, Guwahati, *The Assam Tribune* aired its reservation about the opinion that the society in Assam was basically Mongolian in its origin.[25] The critiquing of Banikanta's fusion theory is also evident in some recent works like Bhaben Barua's *Prasanga : Banikanta Kakati* which argued that Pragjyotish was an Aryan kingdom from the earliest time.[26] On the other hand, the generality of the scholars consider Kakati's works as pioneering contributions in scientific historiography of the region.[27] In fact, Kakati's position was well vindicated in Birichi Kumar Barua's *A Cultural History of Assam* (1951) which brought out the fact of Aryan-non-Aryan continuum in the formation of a composite culture in Assam.[28] Barua found that earliest known inhabitants in Assam spoke in an Indo-Chinese language belonging to the Austric family of languages.[29] Rajmohan Nath argued that a large number of tribes and communities in the region provided the background of the Assamese culture.[30] Amalendu Guha went to the extent of identifying the like of Naraka, Bhagadatta and other rulers in early Pragjyotisa-Kamarupa as 'Aryanized sons of the soil'.[31] It is for Kakati's scientific research methodology and objectivity of approach that Sailen Barkataki looks upon Kakati as a sociologist[32] and Sibnath Barman considers him a sociologist of religion.[33] Reviewing the major works of Kakati, the eminent intellectual of Assam Hiren Gohain[34] says,

> All these books reveal the supreme organizing intelligence of his intellect and his wide and searching erudition. Not only the selection and marshalling of data, the formulation of hypothesis, the impeccable logic of argument, but the crispness and austere beauty of the prose suggest an original and forceful genius at work. After these works Assamese intellectuals found before them a standard with which to judge their own intellectual maturity.[35]

On his part, Kakati's strength was his methodology. As a linguist, he identified the 'Austric substratum in the Assamese language',[36] 'place and personal names in the early land-grants of Assam'[37] and 'certain Austric-Sanskrit correspondence'[38] and linguistically analyzed the word 'Prag-jyotisa'[39] and thereafter, proceeded to explain 'the fusion of the Aryan and extra-Aryan religious beliefs and practices in Assam' by using the available conventional and non-conventional sources.[40] However, Kakati in his 'preface' to *The Mother Goddess Kamakhya* had himself stated that "No conclusion has been hazarded because none is possible at this stage. An attempt has only been made to enlarge the scope of discussion."[41] This was the scientific temper of the scholar in Banikanta Kakati who considered his findings always tentative with an open mind. Moreover, in *The Mother Goddess Kamakhya* he had clearly stated that "Simply because Naraka is said to have settled the twice-born people in ancient Kamarupa, it would be hasty to interpret his adventure as the first attempt at Aryanisation of ancient Assam. Aryinisation of ancient Assam seems to have taken place by slow infiltration of Aryan ideas, and Aryanised gods and modes of worship. Saivism was the prevailing religion of Assam before the advent of Naraka and it must have been introduced by some Aryan or Aryanised people."[42] He further said,

> In all periods of Assam history there is mention of Brahmanas and other twice-born people having been imported into Assam from different parts of Northern India, especially Gauda and Mithila by several reigning monarchs either to signalize their assent to the throne, some victory or the building of some shrine. Naraka must have imported the twice-born to support his regime and his new cult of the goddess Kamakhya.[43]

As a historian

Banikanta Kakati is indeed better known as a scholar of extraordinary stature in his own field, i.e. language and literature. His *Assamese : Its Formation and Development* (1941) and his other works on old Assamese texts, which he scientifically studied and edited, resolved an uncalled for colonial controversy regarding the status of Assamese as a language and contributed to its ascendancy to a place of pride among the modern Indian languages. While studying the history of Assamese language and literature, particularly the old Assamese texts, he seems to have found it necessary to study the cultural history of the region, particularly the ethnic components of languages, and in the process, he discovered the fact of plurality in cultural life of the local communities by using the linguistic tool. The use of this scientific method was always a strong point in his works in history. In fact, the application of linguistics as a tool in historical inquiry was the most significant contribution of Banikanta Kakati to the historiography of Northeast India. He used literary sources – both written and oral, as well as mythology and folklore, and examined the validity of the sources by analyzing the contents linguistically. His works are thus important for understanding the origins of the cultures and the cultural history of the region, for which conventional sources are very few and far between. Thus, he left behind a clue for the historians to work on and to address the origins and development of cultures through the languages for filling up the spectacular vacuums in early history of Northeast India. Kakati's own works like *The Mother Goddess Kamakhya* (1948), *Kalita Jatir Itibritta* (1941) and *Purani Kamrupar Dharmar Dhara* (1955) are major contributions in early history of the region which he wrote after consulting all available sources. The broadness of academic perspective, extensive survey and readings of world literature, and the openness of a universal mind are the distinguishing marks of his scholarship in these works. In *The Mother Goddess Kamakhya* his readers are acquainted with some of the similar concepts and ritual practices in pre-historic Egypt, Syria and many other parts of the globe as in the *kumari* cult in Kamakhya. It is true that he did not follow the hardcore convention of history writing by footnoting the sources and providing a bibliography, but his works are well documented as he mentioned the source within brackets after almost every statement of fact. Finally, the uniquely pleasant literary style in historical works of Banikanta Kakati brought history and literature closer to each other.

Notes & References

1. The Founder Principal of J.B. College, Jorhat and Founder Vice-Chancellor of Gauhati University, Krishna Kanta Handiqui (1898-1982) was a great Sanskrit, Prakrit and Pali scholar and proficient in a number of foreign languages including French, Greek and German. Born in Jorhat, he studied in Jorhat Govt. High School, Jorhat, and Cotton College, Guwahati, graduated from Calcutta Sanskrit College, and did his M.A. in Sanskrit

in Calcutta University and M.A. in Modern History in Oxford University. A brilliant student, he authored several papers in English and Assamese early in his career and gradually earned national and international fame for his scholarship in linguistics and literature by translating with notes and annotations the ancient classics in Sanskrit, Prakrit and Pali, like *Naushada Charita* of Sriharsha (Motilal Banarsi Dass, 1951), and *Setubandha* (Prakrit Text Society. 1976) and his scholarly work on *Yasastilaka* (namely, *Yasastilaka and Indian Culture* (Bharatiya Jnanpith, 1964). A Padmasree (1955) and Padmabhushan (1967) awardee of the Govt. of India and honoured as a Hony. Fellow by Deccan College, Pune (1968), Handiqui's Presidential Addresses to Asam Chhatra Sanmelan (1929), Asam Sahitya Sabha (1937), All India Oriental Conference, Sanskrit Section (1951), Indian Vice-Chancellors' Conference (Madras, 1952) and All India Oriental Conference (1961) are quoted by many till these days as words of a visionary. He contributed a seminal paper entitled "Classical Sanskrit as a Vehicle of Indian Culture" in Vol. II of the four-volume *The Cultural Heritage of India* (1937) prepared and published by the Ramakrishna Mission Institute of Culture, Calcutta, under the Chairmanship of Dr. Sarvepalli Radhakrishnan. As founder Principal of the first non-government college and founder Vice-Chancellor of the first University in the region, K.K. Handiqui set a dignity and vision for higher education management in the Northeast. For details see Abdus Sattar, *Krishnakanta Handiqui*, 1st published 1975, 3rd edition, Sahityika, Jorhat, 2008 and Tabu Taid & Ranjit Dev Goswami (ed), *Banikanta Kakati : The Man and His Works*, Publication Board Assam, Guwahati, 1988.

2. Tabu Taid & Ranjit Dev Goswami (ed), *Banikanta Kakati : The Man and His Works*, Publication Board Assam, Guwahati, 1988, pp. 1-2 ; Sailen Barkataki, "*Samajbijnani Dr. Banikanta Kakati*", *Gariyashi*, 19th Year, no. 2, November, 2011, pp. 43-45.

3. Birinchi Kumar Barua succeeded Banikanta Kakati as Head of the Department of Assamese on premature death of Kakati in November 1952. Barua was instrumental in instituting the Banikanta Kakati Memorial Lectures to be delivered once in every two years by an eminent scholar to commemorate the contributions of Kakati as a scholar and to the development of Gauhati University in its formative years and in organizing the Assamese Department of the University. Barua himself raised funds for instituting the lecture series at the University. The inaugural Banikanta Kakati Memorial Lecture (1954) was delivered by the internationally acclaimed linguist Suniti Kumar Chatterji, then National Professor of India, who was a teacher of both Banikanta Kakati and Birinchi Kumar Barua in Calcutta University and a personal friend of K.K. Handiqui, then Vice-Chancellor of Gauhati University. In his 'Foreword' to the lecture, later on published by Gauhati University as a book, K.K. Handiqui said, "I am grateful to my friend Dr. S.K. Chatterji for consenting to deliver the first lectures on a subject on which both he and Dr. Kakati could speak with authority. Our thanks are due to Dr. B.K. Barua, the successor of Dr. Kakati in the chair of Assamese literature, for organizing the collection of funds for instituting these lectures." (Suniti Kumar Chatterji, *The Place of Assam in History and Civilisation of India*, Gauhati University Publications, 1955, see 'Foreword') The initiative of Birinchi Kumar Barua in honoring and keeping the memory of a senior colleague green is certainly an instance of the value system in the academia of Assam in that generation.

4. Suniti Kumar Chatterji, *The Place of Assam in the History and Civilization of India*, Gauhati University Publications, 1955.

5. *Ibid*, p. 1.

6. For a complete bibliography of the works of Banakanta Kakati see ,Tabu Taid & Ranjit Dev Goswami (ed), *Banikanta Kakati : The Man and His Works*, *op.cit*, pp. 3-9.

7. *Banikanta Rachanavali*, Maheswar Neog ed., Asam Prakashan Parishad, Guwahati, 2003. Banikanta's scholarly essays like "*Rashkridar Guri Katha*", "*Chandradevatar Upakhyan*", "*Radha-Charitrar Abhyuday*" etc. are serious discourses in history.

8. Banikanta Kakati, *Life and Teachings of Sankara Deva*, Saints of India Series, Natesan & Co., Madras, 1923; reprinted in *Chaitanya to Vivekananda*, Natesan & Co., Madras, 1928.

9. Banikanta Kakati, *Assamese : Its Formation and Development*, Department of Historical and Antiquarian Studies (DHAS), Govt. of Assam, Gauhati, 1941.

10. Bani Kanta Kakati, "Dr. Bhuyan's Literary and Historical Output", reprinted in H.K. Barpujari and Maheswar Neog (eds), *Professor Suryya Kumar Bhuyan Commemoration Volume*, Gauhati University, 1965, pp. 1-6.

11. Banikanta Kakati, *The Mother Goddess Kamakhya*, 1st edn. Lawyers Book Stall, Gauhati, 1948; reprints Publication Board Assam, Guwahati, 1989 & 2004.

12. *Ibid*, see 'Preface'.

13. *Ibid*.

14. *Ibid*.

15. *Ibid*, see 'Contents'.

16. Banikanta Kakati, "The Mother Goddess Kamakhya", *Triveni Quarterly*, vol. XXI, No. 8, March 1948.

17. Banikanta Kakati, "The Mother Goddess Kamakhya", *Siddha-Bharati, or Essays of Indology*, Siddheswar Varma Presentation Volume, Hoshiarpur, 1950.

18. Banikanta Kakati, *Purani Kamrupar Dharmar Dhara*, Gauhati, 1955

19. Banikanta Kakati, *Kalita Jatir Itibritta*, Gauhati, 1941

20. Banikanta Kakati, "The Kalita Caste of Assam" in *A Volume of Indian and Iranian Studies* presented to Sir E. Danison Ross, reprinted in Tabu Taid & Ranjit Dev Goswami (ed), *Banikanta Kakati : The Man and His Works, op.cit.*, pp. 225-234.

21. *Ibid.*, pp. 233-234.

22. Suniti Kumar Chatterji, *Kirâta-Jana-Kriti : The Indo-Mongoloids, Their Contributions to History and Culture of India*, The Asiatic Society, Calcutta, 1951; *.The Place of Assam in the History and Civilisation of India*, Gauhati University Publications, Gauhati, 1955.

23. Suniti Kumar Chatterji, *The Place of Assam in the History and Civilisation of India*, Gauhati University Publications, Gauhati, 1955, see Handiqui's 'Foreword'.

24. B.M. Das, "*Kalita Jatir Itibritta*" in Tabu Taid & Ranjit Dev Goswami (ed), *Banikanta Kakati : The Man and His Works, op.cit.*, p. 172.

25. *The Assam Tribune*, 20th July 1947.

26. Bhaben Barua, *Prasanga : Banikanta Kakati*, Guwahati, 2003.

27. Maheswar Neog (ed.), *Banikanta Rachanavali*, Asam Prakashan Parishad, Guwahati, 2003, see 'introduction'.

28. B.K. Barua, *A Cultural History of Assam,* Vol. I, Published by Shri K. K. Barooah, Nowgong, 1951.

29. *Ibid*, p. 2.
30. Rajmohan Nath, *The Background of Assamese Culture*, Gauhati, 1948.
31. Amalendu Guha, "The Ethnic Process in India with special reference to Assam", *Proceedings of North East India History Association*, Xth Session, Shillong, 1989, pp. 106-108.
32. Sailen Barkataki, "*Samajbijnani Dr. Banikanta Kakati*", *Gariyashi*, 19th Year, no. 2, November, 2011, pp. 43-45.
33. Shibnath Barman, "*Dharmar Samajbijnani Banikanta Kakati*", *Awahan*, July-September, 1991, p. 15.
34. Formerly Professor of English at the Gauhati University and currently associated in editorial advisory capacity with a leading English daily of Guwahati, Hiren Gohain is well known as an eminent scholar, intellectual and social activist of Assam, who suffered social gallows during the Assam Movement (1979-85) for critically analyzing the movement and is praised by all well meaning people in the region for his leadership role in civil society initiative in the peace processes. Intellectually alert, socially committed and a powerful essayist in English and Assamese, he is always guided by the courage of conviction to address the contemporary social issues progressively searching the historical roots of the problems. A recipient of the Sahitya Academy Award for his work on Sankaradeva (in Assamese) in which he credited the Saint with development of modern Assamese language and literature and the Assamese nationality formation, Gohain's contribution to secular and scientific historiography in Northeast India is indeed immense. His research papers and articles on themes like middle class, nationality formation and Vaisnavism in Assam published in *Indian Social and Economic History Review*, *Social Scientist* and *Economic and Political Weekly*, besides leading Assamese periodicals, set a new trend in understanding historical development in the region in light of historical materialism as an alternative to the prevailing positivist approach that has been dominating historiography in Northeast India for a long time. He also supervised the doctoral works of some research scholars in history, besides English literature, at the Gauhati University.
35. Hiren Gohain, "Ideology and the work of Banikanta Kakati" in Tabu Taid & Ranjit Dev Goswami (ed), *Banikanta Kakati : The Man and His Works*, *op.cit.*, p. 43.
36. Banikanta Kakati, "Austric Substratum in the Assamese Language", *The New Indian Antiquary*, vol. I, no. 4, July 1938, pp. 259-264.
37. Banikanta Kakati, *The New Indian Antiquary*, "Place and personal names in the early land-grants of Assam", vol. IV, No. 11, February 1942, pp. 388-394.
38. Banikant Kakati, "Certain Austric-Sanskrit Correspondence", *The New Indian Antiquary*, vol. VI, no. 3, June 1943, pp. 49-51.
39. Banikanta Kakati, "A note on the word Prag-jyotisa", *The New Indian Antiquary*, vol. VII, nos. 7-8, October-November 1944, pp. 134-135.
40. Banikanta Kakati, *The Mother Goddess Kamakhya*, *op.cit*, see 'Preface'.
41. *Ibid.*
42. *Ibid*, p. 29
43. *Ibid.*

10

Lairenmayum Iboongohal Singh (1895-1966)

—H. Sudhir

Biographical Sketch

Lairenmayum Iboongohal Singh (1895-1966) was born on 26 March 1895 at Khoyathong Polem Leikai, Imphal, Manipur. He was educated at Government High School (Silchar); Dacca College (Dacca), Cotton College (Gauhati, Assam), Earl Law College (Gauhati, Assam). He became the first B.L (Bachelor of Law) of Manipur. On completion of education he joined the state service of Manipur and served the state in various capacities till he passed away in 1966. The positions held by him from time to time included :

- Member, Sadar Panchayat Court (1926)
- ADC to the Maharaja Sir Churachand Singh, KCSI (1927)
- Additional Member, Manipur State Durbar (1931)
- First Forest Member of the State
- Judge, Chief Court (1944-50)
- Chairman, Hill Bench (1947-50)
- Chairman, Election Tribunal (1948)
- District and Session Judge (1950)
- Member of the Delegation to the Viceroy of India (1932)
- Secretary, Manipur State War Fund Committee (1940-46)
- Organizer, Manipur State National War Front (1944-46)
- Member, Governing Body, Dhanamanjuri College
- Member, All India National Language Convention, New Delhi (1949)

Iboongohal was known more as a historian of Manipur. Among the Manipuris, he was one of the pioneers in the field of historical research. A.C Banerjee's *Eastern Frontier of British India 1784-1826* (1943),[1] according to Lairenmayum Iboongohal Singh[2], "is one of the most up-to-date" in his time. Other works available at the time included those of R.B. Pemberton (1835),[3] McCulloch (1859),[4] R. Brown (1874),[5] Alexander Mackenzie (1884),[6] E.W. Dun (1886;1891),[7] James Johnston (1896),[8] T.C. Hodson (1908;1911),[9] etc. The *Cheitharol Kumbaba* (the royal chronicle in manuscript)[10] and the works of Panditraj Atombapu Sharma[11] were among the indigenous literature[12] available to the researchers.[13] A simple idea that implies behind the argument is the meagerness of available sources. At that embryonic stage of historical research in Manipur, Lairenmayum Iboongohal Singh, as an investigator in historical research, came up with his works, through which Manipur was introduced to the academics and general readers as well. In this backdrop, the paper intends to discuss (a) the prevalent approaches of knowing the history; (b) life and activities of Lairenmayum Iboongohal Singh; and (c) Lairenmayum Iboongohal Singh as a contributor in the historical research of Manipur by way of going through his works.

Historical Tradition, Vernacular History, and the Colonial Style

The people of early Manipur had a strong sense of writing their past and also preserving them. This traditional knowledge of recording the past is well explained by the Meitei word '*puya/puwari*' that means the stories of the forefather. Though myths, legends, folklore, genealogies are all inextricably mixed up, these *puyas* can be considered as the treasure of the traditional Manipuri historiography.[14] History *per se*, in its strict academic sense, had not yet emerged, but the *puyas*, more particularly the chronicles, form the core of historical research even today. However, there is need for historiographical knowledge and historical methods to use the *puyas* in scientific ways as sources of historical reconstructions.

With the Hinduised wave and its subsequent sanskritisation, the past of the Manipuris began to be looked at from the Hindiused perspective. *Haree Mayee* (1930)[15] by Atombapu Sharma is a clear example where a Vedic scholar employs his Vedic scholarship to interpret the Aryan origin of the Meiteis. Till then, academic history as a separate discipline was unseen. It was only with the coming of the vernacular writings in history in the last decade of the nineteenth or the beginning of the twentieth century that the writing history of Manipur began to surface. Haodeijam Chaitanya's *Manipur Itihas* (1890)[16] is regarded as the chronicle based 'first account on the history of Manipur'.[17] Other vernacular writings in history included those of Pukhrambam Parijat (1917),[18] Kaomacha (1933),[19] Mutum Jhulon (1939),[20] Atombapu Sharma (1940; 1952),[21] W. Yumjao Singh (1946),[22] etc.

In the aftermath of the Anglo-Manipur relations, a corpus of colonial writings in various shapes began to emerge: official/non-official reports, memoirs, monographs, gazetteers etc. R.B. Pemberton (1835), McCulloch (1859), R. Brown (1874), E.W. Dun (1886;1891), James Jonhstone (1895), Alexander Mackenzie (1884), T.C. Hodson (1908;1911), J. Shakespeare (1913) have immensely contributed in the areas of historical inquiries. Their writings have culminated to produce the colonial style of knowing the people and culture of Manipur, but the works fall apart from history as such. Irrespective of merits and deficiencies, the colonial writings dominated the academics of historical inquiries. This colonial historiography was used by the later researches as authentic and reliable without cross-checking and re-verification. It was only in the first half of the twentieth century, that a class of educated middle class intelligentsia began to initiate the step to re-write the history of Manipur which they aimed to be scientific. A little time can be given here on how the western education impregnated a class of western educated intelligentsia and the role they played.

The first half of the twentieth century could well be conceded as the turning point of modern Manipur characterized by an innate urge for transition from traditionalism and orthodoxy to democracy and modernity.[23] Of the various factors which had played roles in heralding new ideas, modern western education played a key role. The western modern education in the state was initiated in 1872 under the banner of the Political Agency that was basically aimed at providing rudimentary school teaching to the children of the British employees.[24] An old primary school is recorded to have been managed by the first Political Agent, Captain Gordon (1835-44). But it soon dried up. With the coming of the Johnstone Middle English School under the personal initiative of Sir James Johnstone (Political Agent, 1877-86) in 1885, the formal education arrived in the state. Next decades witnessed a gradual expansion and standardization of primary and junior level education.

The western education created a class of educated natives to serve in the native steel frame of the state. Irrespective of serving in the state service or not, what is but seen as a result of western education is the impregnation of the native intelligentsia with reformative minds. Reading the available early twentieth century works by the Manipuri scholars, readers will certainly find the intellectual anxieties of those scholars to dig up the rich cultural heritage and investigate the past. The formation of the Nikhil Hindu Manipuri Mahasabha and later the Nikhil Manipur Mashasabha can be testified as a platform for the purpose. Reading the resolutions of the sessions of Mahasabha, one finds the concerns of reforms in the state. A very important concern of the Mahasabha as such was to write or re-write the history of Manipur.

It was, more specifically, after the Second World War that the historical writings in better academic sense have sprung up. Written in Manipuri, R.K. Sanahal's *Manipur Itihas* (1947)[25] is a forerunner. Then came, Jyotirmoy Roy's *History of Manipur* (1958)[26] which is written in historical framework and is first of its kind in the historical writing of Manipur. After Jyotirmoy Roy, Iboongohal Singh came up at the scene with a mind to contribute something into the history of Manipur. The idea behind writing this paper is not intended to prove Iboongohal as a historian. This is simply to acknowledge him as someone who had not only shown his commitment to understand the history and culture of Manipur but also introduced it to the academic circle and the general readers as well. Here, an attempt is made to understand the history of this place by way of reading Iboonghohal's works.

Reading his works

Iboongohal Singh had about ten works (both English and Manipuri) to his credit. Some of them were published during his lifetime and which got reprinted later. Some are published posthumously. One manuscript is waiting for publication. The following shows a list of his works.

Published in lifetime

- *Babrubahanpokpa* (1932)
- *Nara Singh-Ava Ngamba* (1941)
- *Manipur* (1956)
- *Introduction to Manipur* (1960)
- *Meaning of Mayang* (1963)
- *Wari Ahumna Tamphasana* (1964)

Published posthumously

- edited *Cheitharol Kumbaba* (with N. Khelchandra Singh), Manipuri Sahitya Parishad, Imphal (1967)
- *Beginners Anglo-Manipuri Dictionary* (1969)
- *Yubaraj Tikendrajit* (1972)
- *Jeevan Charit* (1975)

Unpublished Manuscript

- *English Amashung Manipurda Culturegi Maramda Iba Lairikshing*

With the exception of *Introduction to Manipur* (1960) and *Meaning of Mayang* (1963), all his works are in Manipuri. Among his works, *Babrubahanpokpa* (1932) written in Manipuri was his first attempt. It is a play. It was originally written in 1925. It was first staged in the same year at the royal palace.[27] In the strict sense, two crucial stories are built up in the play. Firstly, Manipur was created by the Lord Mahadev. The second element that is the crux of the drama is on the Aryanization of Manipur. The story goes on narrating the marriage of the Pandava prince Arjun with the Gandharbha princess of Manipur named Chitrangada and the birth of their son called Babrubahan. Then, the story is about separation of Arjuna (his return to Hastinapur) from Chitrangada and then their finale re-union along with their son, Babrubahan. The plots of the drama are weaved around to support that the Manipuris are descendants of the Pandava and the Gandharva.

Nara Singh-Awa Ngamba (1941) is another drama in Manipuri which was originally written while Iboonghohal was reading in the first year of his Law. The drama was first staged on 30 September 1925 at the royal palace.[28] Literally meant, conqueror of Awa

(Burma), the drama highlights the personality and role of the prince, Nara Singh. The plot of the drama is set at the backdrop of the seven years of Burmese rein in Manipur (1819-26). Nara Singh had shown his valour to liberate the soil of Manipur from Burmese imperial yoke. Both the two dramas cannot be totally historic, but the dramas based on history.[29]

Cheitharol Kumbaba (1967) is the royal chronicle of the Meitei kings of Manipur. All the royal records were written and preserved in the school of royal priests. Iboongohal (along with N. Khelchandra Singh) edited and submitted the final form of the *Cheihtarol Kumbaba* for publication to the Manipuri Sahitya Parishad in 1965. It was published in 1967 (subsequent reprints henceforth). Despite criticisms from the modern scholars, this edited chronicle is still extensively used as a source of historical research.[30]

In his *Manipur* (1957), Iboongohal shows the creation of Manipur by the Lord Mahadev. Secondly, he tries to analyse the Meiteis as originated from the Pandava and the Gandharva. In the religious life, his writing shows that the Meities began to adopt Hinduism during the reign of king Charairongba (even before the king Garibniwaj). In the line of his religious *guru*, Atombapu Sharma, he sees the existence of Vedic religion before the arrival of Hinduism in Manipur.

Iboongohal's autobiography *Jeevan Charit* (1975), in contrast with earlier writings in Manipuri, is written in lucid language but is also informative. The beauty of the autobiography is how the autobiographer consciously or unconsciously portrayed the past of his period in such a manner that it enlightens us much more. Readers will have an idea of the socio-economic and political conditions of the time. The photographs themselves show the multi traited personality of Iboongohal Singh.

English Amashung Manipurda Culturegi Maramda Iba Lairikshing (work on the culture of Manipur in English and Manipuri) is in manuscript waiting for publication. Once published, the work is sure to prove handy to the researchers on Manipur for ready references.

Among his writings, it is his *Introduction to Manipur* (1960) which makes him to be known to all. In the field of historical research, after Jyotirmoy Roy, it was Iboongohal Singh who contributed through this book. This is his first attempt in English. The title appears to be aptly selected but the work in the real sense introduces Manipur to both inside and outside readers. This work is still used as a valuable source by the present researchers. The famous indologist and linguist, Suniti Kumar Chatterji observed that in this work "….. some of the chapters are full of new information and are very valuable from the historical as well as from the cultural stand-point."[31]

When Iboongohal wrote his work in the beginning of the second half of the twentieth century, the writings on the history of Manipur, if not non-existent at all, were comparatively meager. Iboongohal Singh was a pioneer on the two specific senses. Firstly, his work (1960) can be described as one of the two pioneering writings on the history of Manipur[32] in

English in comprehensive way.[33] Secondly, he introduced through his work the history of this place to the outside readers. Iboongohal was not professionally trained in academic history, but a keen enthusiast in historical research. This reminds us of what E.P. Thompson (1924-93) says, 'history is not simply the property of academic historians'.[34] His long association with the learned pandits of his time, his own interest in history impinged him to the vistas of historical investigation. His interest in historical research can be well substantiated by the fact that he held the presidentship of the Manipur Historical Research Society (1950-54). He was one of the pioneers from the state who had spent time reading and collecting materials from the National Archives of India (May 1966). Readers reading his autobiography will find his photographs showing him spending time in going through records in the said archives. Despite all these, the interesting point is that his work came out to be a forerunner and was published at a time when every reader was eagerly awaiting for a book on the history of Manipur. As Birinchikumar Barua writes, "I was looking eagerly for a book on Manipur like this introduction. You deserve all our good whishes and appreciation for the present publication."[35] His work became not only a widely read book on the history of Manipur by the outside readers but also highly acclaimed one. P.C. Matheo, one time Chief Commissioner of Manipur commented, "it makes most interesting and instructive reading and the subject matter is such that you are one of the best qualified persons to write…."[36]

It appears that the historical knowledge of Iboongohal Singh was largely shaped by that dominant trend of historiography which was contributed at large by Atombapu Sharma, the prolific vaishnavite scholar. This line of scholarship on analyzing the history of Manipur, according to E. Nilakanta Singh, is 'Vedic centric approach'.[37] This dominant trend continuously persisted for a long time. Similarly, Iboongohal's line of argument weaves around the said Aryan theory of the origin of the Manipuris. His writings show that Iboongohal Singh belonged to the school of vaishnavite scholarship. He begins his analysis on the history of Manipur by discarding the notion that the name of this place was given Manipur at the peak hour of Hinduisation in the 18th century. Rather, he sees the naming episode of Manipur long before the 18th century. He convincingly takes the help of *Janasruti* tradition in his attempt to explain the naming of this place as Manipur. He writes:

> — *Janasruti* prevalent among us cannot be false. The *Janasruti* is that Siva and Durga danced together with their companions seeing the natural beauty of Manipur. Being pleased with the sight, Lord Ananta spread gems from his head. Manipur was looking bright by virtue of the existence of the gems. Then the name of the country was given Manipur by Siva.[38]

He candidly challenges the opinion that attaches the naming of Manipur with the advent of Hinduism. He asserts:

> It seems to me that the new historians are trying to create another new theory of the history of Manipur. Otherwise please come forward bravely and tell and point out with sufficient proofs that the name of our country Manipur is called after the coming of Hinduism in Manipur.[39]

Iboongohal goes on arguing that the present Manipur is mentioned in the *Mahabharata*. It reminds the *Ashwamedha* episode of the *Mahabharata*. It runs that Babrubahan was the son of Arjuna, the great Pandava of Hastinapur and Chitrangada, the Manipuri Princess of the Gandharbha dynasty of Manipur. Babrubahan held the *Ashwamedha* horse of Arjun in captive. In search of his horse, Arjun fought battle with Babrubahan. In the battle, Arjun was killed by Babrubahan. As advised by the Lord Krishna, Babrubahan brought gem from the *patal* and Arjun was brought to life again. The battle, as narrated, was fought at Lamphel.[40] The Manipuris, on the basis of this theory, were projected as the descendants of Babrubahan. To continue his argument, Iboongohal is bold enough to comment that contrast began to be heard of. According to him, "such statements made by others who do not have thorough knowledge of Manipur can not and will not change our true ancestral line from where we are coming down."[41]

He continuously puts:

> I am afraid that the so called historians are trying to alter the history of our Manipur according to their own will. Oh young historian if you want to know the actual facts and incidents that happen in our Manipur then come to us and ask about the incidents happened in Manipur.[42]

Still, a pertinent question remains. Was Manipur of the *Mahabharata* the present Manipur? It has been challenged by many scholars.[43] Does the state chronicle narrate this point? Do the religious beliefs and practices of the people of that time support it? All these different propositions reflect an attempt of antiquitising the Hinduised belief system in the Manipur valley.

As a historian

It may be said that Iboongohal Singh was not professionally trained in academic history. He may not be necessarily a historian per in the strict modern sense. But, he may, unquestionably, be seen as a one of the pioneers who had contributed in the field of historical research of Manipur. It can be rightly established that Iboongohal Singh, without any question, was a keen enthusiast who actively engaged in his attempt to understand and contribute in the history of Manipur. He says, "I have been contemplating to write a book about Manipur for which I have been collecting materials for the last many years".[44] His sense of the history of Manipur, as one finds, has been largely shaped by a combination of the oral narratives transmitted throughout generations and his own research (that is based on his personal reading of the available writings and discussion with the learned local pundits of his time). Despite all these, an interesting point is that the writings of Iboongohal Singh not only show his firm belief in that approach of historical studies i.e., Vedic or Aryan, but he also, in the meantime, absolutely employs the same approach.

Notes & References

1. A.C. Banerjee, *Eastern Frontier of British India 1784-1826*, A. Mukherji & Co., Calcutta, 1943.
2. Lairenmayum Iboongohal Singh, *Introduction to Manipur*, Imphal, 1960, *preface*.

3. R.B. Pemberton, *The Eastern Frontier of India*, Mittal Publications, New Delhi, 2000 (1st edn., *The Report on the Eastern Frontier of British India*, Bengal Govt. Press, Calcutta, 1835; Reprint DHAS, Gauhati, 1966).
4. W. McCulloch, *An Account of the Valley of Manipur*, Gian Publications, Delhi, 1980 (1st edn. Calcutta, 1859).
5. R. Brown, *Statistical Account of Manipur*, Sanskaran Prakashak, Delhi, 1975 (1st ed. London, 1874).
6. Alexander Mackenzie, *The North-East Frontier of India*, Mittal Publications, New Delhi, 1995 (1st edn. *History of the Relations of the Government with Hill Tribes on the North-East Frontier of Bengal*, Calcutta, 1884).
7. E.W. Dun, *Gazetteer of Manipur*, Manas Publishing House, Delhi, 1992 (1st edn. London, 1875).
8. James Johnstone, *Manpur and the Naga Hills*, Gian Publishing House, Delhi, 2002, (1st edn.Calcutta, 1896).
9. T.C. Hodson, *The Meithies*, Neeraj Publishing House, Delhi, 1984 (1st edn. London, 1908); *The Naga Tribes of Manipur*, Low Price Publications, Delhi, 2007 (1st edn. London, 1911).
10. L. Iboongohal Singh and N. Khelchandra Singh, *Cheitharol Kumbaba,* Manipuri Sahitya Parishad, Imphal, 1967, Nithor Nath Banerjee (1904), *Manipur Diary* (Microfilm), Manipur State Archives, Imphal..
11. Lairenmayum Iboongohal Singh, in the said preface of his *Introduction to Manipur*, simply mentions the 'works', but does not spell out the works of Atombapu Sharma. For a detailed profile of works by Atombapu Sharma, see. E. Nilakanta Singh, *Pandit Atombapu Sharma*, Sahitya Akademi, New Delhi, 1998, pp. 39-42.
12. There were already some vernacular writings in the ways of contributing towards the history of Manipur, but Iboongohal Singh had missed out from mentioning them in his preface to *Introduction to Manipur*. These writings in vernacular are mentioned in the text of this paper.
13. Lairenmayum Iboongohal Singh, *Introduction to Manipur*, Imphal, 1960, *preface*.
14. Gangmumei Kamei, *On History and Historiography of Manipur*, Akansha Publishing House, New Delhi, 2006, pp. 23-24; N. Khelchandra Singh, *Ariba Manipuri Sahityagi Itihas*, Imphal, 1969.
15. Atombapu Sharma, *Haree Mayee*, Imapal, 1930.
16. Haodijam Chaitanya, *Manipur Itihas*, Imphal, 1890.
17. Gangmumei Kamei, *On History and Historiography of Manipur*, *op.cit*, p.25
18. P. Parijat Singh, *Manipur Purabritta*, Imphal, 1917.
19. K. Kaomacha, *Manipur Ittibritti*, Imphal, 1938.
20. M. Jhulan Singh, *Manipur Itihas*, Imphal, 1939.
21. Atombabu Sharma, *Manipur Itihas,* Imphal, 1940; *Pakhangba*, Imphal, 1952.
22. W. Yumjao Singh, *Manipur Itihas*, Imphal, 1946.
23. R.K. Mani, *Khwairakpam Chaoba Singh*, Sahitya Akademi, New Delhi, 2002, p. 1.
24. Major General W.F. Nuthal, Political Agent of Manipur, established a vernacular school in Imphal in 1872.

25. R.K. Sanahal, *Manipur Itihas*, Imphal, 1947.
26. Jyotirmoy Roy, *History of Manipur*, Eastlight Book House, Calcutta, 1958.
27. Lairenmayum Iboongohal Singh, *Jeevan Charita*, Imphal, 2008 (1st edn. 1975), p .69.
28. Lairenmayum Iboongohal Singh, *Nara Singh- Awa Ngamba*, Imphal, 1941, *Bhumika*.
29. Pandit Atombapu Sharma goes to the extent of saying the *Nara Singh-Awa Ngamba* a 'historic drama'. These two dramas were prescribed for matriculation under the Calcutta University.
30. Now state chronicle in English are also available in the market. See L..Joychandra, *The Lost Kingdom – Royal Chronicle of Manipur*, Prajatantra Publishing House, Imphal, 1995 and Saroj Nalini Arambam Parratt, *The Court Chronicle of the Kings of Manipur: The Cheitharon Kumpapa,* Routledge, New York, 2005.
31. Letter to L. Iboongohal.
32. R.K. Jhalajit, *A Short History of Manipur* (Imphal, 1965), is another forerunner in the fray.
33. Before, there were already a few writings on the history of Manipur both in vernacular and English. But, they stand scattered and incomplete.
34. Marnie Hughes-Warrington, *Fifty Great Thinkers on History*, Routledge, London, 2004, p. 311.
35. Letter to L. Iboongohal.
36. Letter to L. Iboongohal.
37. E. Nilakanta Singh, *Pandit Atombapu Sharma*, Sahitya Akademi, New Delhi, 1998, *proloque.*
38. Lairenmayum Iboongohal Singh, *Manipur*, Imphal, 1957, pp. 11-12.
39. English translation of some portions of *Manipur*, p. 17.
40. Identification of 'Manipur of the *Mahabharata*' with the present Manipur has been a debate. While R. C. Majumdar favours it, Dr. Cunningham and E.W. Gait locate 'Manipur of the *Mahabharata*' is somewhere in Kalinga (Orissa). See R.C. Majumdar, *Expansion of Aryan Culture in North Eastern India*, Imphal, 1996, pp. 43-45; Suniti Kumar Chatterji, 'Kirata Jana Kriti: Contribution of the Indo Mongoloid People to Indian Culture', *Journal of the Asiatic Society of Bengal*, 16:2 (1950); R.K. Jhalajit, *Manipur*, Publications Divisions, Ministry of Information and Broadcasting, Govt. of India, New Delhi, 1975; *A History of Manipuri Literature*, Imphal, 1987; *A Short History of Manipur*, Imphal, 1965; E. Nilakanta Singh, 'Ramayana in Manipuri Literature and Folklore', *Quarterly Journal*, Vol. 2:2 (1976).
41. Lairenmayum Iboongohal Singh ,*Manipur*, Imphal, 1957, pp. 5-6.
42. *Ibid*, pp. 17-18
43. For example, see J. Roy, *History of Manipur*, Calcutta, 1958, p. 4.
44. Lairenmayum Iboongohal Singh, *Introduction to Manipur*, Imphal, 1960, *preface*.

[**Acknowledgement:** I must thank Lairenmayum Hemango Singh (son of late Lairenmayum Iboongohal Singh) for providing me the works of Lairenmayum Iboongohal Singh and allowing some papers preserved in the family. Co-operation from his family members is gratefully acknowledged.]

11

Moidul Islam Bora (1899-1944)

—Anowar Hussain

Biographical Sketch

In the world of contemporary Assamese history and literature, Moidul Islam Bora is remembered for his scholarship in Persian language and literature and medieval Indian history and for the distinction of being the first Doctorate among the Assamese in London University. He embodied the ethos of his people, possessed a highly inquisitive mind and contributed immensely in enriching the history, literature and culture of Assam. Born on 22 September, 1899 at Jengonikatia village in the outskirts of Sibsagar town, Bora had his early education in Sibsagar and did his Matriculation of the Calcutta University from Sibsagar Govt. High School in 1917 in first division, got a scholarship, and took admission in Cotton College, Guwahati. He passed B. A. in 1921 with Honours in Persian and again qualified for a scholarship for post-graduate studies. He took admission at the newly established Dacca University for his post-graduation in Persian language and literature. He obtained the first class first position in M A in 1923 and at the same time completed Bachelor of Law (BL) from the Dacca University. As a student Bora had impressed his teachers so much that immediately after his M. A. he was appointed as a Lecturer in the Department of Persian at the same University. In 1929, he proceeded to London for his doctoral research in the School of Oriental and African Studies (SOAS) in London University under the guidance of a renowned Persian scholar, Sir Edward Dennison Ross. His topic of doctoral research was "Life and Works of Amir Hassan Dihalve". He completed his work within the stipulated period of two years and was awarded Ph.D. by the London University in 1931. He had the distinction of being the first amongst the Assamese people to receive the Degree of Doctor of Philosophy from the London University. In this glory he was followed by a galaxy of renowned Assamese scholars consisting of the legends like Suryya Kumar Bhuyan, Birinchi Kumar Barua, Heramba Kanta Barpujari and others who also successfully pursued their Ph. D. works in the same University.

After completing his Ph. D. at the London University, Moidul Islam Bora returned to India and once again joined the faculty of the Dacca University. He continued to teach in the department of Persian and Urdu, but closely interacted with the department of history which had in its faculty at that time some of the stalwarts of medieval Indian studies like Sir Jadunath Sarkar, K.R. Quanungo and S.N. Bhattacharyya. A good number of students from East Bengal and Assam did their doctoral research in Persian literature and medieval Indian history under his supervision. It was due to his scholarly genius and efficiency that Moidul Islam Bora became the Professor and Head of the Department of Persian and Urdu in the same University at a comparatively young age. He also helped his University from time to time by temporarily holding administrative positions, in addition to his normal assignment in the department of Persian and Urdu, and in 1943-44, served for a brief period as the officiating Vice-Chancellor of the University.

Despite his deep involvement in his service away from home at the Dacca University in East Bengal, Bora maintained regular contacts with home and actively participated in literary and cultural life of Assam. He delivered the Pratibha Devi Memorial Lectures at Guwahati in 1935 and presided over the eighteenth session of Asom Sahitya Sabha at Jorhat in 1940. Bora died prematurely at the age of 45 on 5 May 1944. On his death, Assam lost a great literary genius and a brilliant scholar who would have contributed much more to the intellectual life and study of literature, culture and history of Assam.[1]

Contributions to history

Moidul Islam Bora taught Persian language and literature at the Dacca University and did his doctoral research at the London University under the supervision of a renowned Persian scholar, Sir Edward Dennison Ross, who was then a Professor in the School of Asian and African Studies, London University. Bora's doctoral dissertation was on the 'Life and Works of Amir Hassan Dihalve', a giant of Persian literature of his time. The doctoral thesis of Bora was, later on, published in an abridged form in the *Journal of the Asiatic Society of Bengal* (Calcutta) in 1941 and it bears the stamp of his scholarship in medieval Indian history as well.

The study of Persian naturally made Bora interested in medieval Indian history and culture. In fact, he had extensively studied the medieval Indian history and the history of Assam. During his stay in London he took up the work of translating *Baharistan-I-Ghayabi*, originally written in Persian by Mirza Nathan, which is a chronicle of the Mughal invasions against Coach Behar, Assam and Cachar and a very important source book for the history of medieval Northeast India. Bora did the translation under the able guidance of his supervisor Sir Edward Dennison Ross. Later on, he edited and published the work in two volumes.[2] It was indeed a monumental work of M. I. Bora which is being used by the historians for studying Assam and Bengal in the medieval period. Though he was a scholar of Persian language and literature, this work shows that Bora was equally interested in history and he had earned remarkable knowledge and expertise in the medieval history of India, including Bengal and the Northeast.

The translation of *Baharistan-I-Ghayabi* was a difficult task. The only extant copy of the manuscript was available in the Biblotheca National of Paris. Bora had to work hard to translate and then to edit and get the chronicle published. The *Baharistan-I-Ghayabi*, translated by Bora, is indeed invaluable as a mine of information for the students of Mughal history, as it vividly projects the details of the hostilities of the Mughals with Assam, Bengal and Orissa during the first three decades of the seventeenth century. The minute details of the political conditions in the Ahom and Koch kingdoms, their relations with the Mughals, minor skirmishes as well as significant wars, and side-lights on social and economic organizations of the areas, are of great value for interpreting the history of Assam and Northern Bengal during that period. As regards the war tactics of the 'Assamese', for example, it said, "it is the custom of the Assamese that whenever they engage in a war they perform some sorceries a day previous to the battle. In this way, they send some magic object floating down the river towards the enemies' side. If it floats down towards the enemies' side they take it as a good omen. If it travels up stream of its own accord, they take it as foreboding something against them and consider it as a sign of their defeat and they do not go out for battle."[3] Bora's use of the word 'Assamese' in this translation is significantly indicative of his pride in own identity. His translations with notes and annotations became helpful for the historians to use the chronicle as an important source of information in their works. The great masters of medieval Indian history drew the source materials from this chronicle in their works on Bengal and Assam. Sir Edward Gait in second edition of his *A History of Assam* had used Sir Jadunath Sarkar's translation of the *Baharistan-I-Ghaybi*.[4] S.N. Bhattacharyya's *History of North-East Frontier Policy of the Mughals* (1929) was largely based on *Baharistan-I-Ghaybi* and other Persian sources.[5] However, the publication of Bora's translation in 1936 made *Baharistan-I-Ghaybi* handy as a source-book and the historians made extensive use of the work. The historians who worked on aspects of the history of medieval Assam, including Suryya Kumar Bhuyan and Jagadish Narayan Sarkar, found the work indispensable. S.C. Dutta extensively used it in his *North-East and the Mughals*.[6] J.B. Bhattacharjee identified the route of Mughal operations against the Kachari kingdom of Maibong, from Dhaka via Sylhet and Cachar, on the basis of Bora's translation of *Baharistan-I-Ghaybi*.[7] For this outstanding translation work of *Baharistan-I-Ghaybi*, the well known historian S.K. Bhuyan, in his 'preface' to the publication, said, "it is a matter of special gratification that the present translator, an Assamese by birth, employed his Persian scholarship in translating this valuable source book of his country's history, for there will be men all over the world to expound the mysticism of Sufi poets or delineate the scholarly zeal of Abbasids but who will exert the past history of Assam except her own children."[8] Bhuyan had also observed that the publication of the *Baharistan-i-Ghaybi* constituted a distinct landmark in the history of the Department of Historical and Antiquarian Studies, Assam.[9] Mohamad Taher, a well known geographer, also paid glowing tributes to Bora's knowledge of Assam and his scholarship.[10]

Bora's knowledge of the history of Assam, particularly the sources of medieval history, became evident in the 'Pratibha Devi Memorial Lecture'[11] which he delivered in November 1935 at Cotton College, Guwahati. The topic of the lecture was *History of Assam as told by the Muslim Historians*. In this lecture, he dwelt on the history of Assam, sources for study of the political contacts between Assam and the Muslim rulers of Delhi, and the people of Assam as depicted in the famous Persian chronicle *Baharistan-I-Ghaybi*. The lecture was divided into five parts; viz. (i) (a) Sources of study, and (b) Pre-Mughal relations (of the Delhi Sultanate) with Assam; (ii) Mughal relations with Assam during the reigns of Akbar and Jahangir; (iii) Mughal's hostility with the Ahoms during the time of Jahangir; (iv) Mughal relations during the reigns of Shahjahan and Aurangzeb; and (v) An account of the country (Assam) and its people. Commenting on the lecture, S.K. Bhuyan remarked that Bora had earned a unique distinction by harnessing his Persian scholarship in the unfurling of past history of Assam.[12]

Bora seems to have written some articles in journals and periodicals in English and Assamese, most of which, unfortunately, are no longer accessible to scholars as those were not systematically preserved in any particular location. His "*Asomiyar Ranabal*", which was published in *Asom Sahitya Sabha Patrika* (1929), is a valuable research paper on the war tactics and strategies of the Assamese forces in the seventeenth century. In this article Bora narrated Mir Jumla's Assam invasion, in particular, and other Mughal invasions against Assam and the resistance of the Assamese soldiers in different strategic points, and the construction of forts like Jogighopa, Saraighat, Srighat, Pandu, Chandhara and Simalagarh.. But despite such all out resistance and also the superiority of the Ahom naval forces, Mir Jumla was able to reach and torment the Ahom capital at Garhgaon. To this effect, Bora drew his conclusion that Mir Jumla was the only one Mughal general to achieve this success in his campaign against Assam and, according to him, it was due to the lack of leadership in Assam at that point of time.[13]

Bora also wrote an article in the journal of Asom Chhatra Sanmilan entitled "Hindu-Muslim unity from the cultural point of view". Some of his writings were extracted and included in the souvenir published on the occasion of his birth centenary.[14] However, at least two of his important manuscripts in history, namely, 'Immigration of Persian Poets to Bengal' and 'Jahangir, the man' have not yet been published. He also wrote a book on 'Nature of Persian Language: written and spoken in India during the 13th and 14th Centuries'.[15]

As a historian

Moidul Islam Bora was a scholar of Persian language and literature, but his interest and contributions in history were also significant. The knowledge of Persian enabled him to critically examine the original sources of the history of medieval Assam, besides those in Assamese, and in that area of Assam's history he made spectacular contribution. The translation of *Baharistan-I-Ghaybi* made him well known all over India and it was also his greatest contribution to historical studies in Assam. He seems to have been the first Persian scholar from Northeast India to become a Professor of Persian in a university outside the region and to have translated into English a major Persian chronicle of India, namely, *Baharistan-I-Ghaybi*, without which the sources of history of medieval Northeast India would have been much poorer. His *History of Assam as told by the Muslim Historians*, which he delivered as Pratibha Devi Memorial Lectures in 1935, covered the entire medieval period of Assam's history and focused on the Persian sources which could be used by the historians for further studies in future along with the Ahom and Assamese sources preserved in local *Buranjis*. These contributions in the field of history genuinely earned him the recognition as a historian of medieval Assam.

While presiding over the eighteenth session of the Asom Sahitya Sabha, at Jorhat, in 1940, Bora in his address emphasized the importance of historical research and invited the young generation to engage in historical research and to contribute towards strengthening the regional history of Assam. In his deliberation at the session, he stressed that politics and social work should go simultaneously for the progress of the country and that history always plays a key role in politics and society. He insisted that history was the essential tool to build a strong society in Assam and for the socio-economic and cultural development of the Assamese people. Although the Persian chronicles and local *Buranjis* were invaluable sources of medieval history, Bora believed that folklore and other oral materials also could be important sources of history and that Assam, in particular, has a vigorous tradition of preserving those sources. The oral sources, according to him, included the folk tales, folk songs, *Borgeet*, *Baulgeet*, *Ghajirgeet*, and old *puthis* (hand written manuscripts), which were lying scattered in different nook and corner of the state. Therefore, he made a strong plea for the collection of such materials and their publication, which, he believed, would definitely throw new light in writing history of medieval Assam. Bora also saw the close relationship between history and literature and wanted the historians of Assam to explore literature, both written and oral, for source materials and insights in writing history.[16] It is said that in case of writing history, Bora was greatly influenced by the works of the Assamese literary giant Lakshminath Bezbaruah. Rai Bahadur Kanaklal Barua, an eminent historian and littérateur of Assam, also inspired him to contribute to the cultural development of Assam by writing history and thereafter, he dedicated himself to the task of resurrecting the history of medieval Assam.[17]

Notes & References

1. Jogeshwar Nath Goswami, "*Dr. Moidul Islam Borar Prati Sradhanjali*", in *Dr. Moidul Islam Bora Birth Centenary Souvenir*, Dr. Moidul Islam Bora Birth Centenary Celebration Committee, Dibrugarh, Assam, Lakhimi Press, Dibrugarh, 2000; Anowar Hussain, "Dr. Moidul Islam Bora : Contribution to the Writing of History with special reference to the History of Medieval Assam", *Proceedings of North East India History Association*, 23rd Session, Agartala, 2002, pp. 92-98.
2. M.I. Bora (trans. & ed.), *Baharistan-I-Ghayabi*, 2 vols., Department of Historical and Antiquarian Studies, Govt. of Assam, Gauhati, 1936, reprinted Guwahati, 1992.
3. *Ibid*, vol. ii, p. 487.
4. Edward Gait, *A History of Assam*, 1st edn. London, 1906, 2nd revised and enlarged edn., Thacker Sprink & Co., Calcutta, 1926, see 'Preface'.
5. S.N. Bhattacharyya, *History of North-East Frontier Policy of the Mughals*, Calcutta, 1929.
6. S.C. Dutta, *The North-East and the Mughals*, D.K. Publishers, New Delhi, 1984.

7. J.B. Bhattacharjee, "Miza Nathan's Kachar", *Social Research*, Vol. 2, No. 3, July-September, 1982.

8. See Dr. S.K. Bhuyan's 'Preface' to M.I. Bora (trans. & ed.), *Baharistan-I-Ghayabi*, Department of Historical and Antiquarian Studies, Govt. of Assam, Gauhati, 1936.

9. *Ibid.*

10. Mohamad Taher, "*Dr. Moidul Islam Bora - Jivan Aru Pratibha*", in *Dr. Moidul Islam Bora Birth Centenary Souvenir*, Dr. Moidul Islam Bora Birth Centenary Celebration Committee, Dibrugarh, 2000.

11. Pratibha Devi was a great talent of Assamese literature, who breathed her last at the young age of only twenty-one. Her father, Sarat Chandra Goswami arranged a series of lectures in his daughter's memory known as *Pratibha Devi Memorial Lectures*. The lecture in the series was delivered by Dr. Moidul Islam Bora in 1935. See Jogendra Narayan Bhuyan, *Kriti Aru Smriti*, Guwahati, 1999. Dr. Moidul Islam Bora was possibly the first scholar to deliver the *Pratibha Devi Memorial Lectures*. The lectures in the series were subsequently delivered by some of the stalwarts of Indian history. For example, Dr. Suryya Kumar Bhuyan of Cotton College in 1941 and Dr. Nalini Kanta Bhattasali of Dacca University in 1944. The text of Bhuyan's lecture entitled *The Military System of the Assamese People* has been published as a booklet by Kamarupa Anusandhan Samiti, Guwahati (2010), while that of Bhattasali entitled "New Lights on the history of Assam" was published in *Indian Historical Quarterly* (vol. XXI, 1945, pp. 1-28).

12. Deepali Barua, "Dr. Moidul Islam Bora: A Scholar of Repute", in *Dr. Moidul Islam Bora Birth Centenary Souvenir*, Dr. Moidul Islam Bora Birth Centenary Celebration Committee, Dibrugarh, 2000.

13. Moidul Islam Bora, "*Asomiyar Ranabal*", *Asom Sahitya Sabha Pratika*, 3rd year, 6th edition, Jorhat, 1928-29.

14. *Dr. Moidul Islam Bora Birth Centenary Souvenir*, Dr. Moidul Islam Bora Birth Centenary Celebration Committee, Dibrugarh, 2000.

15. Information given by the grandson of Late Dr. M.I. Bora, who now stays in the Sibsagar residence of Dr. Bora.

16. *Sabhapatir Bhasan*, Asom Sahitya Sabha, Jorhat, 1940.

17. Biren Borkotoky, "Dr. Moidul Islam Bora", in Prem Gogoi (ed.), *Smriti Grantha*, Asom Sahitya Sabha, Sibsagar, 1999.

12

Rajmohan Nath (1899-1965)

—*Jayati Bhattacharjee*

Biographical Sketch

An engineer by education and profession but historian by passion and contribution, Rajmohan Nath was born in his ancestral village Rangauti in Hailakandi subdivision (now district) of undivided Cachar district of Assam in 1899. A brilliant student all through out his career, Rajmohan studied Sanskrit in a *Chatuspathi* in Hailakandi while he was a regular student in Victoria Memorial Govt. High School, Hailakandi. He passed Matriculation from the said high school in 1919 and I. Sc. from M.C. College, Sylhet in 1921, both in first division with merit scholarship, and B.E. from Bengal Engineering College (now University), Shibpur, Calcutta, in 1925, securing first position in first class. Beginning his career in Public Works Department, Govt. of Assam, in 1927 as an Assistant Engineer, he became Executive Engineer in 1942 and Superintending Engineer in 1947, and thereafter, served as Special Officer, Flood Control and River Training in 1954-55, Principal, Assam Civil Engineers' Institute, Jorhat, in 1955-56, and Special Officer, Technical Education Department, Govt. of Assam, in 1956-57, before his retirement from service in 1957. Nath became well known among the civil engineers in and outside Assam in 1942 by publication of the first edition of his *A Handbook for Civil Engineers*, the fourth edition of which came out in 1964 as *Nath's Handbook for Civil Engineers*.

A talented scholar by birth and widely read in a large number of subjects, like history, archaeology, literature, religion, philosophy, astrology, science and technology, one of his lectures on 'modern literature' at Srihatta Sahitya Parishad in 1946 is said to have been a souvenir of his knowledge across the disciplines. It was the inquisitive mind of an ardent devotee of scholarship that might have impelled Nath to study history, archaeology and culture of the local communities and collect visual empirical evidences from various sites during his tours and postings in different places in the undivided province of Assam and eventually use those for his major works like *The Background of Assamese Culture* (1948), *Glorious Assam* (1949) and *Anquities of Cachar* (1981), which deservingly earned him the fame of a historian of Northeast India. He presided over history session of the Asam Sahitya Sabha at Tinsukia in 1951, which was indeed a great recognition of his contributions in the field of history. In the printed cover page of some of the books authored by him 'B.E., Tattabhushan' followed the name of the author. This *Tattvabhushan* is an honorific title said to have been conferred on him by an organization of enlightened literati in Nabadweep for his extraordinary scholarship and stupendous knowledge in Indian heritage. The Rajmohan Nath Archaeological Garden at Jogijan, near Hojai, in Assam stands in his name and some of the master pieces of art objects of Assam discovered by him in the Kapili-Jamuna-Doiyang area are parked in this garden. Some of the ancient sculptures exhibited in the galleries of the Assam State Museum, Guwahati, were also recovered by Nath from nooks and corners of the state. He was a member of the planning and managing committee of this museum for many years and his personal efforts enormously enriched the collections for the museum. His *Glorious Assam* (1949) contains one hundred and thirty photographs of images and art objects that he had collected from various districts of Assam. The author of many books and large number of articles in English, Assamese and Bengali in a wide range of subjects, Rajmohan Nath passed away at his own residence (Mimosa Ridge) in Nongthymmai, Shillong, in 1965.[1]

Contributions to history

Rajmohan Nath wrote a large number of books and booklets in English, Assamese and Bengali on variety of topics, some of which were published posthumously and few more are yet to be published.[2] Of these, *The Background of Assamese Culture* (1948), *Glorious Assam* (1949), *A Clue to the Indus Valley Script and Civilisation* (1959), *The Background of Assamese Architecture* (1959), *Antiquity of the Kapili and the Jamuna valleys* (1981), *Antiquities of Cachar* (1981), and *Ruins of Na-Vanga* (1981) in English, *Bir Chilaray* (1940), *Sri Sri Sankardev-Madhavdev Charit* (1947), *Gauravmoy Asom* (1949), *Pandavgeeta aru Kamrupi Vaisnavgeeta* (1950), *Nathyogi Tattva* (1958), *Pragvaidik Kamrup* (1958), and *Kadali Rajya* (nd) in Assamese, and *Katapara Vamsa* (1941), *Kadali Rajya* (1941), *Asamer Katha O Kahini* (1945), *Sonadhaner Geet* (1947), *Sarparajni Manasa* (1957), *Gorokshabani*, vol. I (1958), *Nathyogi Tattva* (1958), *Bangiya Yogijatir Dikdarshan* (1960), *Mohenjodaror Lipi O Savyata* (1961), *Bangasanskriti O Nathpantha* (1961), *Yogijati* (1961), *Bangiya Nathsahitya* (1961), *Gopichandrer Gan* (1962), *Bangiya Nath Panther Prachin Puthi* (1964) in Bengali are essentially contributions to history, archaeology and cultural heritage of the Northeast. He also wrote some articles in newspapers and weeklies and presented papers in seminars and conferences.[3] However, his *The Background of Assamese Culture* (1948) is the *magnum opus* which covered the historical legends, origin myths and cultural heritage of almost all the areas and tribes and communities inhabiting different parts of erstwhile British Assam and its neighbourhood.[4] The *Glorious Assam* (1949), and its Assamese version, *Gauravmoy Asom*, published in the same year, is in the nature of a pictorial album of important monuments and sculptures, with scholarly notes and annotations by the author that are useful guides for further studies.[5] The articles and booklets on antiquities and ruins of Kapili and Jamuna valleys and Na-Vanga are also source books for the same reason. The *Antiquities of Cachar* (1981) is another significant contribution which not only describes the details of almost all the major pre-historic and archaeological sites in the Barak valley or erstwhile Cachar but also discusses the historical background of the sites preserved in myths and legends as well as the literary references.[6] His last major work was a history of Cachar in Bengali.*

The articles written by Rajmohan Nath were on a variety of subjects.[7] He was a member of the Indian History Congress and actively participated in some of its sessions. His article "The Background of Assamese Architecture" was published in the souvenir of the Guwahati session (1959) entitled *Heritage of Assam*, edited by H.K. Barpujari.[8] He also presented a paper in the same session entitled "A Clue to the Indus Valley Script and Civilisation".[9] In the next session at Aligarh, he presented "Two Seals of Lothal".[10] In Kamarupa Anusandhan Samiti also Nath's involvement was very intimate. In the Samiti's journal, called *Journal of Assam Research Society* (*JARS*), he was a regular contributor for many years. "Ruins of the Siva temple at Numaligarh",[11] "Mohenjodaro and Nathism",[12] "Digaroo Plates",[13] "Sankaracharyya and Buddhism in Assam",[14] "Kalapahar and the Kamakhya temple",[15] "Notes on certain words in the Nidhanpur Copper Plate",[16] "Cachar and Hidimba",[17] "Antiquities of the Kapili and Jamuna Valleys – Durjaya and Varasana, Sitajakhala, Mahadeosal, Vasundhari, Matharbori, Changchowki, Kawaimari, Jugijan, Amtala, Gosainjuri, Gachtol, Daboka, Mikirati, Akashiganga, Urdhangang, Badaganga, Mahamaya temple, Pudgosain Sthan, Hojai and Odddiyana",[18] "Dates of the Bhatera Copper Plates",[19] "Ancient Remains at Singri in Darrang",[20] "Early Vaisnavism in Kamrup",[21] "Worship of the Jackal and the Dog in India",[22] "Further Antiquities of the Kapili and Jamuna Valleys - Mondauga",[23] "Kondoli and the Kapili Kingdom",[24] "Luipada and Matsyendra Nath",[25] "Ruins at Na-Bhanga",[26] "Antiquities of the Kapili and the Jamuna Valleys – Bhoi Parbat, Ganesh Parbat, Teteli Pukhuri, Tarab",[27] "The Deopani Ruins"[28]

---

* Rajmohan Nath wrote a book on history of Cachar in Bengali, entitled *Kacharer Itihas*, which was under print in a press in Calcutta at the time of his death in 1965. The proof copy of 176 pages (eleven forma), received and seen by him, was in his house in Shillong. The 176th page ends abruptly in the midst of seventh chapter of the book while discussing the reign of Heramba king Krishnachandra (1780-1813). The book begins with a geographical description of Cachar and its neighbourhood, first five chapters are on history of the Cachar plains before the hegemony of the Heramba Dynasty extended to the area, discussing the legendary period and early inhabitants and rule of the Tripuri, Samatata, Kamarupa, Chandra and Srihatta kings, and sixth and the incomplete seventh chapter are on Heramba rule. Those printed pages were handed over to the editor of this volume by Mrs. Bharati Nath (wife of Late Rajmohan Nath) and their youngest son Anjan Nath sometime in early eighties to explore the possibility of updating and publishing the book. The Research India Publications, Calcutta, agreed to undertake the publication subject to completion of formality, while Anjan offered to buy two hundred copies for his family, relatives and friends once the book is published. With the help of Dr. Amalendu Guha (then a Professor in CSSS, Calcutta) and the West Bengal Publishers Guild attempts were made to recover the manuscript from the press or at least to obtain 'no objection' for reprinting elsewhere. It transpired in the process that the printing work was stopped due to some disputes which could not be resolved due to failing health and sudden demise of the author. In the meantime, the manuscript was also possibly lost from the press. It is indeed sad that things did not move beyond. The printed portion of 176 pages is still carefully preserved in possession of the editor of this volume with the hope that some way out can be found some day. [*Editor's Addendum]

are amongst his papers published in *Journal of Assam Research Society*. As it may be evident from the titles and contents all these papers were relevant to history, archeology and culture of Northeast India and most of these were based on primary data that he gathered from the field. It appears from his different bibliographies that some of these articles were also re-issued as booklets.[29] In *Srihatta Sahitya Parishat Patrika*, he contributed at least seven articles in Bengali[30] and amongst those *"Tantric Dharmer Prachinatva"*[31] and *"Prachin Kamruper Shasanniti"*[32] are important for understanding Rajmohan Nath as a historian of the region. Similarly, he contributed a large number of articles in Assamese in *Asom Sahitya Sabha Patrika* and other journals and periodicals.[33] *"Kachari Rajya"*,[34] *"Prachin Kamrupat Kaivarta"*,[35] *"Bhismaknagar"*,[36] *"Mahamanikya"*,[37] *"Gachtalar Shilalipi"*,[38] *"Kamakhyat Shhikguru Tegbahadur"*, [39] *"Balavarmadevar Tamrashasan"*,[40] etc published in *Asom Sahitya Sabha Patrika* are in the field of history and archaeology. He also contributed some papers in reputed national level research journals, amongst which "Chronology of Kamarupa Kings"[41] in *Indian Culture* deserves special mention.

Nath seems to have written a large number of popular articles on historical and cultural themes in daily and weekly newspapers. Among those a series of fourteen articles in *Organiser* was on culture and civilization, religion and related practices in ancient India.[42] He wrote "The Black Art of Assam"[43] and "Trade Routes in Ancient Kamrupa"[44] in *The Assam Tribune*, "Romance of the Tower of Monarai (Sylhet)"[45] in *The Sylhet Chronicle*, and "Northern Boundary of Assam – Archaeological proof of NEFA as Indian Boundary"[46] in *The Democratic Review*. He contradicted K.M. Munshi's views on 'Bhagawan Parasuram'[47] and 'Ancient Sages'[48] by letters to the editor in *Bhavan's Journal*, reviewed Hem Barua's *The Red River and the Blue Hill* in *Amrita Bazar Patrika*,[49] and wrote an article entitled "Kanaklal Barua as a Historian"[50] in *The Times of Assam* after the death of his former colleague in Kamarupa Anunsandhan Samiti, who was also the founder editor of *Journal of Assam Research Society* (*JARS*) and celebrated author of *Early History of Kamarupa* (1933). These are some of the examples of the commitment and concerns of Rajmohan Nath.

Finally, Rajmohan Nath emerged as a scholar of national repute in *The Cultural Heritage of India*, prepared and published by the Ramakrishna Mission Institute of Culture, Calcutta, under the Chairmanship of Sarvepalli Radhakrishnan. The editorial board of the four-volume series[51] was headed by Radhakrishnan and the contributors were the stalwarts of Indian history and culture like Haridas Bhattacharyya, R.C. Majumdar, Jadunath Sarkar, K.A. Nilakanta Sastri, S. Kumaraswami, K.R. Venkataraman, D.C. Sircar, V. Vengacharya, Kalidas Nag, Sukumar Sen, S. Sachidanandan Pillai, Suniti Kumar Chatterji, Nirmal Kumar Bose, A.D. Pulaskar and others whose names are still remembered with reverence by myriad of scholars in India and beyond. Only two scholars from the Northeast contributed in that monumental series – K.K. Handiqui and Rajmohan Nath. Handiqui's paper entitled "Classical Sanskrit as a Vehicle of Indian Culture" was included in Volume II and Nath contributed "Sankardeva and the Vaisnava Movement in Assam" in Volume IV. The later volume, in which Rajmohan Nath contributed his paper,[52] was on Religion and this volume was edited by the famous Indologist Haridas Bhattacharyya, while Bharatratna Bhagban Dass wrote an introduction for the volume. The fact that Rajmohan Nath found a place in that galaxy should be interpreted as an indication of his stature among the contemporary academic luminaries in the country of his time.

As a historian

A graduate in engineering and a serving engineer, Rajmohan Nath made a place for himself as a historian by his interest in the subject and by hard work to pursue that interest. Passion backed by sustained endeavour seems to be the secret of his success. He did not follow any of the standard methods or norms and practices of history writing. He was perhaps not even aware of those. This is apparent from how he titled and formatted his books and articles. No wonder, the works suffered some inherent weaknesses due to lack of methodological training on the part of the author. The principles of verification or criticism of sources and the practices of documentation or profiling and providing a bibliography are missing in his works. In fact, in most cases he even did not declare his sources. No doubt, myths and legends are also sometimes rich in historical contents, but there are standard methods and practices of retrieving data from oral sources and for attesting and using those in history writing. There is no indication of awareness of those conventions and practices in Nath's works. The pride in great Indian traditions and its cultural usages and practices and an integrative approach in writing on Assam were his subjective weaknesses that are not hidden in some of his writings. Not only the tribes and communities in two valleys and the hill districts of British Assam but also those inhabiting the neighbouring areas formed the background of Nath's Assamese culture without explaining the basis of such attributions and analogies. On the other hand, he recovered a vast mass of archaeological materials and art objects directly from the field and did a yeoman service to the cause of historiography in Northeast India by publishing those primary sources of history of the region. A large number of ancient and medieval sculptures and other archaeological and art history objects were explored and reported by him for the first time. As a field engineer, it was an advantage for him to visit even remote areas during official tours and travels and his natural talent and love for history instinctively guided him in recovering the hidden or unnoticed historical objects and artifacts, while the littérateur in him naturally drove him in writing and publishing the materials on a large variety of topics. It is here that Rajmohan Nath made significant contributions as a historian. He was at ease in writing in three languages, namely, English, Assamese and Bengali, and he wrote volumes in all three. His works are still relevant for glimpses of history of Northeast India and the source materials recovered and reported by him can be used by generations of historians.

Notes & References

1. Jiban Nath, "*Kirtiman Purush Rajmohan Nath*" (in Bengali), in Prasun Barman (ed.), *Ninth Column* (11th Year), Maligaon, Guwahati, 2011, pp. 153-60; *Prabaha* (Bengali monthly), 13th Year, No. 3 (Rajmohan Nath Centenary Special Issue), October, 1999.

2. The publications of books and booklets of Rajmohan Nath included *The Background of Assamese Culture* (1948), *Glorious Assam* (1949), *A Clue to the Indus Valley Script and Civilisation* (1959), *The Background of Assamese Architecture* (1959), *Rigveda Summary* (1966), *Sankara Deva and the Vaisnava Movement in Assam* (1966), *Antiquity of the Kapili and the Jamuna valleys* (1981), *Antiquities of Cachar* (1981), *Ruins of Va-Vanga* (1981), *Serpent Queen Manasa* (1981), and *Kachar Zilla* (1981, reprint of a section in *The Background of Assamese Culture*) in English; *Bir Chilaray* (1940), *Sri Sri Sankardevar Bargeet* (1943), *Namdharmar Baijnanik Tattva* (1944), *Sri Sri Madhavdevar Bargeet* (1945), *Kaliyadaman Nat* (1945), *Got-korai* (1945), *Sudarshan*, vol. I (1945), *Sudarshan*, vol. II (1946), *Tenga Doi* (1946), *Sri Sri Sankardev-Madhavdev Charit* (1947), *Gauravmoy Asom* (1949), *Tapat Gakhir* (1950), *Bhaktiratnakar* (1950), *Naradiya Bhaktisutra* (1950), *Shandilya Bhaktisutra* (1950), *Shantisatak* (1950), *Pandavgeeta aru Kamrupi Vaisnavgeeta* (1950), *Khaoli* (1951), *Kahundi* (1952), *Nathyogi Tattva* (1958), *Pokamitha* (1958), *Pragvaidik Kamrup* (1958), *Chechapani* (1959), *Kadali Rajya* (nd), and *Upanishadar Vaidik Byakhya* (nd) in Assamese; and *Katapara Vamsa* (1941), *Kadali Rajya* (1941), *Asamer Katha O Kahini* (1945), *Sonadhaner Geet* (1947), *Sri Sri Brajabihar Kavya* (1954), *Sarparajni Manasa* (1957), *Gorokshabani*, vol. I (1958), *Rajguru Yogivamsadarshika* (1958), *Nathyogi Tattva* (1958), *Upanishad Sadhanar Rahasya* (1959), *Bangiya Yogijatir Dikdarshan* (1960), *Mohenjodaror Lipi O Savyata* (1961), *Bangasanskriti O Nathpantha* (1961), *Yogijati* (1961), *Bangiya Nathsahitya* (1961), *Gopichandrer Gan* (1962), *Gorokshaponishat* (1962), *Gorokshapadavali* (1963), *Shivamohisya Stutram* (1964), *Bangiya Nath Panther Prachin Puthi* (1964), *Atharvaved* (1964), *Charyapader Maulik Byakhya* (1964), *Charyapader Yougik Byakhya* (nd), *Matsyendra-Goroksha Sambad* (nd), *Minnath o Gorokshanather Yogtattva* (nd), *Siddhasiddhanta Paddvati* (nd), *Vaidik Sristi Rahasya* (nd), *Bratyabad (nd), Padankadut* (nd), *Sahaj Kathay Upanishad* (nd), *Vede Bijnancharcha* (nd), and *Vaidik Sristibijnan* (nd) in Bengali. The word 'included' has been consciously used, because the list is not exhaustive.
3. For example, Rajmohan Nath contributed a series of fourteen articles on Harappa and Mohenjodaro and ancient Indian culture in *Organiser* (Delhi), dated 3.12. 1957 to 1.9.1958 and presented a paper on script of Harappa and Mohenjo-daro at 20th Session of Indian History Congress at Guwahati in 1959.
4. Rajmohan Nath, *The Background of Assamese Culture*, Dutta Barooah & Co., Gauhati, 1948.
5. Rajmohan Nath, *Glorious Assam* and *Gauravmoy Asom*, Gauhati, 1949.
6. Rajmohan Nath, *Antiquities of Cachar*, published by Lopita Nath, Raj Vila, Silchar, 1981.
7. For a complete bibliography of the books, booklets and articles written by Rajmohan Nath in English, Assamese and Bengali, see *Prabaha* (Bengali monthly), 13th Year, No. 3 (Rajmohan Nath Centenary Special Issue), October 1999, pp. 11-110. It is understood that some of his works are yet to be published.
8. Rajmohan Nath, "The Background of Assamese Architecture" in H.K. Barpujari (ed.), *The Heritage of Assam*, Reception Committee, Indian History Congress, 20th Session, Guwahati, 1959, pp. 12-15.
9. Rajmohan Nath, "A Clue to Indus Valley Script and Civilization", *Proceedings of the Indian History Congress*, 20th Session, Gauhati, 1959, pp. 165-171.
10. Rajmohan Nath, "Two Seals of Lothal", *Proceedings of the Indian History Congress*, 21st Session, Aligarh, 1960, p. 120.
11. *Journal of Assam Research Society*, vol. II, No. 1, 1934, p. 7.

12. *Ibid*, vol. III, no. 4, 1935.
13. *Ibid*, vol. IV, no. 1, 1936.
14. *Ibid*, vol. IV, no. 2, 1936.
15. *Ibid*, vol. IV, no. 3, 1936.
16. *Ibid*, vo. IV, no. 4, 1937.
17. *Ibid*, vol. V, no. 1, 1937.
18. *Ibid*, vol. V, no. 2, 1937.
19. *Ibid*, vol. V, no. 3, 1937.
20. *Ibid*, vol. V, no. 4, 1938.
21. *Ibid*, vol. VI, no. 1, 1938.
22. *Ibid*, vol. VI, no. 2, 1938.
23. *Ibid*, vol. VI, no. 3, 1938.
24. *Ibid*, vol. VII, no. 1, 1939.
25. *Ibid*, vol. VII, no. 2, 1939.
26. *Ibid*, vol. VIII, no. 2, 1940.
27. *Ibid*, vol. VIII, no. 3, 1940.
28. *Ibid*, vol. VIII, no. 4, 1941.
29. For example, Jiban Nath, "*Kirtiman Purush Rajmohan Nath*" (in Bengali), in Prasun Barman (ed.), *Ninth Column* (11th Year), Maligaon, Guwahati, 2011, pp. 153-60; *Prabaha* (Bengali monthly), 13th Year, No. 3 (Rajmohan Nath Centenary Special Issue), October 1999.
30. Usharanjan Bhattacharya, *Srihatta Sahitya Parishat O Patrika*, pub. by Anjali Bhattacharya, Purbachal, Salt Lake, Calcutta, 1993, p. 109.
31. *Srihatta Sahitya Parishat Patrika*, 5th Year, no. 4.
32. *Ibid*, 6th Year, no. 4.
33. For the list of articles in Assamese, see *Prabaha* (Bengali monthly), 13th Year, No. 3 (Rajmohan Nath Centenary Special Issue), October 1999, pp. 11-110.
34. *Asom Sahitya Sabha Patrika*, 7th Year, no. 4.
35. *Ibid*, 8th Year, no. 1.
36. *Ibid*, 8th Year, no. 2.
37. *Ibid*, 11th Year, no. 4.
38. *Ibid*, 12th Year, no. 2.
39. *Ibid*, 15th Year, no. 3.
40. *Ibid*, 18th Year, no. 1.
41. *Indian Culture*, Vol. IV, no. 4, April, 1940.

42. *Organiser*, relevant issues of the weekly in 1957-58.
43. *The Assam Tribune*, 14th April 1941.
44. *Ibid*, 10th October 1948.
45. *The Sylhet Chronicle*, 2nd November 1942.
46. *The Democratic Review*, 6th October 1959.
47. *Bhavan's Journal*, 23rd March 1958.
48. *Ibid*, 25th May 1958.
49. *The Amrita Bazar Patrika*, 14th August 1960.
50. *The Times of Assam*, 18th January 1941.
51. Volumes I to III were published in 1937 and Volume IV in 1956. Few more volumes have been added subsequently.
52. Rajmohan Nath, "Sankar Deva and the Vaisnava Movement in Assam" in Haridas Bhattacharyya (ed), *The Cultural Heritage of India,* vol. IV, The Ramkrishna Mission Institute of Culture, Calcutta, 1956, pp. 201-210.

13

Bhaben Narzee (1906-1992)

—*Sekhar Brahma*

Biographical Sketch

Bhaben Narzee, who never claimed himself to be a historian nor does anybody knew him in that profession, silently pursued throughout his life scholarly work to explore the roots of the Bodo culture which came down through generations and thereby he created valuable source materials for studying the social history of the Bodos. An unexposed Bodo scholar, litterateur, linguist and social worker, Narzee was born on 13th *Bhado* of the Bangla year 1313 (1906 AD) in village Khoipagaon of North Abhayapuri in the present Bongaigaon district of Assam. His father Nabin Narzee was a dramatist and popular artist, who wrote Bodo drama, like Bengali *Yatra*, and performed in the Bodo villages, and his mother Sameswari Narzee was a kind hearted woman and housewife, expert in weaving, handicraft and in managing the household. His parents were originally from Dotma area of the then Goalpara (present Kokrajhar) district of Assam. After the birth of Bhaben, his parents shifted their residence to Jhargaon near Tamulpur under Rangia police station of Kamrup district. As Bhaben Narzee worked as a pleader's clerk in Gauhati High Court, he temporarily settled at Kharguli in Guwahati. Though his mother tongue was Bodo, he earned fluency in Assamese, English, Hindi and Bengali. In 1990 he was awarded Literary Pension by the Government of Assam for his valuable contribution to investigative literature in Assam. He had a brief stint in politics when he was elected as a Member of the Assam Legislative Assembly, in 1985, as a nominee of the *Asom Gana Parisad* (AGP). In the meantime, he suffered protracted illness and passed away in his Kharguli residence on 3rd November 1992.[1]

Narzee's proficiency in Bodo language was proverbial. He attended the summer and autumn schools in linguistics at the Deccan College, Poona, in 1955, as an informant of grammar, structure and phonetics of Bodo language. His classes were attended, amongst others, by Pramod Chandra Bhattacharya, then a research scholar in Gauhati University under the supervision of Banikanta Kakati. Bhattacharya remarked in his book, "Shri

Narzi proved himself to be an ideal informant in the school of linguistics, Deccan College, Poona. He very eagerly associated with me as the chief informant since the beginning of my learning of this form of Bodo Language in 1952. He has moreover shown outstanding literary talents in the mist of his official and social preoccupation."[2] In the footnote of the same book Bhattacharya mentioned Narzee's *Boro Kacharir Jana Sahitya* as a pioneering study of Boro folklore in Assamese.[3] In fact, Bhaben Narzee was well-known as a social worker and a scholar in the Bodos society. He was privileged to work as associate researcher with renowned Assamese scholars like Pramod Chandra Bhattacharya and Prafulladatta Goswami. His association with these scholars had inspired and trained him to learn research methodology to carry out his subsequent works on the Bodos. While carrying out his work he had always been inspired and appreciated by Suniti Kumar Chatterji, who even gave him a recommendation to pursue further study. He was also in close contact with famous linguists Sukumar Sen and S.M. Karte, who helped him a great deal and Narzee acknowledged the support of all those great scholars in the preface of his works.[4] On the other hand, Narzee's expertise in the field of Bodo language was recognized by the institutions and specialists. This is established by the fact that he was invited twice as an informant to the summer and autumn schools of linguistics, organized by the Linguistic Society of India at Deccan College, Poona, in 1955. The world-famous linguist Suniti Kumar Chatterji said : "Sri Bhaben Narzee whose mother tongue is Bodo, and who is very qualified in Bodo music and dance, also participated in the summer school of linguistic as an informant in Bodo linguistic."[5] The linguists like Banikanta Kakati, Prafulladatta Goswami and Pramod Chandra Bhattacharya utilized his expertise for linguistic research at Gauhati University.

Glimpses of studies in Bodo history and culture

The Boros, who were also known as Kachari to their Assamese neighbours, call themselves as Bodo. Their autonomous area is known as Bodoland Territorial Council and their language is included in the VIIIth Scheduled of the Constitution of India. The word Bodo is believed to have originated in Tibet in the pre-Buddhist period when the land westward of China and north-east of the Himalayas was known as 'Bod'. Suniti Kumar Chatterji had observed that in most parts of present Northeast India, North Bengal and a part of Bangladesh the Bodos for a long time predominated the local population,[6] but the history of the Bodos has never been systematically explored by the scholars. Suniti Kumar Chatterji's *Kirata-Jana-kriti* (1951)[7] seems to be the first scholarly work which threw important light on the history of the Bodos. Chatterji's *The Place of Assam in History and Civilisation of India*[8] is another great work that provides glimpses of Bodo history and culture. But we do not come across any work by any scholar specifically on the Bodo community prior to the works of Bhaben Narzee. However, the Christian missionaries were the first to study about the Bodos. They learnt their language, developed a grammar and recorded information on Bodo language, culture and traditions mainly with the objective to propagate Christianity. Thus, in 1884, Rev. Sydney Endle published a book entitled *Outline Grammar of the Kachari (BARA) language as spoken in the District Darang, Assam.* This was the first book on the structure of Boro language. Endle's *The Kacharis*

(1911) is more important as a source book of Bodo history as it contains a good deal of information about the Bodos in undivided Darrang district of Assam and some folk tales reflecting on the origin and migrations and traditional beliefs and customs of the Bodo people. J.D. Anderson, Deputy Commissioner of Darrang district, also wrote a brief treatise on the Boro society entitled *A collection of Kochari Folk Tales and Rhymes* (1917). Sir Edward Gait, in his *A History of Assam* (London, 1906),[9] no doubt, recognized that the 'Kacharis in the Brahmaputra valley call themselves Bodo' and went to extent of saying that the "Kacharis may be described as the aborigines, or earliest known inhabitants of the Brahmaputra valley", but his chapter on 'Kacharis' is devoted mainly on the Dimasa-Kacharis of Cachar.[10] These are among very few works on the Bodos that deserve mention till about middle of the twentieth century. Since second decade of twentieth century, a section of the enlightened Bodos had taken initiative for the development of Bodo language and literature, but no effort was seen to rediscover the past and to explore the source materials to study the society, culture and history of the Bodos. It was only in the middle of 20th century that Bhaben Narzee single-handedly took upon himself the task of exploration and documentation of the heritage of the Bodo people.

Contributions to Bodo history

A social worker turned researcher, Bhaben Narzee worked mainly to highlight the social history and values of the Bodo society when the Bodos were not much known to the outsiders and the common Bodos themselves were confused about their origin and identity. In the preface of his book *Boro Kacharir Samaj Aru Sanskriti* (1966) Narzee took a position that without studying the society and culture of a community it would not be possible to understand the problems of their day-to-day life. It would be a great advantage for an independent country like India to know the society and culture of every community, which would help the leaders of the country in protecting every community and giving social security to every individual and social justice to all people. For the development of a tribal community it is necessary to understand their society and culture and to appreciate their traditions and value system. The lack of mutual appreciation and recognition might lead to chaos and conflicts. As the Boro-Kacharis are living side by side with different communities and they have been sharing their ideas and way of life with others, it is necessary that their history, society and culture should be understood by others. This, according to him, was the objective of his studies and the reason why his works are mostly in Assamese and Bodo languages. His major works are (i) *Boro Kacharir Jana Sahitya* (1957), (ii) *Boro Kacharir Samaj Aru Sanskriti* (1966), (iii) *Boro Kacharir Geet Maat* (1983), (iv) *Sankipta Boro Bhasa Sikhya* (1988) and (v) *Boro Rao* (1990). He also contributed articles in various magazines, weeklies and periodicals. Some of his important articles are (i) *Boro Kacharir Janma Prakaran*, (ii) *Boro Kacharir Mrityu Prakaran* (published in *Asom Bani*, Assamese newspaper), (iii) *Boro Kacharir Chikarar Pranalee* (published in weekly *Amar Pratinidhi*). Some of his articles, particularly in Boro language, were published by Bodo organizations, like Bodo Sahitya Sabha, but most of those articles are scattered in magazines and newspapers and no attempt has so far been made for the collection and preservation of his writings. An article entitled "*Boro Kachari*", in a collection edited by Pramod Chandra Bhattacharya, is an important contribution to Bodo history.[11]

Narzee was concerned with studying the social systems of the Bodos, historical accounts of the community, folk literature, and grammar of the Bodo language. His works are based on field investigation for which he extensively toured the remote areas inhabited by the Bodo people in Assam and West Bengal. He gathered tales and fables, folk-songs, proverbs, riddles, etc. of the Bodos which are fundamental for reconstructing history from below and also studied the social and cultural practices and the belief systems of the community as prevalent among them in the 20th century. His first book *Boro Kachari Jana Sahitya* (1957) was based on folk literature and traditional beliefs and festivals of the Bodos. Prafulladatta Goswami, a pioneer folklorist of Assam, commented on the book : "The importance of Bhaben Narzi's work in term of Assamese culture may be understood if a note is added on Bodo culture in general and its relationship with Assamese culture... *Boro Kacharir Jana-Sahitya* is Shri Narzi's first work as it is the first important book on folklore to be prepared by a Bodo Kachari gentleman."[12] In fact, the Bodo folk literature seems to have a rich treasure of heritage of the community, which had been passing orally through generations as inherited from their ancestors in the form of tales, songs, proverbs, rhymes, rites and rituals, festivity, dances, economic practices, beliefs, etc. Though many of those have already sunk into oblivion, Bhaben Narzee made great endeavor to retrieve and record them to reconstruct the historical past of the Bodos.

Narzee's second book entitled *Boro Kacharir Samaj Aru Sanskriti* (1966), is a masterpiece in the field of Bodo social history. The first chapter of this book is devoted to early history of the Bodos. He described the physical features and origins of the Indo-Mongoloid Kiratas and observed that the Bodos belong to the Mongoloid group of people, physically and linguistically. The distinct Mongoloid features, according to him, were the flat nose, short head, wide forehead, scant beard and yellow complexion. Around 2000 BC, this group was wandering in Siberia and Mongolia and, in course of time, they moved towards three directions : first group travelled towards Europe (Italy and Turkey); second group went towards Japan and North America; and the third group travelled around Huang Ho valley, Tibetan plateau and spread to Bhutan, Nepal and the foothills of the Himalayan region. From that region a section came to the Brahmaputra Valley for silk-trade and settled down in the area permanently. Around 1000 BC, the Gangetic valley and southern and western India were under influence of the Aryan, Dravidian and Austric people, but Northeast India was predominated by the Mongoloid culture. These Mongoloid people entered into India from three directions. One group settled in South Bihar and North Bengal and spread to the Gangetic valley. Second group entered through the valley of the north-eastern tributaries of the Brahmaputra and spread to the Assam valley. The third group entered Tripura, and sections of them spread to Saptagram, Maimonsing, Dhaka and other places in East Bengal where they were later on converted to Islam. Narzee also reflected on a traditional belief of the Bodos that they did not migrate from outside. Such migration is not supported by any myth, tale or legend of the Bodos. He referred to a popular myth of the Bodos according to which the Almighty (*Ahamguru*) created a couple of birds with a view to create human and land. The female bird laid three eggs and hatched the eggs for thousands of years, but nothing originated from them. Then she broke an egg but failed to see any sign of life. Suddenly she heard the prophecy from Almighty not to break the remaining two eggs; otherwise the earth will be destroyed, and asked her to sprinkle the broken egg around. The spread of egg-drops originated into ghosts, spirits, insects, trees, creepers, etc. But there was then no land in the *Martyalok* (earth) and the world was full of water. So, Almighty sent birds and beasts to fetch soil from the *Patalpuri* (world beneath the earth) but no one could bring soil from there because of the strong vigilance of the king's soldiers. The Almighty then sent a couple of old *magur* fishes to bring soil, but when coming back carrying huge mound of soil the *magurs* were caught by the soldiers who seized the mound and punished them severely. After many years when the Almighty remembered the *magurs* he asked all birds and bitches to search for them. A crow saw the dead *magurs* floating on the water and informed the Almighty who by beating with his *jiya tangon* (live stick) and *mara tangan* (dead stick) resurrected the *magurs* and with the little soil that remained in their mouth he created the earth. After thousands of years, two human couples took birth from two other eggs. *Monsinsing Bwrwai* and *Monsinsing Bwrwi* originated from the first egg, while from the second egg, *Diba Bwrwai* and *Dibi Bwrwi*. They prayed to the Almighty to allow them to go to heaven. However, on way to the heaven *Diba* and *Dibi* heard screaming of creatures of this earth and looked back, as a result of which they fell back on the earth. They cried before Almighty for food, but Almighty consoled them that the offspring of *Mansinsing Bwrwai* and *Mansinsing Bwrwi* would come to dwell on this earth and will worship them offering eatables. The Boro-Kacharis believe themselves to be the descendants of first human *Mansinsing*. The Bodos narrate this story with the tune of *Sifung* (flute), *Kham* (big drum) and *Jatha* (cymbal) on religious ceremonies.

Narzee referred to another Bodo myth about origin of the universe[13] which recounts that there was no sun, moon, earth or stars in the universe. The eternal deities *Anan Gosai* and *Binan Gosai* were also in dormant and formless state. On one sacred moment the Almighty woke up, took his shape and wished to regulate the universe. He uttered a sentence - *'laoba laswm khaoba khaswm ada gwswm dwiao barswm'*.[14] Then a luminous body appeared in the space and *Anan Gosai* and *Binan Gosai* got new name *Sibrai*, the prime god of the Bodos. Narzee found that some of the origin myths of the Dimasa-Kacharis were similar to those of the Bodo-Kacharis, Lepsas and Limbus and cited a common tradition of the Lepsas and Limbhus about their origin and migration which states how they were separated from the Meches (Bodos).[15] Narzee mentioned about the works of eminent scholars like Birinchi Kumar Barua and Bisnu Prasad Rabha, who were of the opinion that the Bodos immigrated from Tibet by the tributaries of the Brahmaputra for silk trade and introduced themselves as Tibod or Bod, and, therefore, it is believed that the word Boro (Bodo) is derived from Bod or Tibod.[16] Narzee, thus, discussed the secondary sources also to arrive at his conclusions.

Bhaben Narzee's description of the social systems and practices, religious beliefs, economic institutions, festivals, rituals, food habits, dresses, etc. of the Bodos and the contemporary changes in the society in *Boro Kacharir Samaj Aru Sanskriti* is such an important documentation that the researchers find it handy to write on the community. This monograph on the Bodo society is indeed comprehensive. The author not only used the data he gathered from his field-work over a long period of time, but also took cognizance of the secondary materials and the views of other scholars. For example, he dwelt at length with the observation of Birinchi Kumar Baruah that the Boro-Kachari society was originally matriarchal and it had influenced the Assamese society to allow more freedom to women, but later on under influence of Aryan culture the Bodos turned to be a patriarchal society. Narzee did not rule out the possibility. He observed that the bride-price was an important custom in Bodo marriage. The father of the bride and elders of the village decided on the *Malsa* (money payable to the village society of the bride) before handing over the bride to the groom. The amount was fixed on the basis of the social status of the bride. If the parents were not alive, the maternal uncles of the bride were entitled to realize the bride price. Among the Bodos there is still a system of *Gorjia lakhinai,* according to which the groom stays in bride's house after marriage. In such a marriage the boy renders free service to girl's house for one year before wedding. There is also a system of widow remarriage, known as *Doka Habnai*, in which a widow, to look after her children and property from the expired husband, remarry a man and bring him to her residence by observing traditional rites and rituals. The man who enters such wedding has to surrender all rights and claims on his paternal land and property. On the basis of this female oriented system, Narzee felt that the Bodo society was possibly matriarchal in early times.[17]

The description of the features of a village and homesteads in Narzee's work is like pen-picture of a traditional Bodo village. The author began with the selection of land for setting up a village. It is found that the Bodos generally selected high land for a village, which should not be far away from water-source (river, lake and forest), and to select a plot of land for homestead they performed a ritual during winter standing barefoot on the soil uncovered by grass. If felt hot, it is considered as disease prone and unfit for dwellling. If cool, on a Saturday or Tuesday they clean a small area with water and put a banana leaf on the ground and keep nine *Tulsi* leaves and nine husked rice on the banana leaf and cover it with a *Don* (bamboo basket for measuring rice) over night. The next day after removing the *Don* if rice and *Tulsi* leaves are found scattered the place is considered as *Amongal* or not suitable for dwelling. And if the *Tulsi* leaves and rice are in same position, the place is considered as suitable for homestead. The elders then dig the land around two feet depth and taste the soil by eating. If the soil tastes sweet, it is suitable; if tastes salty or bitter it is medium or average, but if sour, the site is unsuitable for homestead. Building the houses start with *Bakhri* (store-house for keeping rice) in the eastward of the courtyard and the next is *Noma No* (main dwelling house) comprising three rooms, namely, *Ising, Akhong* and *Khopra* in the northward. It is followed by *Chaura No* (sleeping house of young boys and guests) with one door facing outward, because it is believed that people coming from outside should not enter straight to the courtyard. This courtyard is considered sacred because of the presence of *Bathou* (altar of lord *Siva* or *Bathou Brai*) and it is believed to be the place of gaining wisdom. In the main house first room *Ising* has altars of chief deities like *Mahadev Bwrai Bathou* and *Mainao* or *Ai Khamakhya* and it is used for cooking food and a little portion of every cooked food is offered to deities, the second room is *Akhong* for dinning and the third room, *Khopra* for sleeping. The Bodos build *Goli* or cow-shed without wall, but they never build shed for buffalos.[18]

Boro Kacharir Samaj Aru Sanskriti is also a documentation of the traditional economic institutions, technology, beliefs and practices of the Bodos. It provides useful data for economic history as it also discusses the changes brought about by modern science and technology. The main occupation of the Bodos remains to be paddy cultivation for which the Bodos prefer flat and low fields of alluvial soil. High-land is preferred for homestead to avoid flood water. River or lake is a must for fishing and irrigation, grass-field for cattle, while they also need forest or jungle for hunting animal, firewood, timber and other plants for house-building and agricultural implements. If there is lack of any one or more of these components, they migrated to other places where those were available in abundance. This option is now redundant due to the absence of fallow land. They have their own method of selecting and classifying the cultivable lands according to the location, altitude, and source of water. Narzee presented those facts in his works along with traditional folk rhymes and songs which tell the readers how the Bodos in early times gathered experience through a long struggle for adjustment with the nature for livelihood. A proverb says – 'bamboo towards west, duck towards east; betelnut towards north, smoke towards south'. Bamboo is indispensable in building house and for agricultural and domestic implements, fishing and hunting and for observing rites and rituals. So, planting bamboo in the northern side may save the village from destruction by storm from the west. Duck towards east means, river, lake or pond should be in the east by which a family can derive economic support by fishing and poultry farming and cool breeze from the eastern side is hygienic for the villagers. The betelnut trees or betel leaves plants are important not only to entertain the guests but also to perform religious rites and to fetch income from the market. Smoke towards south is meant to keep the south open to get sunshine for sound health. In his *Boro Kocharir Geet-Mat*, Narzee interpreted many such sayings which, according to him, had helped the Bodo society in the past to maintain a self-sustained agricultural economy.[19] They regarded cow as *Lakshi* (goddess of wealth) and most important part of their economy. The birth of cows was thought as the blessings of *Lakshi Devi*. A villager without a cow was considered unlucky and a miserable man, since milk and cow-dung were essential in rites and rituals of the Bodos.[20]

The calendar of festivity of the Bodos was according to the agricultural activities. The Bodos consider the paddy or rice as *Mainao* or *Lakshi* and they perform two types of Kherai *Pujas - Iswnna* or *Maisali Kherai* during the harvesting of paddy in the month of *Mag* or *Aghan* and *Asu Kherai* during the harvesting of *Asu* paddy in summer. *Kherai* is a form of worship to *Sibrai* or *Siva* through dances by female shaman accompanied by the tune of *Kham* (long drum), *Sifung* (flute), and *Jatha* (cymbal) around the altar of *Bathou*. These *pujas* are performed for whole night with a view to get blessings from *Lakshi* and *Siva*, in which people from the village and neighboring villages take part. After the *Kherai puja,* the *Mainao* or *Lakshi Devi* is ceremonially placed on the altar of *Ising*.[21] *Bwisagu* is another important festival observed in the beginning of *Boisag* month. On the *Sangkranti* (last day of the month) of *Chaitra* the cattle are taken to bathe in the river. Their horns are polished with mustard oil; they are garlanded with wreath of brinjal and gourd, and fed with rice grains. On the first day of the *Boisag* the Bodos worship their deities, gurus, ancestors and bid farewell to the old year. After worshipping for the progress and well-being of the family, they join the festivity by dancing and singing *Bwisagu* songs. Even if for a short time, they forget rich or poor, old or young and enjoy drinking rice beer. This festivity lasted for seven days in the past. First five days, they performed dance, music and songs in every house and collected small gifts as a token of blessing in cash or kinds, especially rice, eggs or other eatables. Next two days they arranged grand feast with the collected items; bid *Bwisagu* farewell and devote to agricultural activity.[22]

Another important festival of the Bodos is *Domasi*; observed in the beginning of the month of *Mag* after harvesting. On the last day of *Chaitra* every family makes various food items of agricultural products but they do not prepare *Tekeli Pitha* (steamed rice cake) as they believe that it may cause tumor to cows. During *Domasi* cowherds build a hut with straws of rice and bamboos, known as *Belagur*, in the paddy field and enjoy whole night by singing and dancing and at the late-night they enjoy feast and then burn the *Belagur*. Generally *Belagur* is built near a river, lake or pond because on 1st of *Mag*, cowherds take bath before the crow wake up and then warm up their frozen body near the burning flames of *Belagur*. It is believed that any one taking bath after the crow wake up would be infected by skin allergy. After bath, they sing traditional hymn around bonfire for the wellbeing of the villagers and well-wishers and rebuke those who tortured them for nothing. In the morning they go house to house and eat different types of food made for the occasion. The villagers eat, drink, sing and dance during the festival.[23]

Bhaben Narzee discussed the details of traditional Bodo festivals in his first Book *Boro Kocharir Jana Sahitya*, published in 1957, and interpreted the rites, rituals, values and significance of songs, dances and mode of observance, which are important for reconstructing the history of the Bodos. He also studied the methods of hunting and fishing which formed part of the Bodo culture and found similarity with those of the Lepsas of Tibet and Sikkim and Limbus of Nepal. The Bodos believe that there is a couple of deities, known as *Jwmwn Jwla* and *Jwmwn Buri*, who tend wild animals in the jungle and they worship these deities before setting out for hunting. Even during *Kherai puja* these deities are provided separate altars. In a new year when the Bodos first go for hunting they sacrifice a cock in the name of *Jwmwn Jwla* and *Jwmwn Buri* to worship them. If they slay animal during that hunting they prepare meat curry with heart and blood of the slain animal and cook rice to propitiate deities by offering these. The children or women cannot take part in such worship. In the first worship the Bodos appeal to deities and fix the number of animals to be slain in the year. If they exceed the fixed number they worship *Jwmwn Jwla* and *Jwmwn Buri* for forgiveness. This shows the awareness about conserving wild animals and maintaining ecological balance. The hunting was of two types – first by bow and arrows by individuals known as *Folan* and second, the community hunting, where nets made by the fibers of *Odal* tree or jute-rope and pointed bamboos are planted in running track of animals on one side and the people chased the animals from three other sides with spear, *dao*, etc. and by making loud noise. Narzee described the art of knitting hunting net and technique of planting it and pointed bamboos and observes that the Bodos knew the time and routes of movements of the animals and could identify the footprints and stool of different animals. They also knew the art of taming the animals, like beer, by chanting *mantra*. Like hunting, he identified two types of fishing, namely, individual fishing and community fishing, and described the equipments and methods of those activities. He also described the popular food habits of the Bodos and the method of preservation of dry-fish and dry-meat.[24]

Narzee studied the traditional religion of the Bodos, including deities, beliefs, rituals and practices, and also the changes that came over time through outside influences. He identified the principal deity or supreme god *Bathou* as *Siva*, who was known under different names, like *Sibrai, Bathou Bwrai, Kwria Bwrai, Gila Dambra*, etc. and the festivals (*puja*) were intended to propitiate that god. The community worship is called *Garja Puja* for which every family in the village contributes rice and money. The place of worship, called *Garjasali*, in the outskirt of the village remains covered with big trees. It is intended to avert famine, epidemic or any other calamity by purifying the village of any evil or impure act during the preceding year. The sanctity of the village is checked one day ahead of the *puja* through a ritual in which a place in the *Garjasali* is sanctified with holy water, a top portion of a banana leaf is placed on the ground, a pair of *Tulsi* leaves and nine husked rice are placed on the banana leaf and then it is covered with a *Don* (bamboo basket for measuring of rice). The *Siva* and other deities are then invoked for forgiveness for misdeeds. After removing the basket next morning if it is found that rice or *Tulsi* leaves are scattered it is confirmed that some man and woman in the village are involved in illicit relations. The offenders are detected and punished by the village court and purified by customary rituals before *Garja Puja* can take place. There are nineteen *Garja Pujas* in which two categories of deities are propitiated along with *Siva*, namely, *Boroni Mwdai* (deities of Boro-Kachari) and *Harsa Mwdai* (deities of Aryans). The Bodo deities are *Maothansri (lakshidevi), Bathou Bwrai (Siva Mahadev),Akhaisri, Jwmwnjwla, Barmali, Sainasi, Budaru, Jekhaibwrai, Khobaibwrai, Gambari, Dwhwnsri, Mwnsri, Mayodbwrai, Mayodburwi, Ai Khamakya*, while the Aryan deities (to whom separate alters are provided) are *Baro Gopal, Baro Gopini, Thakurani, Laokhargosai* (cowherd deity or *Krisna*), *Langthiyagosai, Barmali, Mahadeo Bwrai, Sallasha Gopal, Sallasha Gopini, Jagatguru, Jagatnath, Mahamaya*. Nazee's categorization of the deities makes it clear that one category consisted of the traditional Bodo tribal deities and another of those the Bodos adopted after Hinduisation. A third, *Phir Chahab* (Islam) was possibly taken much later from the Muslim neighbours in the area. In the *Garjashali* the alter of the *Bwrai Bathou (Siva)* is build as *Chang Ghar* (elevated house) with ladder and smaller houses are made for other deities and alters inside stretching on the left of *Bwrai Bathou*. They are worshipped with the sacrifice of fowls and offered earthen-pot full of rice beer. After chanting *mantras*, three pigeons are flown in the sky in the name of Aryan deities. Each deity gets a sacrifice of fowl, rice beer and other eatables. After the *puja, Deoris* (priests) sprinkle the holy water in the houses of every family in the village. Among the household worships, the *Kherai Pujas* are observed for three reasons, viz. *Asu Kherai* for the growth of *Asu* cultivation or summer crops; *Sali Kherai* for the growth of *Sali* cultivation or winter crops; and another *Kherai Puja* is observed for recovery from incurable diseases. The primary requirements are a pair of pigeons, a chicken, a cock, a pig, a pair of eggs and all usual needs for a *Puja*. The exclusive musical instruments for *Kherai Puja* are : a pair of *Sifung* (flute), a pair of *Kham* (big drum) and a pair of *Jatha* (cymbal). The tune of music continues whole night along with shamanistic dance till the end of the *Puja*. The female shaman dances in trance with weapons, sword and shield. In case of diseases the *Kherai Puja* is organized within compound of the house and in case of growing of crops it is arranged in a convenient part of the field. After ritual purification of the place the alter for the *puja* is built around ten inches high and two feet width encircling a bamboo fence with five level of horizontal bamboo reefs and crisscross in the front having an entrance. A stem of *Sijou* tree and *Tulsi* are planted in the *Bathou* alter and a round stone is placed under *Sijou* tree keeping an egg on it. This stone is a symbol of creation of universe. A bamboo tree, without any cut towards the top, is also planted with a white flake as a symbol of peace, which is called *Jatha*. The priest chants *mantras* along with the tune of music and is followed by *Daudini mwsanai* (shamanistic dance). The deities of the *Kherai Puja* are; *Khwria Bwrai (Siva), Khwria Burwi (Kamakhya), Aileng* (Bodyguard of Siva), *Agrang* (soldiers' chief), *Khwila* (messenger of *Siva*), *Kazi* (minister), *Abla Kungur, Rajputur* (son), *Rajkhandra* (grandson), *Songraja* or *Jwmwnjwla* and *Songrani, Mwnasw* (deity of Manas river), *Alaikhungri* and *Bilaikhungri* (daughters of Siva), *Bhandari* (deity of water), *Kumari* (deity of diseases), *Basamuthi Chaudri, Ransandi* (deity of war), *Bwliburi* (deity of *mantras* and medicine), *Laokhar Gosai* (deity of cowherd). After the *puja, Mainao* or deity of wealth is raised up and placed in the *Ishing*. Narzee shows that the deities are both traditional as well as those adopted after Hinduisation, including a few humans with supernatural powers. He also dealt with *jadu mantra* (magic), love-charm, witchcraft, etc and also dress, weaving and spinning (*endi* or *muga*), bamboo-crafts, ornaments, curse and blessings, etc. in his works.[25]

As a historian

Bhaben Narzee was not a trained or professional historian, but his works are based on the life-long field studies on the origin and growth of Bodo society and culture, including family system, social behaviors, religious practices and beliefs, social institutions, economic activities and almost every aspect of the society. His *Boro Kacharir Jana Sahitya* (1957) is a wonderful collection of folk literature of the Bodos, including folk-tales, maxims and riddles, with authoritative interpretations. His *Boro Kacharir Samaj Aru Sanskriti* (1966) is a documentation on the social history of the Bodos, beginning with origin of the Bodo people, migration and settlement, customs and usages, and changes in society over time, including the adoptions and adaptations. Similarly, his *Boro-Kacharir Geet-Mat* (1983) is a testimony of the author's expertise in Bodo folk literature and interpreting those to discern the features of life and conditions in the past and the changes till modern times. The text is also a documentation of the Bodo folk songs and ballads, including songs of festivals, wedding, pacifying, repentance, agriculture field, taunting, teasing, flattering, love, counseling, children songs and those sung in fields in various stages of agriculture. A large number of ballads, maxims and at least five historical folk tales are found in the book. In 'Preface' of the book he admitted that as the Boro-Kacharis are scattered in different places it was difficult to collect all folk literary items and many of those might have gone into oblivion. His *Sankipta Boro Bhasa Sikhya* (1988) in Assamese and *Boro Rao* (1990) in Bodo language are the books on the principle and grammar of Bodo language, but in the introduction the author has given a brief historical account of the ethnic background of the Bodo-speakers. He made no attempt to study the political history of the Bodos. His concern was society and culture, but in the process he has left behind not only the authoritative documentations of the contemporary Bodo society but also the origin and growth of the society and culture, including the changes that have taken place over a long period of time In this context it may be recalled that G.M. Trevelyan regarded social history as a bridging point between economic and political history and remarked that "without social history, economic history is barren and political history unintelligible."[26] Bhaben Narzee was also a social historian, who studied one aspect of 'history from below' by gathering information from the people themselves during his extensive field work in the Bodo inhabited areas in Assam and North Bengal. The researchers in future may write other aspects of Bodo history by drawing information and inspiration from the works of this great historian of Bodo traditions. Finally, it may be mentioned that some of the well known historians of Northeast India have been extensively citing the findings of Baben Narzee in their works.[27]

Notes & References

1. This biographical stretch of Bhaben (alias Babendra) Narzee has been reconstructed on the basis of information gathered from those who knew him intimately, including Sri Taren Boro, an official of Reserve Bank of India, Guwahati, who was a neighbour of Bhaben Narzee in Kharguli and associated with Narzee in social work, and Smt. Indira Boro, Head of the Department of Bodo, Gauhati University, Kokrajhar Campus, who has studied the life and works of Bhaben Narzee in connection with her own research.
2. Pramod Chandra Bhattacharya, *A Descriptive Analysis of Boro Language*, Gauhati University, 1976, pp. 3-4.
3. *Ibid.*, p. 4.
4. See for example, 'Preface' in Bhaben Narzee, *Boro Kacharir Samaj Aru Sanskriti*, Guwahati, 1976.
5. Suniti Kumar Chatterji, "Of the Bodos", an article published in the Souvenir of the 8th Annual Session of Bodo Sahitya Sabha in 1966; edited by Manoranjan Lahary, p. 17.
6. Suniti Kumar Chatterji, *Kirata-Jana-Kriti : The Indo-Mongoloids, Their Contributions to History and Culture of India*, The Asiatic Society, Calcutta, 1951, p. 28.

7. Suniti Kumar Chatterji, *Kirata-Jana-Kriti : The Indo-Mongoloids, Their Contributions to History and Culture of India,* The Asiatic Society, Calcutta, 1951.
8. Suniti Kumar Chatterji, *The Place of Assam in the History and Civilization of India*, Gauhati University Publications, 1955.
9. Edward Gait, *A History of Assam*, 1st edn. London, 1906, revised and enlarged 2nd edn., Thacker Sprink & Co., Calcutta, 1926.
10. *Ibid*, second edition, Thaker Sprink & Co., Calcutta, 1926, pp. 299-310.
11. Bhabendra Narzee, *"Boro Kachari"* in Promod Chandra Bhattacharya (ed.), *Asomar Janajati* (Assamsse), Asom Sahitya Sabha, Jorhat, 1962, pp. 52-68.
12. Quoted in Pramod Chandra Bhattacharya, "An Introduction to Boro Kachari's Society and Culture" in Bhaben Narzee's: *Boro Kacharir Samaj Aru Sanskriti*, reprint Calcutta, 2001, pp. xi-xii.
13. This myth is also found in Dhuparam Basumatary, *Boro-Kacharir Sanskritir Kinchit Abhas*, Guwahati, 1967.
14. *Laoba Laswm* means embracing five elements like air, water, fire, earth and sky (soul) in the living body; *Khaoba Khaswm* means fastening five organs of sense like eye, ear, nose, tongue and skin in the heart; *Ada Gwswm* means black brother/means my heart; *Dwiao Barswm* means Jump to the water/means devoted to duty.
15. Bhaben Narzee, *op.cit.*, pp. 6-14.
16. *Ibid*, p. 16
17. *Ibid.*, p. 21.
18. *Ibid.*, pp. 24-37.
19. *Ibid.*, pp. 43-47.
20. Bhaben Narzee, *Boro Kocharir Geet-Mat*, Guwahati, 1983, pp. 11-12.
21. Bhaben Narzee, *Boro Kacharir Samaj Aru Sanskriti*, reprint Calcutta, 2001, pp. 50-51.
22. *Ibid.*, pp. 212-220.
23. Bhaben Narzee, *Boro Kocharir Geet-Mat, op.cit.*, pp. 2-8.
24. *Ibid.*, pp. 175-204.
25. Bhaben Narzee, *Boro Kacharir Samaj Aru Sanskriti, op.cit.*, pp. 124-144, 194,175-204.
26. G.M. Trevelyan, *English Social History: A Survey of Six Centuries from Chaucer to Queen Victoria*. Indian reprint, New Delhi, 1997 (ISBN 058248488X), Introduction, p. i.
27. For example, see Rabindranath Mosahary, 'Social History of the Bodos of Assam', Ph D thesis, North-Eastern Hill University, Shillong, 1986; The Bodos : Their Origin, Migration and Settlement in Assam", *Proceedings of North East India History Association*, 4th Session, Barapani, 1983, pp. 42-70; Jayanta Bhusan Bhattacharya, *Kachari Rajya : Utthan Aru Patan* (Assamese), Asom Sahitya Sabha, Jorhat/Guwahati, 1993.

14

Padmeswar Gogoi (1907-1979)

—Romesh Buragohain

Biographical Sketch

A pioneer researcher in the history of Tai-Ahoms, Padmeswar Gogoi was born in the month of *paus* (corresponding to December-January) in the North Lakhimpur district of Assam in 1907 and died on 1st September, 1979. A meritorious student, he studied at North Lakhimpur Government High School and passed the Matriculation Examination of the Calcutta University in 1925 securing more than eighty percent marks in three subjects and scoring highest marks in English in the University. He took B.A.(Honours) degree in Economics from Cotton College, Gauhati and M.A. in Economics from the Calcutta University. He began his career as a Lecturer in Economics in J.B. College, Jorhat, which was the first non-government College in Assam and its founder Principal was the eminent scholar, Krishnakanta Handique, who later on became the founder Vice-Chancellor of Gauhati University in 1948. Gogoi served J.B. College from 1933 to 1948. In 1948, he joined the Cotton College as Junior Professor in the newly opened post-graduate class in Economics. After ten months, the post-graduate classes in Cotton College were transferred to the newly established Gauhati University and Gogoi joined the Commerce Department in the University to teach Economics. It was during this period that he successfully did his doctoral research and obtained Ph. D. from the Gauhati University in 1961. In 1964, he joined the Department of Political Science of the University as a Reader and retired from active service in that position in 1967.[1]

In his youth Padmeswar was inspired by the nationalist movement in India under the leadership of Mahatma Gandhi, though he did not actively participate in the movement as he thought that it was more important for him to concentrate on his academic career.[2] However, his sense of political consciousness was always very strong. As it would appear from his activities later in life, he was always guided by two interests that were natural in him. Of these, (i) one was to academically explore the traditions and culture of the Tai peoples, and the other, (ii) to improve the political culture in the state of Assam.[3] It is a different matter that he is remembered today more as a historian and very few may even know that he also had a brief experience in the electoral politics of Assam.[4] The interest in historical research stayed with him till the end of his life. In fact, Padmeswar Gogoi was the first historian who comprehensively explored the Tai-Ahom history. He was also the moving force behind the study and research in Tai history and culture in Assam. To achieve this goal, he founded the Tai Historical and Cultural Society and under its aegis, the publication of a journal - *LIK PHAN TAI* - was launched. Though the journal did not last long due to various logistic reasons, under the care of J.N. Phukan it made a lasting impact in historiography by creating fresh interest in Tai-Ahom history.[5]

Contributions to history

Padmeswar Gogoi authored three major research works, namely, *The Tai and the Tai Kingdoms with a fuller treatment of the Tai-Ahom Kingdom in the Brahmaputra Valley* (1968),[6] *Tai-Ahom Religion and Customs*.(1976),[7] and *Future Status of Assam* (1945).[8] He also authored a number of books in Assamese, mostly meant for the students as text books and references.[9] His essays *"Rajnity Vigyan - Sanmilita Rastrasangha"* and *"Manavar Moulik Adhikar Samuh"* were published in the *Jagannath Barua College Magazine* (1980-82).[10] However, Gogoi published a large number of research papers, both in English and Assamese, on history and culture of Northeast India and those included *"Mung-Ri Mung-Ram"* (*Sangram*, All Assam Ahom Cultural Federation, February, 1949), "Coinage in Old Assam" (*Undergraduate Students Journal*, Gauhati University, Jan-Feb., 1953), *"Manipurar Lagot Taijatir Oitihasik Samparka"* (*Jayanti*, 1953), "Buddhism in Kamarupa under Bhaskaravarman" (*Journal of Assam Research Society*, 1964), *"Kamakhyar itibritti samparke abhas"* (*Awahan*, January, 1967), *"Taradevir upasana" (Awahan*, March, 1967).[11] Gogoi's research in history thus ranged from ancient coinage to modern political systems. He also wrote some popular essays in various newspapers and periodicals on cultural heritage and contemporary political issues concerning the Northeast.[12] Gogoi also wrote a critical introduction to Gunabhiram Barua's *Asam Buranji* (1884) reprinted by Asom Prakashan Parishad, Guwahati, in 1972.[13]

Gogoi's approach to history writing is found in his *Presidential Address* in the fourteenth history session of the Asom Sahitya Sabha, held at Dhing in the Nowgong District, Assam, in 1959.[14] This *Address* is an evidence of his knowledge in the history of history writing since earliest times. It appears that he was much influenced by the Greek historian Thucydides who is considered by many as the 'father of scientific history' and who is also well known for his unbiased views in writing political history. Following Thucydides, Gogoi also believed that the historians should provide genuine information and testimonial evidence of what they claim to have already taken place and insisted that the evidence should always be verified and tested and the facts should be accurately recorded without interpolating the historian's own ideas and beliefs. The interpolation of any sort, according to him, would amount to distortion of facts.[15] In fact, Gogoi rigorously adhered to these principles in all his historical writings. This is particularly discernible in his *magnum opus*, entitled *The Tai and the Tai kingdoms: With a fuller treatment of the Tai-Ahom Kingdom in the Brahmaputra Valley*.[16] On the other hand, Gogoi did not altogether rule out the importance of ancient literary texts, like the *Ramayana* and the *Mahabharata*, as sources of history. He did not consider those to be totally unhistorical. Like many of his predecessors and contemporaries among the historians, he subscribed to the historicity of the Kurukshetra war and the existence of the kingdoms of Ayodhya, Lanka, Anga, Kalinga,

Magadha, Pragjyotishpura, etc. In a similar observation, he argued that the myths of the Ahoms having eight lakhs of gods, as mentioned in the Tai-Ahom chronicle, are no other than the eight lakhs of Tai population (Mao-Shans). Though it might appear mythical to many, Gogoi believed that the Tai-Ahom chronicle is a history of the Mao-Shans. According to him, this chronicle is a genuine record of the origin and spread of the Tai race over a vast land mass of Southeast Asia where the Tai kingdoms had once flourished. Though he believed that the antiquity of Tai culture and civilization might go back to 3000 BC, his own studies of the Tai-Ahom history were mainly concerned with the emergence of the Tai states in Southeast Asia from the third century AD.[17]

It may be interesting to know how his interest in the origin and culture of the Tai-Ahoms made Padmeswar Gogoi a historian of the Tai-Ahoms. He wrote an article entitled "Westward Migration of the Tai", which was published in the *Gauhati University Journal of Arts* in 1950. This article drew attention of the then Dean of the Faculty of Arts, Banikanta Kakati, who asked Gogoi to develop the subject matter of the article to a fuller study.[18] The appreciation of a scholar of the eminence of Banikanta Kakati inspired Gogoi to take up research in the history of the Tai race which was then little known to the scholars. As a matter of fact, the studies in Tai history and culture were hitherto confined only to the Christian missionaries and western scholars. The work of N. Elias, dealing with the Tai migrations towards the west, was one of those which covered the migration of the Ahoms to Assam.[19] In fact, these studies were only in segments. It was only Edward Gait who discussed the Ahom rule in Assam with considerable details in his monumental work *A History of Assam*.[20] Gait did a commendable work on the basis of the sources known in Assam till his time. Although his work was published in 1906 and a revised edition came out in 1926, no historian had significantly gone beyond Gait till Gogoi took up the subject. S.K. Bhuyan had, no doubt, written extensively on the Ahoms in English and Assamese, but the materials he used were limited to Ahom and Assamese *Buranjis* which were locally available in Assam.[21] G.C. Barua made a great contribution by translating and publishing in 1930 one of the Ahom language *Buranjis*.[22] However, Gunabhiram Barua*'s *Asam Buranji* (1884)[23] and Padmnath Gohain

* An Extra Assistant Commissioner and a Magistrate in British Assam, Gunabhiram Barua (1834-1894) was a charismatic personality of the *Jonaki Age* of Assamese literature. He was influenced by the spirit of Bengal renaissance and Vidyasagar's movement for widow remarriage while a student in Calcutta, where he did his FA and Law, and worked for a reformed society and integral nationalism in Assam. His articles in *Orunodoi*, *Jonaki* and *Asam Bandhu* echoed his progressive thought and ideas. *Asam Bandhu*, which he edited and published from Calcutta, laid the foundation for Assamese national revival and inspired a large number of talented and creative littérateurs of his generation. His prose style was forcefully vigorous and set a standard for the modern writers. His two dramas, namely, *Ramnavami* and *Bibah Rahasya*, were on the theme of social reform, widow remarriage and justice to women. Later in life he became a Brahmo and, after the death of his first wife, married a widow. He wrote two textbooks, namely, *Lorar Puthi* (1874) and *Lorar Bhugol* (1879), and edited two other books, namely, *Asomiya Lorar Mitra* (1873) and *Kavya-Kusum* (1884). Gunabhiram's contribution to historiography of Assam is indeed immense. His *'Agar Din Atiar Din'*, published in *Asam Bandhu* in fourteen installments was a historical essay on social change in nineteenth century Assam. Similarly, the article entitled *'Saumar Bhraman'* is replete with his great love for Assam and a sense of pride in its history and culture. His *Anandaram Dhekial Phukanar Jiban Charitra* is a historical biography of a great leader of social reforms in Assam. Finally, Gunabhiram's *Assam Buranji* (1884) was a great work in modern history writing in the standard of nineteenth century vernacular historiography in India. [*Editor's Addendum]

Barua*'s *Asomar Buranji* (1899)[24] laid the foundation of studies in Ahom history in the nineteenth century. The famous Assamese poet and litterateur Hiteswar Barbarua,** who is also well known as a historian, created awareness among the people about Ahom history by his literary master pieces like *Ahomar Din* (1925) in prose and some poetical works, namely, *Kamatapur Dhamsa* and *Yuddhaksetrat Ahom Romani* or *Mulaghauru Kavya*.[25] Sarbananda Rajmukar*** wrote his *Itihase Soara Sasata Basar* on six hundred years of Ahom rule in Assam.[26] A large portion of N.N. Acharya's *History of Medieval Assam*[27] is on the Ahom period, while N.K. Basu's *Assam in the Ahom Age* (1973) was a study of the

---

* An architect of modern Assamese literature and a literary giant, Padmanath Gohain Barua (1871-1946), who presided over first session of the Asam Sahitya Sabha at Sibsagar in 1917, was also a historian of considerable significance. He studied FA and Law in Calcutta and taught and served as Headmaster in several Middle and High schools in undivided Assam. He also presided over annual conferences of Asam Chattra Sanmelan (1918) and the Assam Association (1919). Besides his own immense and voluminous contributions in almost all branches of Assamese literature, he created a large number of young poets and writers as editor of various literary magazines. His *Jibani Samgraha* was an important work in history that contained as many as 27 biographies of important personalities from various walks of life. *Joymati* (1900), *Gadadhar* (1907), *Sadhani* (1911), *Lachit Barphukan* (1915), and *Banroja* (1932) are historical dramas written by him. His *Asomar Buranji* (1899) was a great work in historiography which opened with a brief chapter on pre-Ahom Assam, including the Baro Bhuyans, discussed Ahom period in several chapters, devoted a chapter each on the neighbouring kingdoms like Koch, Chutiya, Kachari, Jaintia, Srihatta, Manipur, etc. and finally, a chapter each on rise of British power and the hill tribes that were integrated into British Assam. Nineteen editions and reprints of the book came out till 1937 and every edition was revised by the author using new sources that came to light. The original work was based mainly on the traditional *Buranjis*, some historical documents, archaeological sources, inscriptions, coins, and other literary sources that were known till that time. He also used Edward Gait's *Report on Progress of Historical Research in Assam* (1897). To facilitate the teaching of regional history in vernacular schools seems to have been one his objectives in writing the book. The 'preface' was in English and he said : "I am to admit that this very preface makes no pretence of the completeness in the few pages of this booklet; but, I hope to increase its usefulness in time if it can earn appreciation of the well-wishers of the Assamese people and their country, and in the event of its being introduced as text-book in Assamese schools." True to his words, Gohain Barua brought out another eighteen revised and enlarged editions of the book in his own life time. Edward Gait's *A History of Assam* (1906/1926), *Buranjis* edited by S.K. Bhuyan and published by DHAS, John Peter Wade's *Account of Assam*, and many other publications, including newly discovered inscriptions, were used in later editions. The popularity of the book even today can be understood from the fact that Asom Prakashan Parishad brought out a reprint in 1976 and thereafter two more, in 2003 and 2004. [* Editor's Addendum]

** A literary giant, Hiteswar Barbarua (1876-1939) was the pioneer of sonnet in Assamese. *Kamatapur Dhamsa Kavya* (1913) and *Yuddhakshetrat Ahom Romani* (1915) were among his epic poems on historical themes and examples of popularizing history through literature. His *Ahomar Din* (1925), written in prose, is an important contribution to history of the Ahom period which discussed political, social and cultural history from the advent of Sukapha to the end of the Ahom rule. He was the first president of the history session of the Asam Sahitya Sabha (1925) and his presidential address set a standard for the future addresses. [**Editor's Addendum]

*** Sarbananda Rajkumar (1909-1968), BA (Hons) in Philosophy and a distinguished civil servant, is well known for his contributions to Ahom history. He contributed over the years a large number of articles in *Bahi*, *Awahan*, *Jayanti*, *Ramdhenu*, *Manideep*, etc Assamese periodicals bearing original findings and interpretations on aspects of Ahom history. *Chutiya, Bhuyan aru Matak Rajya* (1965) and *Itihase Sawora Sasata bachhar : Ahom Yugar Asom Buranji, 1228-1826* (1980) are his major works in history of Assam. He presided over history session of the Asam Sahitya Sabha at Dibrugarh in 1947. [***Editor's Addendum]

polity, society and economy of Assam under the Ahoms.[28] S.L. Barua*'s *Last Days of Ahom Monarchy* (1985) is on the decline of the Ahom state.[29] Nonetheless, the Southeast Asian perspective of the Ahom history did not come into focus in those writings.

Padmeswar Gogoi established the integral affinity of the Ahom kingdom of Assam with that of the other Tai kingdoms of Southeast Asia by using much wider range of source materials than what was available to Edward Gait. Gogoi's *The Tai and the Tai kingdoms: With a fuller treatment of the Tai-Ahom Kingdom in the Brahmaputra valley* is not a history of the Ahoms in Assam only like that of Edward Gait (though a large part of the Gait's book was on the Ahoms), but it is a fuller treatment of the Tai-Ahom kingdom that emerged in the Brahmaputra valley with critical analysis of the Southeast Asian roots of the race. He explored and used the sources hitherto known and unknown to the historians. The vastness of the material could pose a problem of handling but Gogoi's apt and in depth handling of those sources has made his work indispensable to any scholar in the subject.[30] The western scholars thenceforth increasingly realized that without a reference to the Tai-Ahom kingdom in Assam any study on the Tai race of Southeast Asia would remain incomplete. Thus, Gogoi's works[31] went a long way in filling up a major gap in Southeast Asian history and culture, besides comprehensively reconstructing the history of the Tai-Ahoms in Northeast India without missing their Southeast Asian backdrop.[32] The Ahom people of Assam were, thus, for the first time brought into focus in the context of Southeast Asian studies and the term 'Tai-Ahom' came to be popularly accepted.[33]

---

*Formerly Professor of History and Aniruddha Chair Professor, Dibrugarh University, Swarnalata Barua (ne S.L. Barua) is well known as a historian for her significant contributions in history of medieval Assam. Along with Late M.L. Bose and Late Salil Basu, she had been one of the first teachers in the department of history, Dibrugarh University, and one of the main architects of the department, of which she eventually became Professor and Head and served it in that capacity for many years. She was also the first Professor of Aniruddha Chair, Dibrugarh University, and made the Chair prestigious by her academic contributions. A Ph.D. of Dibrugarh University for her thesis on 'Purnananda Buragohain and his times', Barua adopted Medieval Assam as thrust area for further research and immensely developed that field by sustained research. She has been associated with Indian History Congress (IHC) for many years and her involvement in Northeast India History Association (NEIHA) is from the beginning of the organization, and some of her seminal papers have been published in the proceedings of these two most prestigious national and regional forums of Indian historians. He presided over 16th session of NEIHA at Assam University, Silchar, in 1995 and Medieval Section of IHC, 65th Session, at Visva-Bharati, in 2004, and delivered H L Gupta Endowment Lectures at 22nd session of NEIHA at Darrang College, Tezpur, in 2002. 'Historiography of Medieval Assam' is one of her favourite fields and after her retirement from Dibrigarh University, she did a major project on the subject as a Senior Fellow of the Indian Council of Historical Research (ICHR), New Delhi. Barua has published a large number of research papers in both English and Assamese. Her major works in English include *A Comprehensive History of Assam* (Munshiram Manoharlal Publishers Pvt. Ltd., New Delhi, 1985) and *Last Days of Ahom Monarchy*, Munshiram Manoharlal Publishers Pvt. Ltd., New Delhi, 1985. While a Professor, Aniruddha Chair, she edited a book, entitled *Life and Teachings of Sri Sri Aniruddhadeva* (Aniruddha Chair, Dibrugarh University, 2003), which is a major contribution in religious and cultural history of medieval Assam. In her retired life, S.L. Barua is deeply engrossed in her research. [+ Editor's Addendum]

As a historian

In Assam there are many scholars who contributed to the study of history though they belonged to disciplines other than history. The basic discipline of Suryya Kumar Bhuyan was English literature, while Banikanta Kakati, Birinchi Kumar Barua and Maheswar Neog were distinguished Professors of Assamese literature, but they are well known as historians as they contributed immensely to the progress of historical research in Assam. In our own time, Amalendu Guha, whose original discipline was Economics, is an acknowledged authority on the history of mediaeval and colonial Assam. The instances all over the world show that the quality of academic contributions to history is the only criteria that make a scholar a historian. Padmeswar Gogoi's basic discipline was Economics, but he distinguished himself as a historian by his original contributions to the studies in history of the Tai race, particularly the Tai-Ahoms. His *The Tai and the Tai kingdoms: With a fuller treatment of the Tai-Ahom Kingdom in the Brahmaputra valley* emerged out of his doctoral thesis of the Gauhati University and he contributed a good number of research papers on history of Assam in journals and periodicals. His Presidential Address to the history session of Asom Sahitya Sabha (1959) is an index to his perspectives of history and historiography. In his own works, he strictly adhered to historical methods; used standard sources and his works are rigorously documented.

Notes & References

1. For a life sketch of Padmeswar Gogoi, see, *Dr. P. Gogoi: A Brief Introduction*, compiled and edited by B. Chetia, published by B. Chetia on behalf of Dr. Padmeswar Gogoi Memorial Committee, Tinsukia, Assam, 1st September, 1992, pp. 33-36.
2. *Ibid.*, p . 34.
3. *Ibid*, p. 9, see Birendra Kumar Bhattacharyya's note on 'Dr. Padmeswar Gogoi'.
4. Padmeswar Gagoi unsuccessfully contested elections to the Assam Legislative Assembly twice in 1938 and 1952. *ibid.*, p. 7.
5. Though short-lived, the *Lik Phan Tai* played a great role in bringing Tai-Ahom history and culture into focus as a research field of the social scientists.
6. Padmeswar Gogoi, *The Tai and the Tai Kingdoms with a fuller treatment of the Tai-Ahom Kingdom in the Brahmaputra Valley*, Gauhati University, 1968.
7. Padmeswar Gogoi, *Tai-Ahom Religion and Customs*, Publication Board, Assam, Gauhati, 1976.
8. Padmeswar Gogoi, *Future Status of Assam*, pub, by R. Bora, Jorhat, 1945.
9. Those included *Ganatantrik Samajbad* (Oriental Book Company, Gauhati, 1970), *Asomot prachalita pauranik akhyansamuhar mul bichar* (Asom Prakashan Parishad/ Oriental Book Company, Gauhati, n.d.), *bartaman yugat brihat saktibargar arthanoitik bikash* (Secretary, U.C.C.P.T. in Regional Language, Gauhati University, 1st part, 1975 & 2nd part, 1976), *Eknayak tantra* (Secretary, U.C.C.P.T. in the Regional Language, Dibrugarh University, n.d.), *Samaj Vigyan*, Part III (Oriental Book Company, Gauhati, 1977).

10. For the list of publications of Padmeswar Gogoi, see 'Life Sketch' in: *Dr. P. Gogoi: A Brief Introduction, op.cit.*, pp. 36-37.

11. Compiled by Sarat Rajkhowa, *Ibid.*, pp. 47-48.

12. Those popular essays/articles included "*Adhunik Soshan Nity*" (*Sangram*, All Assam Ahom Cultural Federation, February, 1951), "*Manipurar Swaroop*" (*Jayanti*, 1954), "*Tirtha buli kare jalot sudhi*" (*Asom Sahitya Sabha Patrika*, 1957, March Issue), "*Kailashat Kamakhya*" (*Surujmukhi*, October, 1960), " *Sarbak Darshan aru ajir yug*" (*Surujmukhi*, June, 1963), "*Ganatantrik Samajbad aru samajbadi ganatantra*" (*Navadhara*, August, 1964), "*Ganatantra dhanatantrik aru samajtantrik*" (*Janamat*, August, 1966), "*Zorstar ba zorthrastar siksha*" (*Surujmukhi*, March, 1967), "*Bharatar samajik niyantran aru byaktigata swadhinata*" (Akashvani, Guwahati, 1973), "Party Government" (*Janata*, March, 1975), "India's Democratic Experiment" (*Janata*. July, 1977), "The Rule of the Janata Party" (*Janata*, September, 1977), " *Kurushetrar yuddhat arjunar durgastuti*" (*Jyoti*, August-October, 1977), "The Price and Gandhian Solution" (*Janata*, January, 1978), "Forces of Integration and disintegration" (*Northeastern Economic Review*, January-March, 1978), "Whither Indian Socialist" (*Janata*, July, 1979).

13. Gunabhiram Barua, *Asam Buranji*, 1st edn., Calcutta, 1884, reprint Asom Prakashan Parishad, Guwahati, 1972.

14. *Asam Sahitya Sabhar Bhasanavali* (Assamese), Part III, *Buranji*, A Collection of the Presidential Addresses of the History Sessions, Asom Sahitya Sabha, from 1925 to 1961, compiled by Atul Chandra Hazarika and Jatindranath Goswami, published by Maheswar Neog, General Secretary, Asom Sahitya Sabha, Chandrakanta Handiqui Bhavan, Jorhat, 1961, pp.199-207 (herein after *Bhasanavali*). The volume includes the *Presidential Addresses* of Hiteswar Barbarua, Suryyakumar Bhuyan, Pramathnath Chakravarty, Rajanikumar Padmapati, Sonaram Choudhury, Kanaklal Barua, Sarbananda Rajkumar, Benudhar Sarma, Sureshchandra Rajkhowa, Birinchikumar Barua, Rupnath Brahma and Premadhar Choudhury, besides Padmeswar Gogoi.

15. *Bhasanavali*, pp. 200-202.

16. Padmeswar Gogoi, *The Tai and the Tai kingdoms: With a fuller treatment of the Tai-Ahom Kingdom*, Gauhati University, 1968 (herein after *TTK*).

17. *TTK*, p. 125.

18. *TTK,* see 'Preface'.

19. Ney Elias, *Introductory Sketch of the History of the Shans in Upper Burma and West Yunnan*, Calcutta, 1876.

20. Edward Gait, *A History of Assam*, (1st edn. London, 1906) Revised edn. Thacker Sprink & co., Calcutta, 1926.

21. Some of the well known works of S.K. Bhuyan in Ahom history, besides the large number of *buranjis* edited and/or translated by him with long introductions, include his *Lachit Barphukan and His Times*, DHAS, Gauhati, 1947; *Atan Buragohain and His Times*, DHAS, Gauhati, 1931; *The Military System of the Assamese People*, Kamarupa Anusanddhan Samiti, Guwahati, 2010; *Mir Jumla's Invasion of Assam*, DHAS, Gauhati, 1956; *Studies in the History of Assam*, Pub. Lakshewari Bhuyan, Gauhati, 1986; *Ahomar Din*, Jorhat, 1918; *Jaimati Upakhyan*, Gauhati, 1920; *Kowanr-Bidroh*, Gauhati, 1948; *Ramani Gabharu*, Gauhati, 1951; *Rajeswar Singha, 1751-1769*, Publication Board, Assam, Gauhati, 1975; *Mirjumlar Asom Akraman*, Gauhati, 1956; *Lachit Barphukan*, Publication Board, Assam, Gauhati, 1979.

22. G.C. Barua (trans. & ed.), *Ahom Buranji*, Calcutta, 1930.
23. Gunabhiram Barua, *Asam Buranji*, Calcutta, 1884.
24. Padmanath Gohain Barua, *Asomar Buranji*, Lakhimpur, 1899.
25. Banikanta Sarma, *"Sonnet : Madhusudan Aru Asomiya Kabisakalar Obodan"*, *The Heritage*, Vol. I, Issue No. 2, Guwahati, 2011, p. 94.
26. Sarbananda Rajkumar, *Itihase Soara Sasata Basar*, 1st edn. 1980, reprint Banalata Prakashan, Guwahat, 2000.
27. N.N. Acharya, *History of Medieval Assam*, Dutta Barooah & Company, Gauhati, 1966.
28. N.K. Basu, *Assam in the Ahom Age*, Firma K.L. Mukhopadhyay, Calcutta, 1973.
29. S.L. Barua, *Last Days of Ahom Monarchy*, Munshiram Manoharlal Publishers Pvt. Ltd., New Delhi, 1985.
30. Such scholars are Barend Jan Terwiel and Stephen Murray from Australia, Jean Berlie of France, Yuji Baba and Mikike Kure from Japan, and Chatthip Nartsupha from Thailand to mention a few.
31. Another notable work of Padmeswar Gogoi was *Tai-Ahom Religion and Customs* which inspired the Tai-Ahom people to revive their old archaic cults in the celebration of the *Me-Dam Me-Phi* (ancestor worship) religious festival throughout the state of Assam with much enthusiasm. The Govt. of Assam has declared 31st January every year as a state holiday for the purpose.
32. See, Chapter Three: 'The Tai-Ahom Power in Assam', in: H.K. Barpujari (ed.), *The Comprehensive History of Assam*, Vol. II, Publication Board, Assam, 1992, pp. 50-52, 61, 68.
33. The Ahom people now-a-days refer themselves as 'Tai-Ahom' instead of 'Ahom' only, such as Tai-Ahom Students' Union, Tai-Ahom Development Council, etc. It was Gogoi who first introduced this concept which has now got wider acceptance. This term was not in use before the publication of Gogoi's works.

15

Birinchi Kumar Barua (1908-1964)

—*Sagar Boruah*

Biographical Sketch

The task of assessment of a scholar of the eminence of Birinchi Kumar Barua, who in his short span of life of only about fifty-six years had proved himself as a man of infinite energy, imagination and ideas in a vast range of his works, is albeit a difficult task. Born at Puranigudam, nearly 10 kilometers from Nagaon town of Assam, on 10 November 1908, Birinchi Kumar Barua was simultaneously a novelist, dramatist, story writer, and essayist of high caliber. Over and above, he was the pathfinder in objectively writing a cultural history of Assam which remains as the only standard work in the subject for more than last sixty years. He was also a very successful teacher and a skilful academic administrator. Beginning his early education in Nagaon Mission School, Barua studied in Nagaon Sadar Middle Assamese School and Nagaon Government High School. A brilliant student all throughout his career, he passed the Matriculation Examination of the Calcutta University in 1928 in First Division and proceeded to Calcutta for collegiate education. He studied at the prestigious Presidency College, Calcutta, wherefrom he graduated with Honours in Pali Language and Literature in 1932. He had the rare distinction of qualifying for the much coveted 'Ishan Scholarship'of Calcutta University for his brilliant academic performance. He did his M.A. in Pali from the Calcutta University in 1934 securing first position in First Class. After his graduation in Law in 1936, Barua joined Calcutta University as a part-time Lecturer in Pali in 1937 and in the next year, he was appointed as Lecturer in Modern Indian Languages in the same University. However, he soon left Calcutta to join Cotton College, Guwahati, as a Lecturer in Assamese (on 13 September 1938).[1] In 1945, Barua left for London to pursue his research work for the Degree of Doctor of Philosophy at the School of Oriental and African Studies, University of London. He worked on 'Cultural History of Assam' under the supervision of Professor K. De B. Codington of the School of Oriental and African Studies and was awarded Ph. D in 1947 by the University of London for successful completion of the research work.[2]

On his return from London, Birinchi Kumar Barua resumed his service in Cotton College. Meanwhile, Gauhati University was established in 1948 with noted scholar K.K. Handiqui as the first Vice-Chancellor. Barua moved to the University as Reader in the Department of Assamese.[3] Due to the premature death of Banikanta Kakati, Barua had to assume charge of the Head of the Department of Assamese on 1 February 1953. He became a Professor in the same department and served the University as Dean of the Faculty of Arts till 1961. Barua also acted as the Head of the Department of Bengali for a pretty long period of time. In fact, he played the key role of an organizer and one of the architects of the Gauhati University. Before establishment of the University, he took active part in what is known in Assam as 'University Movement', organizing meetings in different places in the state in support of the demand for establishment of a University at Guwahati. A prolific writer and a fine orator, he played the key role in mobilizing the public opinion in favour of the movement for establishment of a University in Assam. In those days of the movement, Barua used to write powerful essays in the newspapers explaining the need of the University and inviting the views and suggestions from the people on the subject. He also organized several public meetings and took out processions in various places demanding the establishment of a University in Assam.[4]

Barua was associated with several academic institutions and organizations of his time. He served in the Department of Historical and Antiquarian Studies, Assam, as the Honorary Deputy Director from 1951 to 1960. He presided over the *Buranji Sammilan* (history session) of the *Asam Sahitya Sabha* at Guwahati in 1955. He visited Colombo and Russia on academic invitations and served as a Guest Professor at the Indiana University, United States of America, in 1964. He also participated in the International Conference of Orientalists, held in Delhi, in January 1964, and acted as one of the Conveners for the 42nd Session of the Indian Oriental Conference at Calcutta. In the midst of huge activities and prime of his academic career, Barua passed away on 30 March 1964 at a comparatively young age of 56.[5]

The untimely passing away of Birinchi Kumar Barua was a rude shock to the academia in the country and a great loss to scholarship in Northeast India. It happened at a time when Barua was fast growing in stature as a scholar in India and abroad. As a tribute to his contributions to Assam and the Gauhati University, *The Assam Tribune* in its editorial note under caption *A Great Loss* said, "In the death of Dr. Birinchi Kumar Barua Assam has lost a historian, litterateur, scholar and educationist of all India repute . . . His association with Gauhati University since its inception and his contribution as the Dean of Faculty of Arts and Secretary of the Post-Graduate Classes cannot be easily forgotten. His participation in hundreds of all-India councils on education and scholastics not only gave him recognition on a national level, but also raised Assam's prestige outside. His erudition was recognised abroad as is shown by the invitation accorded to him by an American University recently to go there as Visiting Professor."[6]

Contributions to history

Birinchi Kumar Barua made significant contributions in different aspects of the history of Assam and the Assamese literature. His literary talent was manifested in some of his creative writings in his school days. While a student of Class IV, he took initiative in establishing a 'Juvenile Association' in his school which brought out a handwritten monthly. He was the editor of the journal. He also established a library called *Balya Pushtakalaya* (children library) in Nagaon in 1923.[7] He used to write stories in *Awahan,* an Assamese monthly. It is said that *bidruhi deka* (revolutionary youth) was Barua's first short story published in *Awahan*. The collections of his short-stories *Pat-Parivartan* (1948) and *Aaghunibai* (1950) are testimonies of his literary creativity and assemblage of critical judgments. His novels *Jivanar Batat* (1944) and *Seuji Patar Kahini* (1950) not only earned him name and fame as a great novelists but these are also important milestones in the development of Assamese novels. He wrote a drama *Abelar Nat* (1955) under a pen-name. *Switzerland Bhraman* (1948) and *Professor Baruar Chithi* (1968) are his two travelogues. His *Kabya* and *Abhibyanjana* (1941) and *Asomiya Bhasa* (1946) are seminal contributions to the study of Assamese language and literature. He wrote several pieces for the children, among which *Jatakmala* (1938) and *Desh-Bideshar Sadhu* (1948) deserve special mention. He translated *Chitrangada* of Rabindranath Tagore into Assamese. Among the textbooks he wrote for students, *Bharat Buranji, Buranji Katha* and *Sahitya Saurabh* were very popular for a long time. A large number of his scholarly essays in Assamese were published in important literary journals, periodicals and magazines, like *Asom Sahitya Sabha Patrika, Asom Hitaishi, Awahan, Ranghar, Ramdhenu, Jayanti* and *Bordaisila.*[8]

A great literary genius, Barua's works in Assamese literature are important for understanding history and culture of Assam. He edited a number of old books and among those *Ankiya Nat* (1940), *Mahabharatar Adi Parba* (1962), *Mahabharatar Sabha Parba* (1963), *Arunudoir Dhalphat* (1965), *Manasa Kabya* (1951), *Babrubahanar Juddha* (1959) are important sources for cultural history of the region. His *Asomiya Katha Sahitya* (1950), *Asomiya Bhasa Aru Sanskriti* (1957), *Asomar Loka Sanskriti* (1961) are among his those studies which contain mines of information and insights for literary and cultural history. His *Assamese Literature* (1941), *Studies in Early Assamese Literature* (1953), *Modern Assamese Literature* (1957) and *History of Assamese Literature* (1964) are indeed path-breaking works in history of Assamese literature which are also important for studying intellectual history of Assam. His *Early Geography of Assam* (1952) and *Sankardeva : Vaisnava Saint of Assam* (1960) are invaluable contributions in the history of ancient and medieval Assam. He translated Ambikagiri Ray Choudhury's *Karagarar Geet* into English under the caption *Songs of the Cell*. He also contributed a good number of research papers in history and culture of the region in *Journal of Assam Research Society, Calcutta Review* and *Journal of Gauhati University,* He contributed entries in *Shipley's Encyclopedia of World Literature* (Vol. I), and wrote some popular articles in *The Assam Tribune.*[9] Barua brought out a revised and enlarged version of Edward Gait's *A History of Assam* (1926) in 1963, for which he jointly worked with H.V.S. Murthy of the Department of History, Gauhati University.[10]

The most acclaimed work of Birinchi Kumar Barua in the field of history is his *A Cultural History of Assam* (Early Period) for which he shall always be remembered as a historian of Northeast India. It was a pioneering work in cultural history of the region and till today it remains the only standard work in the subject. Barua himself wrote in the preface of the book that "Systematic investigations have not yet been carried out in various aspects of early Assamese life."[11] Till that time, there was no scholarly work on the cultural history of the region. In Edward Gait's *A History of Assam* (1906/1926)[12] the treatment of the ancient period was only sketchy. Among the works of the mainstream Indian historians, *The Dynastic History of Northern India* (1931) of H.C. Ray[13] and *History of North-Eastern India* (1931) of R.G. Basak[14] were only two books which are worth mentioning for references to ancient Assam (Kamarupa), but the treatment of cultural history in those works was only casual. Rai Bhadur Kanaklal Barua no doubt discussed the cultural life of the people of Assam in his *Early History of Kamarupa* (1933),[15] but in that valuable work also the attention was mainly on the reconstruction of dynastic or political history of the region. Babu Nagendranath Vasu's *Social History of Kamarupa* (Vols.1-3; 1922, 1926, 1933)[16] contained a vast mass of information, but a lot remained for critical examination and historical analyses. Banikanta Kakati's *The Mother Goddess Kamakhya* (1948),[17] though an analytical scholarly work, is more in the nature of an introduction to the religious history of ancient and mediaeval Assam and Kakati himself wrote in the preface of the book, "the present publication is a mere introduction towards the study of the fusion of the Aryan and extra-Aryan religious beliefs and practices in Assam."[18] Rajmohan Nath's *The Background of Assamese Culture* (1949),[19] was an outstanding contribution to the evolution of composite Assamese culture but it was based mainly on oral traditions and ethno-archeological data. On the other hand, Birinchi Kumar Barua's *A Cultural History of Assam*[20] emerged out of his doctoral dissertation of the University system and prepared according to internationally accepted historical methods and the norms and practices of history writing. Thus, his work was based on standard historical sources, including literary, epigraphic, archeological etc., principles of documentation and authentication, and historical perspectives. The book is an in-depth study of the socio-cultural, economic and political development in early Assam. It opened the door for further research in cultural history of Northeast India in a scientific manner.

Barua's perception of history was clear and comprehensive. This is evident from his speeches and writings. To him history is essential for the formation of a healthy society and the knowledge of history is essentially required for the progress of the nation. He also suggested that the study of history is an instrument to enlarge the perimeter of literature and it helps in the development of literature. He was clear in his opinion that until and unless the works on history, science, philosophy etc are made available in Assamese language, the perfection and nutrition in Assamese literature cannot be accomplished.[21] He was convinced that "the society, thought and philosophy of a nation are placed on record in the past-history of the country. The experiences of the past, preserved in history are the means of development of the nation. Self-understanding is the great advice of history." [22] In Barua's view, history is the reconstruction of the past with the help of sources called evidences or facts or data, but all data or facts are not historical. It is one of the major responsibilities of the historian that he should carefully examine the reliability and dependability of his facts. It was an advantage for Barua that he was well aware of the literary sources of history of Assam and he could analyse those sources scientifically. He emphasized the writing of scientific history on the basis of facts or data. He suggested that the old-scripts, temples, religious books, information reported in Assamese periodicals like *Arunoday* and the archaeological remains are of immense value in terms of source-material for writing of the socio-cultural history of Assam. Barua also observed that folk-literature and social festivals could be used to reconstruct the socio-religious history of Assam. In his opinion the old Assamese literary works are very useful sources for writing the cultural history of Assam as they speak of the food habit, ornaments, music, dance, agriculture, house system, etc of the Assamese people and the facts for writing history can be traced even from the vocabulary of language. Barua further said that the economic history of Assam could also be compiled with the help of the narration made of the deities.[23]

In emphasizing the utility of the *Buranji*[24] in writing the medieval Assam history, Barua said, "The *Buranjis* contributed largely towards the enrichment of Assamese vocabulary in its various ramifications in diverse fields. They incorporate a large number of administrative and legal terms current in the Ahom court. Words from the Ahom language are also not rare. Such words are used to denote things and institutions which are distinctly connected with Ahom life and culture."[25] Viewing that the six hundred years of Ahom rule in Assam presented a panorama of growth in all departments of life, Barua observed, "the most distinctive aspects of the period ... were the geographical institutions, organization of the economic, social and religious systems, and the cultural nationalism . . . The nationalistic temper of the age had a direct effect on arts and literature, which contributed a good deal to the life of the people."[26] He considered it needless to say that *Buranjis* are very helpful for writing the history of medieval Assam, but he regretted that "only the political history is compiled so far from *Buranjis.* It is necessary to collect the facts from *Buranjis* to write the social, religious, economic and academic history of the province."[27] Nonetheless, he said that "it is a matter of pride that Assam has a tradition of *Buranjis* (history) since ancient time."[28] Quoting Alberuni, who had said that "Unfortunately the Hindus do not pay much attention to the historical order of things, they are very careless in relating the chronological succession of their kings, and when they are pressed for information and are at a loss, not knowing what to say, they invariably resort to telling tale", Barua had observed that "Assam is fortunately free from such type of lacking."[29] Barua suggested that the *Vansavalis* are useful documents to compile the history of Assam. Besides recording the genealogy of different families of the nobles these *Vansavalis* give sketches of their lives and careers. He observed that old Bengali and Oriya literature, the Sanskrit scripts and the Persian accounts are also useful sources to write the history of early and medieval Assam. However, Barua suggested that the historian can write proper history only through just evaluation of the sources and interpretation of his facts. Interpretation, according to him, is a basic element in research and essential to write history. He was of the opinion that a historian should not be blind at the time of the interpretation of facts and he should be mentally free from class and caste and the blind national prejudices.[30]

Explaining the meaning of history, Birinchi Kumar Baruah said that "it is (history) not only the story of diplomacy or war or a national story; but it is the reflection of the social and cultural life of a nation; a document of thought."[31] It may be assumed that this own viewpoint of history led Barua to work on cultural history of Assam. Indeed, Barua examined the history of Assam from the national point of view. As a historian, he attempted to highlight the Assamese culture as a part of greater Indian heritage. He showed that 'Assam is a small unit of India but it played a most distinct and important role as a transmitter of Aryan civilization in lands like Tibet, Nepal and Burma' and that 'Assam is the frontier outpost of Indian Civilization'.[32] He was convinced that the land of Assam was an integral part of the geographical boundary of the *Ramayana* and the *Mahabharata*. Since the days of the Mauryas Assam had a relation with Northern India and in the age of the Guptas it had reached its zenith. He said, "Assam had contacts with India since Mauriyan times; in the Gupta Age these contacts became stronger. The manner in which the Assam kings made an attempt to consolidate their political power shows how they imitated the Gupta expansionist measures. Bhaskaravarman not only took part in pan-Indian political affairs but also attempted to have suzerainty admitted on an all-India basis."[33] Barua argued for the idea of 'greater India' by showing that 'the political outlook of Assam kings was not limited to their immediate domain but was to some extent pan-Indian' and while explaining the trade and commercial aspects of early Assam, he further argued that Assam had from very early times close relations with the heartland of India. The commodities like silk and *aguru* of Assam had a ready market in India as well as outside. There were trade relations with Tibet, Burma and the south of China. The Indian trade route to northern Mongolia lay through Assam.[34] In his words, "As a frontier province Assam did not have to maintain an exclusive existence, rather there were frequent exchange with other zones of India in matters of economy and culture. For this very reason the standard of life in Assam had come to an all India level."[35]

In the context of socio-religious history of Assam, Barua showed that Assam had close cultural contacts with other parts of India since early times and that the process of Aryanisation in Assam started during the days of *Ramayana* and *Mahabharata*. Regarding the coming of the Aryans to the province Barua was of the opinion that "At what period of history the Aryan speakers came into the valley of the Brahmaputra we can not say. But there is hardly any doubt that they arrived at a fairly early period either as the result of invasion or by means of peaceful penetration."[36] As elsewhere in other parts India, in Assam too the *varna* system contributed to the development of a new pattern in the socio-religions life of Assam. He further said, "But because Assam is a border region and its relations are mostly with Kirata or Mogoloid peoples, the Aryanised social form and the Vedic customs and rites do not adhere to any rigid pattern. For the same reason the number of Brahmanas here is small and its inherence not dominant and, further, racial discrimination or the caste system is not rigid."[37] He also examined the background and the development of 'the fundamental of streams of the Brahmanical religion' in the early period in Assam and showed how Saivism, Saktism and Vaisnavism developed in Assam in various forms. Barua assumed that the contribution of the Dravidians to the Assamese culture cannot be insignificant and proposed to do more work on this issue, because the influence of the Dravidian custom may be guessed in some manners and customs of Assamese marriage system. On the line of Kanaklal Barua, Birinchi Kumar Barua also was of the opinion that the expressions of *dharma* and *tathagata* which occur respectively in Bhaskaravarman's and Indrapala's grants have led some scholars to believe that Buddhism did exist in Assam at an early period. He also referred to the fact that Nagarjuna and Luipa, known as Minanatha, who promulgated the doctrine of *Yogini-Kula*, belonged to Kamarupa and the same Minanatha composed *Budhi Chitta Bandhupadesha* in old Assamese language.[38]

Barua made in-depth study of the process of growth and development of demographic pattern of Assam and the Assamese language and observed that "linguistic and ethnographic evidences including some ancient place-names of the province indicate that the earliest inhabitants of Assam spoke an Indo-Chinese language of the Mon Khmer family... a branch of the Austric family of languages. The date when the Austric speakers began to infiltrate into Assam is not known, but it must have occurred several hundred years B.C. and certainly long before the advent of the Aryans from the west."[39] He suggested that it is hard to define the contribution of the Austric-speaking Mongolian peoples to the ethnological structure of Assam; but such influence is manifest in many existing cultural institutions, customs and manners of the Assamese people. The next wave of the Indo-Chinese comprised of various people speaking Tibeto-Burman tongue. This group of people entered into Assam from north-west China. Some of them proceeded toward the Garo Hills and the state of Hill Tippera, while some of them entered into the valley of the river Kapili. A large section of Tibeto-Burman people settled in the valley of the Brahmaputra. Among those the Bodo group was the largest. Barua's view is that "The Bodo group includes the Koch, the Kachari, the Lalung, the Dimacha, the Garo, the Rabha, the Tipura, the Chutiya and the Maran tribes."[40] The Bodos established themselves in the vicinity of rivers, and so most of the names of rivers in eastern Assam are of Bodo origin. They even rechristened river names of earlier Austric origin by prefixing them with *di*, their own equivalent for water. Barua also examined the settlement of other groups of people like the Ahoms, the Khamtis, the Phakiyals etc and observed that geography was very important in shaping the linguistic and cultural history of a country. He compared the river Brahmaputra with Nile of Egypt and said, "In a sense it is (Brahmaputra) the life-giving blood of Assam, as the Nile is that of Egypt; and Assam's whole history and culture are intimately connected with the Brahmaputra."[41] Barua is of the opinion that "the Assamese language developed out of the Sanskrit language as early as in the 7th century A.D." He further observed that Assamese, being a living and growing language, has borrowed a great number of words from other Indo-Aryan languages. It has also received some Persian and Arabic words, chiefly administrative and legal terms. All these factors, according to Barua, have contributed towards the full-fledged development of the Assamese language, and made it a subtle and powerful medium of expression.[42]

As a historian

Brinchi Kumar Barua was a path-breaking researcher in cultural and literary history of Assam. He was a doyen among the contemporary scholars of the country, enjoying national and international fame. His works, particularly *A Cultural History of Assam* and *History of Assamese Literature*, are indeed fundamental contributions which have continued to inspire researches in socio-economic and cultural history of early and medieval Assam. He not only used all available conventional sources of history and adhered to standard methods, norms and practices of history writing but also showed how non-conventional sources can be helpful in reconstructing history in the absence of conventional sources. The tradition of using linguistic tools, customs and manners, rites and rituals in studying cultural history in Assam owes its beginning to Banikanta Kakati and Birinchi Kumar Barua who successfully interpreted the living cultural traditions of the people to retrieve their cultural past. On the basis of historical evidences and by using comparative method, Barua strongly argued that the Assamese culture was an integral part of Indian culture, although he pointed out that the Assamese culture took a new shape due to the admixture of Aryan and non-Aryan elements.

Notes & References

1. Somnath Bora (ed.), *Birinchi Kumar Barua: Jeevan Aru Karma* (in Assamese), Krantikal Prakashan, Nagaon, 2008, pp. 29-30.
2. B.K. Barua, *A Cultural History of Assam*, Vol. I, Published by Shri K. K. Barooah, Nowgong, 1951, p. vii (Preface).
3. Somnath Bora (ed.), *Birinchi Kumar Barua: Jeevan Aru Karma* (in Assamese), *op.cit*, p. 30.
4. *Ibid*, p. 30-31.
5. Upendranath Sarmah, *"Birinchi Kumar Baruah : Jeevan aru Kriti"* in *Gariyoshi* (a monthly Assamese magazine), Vol. xv, No 8, May, Guwahati, 2008, pp. 15-17.
6. *The Assam Tribune,* 31 March, 1964.
7. Nagen Saikia, *"Nakhyatra Sarup Birirnchi Kumar Barua"* in *Goriyashi,* Vol. xv, No 8, May, 2008, p. 19.
8. *Ibid*, pp. 16-18.
9. Upendranath Sarmah, *op.cit.*.
10. Edward Gait, *A History of Assam*, (1st pub. London, 1906, 2nd revised edition Calcutta, 1926) revised, enlarged and edited by B.K. Barua & H.V.S. Murthy, Thacker Sprink & Co., Calcutta, 1963.
11. B.K. Barua, *op. cit,* p. vii.
12. Edward Gait, *A History of Assam*, (1st pub. London, 1906) 2nd revised edition Calcutta, 1926; reprinted EBH (India) Pvt Ltd., Guwahati, 2008.
13. H.C. Ray, *The Dynastic History of Northern India*, Calcutta University, 1931.
14. R.G. Basak, *History of North-Eastern India extending from the foundation of the Gupta Empire to the rise of the Pala Dynasty of Bengal (c. A.D. 320-760)*, 1st edn. Calcutta, 1934; reprint Firma K.L.M., Calcutta, 1967.
15. K.L. Barua, *Early History of Kamarupa*, 1st edn. 1933; reprint Lawyers Book Stall, Gauhati, 1966.

16. N.N. Vasu, *Social History of Kamarupa*, 3 vols., Calcutta, 1922, 1926, 1933.
17. Banikanta Kakati, *The Mother Goddess Kamakhya*, Lawyer's Book Stall, Gauhati, 1948.
18. *Ibid*, see Preface.
19. Rajmohan Nath, *The Background of Assamese Culture*, Dutta Barooah & Co., Gauhati, 1948.
20. B.K. Barua, *A Cultural History of Assam*, Nowgong, 1951.
21. For Birinchi Kumar Baruah's concept of history, see his 'presidential address' in Atul Chandra Hazarika and Jatindranath Goswami (ed), *Asam Sahitya Sabhar Bhasanavali* (in Assamese), Guwahati, 1961, p. 148.
22. *Ibid*, pp. 148-49.
23. *Ibid*.
24. *Buranji* is a kind of chronicles of the Ahom Court composed under the patronage of the Ahom kings.
25. B.K. Barua, *History of Assamese Literature*, (1st pub. Gauhati 1964) reprinted New Delhi, 1978, p. 100.
26. *Ibid.*, p. 102.
27. *Ibid.*, p. 101
28. *Ibid*.
29. *Ibid*.
30. Lila Gogoi, *Buranji Sahitya* (in Assamese), Dibrugarh, 1988, pp. 154-59.
31. Cited in *ibid*, p. 154.
32. B.K. Barua, *A Cultural History of Assam*, *op.cit.*, p. 230.
33. *Ibid*, p. 227.
34. *Ibid*.
35. *Ibid.*, p. 8.
36. *Ibid.*, pp. 7-8.
37. *Ibid.*, p. 8.
38. *Ibid.*; Also see Lila Gogoi, *op.cit.*, p. 7.
39. B.K. Barua, *History of Assamese Literature*, *op. cit.*, p. 2.
40. *Ibid.*, pp. 3-4.
41. *Ibid.*, p. 5.
42. *Ibid.*, p. 8.

16

Heramba Kanta Barpujari (1912-2002)

—*Shrutidev Goswami*

Biographical Sketch

Acclaimed as 'the doyen among historians of Northeast India' and formally honoured by the Asom Sahitya Sabha (prestigious literary and intellectual body of Assam) as *Itihas Acharya*, Heramba Kanta Barpujari (*ne* H.K. Barpujari) was born in Dibrugarh on 31 August 1912. His father Padma Kanta Barpujari was a Sanskrit teacher in the Government High School, Golaghat, and his mother Basanta Malati Devi was the daughter of Sivanath Bhattacharya of Dibrugarh. Barpujaris belonged to Jorhat. On the premature death of Padma Kanta the guardianship of the family fell on his elder brother, Chandrakanta Barpujari, who was a renowned Sanskrit scholar and Head Pundit of the Government High School, Jorhat. Heramba Kanta had his early education in Nakari Primary School (Jorhat) and Jorhat Government High School, passed the Matriculation Examination of Calcutta University in 1931, graduated from Cotton College (Guwahati) with Honours in History in 1935 and did his M A in Modern History from the Dacca University in 1938. The eminent Indian historians like Jadunath Sarkar, R.C. Majumdar, N.K. Bhattasali and K.R. Qanungo were among his teachers in Dacca University. He was awarded the Degree of Doctor of Philosophy by the London University in 1949 for his thesis 'The British Administration in Assam (1826-45)' under the supervision of Professors Sir C. H. Phillips and D.G.H. Hall.

Barpujari began his teaching career in 1940 as Lecturer in History in J. B. College, Jorhat. In 1941, he joined the Assam Education Service (AES) and was posted in M. C. College, Sylhet, as Assistant Lecturer in History. In 1943, he was promoted as a Lecturer and transferred to Cotton College, Guwahati. On a scholarship of the Government of Assam, he was in the School of Oriental and African Studies (SOAS), London University, in 1947-49 for his doctoral research. On his return in 1949, he became Professor of History in Cotton College. In 1952-55, he served as Assistant Director of Public Instructions, Assam, at Shillong. In 1955, he rejoined Cotton College as Professor and Head of the Department of History. He became the Vice-Principal of the College in 1961 and served also as Principal for sometime before joining the Gauhati University, in July 1963, as Professor and Head of the Department of History. He was the Dean, Faculty of Arts, of the University during 1968-71. Barpujari retired from active service in March 1976, but rejoined the Gauhati University in 1977 as UGC Professor of History to work till March 1982. In recognition of his distinguished service to the University, the Gauhati University conferred upon him the honour of a Professor Emeritus in 1989.

Barpujari's literary talent and aptitude of a writer became manifest in his school days when he wrote some articles in school magazine and local papers. While a student in Dacca University, he authored a text book in geography, *Bhugol Prabeshika*, which was prescribed by the Calcutta University for the matriculation standard. His *Bhugol Prabeshika* and a series of geography books for various classes, called *Natun Bhugol*, were prescribed as text books for more than forty yeas in the Assamese medium schools by the Government of Assam. On his return from England in 1949 he began to publish research papers and articles in history in various journals and proceedings. He also regularly attended the annual sessions of Indian History Congress and the Indian Historical Records Commission. The historian in Barpujari bloomed in public view with the publication of the *Cotton College Golden Jubilee Volume* in 1952, which he edited with a long introduction. The volume included his own article on the history of higher education in Assam, which is quoted by many even these days. As the Local Secretary of the Guwahati session (1959) of the Indian History Congress, he published a souvenir entitled *Heritage of Assam* highlighting the historical and archaeological sites and cultural traditions of the region. The publication of the *Suryya Kumar Bhuyan Commemoration Volume* (Gauhati, 1966), which Barpujari edited jointly with Professor Maheswar Neog, was another milestone in historical research in the Northeast.

The first book of H.K. Barpujari, *Assam : In the Days of the Company* (Gauhati, 1963) was published soon after he joined the Gauhati University. His next book, *Problem of the Hill Tribes : North East Frontier*, came out in three volumes, Vol. I (1822-43), Vol. II (1843-73) and Vol. III (1873-1962) (Gauhati, 1970, 1976 and 1981). *The Political History of Assam*, Vol. I (1826-1919), was published by the Govt. of Assam in 1977 under the General Editorship of Professor Barpujari. Among his remarkable publications in the later years are *The American Missionaries and North-East India, 1836-1900* (Guwahati, 1986), *An Account of Assam and Her Administration, 1603-1822* (Guwahati, 1988), *Francis Jenkins : Report on the North East Frontier of India* , 1831-32 (Guwahati, 1988) and *India's North-East : Problems, Policies and Prospects* (Guwahati, 1998). Barpujari also wrote three important books in Assamese, viz. *American Misonerisakal aru Unavimsa Satikar Asom* (Jorhat, 1981), *Asamar Nava-Jagaran : Ona-Asamiyar Bhumika* (Jorhat, 1987) and *Itihas : Rachanavidhi aru Cromovikash* (Guwahati, 1988). *The Comprehensive History of Assam*, published by the Publication Board, Assam, in five volumes (1990-1991), covering the period from pre-historic times to 1919, under the editorship of H.K. Barpujari, is another monumental work which is first of its kind in the Northeast. It is indeed to the credit of Barpujari that he could persuade some of the stalwarts of Indian historians like H.D. Sankalia, B.N. Puri, Sudhakar Chattopadhyaya, S.K. Saraswati, D.C. Sircar, Jagadish Narayan Sarkar, A.C. Banerjee, Tarasankar Banerjee and B.N. Mukherjee, besides others from within the region, to contribute chapters in *The Comprehensive History of Assam*, and this explains Barpujari's stature as a historian among his illustrious contemporaries in the country. The last few years of his life, he was engaged in writing *Kuri Satikar Kahini* (Kolkata, 2010), an autobiographical work in Assamese, which has been posthumously published by the Institute of Northeast India Studies, Kolkata.

Besides the books written by him, Barpujari contributed a large number of research papers in journals and proceedings, including *Journal of Indian History*, *Indian Archives*, *Proceedings of Indian History Congress* and *Proceedings of Indian Historical Records Commission*.[1] He contributed a chapter on 'Frontier Policy : Policy towards the Hill Tribes, North East Frontier' in Vol. XXII of the *Comprehensive History of India* edited by Professor Biseswar Prasad and published by the Indian History Congress. He was one of the research supervisors for the monumental *Dictionary of National Biography* (4 vols), edited by Professor S P Sen and published by the Institute of Historical Studies, Calcutta (1972-74) and supervised all the entries from the Northeast. Barpujari's last paper was the Keynote address he delivered to the tenth session of the North East India Political Science Association at the Gauhati University, Guwahati, in December, 2000, entitled "Unabated Immigration: The Burning Issue of the North-East".

Barpujari was intimately involved in a large number of academic bodies and organizations in the country, like Indian History Congress, Indian Historical Records Commission, Indian Institute of Public Administration, Institute of Historical Studies, Punjab History Congress, Assam Research Society, North-East India Council for Social Science Research, and North East India History Association, and served these organizations from time to time as member of the executive committee or academic committee and in various other capacity. Besides his phenomenal contribution to history as a scholar, Barpujari also earned the rare distinction of generously financially supporting the promotion of advanced studies in history out of his own income as a teacher and an author. He disposed of a major part of his self-acquired immovable property in the heart of Guwahati city and created the H K Barpujari Endowment Trust which provided handsome funds to the Indian History Congress for the creation of a biennial 'National Award' for outstanding contributions to Indian History, to Gauhati University for a Professorship in Modern Indian History, and to Institute of Historical Studies (Calcutta), Dibrugarh University, North-Eastern Hill University, Asam Sahitya Sabha, and North East India History Association for instituting biennial/triennial lectures on aspects of history and culture of Northeast India. Few years before his death, he made another handsome donation to the Gauhati University out of his last savings for establishing an Institute for Northeast India Studies.

While Barpujari contributed immensely as a historian and for the promotion of historical studies, the academia in India and abroad recognized his scholarship in various ways. He was honoured to preside over the Modern India Section of the Indian History Congress (Muzaffarpur, 1972), History section of Asam Sahitya Sabha (Dhubri, 1972), Punjab History Congress (Patiala, 1979), North East India History Association (Shillong, 1980), and Academic Session of the Indian Historical Records Commission (Bikanir, 1987). He was the Local Secretary of the only session of the Indian History Congress held in Northeast (Guwahati, 1959) and the only historian from the Northeast to be elected as its General President (56th Session, Calcutta, 1995). He was one of the first members of the Indian Council of Historical Research (ICHR) and subsequently held three terms in the Council. His academic visits abroad included UK, USA, USSR, Canada, France, Switzerland, Italy, Thailand, Japan, Hong Kong and Singapore to attend seminars, to deliver lectures or to collect source-materials on history of Northeast India. In 1972, ICHR sponsored his visit to USSR to deliver a series of lectures in Soviet universities on Indian national movement on the occasion of silver jubilee of India's independence. He was the only historian to be honoured as *Itihas-Acharya* by the Asam Sahitya Sabha (1997). The North East India History Association published a felicitation volume in his honour (*Studies in History of North East India*, NEHU Publications, Shillong, 1986). The Archaeological Society of India, the Numismatic Society of India and the Indian History and Culture Society in a joint session held in Guwahati in 1985 honoured him with a *Tamra-Patra* for his outstanding contributions to Indian history. The Baptist International felicitated him in 1985 at Valley Forge, Pennsylvania, for his contribution to Baptist Studies. The Institute of Historical Studies felicitated him in a special function in Calcutta in 1992 with a citation for his life-long achievements as a historian. Anundaram Barooah Institute of Language, Art and Culture, Guwahati, honoured him with the '*Anundaram Barooah Bata*' in 1998. His *India's North-East : Problems, Policies and Prospects* (Guwahati, 1998) won him the first Srikant Dutt Memorial Award for the best book on Northeast India in 1999.

The tallest personality of Indian academia from the Northeast in the person of H.K. Barpujari passed away in his Guwahati residence on 16 April 2002. The news of his death and condolence meetings held in various institutions and organizations all over the country were extensively covered by the electronic and print media. The local channels also telecast features on the life and works of the doyen among the historians. The North-East India Council for Social Science Research brought out a commemorative special issue of its journal, *Journal of the North-East India Council for Social Science Research* (Vol. 26, No. 2, Shillong, October 2002), containing articles on Barpujari as a historian and his contributions to history, and the North East India History Association organized a symposium on 'Contribution of Professor H,K, Barpujari towards Historical Study' at its annual session at Agartala in October 2002. The Kamarupa Anusandhan Samiti, Guwahati, published a commemorative volume of the *Journal of Assam Research Society* (Professor H K Barpujari Commemoration Volume, vol. xxxvii, Nos. 1 & 2, 1998-2000, Guwahati, 2005.). The *Shradhanjali*, published by A.C. Bhuyan, Ranju Bezbaruah and Priyam Goswami on the occasion of his *Adya Shraddha* ceremony (26 April 2002), and *Prof. H.K. Barpujari : Tributes* (Guwahati, 2003), edited by Reeta Baruah, contain eloquent testimonies of the eminent academic personalities of the region to Barpujari's scholarship and his outstanding contributions to historical research in Northeast India.[2]

Contributions to history

The thrust area in Barpujari's historical writing was Northeast India. In this respect he was a successor of S.K. Bhuyan. Whereas Bhuyan made medieval Assam history known to the outside world, Barpujari made modern Northeast the central theme of his studies and made pioneering contributions in this field. The region, its rich historical roots, diverse people, their languages and the fast changing cultural ethos, different political and social institutions and above all, their economic disparities and ever increasing political problems drew his attention for a considerable period of time. *"An objective and impartial historian"* (emphasis ours), Barpujari asserts, "will have to judge the developments in the light of what prevailed in north-east India prior to the advent of the British or in comparison with developments in other parts of the country, not in terms of present context or of thoughts and ideologies."[3] He found that earlier works on these subjects, mostly by European writers, were useful but not necessarily objective. As early as 1972 he wrote :[4]

> ... Studies in frontier policy necessarily demand a closer examination of the life and conditions of the people living in border areas. Scholar-administrators like J.P. Mills, J.H. Hutton, Verrier Elwin have mae in several monographs invaluable contributions in these fields. Mere description of customs, manners, food, dress, ornaments etc, will not bring out the main trends and developments of the socio-economic life of a community. What is needed is an integrated approach covering a period of years on different aspects of tribal society. Economic transition of the tribal areas in general or group-wise may well be attempted by one or several scholars.

In his presidential address to the first session of North East India History Association (NEIHA) in 1980 he further observed :[5]

> The changing patterns of the society whether in the plains or in the hills need be studied from Medieval to Modern times. In the plains, the degradation and ruination of the old gentry or the official aristocracy following the equalizing policy of the British rulers led to upliftment of the communities which had hitherto been looked down upon; some of them even bear disgraceful marks in their person. A socio-economic study of the so-called backward or weaker section will be interesting as well as instructive. The discredited nobility or higher echelons of society, both in hills and plains, paved the way for the leadership of the middle class elite. How and to what extent this intelligentsia succeeded in regenerating their countrymen socially, economically and politically, need to be properly assessed. The influx of new-comers and consequent tension between the original and new settlers, which has continued with occasional break till our times, require impartial and objective studies. The attention of our researchers should likewise be directed to communal relations in Assam and neighbouring areas and their impact on the course of political and constitutional development.

Barpujari's illustrious career as a historian began with his first major work in English *Assam : In the Days of the Company* (1826-1858) (Gauhati, 1963) which grew out of his Ph.D. thesis *'The British Administration in Assam, 1826-45'* approved by the London University in 1949. This book which is a critical and comprehensive account of Assam during the last phase of the East India Company's rule also 'throws', as the author claimed in the preface to the first edition, "sidelights on the declining fortunes of the ruling families, their relations with the frontier tribes, and also to the contribution of early administrators and benefactors some of whose bones are strewn in different parts of the province, but whose very names may not be known to many of the present generations."[6] It may be kept in mind that when Barpujari began working on this subject he virtually stepped into a virgin area of research as barring A.C. Banerjee's *Eastern Frontier of British India* (Calcutta, 1943), S.K. Bhuyan's *Anglo-Assamese Relations, 1771-1826* (Gauhati, 1949), R.M. Lahiri's *The Annexations of Assam, 1824-1854* (Calcutta, 1954), and of course, E.A. Gait's pioneering *A History of Assam* (London, 1906), there was no other researched study on the history of modern Assam. In this background the publication of this highly useful book, demonstrated Barpujari's competence in marshalling all available sources in English and Assamese languages. *The Quarterly Review of Historical Studies* paying rich tribute to Barpujari's historical craft wrote : " Professor Barpujari as a historian has produced a good example of how administrative history of an Indian region should be written... Barpujari shows a greater capacity for comprehension than the well known and more elegant British administrative historians from the time of Dodwell to that of Beaglehole."[7]

Barpujari's next valuable work *Problem of the Hill Tribes : North East Frontier* in three volumes, 1822-42, 1843-72 and 1873-1963 (Gauhati, 1970, 1976 and 1981 respectively) is an attempt to objectively study the stages of colonial penetration into the hill areas of the Northeast. In writing these volumes Barpujari was aware of the fact that though territorial expansion was the keynote of the British policy in the plains of Assam, it was one of slow but steady penetration in the hills. In the first two volumes he had shown how non-intervention 'which had been the watchword in the earlier period gradually gave way to intervention, and intervention to annexation', whereas in the third volume he attempted to define the actual status of the McMahon line in the context of the rival stands taken by the two neighbours, India and China. The publication of the first volume of '*Problem of the Hill Tribes*' immediately drew attention of the frontline historians of the country who did not fail to note the change in perspective in studying the 'problem' from that of the earlier British administrator-historians like Alexander Mackenzie[8] and Robert Reid.[9] R.C. Majumdar considered it "a great service to Modern History of India by the thorough study of a hitherto neglected subject which is gradually growing in prominence in view of the recent political events both in and outside India."[10] Majumdar said, "I felt the need of such a book while writing Vol. IX of the Bombay History",* and went further to write, "If I have to revise Vol. IX I shall make full use of your book."[11] K.K. Dutta's observation was that "The policy followed by the British Government and the measures adopted by it for the solution of the problem have been lucidly explained."[12] Barpujari maintained his same approach in next the two volumes of the '*Problem of the Hill Tribes*' published subsequently in 1976 and 1981 respectively.

---

* R.C. Majumdar's 'Bombay History' is his celebrated Bharatiya Vidya Bhavan Series, Bombay, vol. IX of which, entitled *The British Paramountcy and Indian Renaissance*, served as a text Book for Modern India at post-graduate level in most of the Universities, including Gauhati University, for many years.

Some of the later works of Barpujari, *The American Missionaries and North East India,* 1836-1900 (Guwahati, 1986), *Francis Jenkins : Report on the North East Frontier of India* , 1831-32 (Guwahati, 1988) and two of his masterpieces in Assamese, *American Misionerisakal Aru Unabingsha Satikar Asom* (Jorhat, 1983) and *Asomor Nabajagaran : Ona Asamiyar_Bhumika* (Jorhat, 1987) were undoubtedly the results of his intense knowledge and in-depth study of the diverse historical and social facets of the Northeast. The last named book, in particular, in the words of Dipankar Banerjee "was a clear deviation from the stereo type and very often politically motivated analysis of Bengali immigration in Assam."[13] In this book Barpujari boldly declared that the so-called Bengali *amlah* conspiracy theory of substituting Assamese language by the Bengali language in the schools and courts of Assam in the 1830's was not based on facts. Banerjee wrote, " He (Barpujari) was bold enough to put on records, and with evidence, that at a certain point of time after the British annexation of Assam, Bengali was made the official language of Assam not because of the so-called 'Bengali conspiracy' but because of the British bureaucrats of Assam who introduced the Bengali language in their own administrative interests."[14]

As a writer of medieval Assam history Barpujari has no mean a contribution. His book *An Account of Assam And Her Administration*, 1603-1822 (1988), though basically a study of the Ahom system of administration, also throws, as the author himself claimed, "a flood of light on the process of decline and degeneration of the Ahom monarchy... the strong and weak points of the kings and members of the royal family, of the grandees of the realm and their under lings, of their intrigues and conspiracies leading to the civil wars and foreign invasions."[15] Historian Jagdish Narayan Sarkar was so highly impressed by Barpujari's style of writing and his mastery over the subject matter that he complimented the author in the following words, "Professor Barpujari's work constitutes a milestone in the historiography of medieval and pre-British Assam. It is a valuable source book of unimpeachable testimony which scholars and laymen would like to keep by their side."[16] His two edited works *Political History of Assam*, vol .I. 1826-1919 (Gauhati, 1977) and *The Comprehensive History of Assam* in five volumes (Guwahati, 1990-93), dealing with a full length history of the province from the pre-historic times to 1919, were published by the Publication Board, Assam. Political events apart, these volumes provide an in-depth account of the art, sculpture, architecture, religion, administration, socio-economic changes, relations with the hill tribes and many other aspects of the rule of the successive rulers of the region. Written critically, objectively and dispassionately by several leading historians of the country, these volumes are indispensable for the reconstruction of the history of India.

As a writer Barpujari followed a highly conservative style laying great emphasis on using official records lodged in the archives of India and abroad. He often said to his scholars, "It is not scarcity but profusion of materials that pose a problem to a researcher in Modern period." However, such records should not be used blindly but with care and precision, he asserted. Along with official documents, Barpujari urged that a research worker should also try to locate and use non-official records like private papers, diaries etc. of private individuals in order to present a fuller view of the work done. Barpujari's over-emphasis on the use of archival records was not supported by many eminent historians of yesteryears. But he was unmoved by all the criticisms and remained firm in his views till his last days. A silent and dedicated worker he was an epitome of strength and inspiration. Shy of publicity he lived a simple, disciplined and active life, spending several hours of the day in his personal library till such time when he was incapacitated by old age ailments. Interestingly, one of his best known works, *North-East India : Problems, Policies & Prospects* (Guwahati, 1998) which "seeks to identify the problems of North East India and analyse and assess the policies of the Union and State Governments to ensure peace, stability and security of the strategically important sensitive region" was published only four years prior to his death. In this monumental work he has authoritatively shown how the unabated influx of Bangladeshi migrants in the post-independence period in particular had created an "explosive situation upsetting the demographic balance of the entire region", and the role of the political parties as well as the State and the Union Governments in tackling this "volatile and emotive issue."[17] He opined that the entire region today is "seething with secessionism, militancy and insurgency bred by a sense of alienation, deprivation and neglect" and suggested that the policy of the Government "should be conciliatory, but firm",[18] cautioning it at the same time by predicting that "If conciliation fails, the divisive and secessionist forces must be brought under control with an iron hand and in the process, care should be taken that the innocents should not be punished along with the guilty."[19] No wonder, Barpujari's bold and straight forward views on the foreigner's issue in Assam and the suggestions he put forward to tackle the problems earned him supporters as well as critics.

Though a patron and promoter of regional history Professor Barpujari deprecated the tendency of some writers of regional history to exaggerate regional achievements, exalt local heroes and heroines and glorify, out of proportion, one's own customs, manners, language, etc. Way back in 1980, in his presidential address to the first session of North East India History Association he sounded a note of optimism:[20]

> Regional study should be complimentary and not competitive. It should be undertaken as part of the Indian history as a whole; in fact, a comprehensive history of India would be possible only on the bed-rock of regional history. A proper understanding of psychological background and literary sources can best be studied; doubtless by persons of the locality. But that does not mean that local studies cannot be undertaken by persons non-resident therein... Such studies by a scholar outside the region will be conducive to better regional understanding. A true historian, needless to say, rises above provincial patriotism, racial prejudice and regional bigotry. He is a citizen of the world, brother of every other man. His only mission is the exploration of the truth, the whole truth and nothing but the truth.

Equally serious was his concern for the spurt in violent and disruptive activities by a section of the disgruntled youth. He was pained to find that such tendencies have emerged on consideration of narrow regionalism, communalism and linguism, rather than on any other grounds. "At this critical juncture", he declared, "the historian can not afford to be a silent observer of the scene; he has an important role to play. It is up to him to trace the causes of the present malaise in order to find out a rational solution to the problems that have confronted the nation."[21] It should be kept in mind that Barpujari condemned violence committed by the cadres of the various militant outfits operating in the Northeast in the strongest possible terms; but as a historian and citizen of a free nation he could not be unmindful to the historical roots of insurgency in this part of the country. In his presidential address to the fifty-sixth session of the Indian History Congress he lamented :[22]

> Above all, insurgency in the north-east is a symptom of the growing disease that the body politic of every State in the region is rickety to the extreme with rampant corruption, disparity in income and total lack of industrial, agricultural and economic development which alone could have provided useful employment to the misguided youths. This will necessarily demand a radical change in the system of governance without which it will be a cry for the moon to curb insurgency in north-east India.

How correct was Barpujari's futuristic perception of the prevailing situations in the Northeast can be perceived from the views he expressed in the last few sentences of his book *North-East India ; Problems, Policies & Prospects*:[23]

> The alienation of the ethnic groups and growing insecurity of the sensitive and strategic North-East has made of late a marked departure from the earlier policy of the Union Government. There had been frequent visits of successive Prime Ministers and allocation of huge funds, for overall development of the entire region. Will the policy of the government remain unaltered with the change in leadership? In any case the war is to be waged at two fronts : terrorism and corruption from the top to the bottom. This will necessarily demand a radical change in governance. if need be, by a spell of emergency, to curb effectively divisive and secessionist forces. This will smoothen the path for a government with accountability, corruption-free, transparent, dynamic, responsive to the needs and aspirations of the people.

As a historian

H.K. Barpujari, the doyen among historians of Northeast India and enjoying international reputation for his many-sided contributions to regional history, was known in historical circles as a strong disciplinarian and as one who hardly compromised with his views, however unpalatable these might be to others. As a historian he was bold and fearless, never ruffled by any pressure, from within and outside. His whole life was a mission in the pursuit of knowledge of history. History had been his first love, and he had shown myriads of historians of our time how history is to be read and written. He had shown us how a historical superstructure can be built on a solid foundation of evidence. He often said, "There is nothing like a final verdict in history, for a better perspective and understanding history is being reassessed, reinterpreted and reconstructed from time to time in the light of new sources unearthed." The commitment, steadfastness and single minded devotion with which he pursued his research, had left behind him an indelible mark on the succeeding generations of historians. It was perhaps this role of a 'fearless truth seeker' in the discipline of history which enabled him to reject views which were not tenable and not based on facts. He repeatedly stated "A historian is no respecter of persons or political organisations. He is to lay bare facts or pass a judgment without fear or favour, under no circumstances should he suppress or distort facts to suit interest or 'ism'." Barpujari further asserted, "... his (historian's) findings must serve the interest of the community by removing misunderstanding, strengthening views and enlightening the public on both its strong and weak points."[24] In his works he followed a methodology which was strictly in conformity with the accepted norms of historical research. A true disciple of Leopold Von Ranke, Barpujari followed the Rankean style of pursuing truth in history writing by asserting his views boldly and with conviction. It was a common practice for every research scholar willing to work under him to undergo a rigorous methodology course before setting out for data collection. In fact, he made research methodology popular and known to all and sundry by himself writing a book entitled *Itihas Rachana-bidhi Aru Cromobikash,* the first and the only book on the subject in the Assamese language. A beginner in research would find this book very handy.

As a historian and a research guide Professor Barpujari made an indelible impression in the minds of his scholars. I was fortunate to have him as my supervisor for my Ph.D. work and I distinctly remember the interest he had taken in my work. An erudite scholar of history and a meticulous supervisor, Professor Barpujari was possibly the first person after Professor S.K. Bhuyan to have emphasised on the use of primary sources, both oral and written, for writing the history of modern Northeast India. In the same manner, he was perhaps the first historian of the region who understood the need of using archival and other official records in historical research. However, such sources, he cautioned, are to be used very carefully and only when the scholar is hundred per cent sure of their authenticity. Young scholars who have had little or no knowledge of working in an archive received preliminary instructions from him before visiting an archive. In his writings Barpujari was never influenced by any external factors, nor did he allow himself to be carried away by emotions and criticism, good or bad. To him a sensible historian should not only be familiar with his sources, but should also know how to use them. In other words he wanted every historian or research scholar to distinguish the 'essentials' from the 'non-essentials.' He was a firm believer in what is called 'eclectic' or 'pluralistic' theory of writing history. He deprecated the tendency of a section of young historians to copy the style of Marxian historians without understanding the essence of Marxism. To him Marxian interpretation of history is useful, but it is not always fool proof. In his opinion Marxism is best understood in 'a colonial and exploitative society', but he wonders how an objective history is written if "for ideological reasons… facts contrary to the formulation of a theory were deliberately suppressed or conflicting details are ironed out by twisted arguments and interpretation."[25] As a historian Barpujari's objective was the presentation of a narrative based on facts. He always laid stress on exploring the truth, which, in his own words is 'nothing but the whole truth.' Like Allen Nevins, Barpujari believed that a novelist or a fiction-writer is free to invent past events and interpret them as he liked. But a historian on the other hand, restricts himself to such events and changes which had actually occurred as he does not have the freedom to resort to any type of imagination. He has to separate facts from fictions; the explanations and interpretations he offers must be supported by facts. To the generality of historians in Assam as elsewhere, Barpujari cautioned, "under no circumstances should facts be suppressed or distorted by a historian to conform to a particular theory… It would be however an anachronism to interpret the past in the light of present thoughts and developments. The role of a historian is that of a Judge, not an Advocate. If search for truth is the *sin qua non* of historical research the primary task of a historian is the collection of all available data, primary and secondary, examination and marshalling of facts and then to evolve a well reasoned theory - geographical, biographical, spiritual, pluralistic or materialistic - to explain the course taken by the events. There is no finality or last word in history."[26] In my humble opinion impartiality and critical objectivity were the hallmarks of Barpujari's writings. J.B. Bhattacharjee's observation made twenty-five years ago in this respect is worth mentioning:[27]

> The most striking feature in the writing of Professor H.K. Barpujari is the consistency in style, approach and views that he has maintained in his voluminous works. In every piece of writing there is an improvement over the previous one, but without a departure in methodology. The objectivity is his supreme consideration. He is extremely cautious about the '*critism*', external or internal, and his footnotes are rigorous in detail and uniformity. Every statement of fact is adequately documented, and lucid literary style contributes to readability. The political, social and economic aspects find balanced share in his treatment. He would not allow one branch of history to overshadow the other. He emphasizes facts, but his presentation is not mere narration of events. One finds in his works a powerful content analysis and a critical interpretation of facts that distinguish him as a great historian.

Indeed Professor H.K.Barpujari has been a torch-bearer for hundreds of historians and research scholars of our country. He became a Living Legend for his Ideas of History, his Research Methodology and his Works in Regional History of Northeast India. In Barpujari's hands, as Amalendu Guha rightly said, "the historian's craft has always remained one of high order, free from unscientific prejudices and compromises with obscurantist pressures."[28] He was a doyen among historians, enjoying national and international reputation for his great contributions in the field of regional history. He was a self made man, loved and respected by one and all for his scholarship, academic honesty, personal integrity and bold and independent views. As a historian his greatest contribution was his ability to focus the history and culture of Northeast India as an integral part of the country's history, thereby winning for it a respectable place in Indian historical texts. To many of us, his former students and research workers, he was not just a teacher or research guide, he was an institution by himself. He was a *Karmayogi* whose life was an unending journey towards breaking new grounds and exploring new domains of history.

Notes & References

1. For Select Bibliography of H.K. Barpujari's publications compiled by editor of the volume see Annexure.
2. The section on Biographical Sketch has been added by J.B. Bhattacharjee [Editor of the volume]. For more details see his papers, "H.K. Barpujari (1912-2002) : An Obituary", *Proceedings of the Indian History Congress*, Amritsar, 2002, pp. 1026-28 and "Professor H.K. Barpujari (1912-2002) and Historical Research in Northeast India", *Journal of the North-East India Council for Social Science Research*, Vol. 26, No. 2, October, 2002, pp. 1-12.
3. H.K. Barpujari (ed.), *The Comprehensive History of Assam,* vol. V, Publication Board Assam, Guwahati, 1993, p. viii, preface.
4. H.K. Barpujari, 'Presidential Address', Modern India Section, Indian History Congress, *Proceedings of Indian History Congress,* Muzaffarpur, 1972, p. 15.
5. H.K. Barpujari, 'Presidential Address ',*Proceedings of the North East India History Association*, First Session, Shillong, 1980, p.7.
6. H.K. Barpujari, *Assam : In the Days of the Company*, 1826-58, 1st edition, Lawyer's Book Stall, Guwahati, 1963; second edition, 1980, p. vi.
7. *The Quarterly Review of Historical Studies*, vol. III, No. 2, 1964, p. 57.
8. Alexander Mackenzie, *History of the Relations of the Government with hill tribes on the North-East Frontier of Bengal* , Bengal Govt. Press, Calcutta, 1884.
9. Robert Reid, *History of the Frontier Areas Bordering on Assam from 1883-1941*, Calcutta, 1942.
10. R.C. Majumdar's letter to H.K. Barpujari dated 30th August 1970. For full text of the letter see Reeta Baruah (ed.), *Prof. H.K. Barpujari : Tributes*, Guwahati, 2003, p.19.
11. *Ibid.*
12. *Ibid*, p. 20.
13. Dipankar Banerjee, 'In Memoriam', in Reeta Baruah (ed.), *Prof. H.K. Barpujari : Tributes*, Guwahati, 2003, p.102.
14. *Ibid.*
15. H.K. Barpujari, *An Account of Assam and Her Administration*, Spectrum Publications, Guwahati, 1988, p. iv.
16. Reeta Baruah (ed.), *Prof. H.K. Barpujari : Tributes*, Guwahati, 2003, p.23.

17. H.K. Barpuijari. *North-East India, Problems, Policies & Prospects*, Spectrum Publications, Guwahati, 1998, p. vi, preface.
18. *Ibid.*
19. *Ibid.*
20. H.K. Barpujari, 'Presidential Address' *Proceedings of the North East India History Association*, First Session, Shillong, 1980, pp. 12-13.
21. H.K. Barpujari, 'Presidential Address', Punjab History Congress, Thirteenth Session, Patiala, 1979.
22. H.K. Barpujari, 'General President's Address', Indian History Congress, Fifty-sixth Session, Calcutta, 1995, p. 63.
23. H.K. Barpujari, *North-East India, Problems, Policies & Prospects,* Spectrum Publications, Guwahati, 1998, Pp. 141-42.
24. *Ibid.*, p. vi, Preface.
25. H.K. Barpujari, 'Presidential Address', *Proceedings of the North East India History Association*, First Session, Shillong, 1980, p.12.
26. H.K. Barpujari (ed.), *The Comprehensive History of Assam*. Vol. IV, Publication Board Assam, Guwahati, 1990, p. x, preface.
27. J.B. Bhattacharjee (ed.), *Studies in the History of North-East India*, Essays in honour of Professor H.K. Barpujari, NEHU Publications, Shillong, 1986, pp. xxiii-xxiv, Introduction.
28. Amalendu Guha, 'Presidential Address'; *Proceedings of the North East India History Association,* Second Session. Dibrugarh, 1981, p. 2.

Annexure

Published Works of Dr. H.K. Barpujari

A. English

(i) Original Works

1. *Assam : In the Days of the Company*, Lawer's Book Stall, Gauhati, 1963.
2. *Problem of Hill Tribes : North East Frontier*, 3 volumes, Lawyer's Book, Stall, Gauhati, 1970-1981.
3. *The American Missionaries and North-East India, 1836-1900*, Spectrum Publications, Guwahati, 1986.
4. *An Account of Assam and Her Administration, 1603-1822*, Spectrum Publications, Guwahati, 1988.
5. *Francis Jenkins : Report on the North East Frontier of India, 1831-32*, Spectrum Publications, Guwahati, 1988.

6. *India's North-East : Problems, Policies and Prospects*, Spectrum Publications, Guwahati, 1998.

(ii) Edited Original Works

1. *The Political History of Assam*, Vol. I (1826-1919), Govt. of Assam, Dispur, 1977.
2. *The Comprehensive History of Assam*, 5 Vols., Publication Board Assam, Guwahati, 1990-1993.

(iii) Edited Commemorative Publications

1. *The Cotton College Golden Jubilee Volume*, Cotton College, Gauhati, 1952.
2. *Heritage of Assam*, 'Souvenir of the Gauhati Session, Indian History Congress', Reception Committee, Cotton College, Gauhati, 1959.
3. *Professor Suryya Kumar Bhuyan Commemoration Volume* (edited jointly with Professor Maheswar Neog), Gauhati University, Gauhati, 1966.

(iv) Research papers

1. "A Short History of Education in Assam, 1826-1900", *The Golden Jubilee Volume*, Cotton College, Gauhati, 1951.
2. "Early British Relations with Bhutan", *Proceedings of the Indian History Congress*, 1951.
3. "Papers relating to History of Education in Assam in the Days of the Company", *Proceedings of the Indian Historical Records Commission,* vol. XXIX, part II, 1953.
4. "Annexation of Jayantia (1835)", *Proceedings of the Indian Historical Records Commission,* vol. XXX, part II, 1954.
5. "The Early Phase of Resistance Movement in the North-East Frontier, 1828-31", *Proceedings of the Indian Historical Records Commission,* vol. XXXI, part II, 1955.
6. "New Light on the Resistance Movement in North-East Frontier", *Proceedings of the Indian Historical Records Commission,* vol. XXXII, part II, 1956.
7. "The Echoes of the Mutiny in Upper Assam", *Proceedings of the Indian Historical Records Commission,* vol. XXXIII, part II, 1957.
8. "Survey and Operations of the Petroleum Springs and Coal-beds in Assam", *Proceedings of the Indian Historical Records Commission,* vol. XXXIV, part II, 1958.
9. "Tariff Walls in the North-North Frontier, 1826-58", *Journal of Indian History* (Trivandrum), vol. I, 1959.

10 "The real causes and character of the insurrection of the Khasis under Tirot Singh", *Proceedings of the Indian History Congress*, 1959.

11. "The Genesis of NEFA", *Proceedings of the Indian Historical Records Commission,* vol. XXXV, part II, 1960.

12. "The Attempted Traffic with the Chinese through the North-East Frontier", *Proceedings of the Indian History Congress*, 1961.

13. "Management and Control of the Religious Endowments in Assam, 1825-58", *Journal of the University of Gauhati*, Arts, vol. XV, 1964.

14. "Early Judicial Panchayats in Assam", *Proceedings of the Indian Historical Records Commission,* vol. XLII, 1964.

15. "Pemberton's Mission to Bhutan : Immediate and Ultimate Objectives", *Proceedings of the Indian History Congress*, 1966.

16. "Historical Researches in Assam (Modern Period) : Retrospect and Prospect" in S.P. Sen (ed.), *Studies in Modern Indian History : A Regional Survey*, Institute of Historical Studies, Calcutta, 1969.

17. "Facts Behind the Jayantia Rebellion, 1861-64", *Journal of Indian History*, vol. II, pt. II, 1973.

18. "Emergence and Role of Middle Class in Assam", in B. Datta Ray (ed.), *The Emergence and Role of Middle Class in North East India*, New Delhi, 1979.

19. "Slavery in Assam : Problem of its Emancipation", *Golden Jubilee Souvenir*, Department of Historical and Antiquarian Studies (DHAS), Guwahati, 1979.

20. "The Siege of Kohima", *The Custodian* (Shillong), 1979.

21. "The New Light on the proposed Crown Colony : North-East India", *Proceedings of the Indian Historical Records Commission,* vol. LIII, part II, 1990.

22. "Quest for Identity :Hmar Demand for Homeland", *Journal of the North-East India Council for Social Science Research*, Vol. 22, No. 1, April, 1997.

23. "Insurgency in North-East India : A Case Study of NSCN ", in B. Pakem (ed.), *Insurgency in North-East India*, New Delhi, 1997.

(v) Presidential Addresses

1. *Problems of the North-East Frontier*, Section III, Modern India Section, Indian History Congress, Muzaffarpur, 1972.

2. *The Sikh Gurus and Assam*, Punjab History Congress, Patiala, 1979.

3. *Historical Research in North-East India – Retrospect and Prospect*, North East India History Association, Shillong, 1980.

4. *North-East India : Problems and Policies since 1947*, Indian History Congress, Calcutta, 1995.

(vi) Reviews & Reminiscences

1. "Book Review – Karunakar Gupta's *The Hidden History of Sino-Indian Frontier*, Calcutta, 1974", *The Indian Historical Review*, vol. II, no. 1, 1975.

2. "Book Review – *A General Guide to the India Office Records*", *Indian Archives*, vol. XXXVII, no. 1, Jan.-June, 1988.

3. "Reminiscences – Professor J.N. Sarkar", *Studies in Cultural Development of India*, Calcutta, 1991.

4. "My Reminiscences – National Archives of India", *Indian Archives*, vol. XXXXIII, no. 1, 1995.

(vii) General Articles

1. "British Policy Towards Hill Tribes in the North-East Frontier", *The Assam Tribune*, 11 April 1952.
2. "Early Tea-plantation in Assam – A State Enterprise", *The Assam Tribune*, 6 July 1952.
3. "Assam-Nagaland Border Dispute (a summary of the note submitted to Sundaram Commission)", *The Assam Tribune*, 5 August 1969.
4. "Thoughts on Ambari Excavation", *The Assam Tribune*, 12 June 1988.
5. "Separation of the Barak Valley", *The Assam Tribune*, 11-12 August 1988.
6. "Our Neglected Archaeological Remains", *The Assam Tribune*, 18 August 1989.
7. "The Need for Archive Directorate in Assam", *The Assam Tribune*, 6 February 1990.
8. "Lachit Barphukan : his place in history", *The Assam Tribune*, 8 November 2000.
9. "Alien Abuse", Interview taken by R. Dutta Choudhury, *The Assam Tribune*, 3 February 2001.

B. Assamese

(i) Original Works

1. *Amerikan Misonerisakal aru Unavimsa Satikar Asom*, Jnandabhiram Barua Lectures, Asom Sahitya Sabha, Jorhat, 1981.
2. *Asomar Nava-Jagaran : Ana-Asomiyar Bhumika*, Asom Sahitya Sabha, Jorhat, 1987.
3. *Itihas : Rachanavidhi aru Cromovikash*, Guwahati, 1988.
4. *Kuri Satikar Kahini*, Institute of Northeast India Studies, Kolkata, 2010.

(ii) Historical Essays

1. "Karnasubarnat Kumar Bhaskarvarman", *Awahan*, vol. 11, 1935.
2. "Kamrupar Pararastraniti", *Awahan*, vol. 11, 1935.
3. "Saumarat Matakrajya", *Saumar Jyoti*, December, 1949.
4. "Thal-Parbatar Sammandha", *Asom Sahitya Sabha Patrika*, December, 1964.
5. "Nathan Brown Aru Asomiya Bhasa-Samaskriti", *Prakash*, July, 1985.

6. "Sarkari Nathi-patra : Kendriya Aru Rajyik", *Prakash*, May, 1986.
7. "Besarkari Nathi-patra : Samasya Aru Samadhan", *Prakash*, June, 1986.
8. "Vaisnav Niryatan Aru Moamaria Vidroha", *Prakash*, 3 installments in February, March and April issues, 1989.
9. "Asomat Itihas Charchar Eti Abhas", *Sutradhar*, 1-15 January, 1991.

(iii) Presidential Address

Sabhapatir Avibhasan, Buranji Sanmelan, Asom Sahitya Sabha, Dhubri, 1972.

17

Maheswar Neog (1915-1995)

—*Rajen Saikia*

Biographical Sketch

Maheswar Neog was born on 7 September 1915 at Kamarphadia by the side of the river Dikhaw, a village under the shadow of the old capital city of Rangpur; that is, Sibsagar in upper Assam. His parents Manikchandra Neog and Chandraprabha Neog had one daughter and three sons. As parents they were happy to observe that their two sons Dimbeswar and Maheswar had shown great literary promise from their school days. These two brothers had the rare distinction of being elected Presidents of the Asam Sahitya Sabha for the annual sessions held at Nalbari (1965) and Mangaldoi (1974) respectively.

For Maheswar, his elder brother Dimbeswar Neog, sixteen years elder to him, was a literary role model. He passed out his matriculation in 1934 from Jorhat Government High School with distinction. He then moved to Cotton College and enrolled himself in the science stream. He obtained a first division in Intermediate of Science and then opted for English Honours with Sanskrit and History as elective subjects. By that time, it seems he developed a mind of his own to choose a career in language and literature. It is apt to recall that under instruction from his teacher, the historian Suryyakumar Bhuyan, Maheswar Neog translated into Assamese the historic document *A Few Remarks on the Assamese Language and on Vernacular Education in Assam* (1855), authored by Anandaram Dhekial Phukan under a pen-name 'A Native', and serialized it in the journal *Awahan* with a brief introduction. As an undergraduate young man he could feel his guru's trust in him.

Maheswar Neog graduated in 1939. As he needed money for further education he engaged himself in teaching for a couple of years. He joined Phuleswari Girls' High School, Sibsagar, as an assistant teacher.[1] Though now confined to a small mofussil town he did not allow his talent to rust. He published articles on Assamese literature and Assamese marriage songs in the well-known journal *Indian Review* published from Madras. Occasionally he contributed articles to *The Hindustan Standard* (Calcutta) and the *Times of Assam*. The Sibsagar Natya Samaj and the Sibsagar Sahitya Sabha provided him outlets for social work. Later he reminisced about his life there with a sense of fulfillment.

In early 1945 Maheswar Neog received a call from the Gauhati University Trust Board headed by Lokpriya Gopinath Bardoloi to work for the establishment of the first university in Assam. Very soon, the 'university movement', as they called it, became an integral part of his life; as if one did not exist without the other. In fact, the demand for a university in Assam was first heard in 1917. The year marked the beginning of cultural nationalism in Assam which looked for recognition and support from a wider world. The Asam Sahitya Sabha was founded in 1917 at Sibsagar and soon it became the sanctum sanctorum of Assamese nationalism. It was from Sibsagar again that the decisive step for a university was taken. In the wake of the annual session of the Asam Sahitya Sabha held at Sibsagar in October 1944 the Gauhati University Trust Board was constituted. Maheswar Neog did not escape the notice of the leaders. On his part, full of energy and self-assurance, he was too ready to join them with a soldierly resolve. It was a turning point of his life and what he did do about this time placed him in the direction to make it to the peak of his career. A great team with people like Saratchandra Goswami, Krishnakanta Handiqui, Bhubaneswar Barua, Faiznur Ali, Rohinikumar Chaudhury, Herambaprasad Barua, Sailendraprasad Barua, Hiranyachandra Bhuyan, Rameshchandra Chaudhury, Rohinikanta Barua, Hariprasad Barua, Birinchikumar Barua, Hem Barua, Devkanta Barua and Suryyakumar Bhuyan, under the leadership of Gopinath Bardoloi, started its work in right earnest. Much help came their way from some other persons as well. Fakhruddin Ali Ahmed, later the President of India, then a young barrister, was appointed secretary of the Trust Board. Madhabchandra Bezbarua was the stormy petrel of the movement; Maheswar Neog was his close confidant. Together they moved from place to place, in the upper Assam districts, collecting fund for the proposed university. The principal fund raiser was of course Gopinath Bardoloi himself. Young Maheswar enjoyed the confidence of Lokpriya Bardoloi and his team.[2]

The Gauhati University came into existence on 1 January 1948. Maheswar Neog always placed a high premium of his experience with those men and their movement. He wrote about them with verve and passion. New possibilities of life were opening up for him at Guwahati. He passed his M.A. in Assamese in 1948 as a private candidate from the Calcutta University securing the first position in the first class. He had Pali, Prakrit and Bengali as compulsory papers and he did remarkably well in those subjects. He joined as the only Lecturer in the department of Assamese in the Gauhati University on 1 December 1948, the very day the department of Assamese was born. The department was very soon to blossom with Birinchikumar Barua as Reader and Banikanta Kakati as Professor. The first phase of his journey to the university was over and the second phase of his journey from the university had begun. The second phase was the brilliant justification of the first. He served the university for nearly three decades.

Immediately after retirement from the Gauhati University, Maheswar Neog had to go to the Punjabi University, Patiala and joined there, on 1 March 1978, as Director and

Professor of the newly created Sankaradeva Chair in the Guru Govinda Singh Department of Religious Studies. The fruits of his labour at Patiala were *The Bhakti-ratnakara of Sankaradeva* and *History of the Concept of Bhakti* (1982). After a sojourn of five years he returned to Assam in May 1983. Neog believed in creative rest and very soon he settled down at his table. He brought out some twenty books in Assamese and English taking in his stride not so pleasant interventions of long travels, lecture programmes and indifferent health. Rare distinctions were conferred on him by the Government of Assam, the Government of India, the Sangeet Natak Akademi, the Asam Sahitya Sabha and the Gauhati University. He breathed his last on 13 September 1995, six days after his 81st birthday.

Contributions to history

The first vice-chancellor of the Gauhati University, Krishnakanta Handiqui with his experience in Oxford University and idea of European scholarship tried to create a stimulating intellectual atmosphere in the university as far as it went. Maheswar Neog tried to imbibe the spirit in a modest way. He began to publish articles on different subjects in *Journal of the Asiatic Society* and *Indian Historical Quarterly* (Calcutta), *Journal of Oriental Research* and *Journal of Music* (Madras), *Poona Orientalist* (Nasik), *Eastern Anthropologist* (Lucknow) and *Man in India* (Ranchi). With those endeavours, he really wanted to deepen his roots and gradually he moved to formal research. The result was *Early History of the Vaisnava Faith And Movement in Assam: Sankaradeva And His Times* (from now *Sankaradeva And His Times*).

The pioneer of Sankaradeva Studies in modern Assam was Lakshminath Bezbaroa. Banikanta Kakati gave a nice touch to it. *Sankaradeva*, authored by Bezbaroa (1911), highlighted the rich corpus of literature produced by the saint. It also aimed at blowing away the cobwebs created by some wrongheaded enthusiasts to blur the singularity of the Sankaradeva school of Vaisnavism in relation to the Chaitanyadeva school. An exhaustive version of this work called *Mahapurusha Sri Sankaradeva aru Sri Madhavadeva* came out in 1914. It was a howling success. Banikanta Katati's *Sankara Deva* (Madras 1923) reached out to a larger readership. Sankaradeva had, by then, become a burning flame of faith and passion.[3]

Sankaradeva and His Times by Maheswar Neog is at one level the cultural history of medieval Assam. It may be accepted as a follow-up programme of Birinchikumar Barua's *A Cultural History of Assam* (Early Period).[4] Maheswar Neog prepared his doctoral thesis under the supervision of Banikanta Kakati, and on his sudden death, it was completed under Birichikumar Barua in 1955.* The uninterrupted chain of *charit-puthis* or biographical

* Maheswar Neog was awarded Doctor of Philosophy (then abbreviated as D. Phil), along with Satyendranath Sarma and Prafulladatta Goswami on the same date, in 1955. They were the first three doctorates of Gauhati University and all of them eventually became Professors in the same university and made mark as scholars of national repute from Assam. Sarma was Professor (later on, Rabindranath Tagore Professor of Modern Indian Literature) at the department of Assamese and Goswami at the

(Contd...)

accounts beginning with Daityari Thakur running well into more than three hundred years, the study of Sankaradeva (1449-1568) and Madhavadeva (1489-1586) had a force of tradition. This could make research on Sankaradeva much easier because the quarry lies right in front of the researcher; but it was all the more difficult for the problem of plenty. This is because in medieval time an 'author' in term and practice meant 'authority'.[5] By rigorously questioning the data and employing other methods like textual criticism, conjectural emendation etc., Maheswar Neog produced a complete work on Sankaradeva.

A.J.P. Taylor once said, 'Inside every historian there lies concealed a biographer struggling to get out'.[6] Neog was able to keep the historian and the biographer in him on an even keel. As an historian he studied the political situation of the country before and during Sankaradeva's time, analyzed the socio-economic background of the Vaisnava movement in Assam and then he wrote the complete biography of Sankaradeva — the man and the saint, focused attention on his genius, his role as an institution builder, and assessed his contribution in the context of the Bhakti movement in India. He rejected the myth dearly held to their heart by the disciples of Sankaradeva but not supported by evidence.

Maheswar Neog's research established Sankaradeva as an extraordinary phenomenon of medieval Assam. He recorded the lasting impact of his work in these words — 'Assam discovered herself as an integral part of the holy land of Bharatavarsa, and gloried in that discovery. The holy books in Sanskrit, ... could no longer be sealed to the common man's view by a rigid oligarchy..... The use of Assamese, an Indo-Aryan tongue, which formed but an island in a Tibeto-Burman ocean, as the medium for the propagation of the neo-Vaisnava faith led to its emergence as the language of all people'.[7]

In course of his research Maheswar Neog discovered the cultural treasure of Assamese Vaisnavism. As an Indologist he felt that Assam could claim cultural equality with the developed cultural zones of India. He, therefore, began to project the cultural forms of Assamese Vaisnavism before the connoisseurs of Indian art, painting, music and dance. The fact that the Satriya dance form secured recognition as an Indian classical dance was largely due to his effort.[8] It is but natural that cultural components have assumed greater importance in the current discourse on national integration.

---

department of Folklore Studies. Professors Sarma and Goswami also made significant contributions in historical studies in Northeast India. Sarma's *Asamiya Sahityar Itibritta* (1959), *The Neo-Vaishnaviete Movement and the Satra Institutions of Assam* (1966) and *Socio-Economic and Cultural History of Medieval Assam* (1989) and Goswami's *Spring Bihu of Assam* (1966) and *Ballads and Tales of Assam* (1970), among their many other books and research papers, are essentially in the field of history and these works are used by the historians. The regional and national seminars on history of Northeast India were always enlivened by their gracious participation. Maheswar Neog, Satyendranath Sarma and Prafulladatta Goswami were trained in their research career at the department of Assamese, Gauhati University, at a time when that department under the leadership of Banikanta Kakati and Birinchi Kumar Barua emerged as an important centre of historical studies in the region. Like Neog, Sarma and Goswami are also in great beyond but their contributions to historiography of the Northeast can never be forgotten. [*Editor's Addendum]

Neog's another research field was epigraphy. The publication of the Journal *Epigraphia Indica* by the Government of India from 1888 aroused the interest of many putative epigraphists to move in search of quarry. The discovery of numerous cave, pillar and stone inscriptions by more than half a dozen of British civil and army officers from 1785 onwards provided enough reason for the government to bring out a journal like this. Nationwide scholarly enthusiasm, including serious polemics, channeled through the *Epigraphia Indica*.[9] In Assam, Padmanath Bhattacharyya Vidyavinod was the pioneer of epigraphic study. *Kamrupa Sasanavali* edited by him with text, meaning and interpretation of twelve copper plate and stone inscriptions was published by the Rangpur Sahitya Sabha in 1931. The book was in Bengali. A later version of the *Kamrupa Sasanavali* was published in 1981 with addition of 27 inscriptions discovered during the intervening period, thoroughly edited and translated into English by Dimbeswar Sarma. He secured some assistance in translation from Premadhar Chaudhury and Rajanikanta Dev Sarma. *Inscriptions of Ancient Assam* edited with notes and translations by Mukunda Madhava Sharma (1978) is a notable contribution to Indian epigraphy.

Prachya Sasanavali, compiled and edited by Maheswar Neog (1974), is a useful collection of royal documents inscribed on stone, copper etc. of Kamarupa, Saumara (upper Assam) and Koch Behar covering a long period from 1205 to 1847 CE.[10] It is a collection of 156 documents. The scheme of the book calls for enormous amount of hard labour that only a few scholars of his eminence and wide linguistic repertoire can really put in. Though the title page is in Assamese character, this is out and out a bilingual book - Assamese and English; giving no short shrift to the English version. One is as complete as the other. The long introduction, which itself carries the weight of a book in either language, introduces the readers to the documents, showing each in its historic and linguistic distinctiveness with a brief history of the document—how it was discovered and deciphered with translation and where necessary, with editor's own analysis of the competing interpretations of documents. His knowledge of Sanskrit came handy. Let us take one example of how he dealt with them. Take for instance, the Rock Inscription of the Nilachal Kamakshya Temple of 1487 *Saka* era (1565 CE). After giving the exact location of the inscription (really there were two), in this case, in the *antarala* or entrance chamber leading to the principal shrine of the Devi, Neog went on to say (I) that Khan Chowdhuri Amanatullah Ahmed gave the full text of the inscriptions in his well known book *Kochbeharer Itihash* (vol.1); (2) that Sir E.A. Gait in his book *A History of Assam* also gave a translation of the text assuming that it was only one inscription; (3) that Hemchandra Goswami wrote an article on the Kamakshya temple in the *Bangiya Sahitya Parishad Patrika* (1325 B.S.) where he provided the copy of the inscription; (4) that another article by him with the text of the inscription was published in the Assamese Journal *Chetana* edited by Ambikagiri Roychaudhury (1845 *Saka*); (5) that Sonaram Chaudhury referred to an article on the same subject by Babu Puranchand Nahar (n.d.); and (6) Dharanikanta Dev Sarma in his book *Kamakshya Tritha* (1357 B.S.) published the text of the inscription.

The documents in the collection deal with a variety of subjects giving clues to historic events. For instance, the *Kanai Barasi Bowa* rock inscription of 1205 CE. in Assamese script bears ample evidence that the script was already in existence at least from the late twelfth century. However, Neog says, 'the first epigraphs in clear and modern Assamese language' comes to light with the discovery of Chamdhora Rampart rock inscription of 1616 CE which recorded the victory of the Ahom ruler over the Mughal army. He is also of the view that the words *Asam* (the land) and *Asamiya* (the people) 'derive themselves from the name of the ruling race,'—that is the Ahoms.

Though the word *'sasanavali'* is used here, all the inscriptions are not royal injunctions. Yet every inscription is important in its own way. The religious beliefs and practices of the ruler and the ruled; how land grants were made with a myriad of pious resolutions, how battles were fought, ramparts built; how vaisnava, sakta and saiva temples were constructed and managed - all these and similar things constituted the subject-matter of the documents. There are scores of exceptionally interesting records which look somewhat tangential, but when placed by the side of larger matters of historical enquiry every document in context brightens up some truth. As regards 'types', they are identical with the 'donative, dedicative and commemorative inscriptions' discovered elsewhere in the country.[11] But genealogical accounts are sparse and patchy.

Neog made two important observations which must go on record - (1) the use of only Saka era in all the epigraphs except one which 'possibly' refers to the year of the reign of the king, and (2) 'The epigraphs stand testimony to the study of Sanskrit through the centuries in Assam. A literary flourish comes not unexpectedly in some of the compositions. Some of the poets of the epigraphs have used Sanskrit metres with much skill;.....'. His interest in epigraphy did not end with that book. He published at least another five essays on copper plate inscriptions of Assam. They include papers presented in the All India Oriental Conference; *Indica,* Heras Institute of Indian History and Culture, Bombay; *Vishveshvaranand Indological Journal* (Vol. XII), Hoshiarpur; annual Congress of the Epigraphical Society of India and *Journal of Gauhati University.* His epigraphical research is an invaluable contribution to the historiography of medieval and early modern Assam.

Maheswar Neog was and still is the widely read historian of Assamese literature. The fact that Assamese language came under a calumny from 1837 to 1873 when it was replaced by Bengali in the schools and in court under government instruction had a lingering effect on the Assamese mind until recently. Whosoever writes the history of Assamese literature would refer to the antiquity of the language and its phonological and morphological peculiarities. When the Sahitya Akademi under the presidentship of the then prime minister Jawaharlal Nehru, sponsored histories of Indian literature, Sukumar Sen wrote *History of Bengali Literature* (1960) and Birinchikumar Barua wrote *History of Assamese Literature* (1964). Barua referred to the linguistic traits of Assamese noted above which Sukumar Sen did not do in his work. This language sense, if we may say so, had always a strong presence in the histories of Assamese literature. The study of language and literature was complementary to one another.

The first attempt at writing a history of Assamese literature was made by Debendranath Bezbarua. His book *Asamiya Bhasa aru Sahityar Buranji* was published in 1911. The very next year came Devananda Bharali's *Asamiya Bhasar Maulik Vichar aru Sahityar Chinaki*. These books held sway for more than two decades as the standard works on the subject. Kaliram Medhi brought out his *Asamiya Vyakaran aru Bhasatattwa* in 1936. Dimbeswar Neog published his *Adhunik Asamiya Sahityar Buranji* next year. But his *New Light on the History of Asamiya Literature* published in 1962 was a more valuable contribution. In the meantime, Satyendranath Sarma had published his *Asamiya Sahityar Itibritta* in 1959.

Maheswar Neog brought out his *Asamiya Sahityar Ruprekha* in 1962.[12] It was an instant success. True to form he approached his subject from the evolution of the Assamese script and the development of the Assamese language; he brought forth a chronological account of Assamese literature based on admirable thematic structure. Even for lay readers it is a breezy read. By the turn of the century, the book ran into more than ten editions. To be sure enough he had already made a mark as a scholar with his earlier publications, of which (1) *Purani Asamiya Samaj aru Sanskriti* (1957), (2) *Asamiya Geeti Sahitya* (1958) and (3) *Svarrekhat Bargeet* (with Birendrakumar Phukan and Purosottam Das, 1958) are important.

An uncommonly tall man among his fellow Assamese, Maheswar Neog had a demonic power for work. He wrote 20 books in Assamese and 20 in English on literature, culture, religion, epigraphy, social history, art, painting, music, dance etc. He acquired such an authority on the social and cultural history of medieval Assam that popular imagination conceded that what he did not know is what nobody ever knew. He was also a poet, playwright and resourceful biographer. His autobiography *Jivanar Digh aru Bani* - the warp and weft of life - is an engaging portrait of the outer dimension of his life. In the art of editing book, Neog had no peer. He edited thirty nine books both in English and Assamese and compiled another six.[13] He was the Chief Editor of two authoritative Assamese dictionaries - *Chandrakanta Abhidhan* published by the Gauhati University (1988) and *Chalanta Abhidhan* published, posthumously, by the Government of Assam (2001). Though all his editorial essays make delightful reading, three editorial articles written for *The Hastamuktavali* of Subhankara (1979), *Orunodoi* (1983) and *Guru-charit-Katha* (1987) marked by his elemental grasp of things, exegetical rigour and commendable profundity outdistance the rest. Neog had, as the Germans called it, an exceptional sprachgefühl — a feeling for language the way someone speaks or writes. His *Nika Asamiya Bhasa* (1990) - neat Assamese - is a valuable guide for those who care.

As a historian

As an historian, Maheswar Neog was no believer of fanciful theories. He was asked to deliver the third Sakharam Ganesh Deuskar Lecture by the Centre for Studies in Social Sciences, Calcutta. The first two lectures were delivered by A.R. Desai of Bombay and Irfan Habib of Aligarh. Maheswar Neog spoke on the Mayamariya Vaisnava uprising where he expressed his disagreement with tendentious Marxian interpretation of the event not supported by fact.[14] In a tribute to Leopold von Ranke, A.J.P. Taylor remarked,

'Impartiality would not have carried Ranke so far, if he had not been accurate as well; and may be he would not have been accurate without his worship of the elusive fact'.[15] Put Neog at Ranke's place and he will justify every word of the statement.

To form an estimate of Maheswar Neog as an historian one has to be a little charitable, because he was not a traditional type of historian. At the beginning of his autobiography (1949) G.M. Trevelyan observed that he 'tried to keep up to date a family tradition as to the relation of history to literature' but as he entered upon an age of 'scientific' history, he thought, his ideas and practice could have some value only as counterpoise. When Maheswar Neog set about research he fell upon an era of 'scientific' history and he equipped himself accordingly. Pithily expressed, he was obliged to study the relation of literature to history. In writing history he made use of the precedents that he, like others, inherited and he too had set many of them for the use of those who would come after him. He spent his early manhood in tumultuous times from the Civil Disobedience to national freedom through Gandhi-Nehru-Ambedkar-Jinnah phenomena. But he kept away from the political firmament. This helped him form a mental habit and made him a dispassionate observer. He did not ever fall for a straitjacket view of history. His gift for a narrative style made his writings all the more attractive and different from others.

On studying the life of Savonarola, Leopold Von Ranke remarked that each nation had periods of its history which were of universal significance and it was the duty of the historian to give prominence to those. Sankaradeva answered a similar prayer for Maheswar Neog. As an interpreter Neog was objective, critical and argumentative but far from judgemental. His two major works are over half a century old, yet no historian has so far made them object of explicit critique. Nobody refuses leap service to truth of history, but few realize the strength of truth in history. Maheswar Neog was a relentless seeker of that truth. It is no wonder, therefore, that he left his mark on his times.

Notes & References

1. Maheswar Neog was married to Nirmala Barua, then a teacher at Sorojini Girls' High School, Jorhat, on 3 December 1943. They had four children—Madhumalati, Pranavsvarup, Snigdhamalati and Navamalati.

2. Maheswar Neog, 'Eta Visvavidyalayar Swapna', *Visvavidyalay, Bhasa, Bhasan aru Bhraman,* Guwahati, 1974, pp. 1-43

3. Dr. Maheswar Neog gave an institutional shape to Sankaradeva Studies by setting up the Forum for Sankaradeva Studies in 1987. After Dr. Neog, the Forum headed by Professor Ranjitkumar Dev Goswami, is keeping up the tradition by organizing a series of lectures leading to a meaningful convergence of multi-faceted Oriental scholarship and Sankardeva Studies.

4. Birinchikumar Barua, *A Cultural History of Assam* (Early Period), Nagaon, 1951.

5. Beryl Smalley, 'The Conditions', *Historians in the Middle Ages,* London, 1974, pp. 9-13.

6. A.J.P. Taylor, 'The Historian as a Biographer', *From Napoleon to the Second International,* London, 1995, pp. 24-35.

7. Maheswar Neog, *Early History of Vaisnava Faith and Movement in Assam: Sankaradeva and His Times,* 3rd edition, 1998. I have used the Reprint edition, Guwahati, 2008, p. 378
8. Eventually the recognition came on 15 November 2001. Notable contributions in this regard were made, among others, by Maniram Bayan Muktiar (Sr), Dr Keshabananda Dev Goswami, Raseswar Saikia Barbayan, Narayanchandra Goswami, Ghanakanta Bora Barbayan, Indira P.P. Bora, Garima Hazarika and Saradi Saikia.
9. D.C. Sircar, *Indian Epigraphy*, Motilal Banarsidass, Delhi, 1965.
10. Maheswar Neog, *Prachya Sasanavali*, Guwahati, 1974. Two more editions have come out in 2003 and 2008.
11. Upinder Singh, *A History of Ancient and Early Medieval India: From the Stone Age to the 12th Century*, Delhi, 2009, p. 47.
12. Now included in *Maheswar Neog Rachanawali* Vol.1, Guwahati, 2nd ed. 2009.
13. Dr Maheswar Neog Memorial Trust headed by Professor Nagen Saikia and Professor Pradipjyoti Mahanta, among others, has so far published seven volumes of his works. Vol. I, 2nd ed. 2009, Vol. II, 2nd ed. 2009, Vol. III, 2nd ed. 2010, Vol. IV, 2008, Vol. V, 2009, Vol. VI, 2009 and Vol. VII, 2009. The seventh volume (pp. 1196) contains altogether 46 essays and addresses on history. The Trust plans to cover the rest of his works in another three volumes. These volumes have been compiled by Pranavsvarup Neog.
14. Included in *Rachanawali*, Vol. VII, *op. cit.* pp. 129-212.
15. A.J.P. Taylor, 'Ranke: The Dedicated Historian', *op. cit.* pp. 258-266.

18

R. Vanlawma (1915-2006)

—*Sangkima*

Biographical Sketch

Mizoram has produced a number of great personalities who immensely contributed to the enrichment of history, culture and literature of the Mizo people and R. Vanlawma was undoubtedly one of them. His philosophy of life was fully conceived in his love and compassion for Mizoram and he lived by that principle. His impulse for the love of Mizoram was the driving force that made him to study more about the people by going into the history of their roots. The same impulse also urged him to work tirelessly for the socio-economic and cultural development of the people so that they might achieve a certain level of political identity. This became necessary because he was born at a time when Mizoram was only a district (first called Lushai hills and later on, Mizo hills) in Assam and in that large province of British India, consisting of a large number of ethnic and linguistic identities in various districts, the Mizo identity could not come into focus. R. Vanlawma had to involve himself in a life long struggle to assert the distinct identity of his people through social and political movements and by writing books and articles on the history and culture of the Mizos, their economic and political problems and aspirations. Therefore, it may not be wrong to say that he sacrificed his today for the tomorrow of the people of Mizoram. Thus, Vanlawma may appropriately be introduced as a historian, politician and writer, and above all, as a nationalist who struggled for the cause of his people. His 'Zalen Cabin', a replica of Lincoln's 'Log Cabin', is a true attestation of his character.

R. Vanlawma was born on 10 January 1915 out of the wedlock of Suaka Ralte and Dengthuami Vanchhhawng. His father Suaka, a teacher by profession, was an employee of a Christian Mission. Maubuang village, the birth place of R. Vanlawma, occupies a significant place in the history of modern Mizoram for two reasons. First, its chief Khawvelthanga Sailo was the first Christian convert among the Mizo chiefs and he is fondly remembered as the chief who was the first to free his *Bawis*.[1] For this reason Maubuang has earned the name as a place for emancipation of *Bawis*. Second, Maubuang is the birth place of Awithangpa, a great poet and a popular composer, who became a legend in Mizo literature. R. Vanlawma was married in 1953 with Vawmmanthangi and they had seven children - four boys and three girls. The initial 'R' stands for 'Ralte', a clan among the Mizo tribes, while Vanlawma is his first name. He made Aizawl his permanent home since 1939 when he joined government service as a circle staff in the office of the District Superintendent.

The educational career of R. Vanlawma began in his own village, Maubuang, where he received his primary education. In fact, in Mizoram (then Lushai hills district of Assam) primary education was under complete control of the government till 1902. In 1903, by an understanding with Christian Missions, the government transferred the management of education to the Christian Missions. This was a landmark in the history of education in Mizoram. Maubuang village (founded in 1903)[2] attracted the attention of the Missionaries as an ideal site for a school in 1910.[3] Khawvelthanga, the chief of Maubuang, was a staunch supporter of Dr. Peter Fraser, a missionary, who vigorously campaigned for emancipation of the *Bawis*. He is said to have been the first Mizo chief who freed his *Bawis*. As recognition of this initiative, a lower primary school (up to class III) was opened at Maubuang. It was in this school that Vanlawma began his education. Being a son of a school teacher, Vanlawma started his schooling early. He finished his lower primary when he was only 10 years old. He then moved to another school at Sialsuk village, where he completed his upper primary (class VI) in 1927. After that he continued his studies in Aizawl, where from he passed middle school (class VII) examination in first division in 1929. There was no high school in Mizoram at that time. Therefore, after a short break, Vanlawma moved to Shillong, studied in the Shillong Government High School, and he passed the Matriculation Examination of the Calcutta University in first division in 1939 from that school. In Shillong, he stayed in Earle Hostel.

Vanlawma's aim in life was to run a business and to join politics. During his stay in Shillong, he actively involved himself with the Lushai Students' Association, enrolled himself as a member of the Boys Scout and attended music classes. The Lushai Students' Association, a precursor of modern Mizo Zirlai Pawl (MZP), was formed in Shillong in 1935, and Vanlawma was actively associated with it from the beginning. As a Boys Scout, he participated in 1st All Assam Jamboree held in Shillong and in 1st All India Jamboree in Delhi. In Delhi, Vanlawma and other boys who represented Assam won first prize in the competition. A natural talent in music, Vanlawma joined church choir at his native village when he was only 11 years old. It was in Shillong that he joined a music class conducted by London School of Music and qualified for a Diploma in Music.[4]

The Shillong experience in students association was the beginning of Vanlawma's political career. However, on his return to Aizawl, in 1939, he joined the government service as a circle staff in the Superintendent's Office. In addition to his normal duty, he was made a member of the district level board which used to conduct examination for the non-Mizo employees of the government of their proficiency in Mizo language. While preparing the results, Vanlawma had to share the same table with Superintendent of the district,

A.G. McCall, which he later on considered as a memorable event in his life. Vanlawma was also assigned the duty of recruitment of cadets to the 'Hospital Corps', a war-time organization known in Mizo as *Ruangla* (meaning collectors of dead bodies). After some months, Vanlawma was transferred to P.W.D office as a clerk only to be dismissed from the service within few months. This happened in 1940 when some non-Mizos were appointed against the posts of clerks which were created to meet the additional workload caused by the challenge of the Japanese advance from Burma and those appointments were openly objected by Vanlawma and his colleagues who formed the Young Mizo Employees Association. The objection was on the basis of a circular of the Governor of Assam in 1934 which reserved the vacant posts in the district for local people. The matter was discussed with the Superintendent, but Vanlawma refused to withdraw the memorandum submitted by him and his colleagues. The Superintendent took action by terminating the service of Vanlawma. However, he was soon appointed as a clerk in the Brigade's office when the 109th War Brigade was raised with headquarters at Aizawl. Later on, he was appointed as a clerk in the office of the Civil Surgeon and then transferred to the Department of Forests. Though Vanlawma once revealed that he had joined the government service only as a temporary engagement whereas his real aim in life was to run a business house in Mizoram and to join politics, the experience in government service in early life gave him self-confidence and ultimately proved to be immensely helpful in his real career in social work and as a historian of the Mizos.

Vanlawma had the opportunity to explore the history and culture of the Mizos when he involved himself in social and political organizations and came in close contact with the people. During his tenure as Secretary since 1940, the Young Mizo Association (YMA), which was originally founded in 1935 by the Church leaders to go along the lines of the Church, underwent significant changes in its form and nature of functioning as it gradually assumed a secular character.[5] The separation of the two became formal in 1946 when the Church authorities banned the association of the so-called *Thubelh* group (organ of YMA) with their monthly organ, called *Kristian Tlangau*, published since 1911.[6] Vanlawma and his colleagues had in the meantime decided to convert YMA into a political organization and to provide political training to the young Mizos.[7] In 1945, they invited McDonald, the Superintendent, to an informal meeting with YMA leaders at Govt. M.E. School, Aizawl, and told him that the people in Mizo hills wanted a democratic system of administration. This was followed by a General Conference in 1946 in which the method of dealing with the British was discussed and the chairman of the meeting, a missionary, left the meeting in protest when the issue came up for discussion. The Church-YMA joint project of sending *Chanchintha Dak*, a gospel mail in Mizo language, to the people of Chin Hills in Burma to spread Mizo language in that area was abandoned when the Church realized that the real motive of the YMA in trying to spread Mizo language was promoting the idea of 'Greater Mizoram'.[8] Vanlawma thus succeeded in freeing YMA from influence of the Church.

In April 1946, Vanlawma met the Superintendent for permission to form a political party to be called Mizo Commoners Union. The permission was granted on the condition that the party shall be named Mizo Union to include all sections of the people, since the people in Mizo hills were then known separately as chiefs and commoners (subjects) and both had contributed to the success of the efforts of the government in Second World War. The first assembly of the Mizo Union, held at Aizawl on 24-26 April 1946, elected Vanlawma as its General Secretary. But the party soon witnessed differences of opinion among its leaders on the question of sending representatives to the Assam Legislative Assembly. The difference became wider when the Superintendent interfered in support of those who preferred to join the Assembly. Consequently, the Mizo Union was divided into two factions. The Mizo Union Right Wing led by Vanlawma, which was against joining Assam Assembly, began to preach the idea of 'independence' among the Mizos. Vanlawma also formed another organization, called Mizo Cultural Society, in 1959, to sow the seed of nationalism among the people through cultural activities. However, the Mizo Cultural Society was soon changed into Mizo National Famine Front (MNFF) to help the people during the worst ever famine in the history of Mizo hills. When the famine relief works were over, the MNFF converted itself into a political party known as Mizo National Front (MNF) with Vanlawma its General Secretary. On 1st March 1966, MNF declared the Mizo district as 'independent Mizoram'. However, Vanlawma had already left the party in 1962 and formed the Mizo National Council with 'independence' as its policy. When the MNF launched armed insurrection in 1966, Vanlawma had virtually withdrawn himself from active political life. His last political stint was in Mizo Democratic Front, founded by him in 1977, which contested the 1977 Lok Sabha elections with Sanglianchhungi as its candidate. Mizoram had then already been separated from Assam and the massive participation in the parliamentary election of 1977 was an indication of the change in Mizo politics.

After the Lok Sabha elections of 1977, Vanlawma never took part in politics and till his death in 2006, he concentrated only on exploration of the history and culture of the Mizos and promotion of Mizo literature. His contributions to society and literature has been widely acclaimed and he was honoured with laurels which included the Freelance Writer's Award presented by Mizo Writers' Association (1994), a Special Award by Lunglei District Welfare Committee (1994), Writer of the Year Award by Lelte Weekly (1996) and the Padma Award presented by the President of India (1998).[9]

Contributions to history

R. Vanlawma's literary career began in 1961when he bought a second-hand printing press from the Presbyterian Mission. He was the second individual in Mizoram to own a printing press, after Lalrinliana of Dawrpui, Aizawl. From this printing press, Vanlawma launched the publication of a weekly newspaper, called *Zalenna* (Freedom). It became the mouthpiece of the MNF, which was formed in 1961. When he gave up politics, he was a free man to write and publish from his own press on any subject that came to his mind. However, freedom, patriotism and nationalism were the key words in his writings published in his own paper *Zalen* (Free), which continued to mould the Mizo public opinion. It is said that writing was his natural talent and he had taken to writing much before he retired from politics and thus spent about 60 years of his life in literary pursuits. However, during last 30 years he contributed a large number of articles in different daily, weekly and monthly newspapers and literary magazines and occasional commemorative publications. It has not been possible to ascertain how many articles Vanlawma wrote and published. However, in only one monthly, called *MEICHHER*, published by the Department of School Education, Adult Education Wing, Govt. of Mizoram, he contributed as many as 89 articles, which are mostly on Mizo history, religion, traditional institutions, language, education and society. In this journal, his first article was published in March 1976 and the last article in January 2006. He also wrote many articles in YMA's *Thubelh*. He wrote a number of books in Mizo language. His well known books are the following :

1. *Ka Ram leh Kei* (My Country and I), 1965.
2. *Israelte Chanchin* (The Story of Israelites), 1989.
3. *Awithangpa Chanchin* (The Story of Awithangpa), 1989.
4. *Khawvel Lehlam* (The Other Side of the World), 1992.
5. *Veronik-i* (Veronica), 1991.
6. *Ka Ram leh Kei – II* (My Country and I, Part. II) (being published posthumously).

Vanlawma was not a professionally trained historian, but history was always a strong point in his writings. Although he wrote mostly on the contemporary issues, he provided the facts and examples from the past. As a social and political worker he extensively toured Mizoram and interacted with people from various walks of life. This enabled him to collect information on oral history and gain strong insight into the origin, migrations and settlements of the Mizos and their traditions, institutions and culture. The books listed above contain a lot of history. The word '*chanchin*' in Mizo means 'story', but story of what had really happened in the past is always history. The *chanchin* dominated Vanlawma's works. However, the *magnum opus* of his contributions to history is the book, *Ka Ram leh Kei (My Country and I)*. It was first published in 1965, and the third revised and enlarged edition came out in 1989. He also wrote a second volume of the book, which was not published in his life time and is being posthumously published now at the initiative of the family and some enlightened Mizos who always loved to read the works of Vanlawma.

Ka Ram leh Kei (My Country and I),[10] as originally published in 1965 and revised or enlarged later, is a political history of Mizoram, The book is a testimony to the fact that R. Vanlawma was really competent to do the work, though he did not provide the references. On this, his own position is that he claimed originality of the information which he gathered himself and the interpretations are always his own. In fact, in Mizoram it is acclaimed by the literati as a dependable book on the history of the Mizos. The 418 pages of the book (1989 edition) is divided into 29 chapters. Except chapter I, which deals with the early history of the Mizos, all other chapters are on the modern period and written on the basis of personal experience of the author. Chapter I, consisting of 69 pages, is a short account of the early history of the Mizo in which he discussed history from the earliest times to the advent of the British in a chronological order. While discussing the folk belief of the Mizos about the origins of the tribe from *Chhinlung*, Vanlawma says that *Chhinlung*, which literally means 'cave', was in China but tracing the origin of the Mizos from that cave does not provide any scope of historical connectivity. Some scholars had earlier tried to link one legendary prince, Chienlung, with the *Chhinlung* theory, but Vanlawma rejected this theory on the ground that the time sequence does not match such a possibility since Prince Chienlung emerged on the scene only at the beginning of the 18th century when the Mizos were already well settled in present-day Mizoram. In his opinion, the Mizos and many other tribes in the region had moved in westward direction in course of their migrations and this is very strongly recalled in the traditions of the tribe. However, he clearly stated that it is not possible to be sure about the particular areas through which the peoples entered Mizoram. At the same time, he suggested that Champhai area could be the place through which the Mizo tribes entered Mizoram due to a variety of reasons. In his opinion, an important landmark in the early history of the Mizos is Khampat. In this story, Khampat was a town where the people (Mizo) planted a banyan tree with a firm faith that they would surely return to the place when the branches of the tree touched the ground. The prophecy is said to been more or less fulfilled in the beginning of the 20th century when a number of Mizos returned and settled down in the areas around the Khampat site. While discussing the implications of this story, Vanlawma observed that it may have been coined not by the Mizos themselves but by the Buddhist priests who wanted to make sure that the Mizos did not go back to Mizoram. The policy of the Buddhist priests towards the Mizos worked well and those who migrated to Burma had settled down in the area around Khampat permanently. He also argued that the banyan tree might have died in the meantime and a new sapling might have been planted. Vanlawma himself visited the site in 1963 and he was convinced that the story of the Khampat banyan tree is a true landmark in the early history of the Mizos.

Vanlawma discussed at some length the history of origin and growth of the chiefships, the dominant political system in Mizoram in the pre-colonial period. While tracing the origin of chiefship from Sailo family he highlighted a version of an oral tradition on the birth of Niguite, who is considered as the progenitor of both Sailo and Paihte families. He referred to a tradition which says that Dongula of the Sailo family had illicit relation with his sister Lakiri and this led to the birth of Niguite. Another version quoted by many scholars shows that Dongula's sister was named Lalnemi. However, what emerges from citing different versions is that no historical conclusion can be reached as to which version is correct. Nonetheless, Vanlawma seems to have considered that the social life of the people improved under rule of the Sailo chiefs and the people in general were happy with the chiefs. He also highlighted some of the very important events in the early history of Mizoram, like the migrations of different tribes of the Mizo, the settlements of those tribes in various regions, and the inter-tribal wars and conflicts in course of settlements, like war of the north and the south, war with Sukte tribes, war of the east and the west, and the wars with Pawi and others. These significant events have been highlighted in a historical and chronological order, and the geographical areas occupied by different tribes emerge very clearly in his narratives. 'Lalsawi', an uprising of the people against the chief, is an important event in the early history about which stories are still heard in different parts of Mizoram. Vanlawma took great pains in collecting information about the event and reconstructing the history of the uprising.

The larger part of the book *Ka Ram leh Kei* (My Country and I), as it is said already, is devoted to the modern (colonial and post-colonial] history of Mizoram. To him the period of British rule was the 'golden age' in Mizo history, because, according to him, under the British rule there was dignity of labour and justice to all. This is an observation, which may not be acceptable to all. However, Vanlawma had seen himself most of the events and developments in Mizoram in the later British period. Since in case of some of the events described in the book he was an eye witness, his evidence can be treated as primary source in case of those events. What is important about the book is that his narratives do not come into conflict with the recorded facts in any authenticated document, if such documents are at all available. Since the recorded information is always meagre, Vanlawma's work goes much beyond the documented history. Even about the earlier periods, his book is considered as a dependable work by the people in Mizoram.[11]

Zalen Cabin

Any discussion on the life and works of Vanlawma cannot be concluded without mentioning his 'Zalen Cabin', perhaps a replica of Abraham Lincoln's 'Log Cabin' in which the great American had lived before he became President of the United States of America in 1861 and the emancipation of the slaves in America was his most important achievement. Inside Vanlawma's 'Zalen Cabin' one would find the portraits of Abraham Lincoln and Winston Churchill hanging on the wall and between the two portraits, is the portrait of R. Vanlawma himself. This indicates that Vanlawma was fascinated by the ideas of those two great leaders. 'Zalen Cabin' is a house first built in 1953 of wood, bamboo and iron sheet. It could not stand the mighty hand of fire caused in the bombing of Aizawl city on 5th March 1966. The present Cabin is a new one built upon the ruins of the old cabin. In fact, 'Zalen Cabin' is a term used by Vanlawma to denote 'a place where there is no fear' or 'where the mind is without fear', as mentioned by Rabindranath Tagore in one of his eternal poems. Tagore prayed to God for a Free India, 'Where the Mind is Without Fear'. In the same manner, Vanlawma implored freedom for his people in Mizoram and he wanted that freedom to be without fear. Like Tagore, patriotism, nationalism and freedom were very close to the heart of R. Vanlawma who insisted on those ideals in whatever he did and wrote. This was inherent in him. Therefore, 'Zalen Cabin' stands in Aizawl today reminding the people of Mizoram of the importance of those ideals.[12]

As a historian

It has already been stated that R. Vanlawma was not a professional historian, but his *Ka Ram leh Kei* (My Country and I) is a major contribution to Mizo history, besides his other articles on historical themes. He wrote history out of his personal interest in the subject, and he was mostly guided by his concern for the Mizo people. He did not give any reference while stating facts in his narratives. However, the facts stated by him are generally what the Mizos know about their own history and what has come down to them as oral traditions. His observations that the people were happy with the rule of the chiefs and that the British rule was the 'golden age' in Mizo history are his own opinions and may not stand the serious scrutiny in historiography. This is particularly because in 1940s it was on demand of the commoners that the chiefship had to be abolished in Mizo hills by the government. It is also well known that the British rule in India or any where in the colonies was exploitative and oppressive in character which provoked national movements for impendence in all British colonies. How it could be different in Mizoram, and if it was at all so, it has to be established with facts and evidences. Vanlawma's narrative of the early history is based only on oral traditions, as recorded or archaeological data are completely absent for that period. However, what makes his works special is that he wrote what the average Mizo mind looks upon as the real past and the people in general consider his narratives as acceptable and dependable. Moreover, there is no last word in history writing. Therefore, Vanlawma's book on Mizo history can form the basis of further research in the subject, and here lies the importance of his contribution as a historian. He was in deed a nationalist historian, who nurtured Mizo nationalism in his heart and wanted to inspire the Mizo people with that spirit.

Notes & References

1. R..Vanlawma, *Awithangpa*, Lalchhungkaw Press, Aizawl, 1989, p. 12.
2. *Ibid*, p. 93
3. Rohmingmawii, "Khawvelthanga Sailo, chief of Maubuang", paper presented in a seminar organised by Mizo History Association, on 25-26 November, 2010. It is presumed that Khawvelthanga freed his *Bawis* in 1910.
4. R. Vanlawma, *op.cit.*, p. 104.
5. R.Vanlawma was elected as Assistant Secretary of YMA in 1940 and General Secretary in 1942. He held the post of General Secretary till the second half of 1945. In 1945 election he was defeated. After that, he began to explore the possibility of participating in politics more directly. He became the General Secretary of Mizo Union when it was founded in April 1946.
6. In 1911 the Presbyterian Church began to publish its monthly mouthpiece, called *Kristian Tlangau*. In 1935 YMA contributed the news of its own activities for publication in that monthly .The news published about YMA in that monthly was called *Thubelh*, meaning *Appendix*.
7. Lalzuia Colney; "R.Vanlawma – Politician", *Zalen Cabin*, Mizo Academy of Letters, Lunglei, 2010, p. 52.
8. R.Vanlawma; *Ka Ram leh Kei* (My Couttry and I), Zalen Printing House, Aizawl, 1989, p. 84.
9. For biographical information on R. Vanlawma and various facets of his life, see reminiscences and tributes in *Zalen Cabin*, Mizo Academy of Letters, Lunglei, 2010.
10. This book was first published in 1965, reprinted in 1972, and the edition revised and enlarged by the author himself was published in 1989. R. Vanlawma also wrote volume II of the same book after 1989, but it could not be published in his life time. However, two volumes (Vol. I and Vol. II) are now under print by the Zalen Printing House, Aizawl.

11. The discussions and comments in this section are based on R.Vanlawma; *Ka Ram leh Kei* (My Country and I), Zalen Printing House, Aizawl, 1989. As regards the popularity and dependability of the work of R. Vanlawma, the position has been taken by the author of this paper after ascertaining the views of a large section of the literati in Mizoram.

12. R. Vanlawma; *Ka Ram leh Kei* (My Country and I), Zalen Printing House, Aizawl, 1972, p.84.

19

Debabrata Datta (1918-1998)

—Amalendu Bhattacharjee & Jahar Kanti Sen

Biographical Sketch

In the tradition of historical research in Barak valley, the name of Debabrata Datta is widely acclaimed for his pioneering contributions. He devoted almost the whole of his life to the study of regional history of Barak valley. This popular and immensely successful college teacher of history was born on 7 January 1918 in the well known Datta family of Silchar. His father Suresh Chandra Datta was a lawyer in Silchar court and his mother, Amitabala was a housewife. His student career was initiated in Silchar Mission Girls' School (now Govt. Girls' Higher Secondary School) when he was admitted in the infant class. In those days infants - boys and girls - were taught together in this school which was meant for the girls only in primary onwards. After spending two years in the infant class, he was taken to Abhayacharan Pathsala from where he completed his lower primary education and got himself admitted to the Govt. Boys' High School and passed Matriculation Examination of Calcutta University from that school in 1935 with distinction in History. He passed BA with Honours in History in 1939 from Murarichand College, Sylhet and M.A. in Modern History from Calcutta University in 1941. Datta began his illustrious career as a college teacher in Brindavan College, Habiganj, in 1941, and in 1944 he joined Gurucharan College, Silchar. In 1952 he passed M.A. in Ancient Indian History of the Calcutta University as a private candidate. After serving Gurucharan College for about twenty years, he became the Vice-Principal of the college on 2 January, 1963. For a brief period, he officiated as Principal of the Gurucharan College (21.01.1967 to 23.05.1968). He was appointed Principal of the Cachar College, Silchar, on January 1, 1972; and he retired on March 1, 1979 after serving the college as Principal. He breathed his last on 1 March 1998, after an attack of *coronary thrombosis*.

Debabrata Datta became a legend in his own life time as a popular teacher for his inimitable style of teaching history to the undergraduate classes. The way he made the subject enjoyable in the class rooms was understood from his students refusing to miss his classes. His name became almost house hold in Northeast India for the textbooks he wrote in English and Bengali for the students in colleges and high schools. The textbooks of history written by him used to be prescribed by the government of undivided Assam for the students in secondary and higher secondary schools in the state. A prolific writer of prose in English and Bengali, Datta had performed the avowed purpose of quickening consciousness about history among all classes of the society.[1]

Research Field

The space of Debabrata Datta's historical research was South Assam where research work in the history and society had been initiated by administrators and scholars about four decades before the birth of Datta. The research output centering the region may be divided into two broad sections, viz., (i) the reports of the European officials, and (ii) the studies of the local scholars. The European officials, with a view to knowing the region out of administrative necessity, collected field information about the history and society and occasionally wrote articles and books. In these articles and books, were incorporated details of regional history, society and culture which eventually became important source materials for future researchers. Among these articles and books the following are worth mentioning: R.B. Pemberton's *Report on the Eastern Frontier of British India* (Bengal Govt. Press, Calcutta, 1835); 'Memoirs of Sylhet, Kachar and Adjacent Districts', written by the first Superintendent of Cachar, Thomas Fisher, and published in *Journal of the Asiatic Society of Bengal* (Vol. IV, pt. II, 1840); Frank Ede's 'The Sacred Caves of Cachar' (*JASB*, 1903); A.J.M. Mills' *Report on Cachar, 1853* (Harkaru Press, Calcutta, 1854); W.J. Alllen's *Report on Cachar, 1859* (Harkaru Press, Calcutta, 1859); W.W. Hunter's, *A Statistical Account of Assam* (2 vols., London, 1877); E.A. Gait's *A History of Assam* (London, 1906); and *Assam District Gazeteers*, Vol. I – Cachar, Vol. II – Sylhet, edited by B.C. Allen (Calcutta, 1905). Studies by the local scholars on regional history and culture of South Assam were initiated in the second half of 19th century. In 1879 was published an article entitled *'Srihatter Prachin Bibaran'* in the periodical *Srihatta Prakash* (1886 BS) after the discovery of the Bhattera Copper-plates in 1872. With a view to contending the contents of this article the historian Kailash Chandra Singha wrote an article entitled *'Srihatter Tamrafalak O Kachar Raj Vamsavali'*, published in two installments in *Bharati* magazine, Calcutta (*Kartik* 1288 and *Vaishakh* 1289 BS). Padmanath Bhattacharyya became interested in regional history when he started collecting research materials for the famous folklorist William Crookes of England.[2] Two important medieval manuscripts of Cachar, *'Hedamba Rajyer Dandabidhi'* (Guwahati, 1910), and *Hedamba Rajyer Rindanbidhi'* (Guwahati, 1921) were published in book forms by Padmanath with scholarly introductions. Though *'Srihatter Itibritta'* (*Purbangsa* 1910, *Uttarangsa* 1917) of Achyutcharan Choudhury Tattvanidhi dealt mainly with the history of Sylhet, in the appendix of the book the history of Cachar has also been discussed. In 1911 was published *Cacharer Itibritta* (Dhaka, 1911), written by Upendra Chandra Guha. The book has 14 chapters, an introduction and an 'appendix'. It begins with the Puranic age and moves through the centuries to end at the termination of Dimasa rule in Cachar following its annexation by the British. The book records the political transition of Cachar along with various aspects of cultural life and the demography. In 1914 was established *'Srihatta Cachar Anushilan Samity'* for researching the history of Sylhet and Cachar. The Secretary of the Samity was Jagannath Deb, a teacher in Normal School, Silchar, and the head office of the Samity was in Silchar. The publication of the journal *Shiksha Sevak* by the Silchar Normal School was an important step forward towards researches in the history of Barak valley as the journal regularly contained articles on local history by Jagannath Deb, Padmanath Bhattacharyya, and many others. The Normal School also served the cause of local history by collecting and preserving some old manuscripts of the Barak valley.

After partition and independence of the country, numerous studies have been made on the history of South Assam. In this phase, Debabrata Datta was at the centre of all research initiatives. He studied the records at the District Records Office, Silchar, and collected information from various other sources and wrote articles in magazines and periodicals. As a teacher of history in Gurucharan College, Datta organized 'History Seminar' involving his Honours students, which occasionally organized seminars and published collections of papers. Datta also established the short-lived 'Cachar Anusanddhan Samiti' and published some issues of a journal entitled *Haidamba*. The important personalities, other than Debabrata Datta, who made significant contributions to historical research in the valley, are Rajmohan Nath, J.B. Bhattacharjee, Sujit Choudhury, and Kamaluddin Ahmed. Nath, well known for his *The Background of Assamese Culture* (Gauhati, 1948), wrote several books and articles on history and culture of Assam. His *Kacharer Itihas* (Kolkata, 1965) and *Antiquities of Cachar* (Silchar, 1981) are important contributions on history of Barak valley. Though distinguished as a historian of Modern India, J.B. Bhattacharjee carried out research work in ancient, medieval and modern periods of the regional history of Northeast India. Two of his important works on Barak valley are *Cachar Under British Rule in North East India* (New Delhi, 1977) and *Social and Polity Formations in Pre-Colonial North East India: The Barak Valley Experience* (New Delhi, 1991). From one vintage point, J.B. Bhattacharjee is the heir of Debabrata Datta. Bhattacharjee's first book is a documented history of Cachar during the colonial rule, an area that Datta had brought into focus. Bhattacharjee has written a large number of research papers on Cachar and the adjoining areas in national and international journals and proceedings in last forty-five years. One of his latest papers presented and accepted in the Indian History Congress described the transfer of Sylhet, Cachar and Goalpara to Assam in 1874 as the 'First Partition of Bengal'.[3] Among his latest books on Modern Northeast, which covered Barak valley in relevant thematic contexts, are *Trade and Colony : The British Colonization of Northeast India* (Shillong, 2000) and *Making of British Assam* (Kolkata, 2008). Sujit Choudhury wrote *Folklore and History : A Study of the Hindu Filkcults of the Barak Valley* (New Delhi, 1996) and *Srihatta-Cacharer Prachin Itihas* (Kolkata, 2003), among his other works, in which, along with the conventional materials like copper-plates, archaeological data and literary sources, he used folklore also as a source material for unveiling the ancient history of South Assam. Kamaluddin Ahmed wrote several articles on the medieval period of Barak-Surma valley, and also wrote on art and archaeology of

Sylhet-Cachar in a major work on the art history of Assam (viz. *The Art and Architecture of Assam*, Guwahati, 1994). Another landmark on the recognition of the Barak valley region as a composite and viable research field was the publication of *Srihatta-Cacharer Itihas O Samskritir Ruprekha* (edited by Jyotirindranath Choudhury et. al.), in 1995, in which Jayanta Bhusan Bhattacharyya, Sujit Choudhury, Kamaluddin Ahmed, Manabendra Bhattacharyya, Amalendu Bhattacharyya, and many others from Barak valley, Shillong and Kolkata contributed substantive essays.[4]

Research Contributions

The contributions of Debabrata Datta to historiography of Northeast India may be evaluated under the backdrop of the evolution of his research field. It is worth mentioning that although he worked in ancient, medieval and modern periods, it was Cachar in the British period that was his main area of study. The historians who were his forerunners belonged to the pre-independence period. None of them studied the history of the colonial period. It was Debabrata Datta who had initiated this study in undivided Cachar. In fact, every researcher has a model before him, and Datta was no exception to it. As he revealed himself, he was influenced by the *Bangiya Itihas Parishad,* which was established in Kolkata in 50s of the last century and had declared its objective in the following words:[5]

> To search for the facts of history with the dedication and patience of a devotee, by ascending above the personal prejudices, disinterested and undivided light of observation, to establish the examined and proven facts through mother tongue in the heart of the people—this Parishad was established with these objectives under the patronage of Acharya Jadunath Sarkar. This Parishad, by way of writing historical books and articles in Bengali language facilitating discussion on historical problems and spreading historical truths, endeavor to create interest in history among the people. Apart from this, the Parishad will transpire interest in historical research by publishing the valued research works in the mother tongue. The Parishad will engage its efforts in every way to generate consciousness about history in all the classes of the society. (Trans. ours)

The title of the mouthpiece of the Parishad was '*Itihas*'. In the 2nd issue (1st year) Ramesh Chandra Majumdar in his essay, '*Bangalir Itihas: Madhyayug*' wrote,[6]

> As it is not possible to construct an 'ideal' imaginatively planned house without collecting bricks, woods, iron and other materials, so it is not possible to write an ideal or all-encompassing book of history without collecting enough necessary materials. Abundance of facts is the life of history and all the materials must be abundant and credible. A house cannot be constructed with only bricks, if iron, timber, lime and other materials are not abundantly used there. Again the house cannot be worth living in if these materials are not strong. The re-construction of history will be as complete as the facts and source materials are sufficient and dependable. The house will remain as incomplete and its base shall remain as weak as there is a paucity of source materials. (Trans. ours)

The first publication of Debabrata Datta is *Cacharer Prastarlipi*, published by the Cachar Anusanddhan Samiti in 1957. The 'introduction' says,[7]

> Though Cachar Anusanddhan Samiti was established in 1953, it has not become possible so long for the samity to publish any book. The samiti does not have any fund of its own.

> So we have only been collecting the source materials. We have now published the book *Cacharer Prastarlipi'* spending very small amount of money. We have in our hands enough materials of history to be published in book form. Many letters have been collected from the Records Room of the Deputy Commissioner relating to the early phase of the British period. It is not possible to publish all these in book form without government help. We have been trying to collect letters and documents from the ancient families of Cachar, and we have collected some. (Trans. our)

An appeal was also made to the public for allowing them 'to see' the documents in their possession and to help them 'search the real history of the country'. However, in *Cacharer Prastarlipi* the complete texts of the following stone-inscriptions were re-produced : a. Malbong inscription of King Naranarayan (1498 *Saka*, 16 *Ashad*); b. Maibong inscription of King Harischandra (1683 Saka); c. Khaspur inscription of Rajmata Lakshmiprava Devi (1693 *Saka*); and d. Khaspur inscription of Maharani Lakshmi Devi (queen of Harischandra, 1720 *Saka*, 14 *Jaistha*). The discussions on the contents and historical background of the inscriptions convincingly pronounced Datta's competence in handling the epigraphic records as sources of history.[8]

A student of history and inspired by the thoughts and ideals of *Bangia Itihas Parishad*, Debabrata Datta realized that his predecessors, while working on South Assam, had confined themselves within the periphery of the ancient and medieval periods. None of them had devoted mind and thought to the modern period. Therefore, Datta had selected the modern period, particularly the period of British rule, as his thrust area of study. Realizing the need he engaged himself in the work of collection of dependable source materials, and by doing so, he had prepared the base for the younger researchers. This he achieved by compiling the valuable *Cachar District Records* (Silchar, 1969),[9] a collection of selected documents preserved in the District Records Office, Silchar, which he painstakingly deciphered, sometimes using magnifying class, sitting in the midst of dusty and smelling heaps of papers every working day after his glasses in the college for several hours over the years. The author braved the discomfort of the dingy record room to rummage through the century old official papers with the patience of a devoted researcher. The volume contained the records from 1832 to 1853, and those which were copied by Datta till 1969. He continued the work and some of the records collected by him after the publication of the first volume in 1969 and covering the period 1853 to 1860 were included in a special volume of the *Gabeshana Parishat Patrika*, published by the Barak Upatyaka Banga Sahitya O Sanskriti Sanmelan, coinciding the *Itihas Anusanddhan Barsa* (year of historical research), in 1994-95.[10] The records covered in those two collections and some more that were awaiting publication in Datta's own house have recently been brought out by the Asiatic Society, Calcutta, in two volumes under the editorship of Sunanda Datta.[11] These two new volumes are, in fact, reprints of the earlier editions, while in volume II some unpublished documents have also been included.

The *Cachar District Records*, compiled and published by Debabrata Datta in 1969, is the most referred collection of documents by the researchers in modern history of South Assam. The first and most extensive user was, of course, J.B. Bhattacharjee in his *Cachar*

Under British Rule in North East India (New Delhi, 1977).[12] While Datta was wading through the records in the District Record Room under the guidance of Narendrakrishna Sinha,[13] he came across Firminger's *Sylhet District Records*[14] which helped him in formatting the work. In his own words:[15]

> I worked for many years to compile these records; many years I say, as the reading of these letters was a tough job. Many of them are illegible because of the bad hand-writing of the copyists and many have become illegible in spite of good hand-writing *because of the fading of the ink used.* But more tough was the tracing of the records which are lying untouched, for how many years no one knows, in a prohibited dark and dingy room, into which 'Aklu' has got entrance. I am grateful to the record keepers with whom I had to come into contact for their kind and ungrudging co-operation.

The erstwhile Cachar, a protected kingdom (under the British tutelage since 1824), was formally annexed to British India on August 14, 1832. But the earliest document traced and compiled in the book was dated to June, 1834. This is because all the documents of the first two years of British rule had been gutted by a conflagration. The introduction reads thus:[16]

> Cachar was informally taken over by the British in 1830, and it was formally annexed in 1832. I do not get the records of the years 1830-32, as would be evident from the letter no.220 of 1839, when the Superintendent, Mr.Burn's bungalow was burnt.

Datta also could not make good use of the documents pertaining to the years 1834-36 for certain other reason. As he stated:[17]

> I could not well utilize the records of the years 1834, '35 and '36, as about 8 or 9 years back these were taken away by a political leader of Assam valley, of course with permission of Rana KDN Singh, the then Deputy Commissioner of Cachar. The records were needed by the political leader, I was told, for writing the history of the freedom movement in Assam. I requested almost all the DCs who came to Cachar after Singh to get back the records, but I do not know if ever any step was taken by any one of them of the recovery of the same. I have ceased to pursue the matter when one DC, in reply to my request, said, 'What interest can we have now in the records of the British period?' the records have not been returned yet and I have doubt if ever these will be returned.

Nonetheless, the book *Cachar District Records* has an enduring value. About the significance of these records Datta wrote:[18]

> From the letters published in this volume one will get an idea as to how Cachar had developed as a prosperous district under British rule. Here in the letters we find the fascinating descriptions of the growth of judiciary, the development of police administration, the emergence of the revenue system, the introduction of the modern education, large scale immigration from the neighbouring district, the early relation of the British with the Kokis and the Lushais, and incidentally, interesting information of Cachar under Cachari Rajas.

Debabrata Datta's another remarkable work is the history of Silchar Municipality in Bengali, under the title *Silchar Paurasabhar Itihas* (Silchar, 1982), published on the occasion of centenary of the Silchar Municipal Board. The then Chairman of the Municipal Board, S.M. Dev wrote in its introduction:[19]

> For how long can the people retain the tale of an institution in their memory? ... I believe this book will preserve the history of the Municipal Board and Silchar town from being thrown into oblivion. Sri Debabrata Dutta has written the history of the Municipal Board on our request. (Trans. ours)

The word 'history' figures in the title, but the author is not ready to term the book as a history in true sense of the term. In the 'Author's note' he stated:[20]

> The book has a fatal flaw. It is based only on the proceedings of the Municipal Board. Had the letters sent by the Government been found, many more facts could be brought into light. But I could not trace them.

In fact, *Silchar Paurasabhar Itihas* is not a self-contained work in history. It is the compilation of the proceedings of the Board. However, the way the author presented those proceedings with intervening observations it well served the purpose of a history of the Silchar Municipality for one hundred years. It was indeed the scholarly honesty of the author that he himself admitted:[21]

> I have not attempted any critical analysis of the proceedings. I have simply set down what I found in the records. Researchers would find materials for their research in this book. They will be able to write the complete history of the Municipal Board with the help of the materials compiled here along with more by themselves.

Debabrata Datta wrote a large number of articles in various magazines and souvenirs. A collection of his essays have been brought out in 2005, entitled *Debabrata Datter Nirbachita Prabandha Sankalan* (Collection of Selected Essays of Debabrata Datta)[22] which contains four articles in English and seven articles in Bengali. The articles are on different aspects of the history of Cachar in the modern times. The topics range from the British annexation of Cachar to the beginning of tea industry, and from Cachar Brahmo Samaj to the history of Silchar Govt. High School. The book also contains his essays on Bipinchandra Pal, Mahatma Gandhi in Silchar, biographical sketch of K.K. Chanda, Swadeshi Movement in Silchar, etc. The article on the history of Silchar Government High School covers an overview of the spread of modern education in Cachar.[23] Datta also published a score of articles in different Bengali newspapers and periodicals on the subjects like the envoy of Ahom kingdom to Cachar court, Bhubhan shrine, celebration of Tagore's birth anniversary in Silchar, the impact of Sepoy Mutiny in Cachar, introduction of modern judiciary in Cachar, World War II and Cachar, 19th May, etc. He has also left behind a large number of articles in English on Cachar on topics related to the colonial history of Cachar.[24]

Debabrata Datta had edited a historical magazine, *Haidamba* (in Bengali) which was, of course, short-lived. Only two volumes of the journal were published as *Sharodiya* or *Puja* issues in 1373 and 1375 BS. His companions in the project were not academics by profession, yet they came forward to support him in the venture out of a desire to reveal the cultural heritage of Cachar to its people. These companions were mainly his school class-mates who in later life used to meet every evening for gossip (Bengali *adda*) and between those gossips they conceptualized and executed *Haidamba*.[25] Similarly, *History Seminar Magazine, 1965-66*, of Gurucharan College, edited by Debabrata Datta, included articles written by his undergraduate students, but the volume became a very important source book for the researchers because it included some original documents, namely, one royal order of a Dimasa king, two official letters of the Superintendent of Cachar (dated to 1850 and 1860), and six letters written to Kamini Kumar Chanda by Surendranath Banerjee, Saiyad Samsul Huda, Ashutosh Mukherjee, and Mohammad Ali Jinnah.[26] He had also edited the souvenir published on the occasion of the birth centenary of Bipinchandra Pal (1958), centenary volume of Abhayacharan Pathsala, Silchar, and many such souvenirs commemorating different occasions. In fact, Silchar has a long tradition in publishing souvenirs to commemorate important events and milestones. The 'Gandhi Mela' has been an annual occasion in Silchar since the martyrdom of the Father of the Nation and the organizers of the '*mela*' have been publishing a souvenir every year, almost each one containing an article by Debabrata Datta. These local souvenirs contained invaluable materials in the form of eye-witness's testimony on the socio-political and cultural changes in Cachar during the British colonial period. Some of the articles in magazines and souvenirs, edited by Datta, did not bear the name of the authors as they preferred to remain anonymous or because the editor himself had supplied the source materials for those writers.[27] This explains Datta's efforts to remind the people of Barak valley about their own past and his own commitment to the cause of history.

As a historian

A legendary teacher of history in a premier college and a writer of text books for schools and colleges, Debabrata Datta was well known in Northeast India through his students and the text books he wrote for the entire region. In the Barak valley, he enjoyed great popularity for his vast erudition, oratory skill and commitment for the welfare of the people of the valley which passed through several popular movements since partition and independence of India on issues concerning economic development as well as language, identity and administrative reorganizations. Though always a non-political and non-party intellectual, Datta would never shy away from expressing his own views on all burning national, regional and local issues through press and platforms. As regards the local issues like language, identity, reforms or human rights concerning Barak valley, he always pleaded that those should be resolved taking history of the valley into account, and therefore, argued that the people should be aware of the history of their own land and own people. While presiding over the history session of a non-political parliament, organized by the premier socio-cultural organization in Barak valley, namely, Barak Upatyaka Banga Sahitya O Sanskriti Sanmelan, in 1993, at the District Library Hall, Silchar, he gave his concluding views in favour of the resolution for observing the Bengali year 1401 (1994-95) as the 'Year of Historical Research for Barak valley' (*Itihas Anusanddhan Barsa*), which was proposed by the historian J.B. Bhattacharjee and unanimously passed by the parliament. In spite of his old age ailments, Datta took active part in the various programmes of observing the 'Year of Historical Research' throughout the valley and in involving the academicians and the common public at large in the campaign that was purely academic. His participation added to the grace, dignity and academic contents of the programmes.

Datta's contribution as a historian of Barak valley is also significant, both in volume and content. His *Cacharer Prastarlipi* (Silchar, 1957), *Cachar District Records* (Silchar, 1969) and *Silchar Paurasabhar Itihas* (Silchar, 1982) are major source books that are being used, and shall be used, by the researchers in writing the modern history of Barak valley for a long time. He also contributed innumerable research articles in history, archaeology, culture, language, literature, institutions and great personalities, which not only revealed the source materials but also contained his own interpretations of the sources in situating Barak valley in contemporary histories. The only objection to his writings may be that he never followed the standard methodology of documentation and authentication. However, his own approach was that of a popular writer on historical themes, as he wrote mostly for the common readers in popular magazines, newspapers and souvenirs. On the other hand, his writings were always source-based. The authority of the sources used by him could never be contested. On the contrary, the historians have been citing his writings in their standard institutional works in support of their contentions. This explains the position of Debabrata Datta as a historian.

Notes & References

1. Amalendu Bhattacharya (ed.), *Debabrata Datter Nirbachita Prabandha Sankalan*, Kolkata, 2005, see *'Bhumika'*; News items in *Dainik Yugo Shanka*, Silchar, March 2, 1998.
2. Padmanath Bhattacharyya Vidyavinode, *"Amar Dekha Manush: Mr.Porteos, C.I.E."*, *Shiksha Sevak*, Vol. IV, No. 4, Silchar, 1336 BS, p. 6.
3. J.B. Bhattacharjee, "First Partition of Bengal (1874)", *Proceedings of the Indian History Congress*, Visva-Bharati University Session, 2005, pp. 640-51.
4. Jyotirindranath Choudhury et. al (eds.), *Srihatta-Cacharer Itihas O Sanskritir Ruprekha* (Bengali), Shillong, 1995.
5. Ramesh Chandra Majumdar & Narendra Krishna Sinha, *Itihas*, Vol. I, no.2, Kolkata, 1357 BS.
6. Ramesh Chandra Majumdar, *"Banglar Itihas : Madyayug"*, *Itihas*, Vol. I, no. 2, Kolkata, 1357 BS, p. 73.
7. Debabrata Datta, *Cacharer Prastarlipi*, Cachar Anusanddhan Samiti, Silchar, 1957, see Introduction.
8. *Ibid*.
9. D. Datta (ed.), *Cachar District Records*, Silchar, 1969.
10. Apurbananda Mazumdar *et. al* (ed.), *Gabeshana Parishat Patrika*, Vol. I, (Itihas Anusanddhan Barsa special issue), Barak Upatyaka Banga Sahitya O Sanskriti Sanmelan, Silchar, 1402 BS (1996), pp. 82-102.
11. *Cachar District Records*, vol. I & Vol. II, compiled by D. Datta and edited by Sunanda Datta, The Asiatic Society, Kolkata, 2007.
12. J.B. Bhattacharjee, *Cachar Under British Rule in North East India*, Radiant Publishers, New Delhi, 1977, see bibliography and endnotes.

13. Professor N.K. Sinha of Calcutta University, distinguished historian and celebrated author of *Economic History of Bengal*, 3 vols., who presided over Modern India section of the Indian History Congress in 1961 and became its General President at the Banares Session in 1969.
14. W.W. Firminger, *Sylhet District Records*, 4 vols., Assam Secretariat, Shillong, 1875-76.
15. D. Datta (ed.), *Cachar District Records*, *op.cit*., see 'Introduction'.
16. *Ibid*.
17. *Ibid*.
18. *Ibid*.
19. Debabrata Datta, *Silchar Paurasabhar Itihas*, Silchar, 1982, see 'Foreword'.
20. *Ibid*, see 'Author's Note'.
21. *Ibid*.
22. Amalendu Bhattacharya (ed.), *Debabrata Datter Nirbachita Prabandha Sankalan*, *op.cit*.
23. Content-wise the articles in English are entitled "Annexation of Cachar, 1832", "Cachar Mela", "Beginning of the Tea Industry in Cachar", and "History the Silchar Government Higher Secondary School " and those in Bengali, *"Silchare Bipin Chandra Pal"*, *"Silchare Gandhiji"*, *"Kamini Kumar Chanda"*, *"Cachar Brahmo Samaj"*, *"Abyayacharan Pathshalar Itikatha"*, *"Sarkari Ucchatara Bahumukhi Balika Bidyalayer Kichu Katha"*, *"Silchar Paurasabha O Swadeshikata"*.
24. Personal knowledge of the authors of this paper who had the opportunity to go through those articles in the personal collection of Late Debabrata Datta in his residence at Ukil Patty, Silchar. Content-wise some of those articles in English are entitled "Cachar at a Glance", "Bandemataram in Cachar", "A New Chapter in the History of Silchar Sports", "Cross Roads on Cachar's onwards march to education", "Higher Education in Cachar and Late Bishnucharan De" and in Bengali *"Ahom Duter Chokhe Cachar"*, *"Bhuban Tirthe"*, *"Silchare Rabindra Jayantir Adiparva"*, *"Unishe Me"*, *"Sipahibidroha O Cachar"*, *"Dwitiyo Biswayuddha O Cachar"*, *"Cachare Ingrej Bichar Byabastar Arambhakal"*, and *"Cachare Pratham Durgapuja"*.
25. Debabrata Datta (ed.), *Haidamba*, Vol. I, 1373 BS; Vol. II, 1375 BS. Contents in Vol. I included *"Cacharer Durgotsav"* – Bhuban Chanda, *"Amar Rajnaitik Chetanar Unmesh"* – Ajit Das, *" Fulertaler Anarash"* – Manindra Kumar Das, *"Cacharer Kaithyabhasah"* – Debabrata Datta, *"Cacharer Cha-Shilpa"* – Cha-Kar, *"Tikendrajit"* – Samarjit Gupta, *"Srihatta-Cachar O Rabindranath"* – Juthika Das and *"Ekti Chithi, Ekti Adesh, Ekti Report"* (three documents on Cachar) – Editor. Vol. II included *"Amar Diner Katha"* – Shrimati, *"Cacharer Cha-Shilper Adikatha"* – Manindra Kumar Das, *"Rajkumar Nandi Majumdar"* – Salil Majumdar, *"Cachare Ingreji Shikshar Gorar Katha"* – (anonymous), *"Cachare Pratham Inreji Adalat ebong Puratan Vakil"* – P.B., *"Haidembaswarer Shesh Nihshash"* – Ragabendra Bhattacharyya, *"Pangan"* – Hamid Ali Choudury, and *"Baniparar Katha"* – Tapan Kumar Datta.
26. *History Seminar Magazine*, 1965-66, Gurucharan College, Silchar, 1966.
27. Personal knowledge of the authors, as explained in n. 24.

20

Lakshminarayan Chakravarty (1919-2006)

—Sarbani Bhattacharjee

Biographical Sketch

A pioneer researcher in history and archaeology of Arunachal Pradesh, Lakshminarayan Chakravarty was born on 1March 1919 to Dwijadas Chakravarty and Kusumkamini Devi in their ancestral village Baniachang in Habiganj sub-division of the Sylhet district of undivided Assam. While a child, he was shifted to Shillong for education where a part of the family was placed for a long time. He passed his Matriculation of Examination of the Calcutta University from the Government High School, Shillong, in 1935, graduated from Murarichand College, Sylhet, in 1939 and thereafter, proceeded to Calcutta for his post-graduate education. He studied in the department of Ancient History and Archaeology, Calcutta University, where R.C. Majumdar, D.R. Bhandarkar, S.K. Saraswati, Nihar Ranjan Ray and D.C. Sircar were among his illustrious teachers who made a deep impact on his idea of history. He became very close to D.C. Sircar, who was then a young teacher in the department, and this association between the two continued for the rest of their life. One of his classmates in college and in the university was Debabrata Datta of Silchar, who eventually distinguished himself as a legendary teacher of history and a historian. Chakravarty passed his M.A. in 1941. As a student in Calcutta he was inspired by the on-going national movement, particularly the heroic escape of Subhas Chandra Bose from the clutches of the British vigilances, and decided to join the movement. On his return to the ancestral village in Sylhet he had a brief stint in political life. He participated in the Quit India Movement as a volunteer of the local congress committee in Baniachang and, later on, also campaigned for the retention of Sylhet in Assam during the infamous Sylhet Referendum in June 1947. In the meantime, he married Binapani Devi, daughter of a renowned Sanskrit scholar Pandit Rebatiraman Tarkaratna of Kayasthagram in Karimganj (Assam) in 1945.

Chakravarty finally shifted to Shillong, the city of his adolescence, with family in 1947 and for sometimes, he taught history as a part-time Lecturer in St. Anthony's College and Lady Keany College as he could not immediately find a regular employment. During that period he became involved in the short-lived Shillong History Society which was organized by a handful of enlightened citizens and officials who belonged to the discipline. He compiled for the Society a bibliography of articles on Assam and the neigbouring areas which were till then published in various journals and periodicals. This bibliography drew attention of the famous anthropologist and scholar Dr. Verrier Elwin, who was then Adviser to the Government for North-Eastern Frontier Agency (NEFA). A turning point in Chakravarty's career came in 1951 when he was appointed as a Research Officer (History & Archaeology) in the Office of the Adviser, NEFA Secretariat, Shillong, and had the opportunity to work under the guidance of Dr. Elwin who took keen interest in the work of the research unit. Within few years, the research unit became the Directorate of Research (called Research Department) of NEFA (later on, Arunachal Pradesh), and Chakravarty became the Deputy Director (History & Archaeology). B. K. Das Shastri was the first Director of the Research Department after whose retirement Chakravarty became the Director in 1973. During the tenure of Chakravarty as Director, the department grew larger with three Deputy Directors, appropriate number of Assistant Directors, Research Officers and research assistants and Visiting Fellows, besides the full complement of supporting staff. Three Deputy Directors during the Directorship of Chakravarty were Dr. I. M. Simon (Philology), Dr. P. C. Dutta (Culture) and Dr. Y.S. Raikar (History & Archaeology). Dr. Simon and Dr. Dutta succeeded him in turn as Director of the department. T. K. Bhattacharjee, N. Sarkar, B.B. Pandey, A.K. Das, and K. Dasgupta were among senior officers in the department who produced books and monographs on Arunachal Pradesh. Subid Chatterjee, then an officer of the Archaeological Survey of India, was also associated with Research Department. Some of the short-term Visiting Fellows in the department later on became well known scholars in the country and abroad in their respective fields. Among them are the great anthropologists Professor Lakshman Mahapatra, Professor B.K. Roy Burman and Professor Usha Deka Mahapatra. Professor Mahapatra and Professor Roy Burman were among his life long friends who visited him several times in Shillong in his retired life. Another such friend was Professor Ram Rahul of the Jawaharlal Nehru University, New Delhi, who frequently visited the Research Department at Shillong and travelled throughout NEFA with Chakravarty while working on the 'Himalayan Borderland'.

Though the headquarters of the Research Department was located in Shillong, the department undertook extensive field work in Arunachal Pradesh, including archaeological excavations, and its credibility came to be recognized through a large number of monographs published in that period. Chakravarty extensively toured Arunachal Pradesh, including the remote and inaccessible villages, some of which he was the first officer of the government to visit, and endeared himself to the local people while studying their cultures and traditions. He personally explored and excavated several archaeological and pre-historic sites in the state, for which he and his supporting technical staff had to encamp in tents for weeks and months together braving the difficult terrain, sensitivity of the area and the mid-night ravages of wilds elephants. As Director of the Research Department, Chakravarty launched the publication of an official journal of the department, called *Resarun*, to publish the research findings of the colleagues and research associates in the form articles. He also introduced the practice of an annual research seminar to be organized by the department in which the researchers in the department were required to share their findings with the invited scholars from research institutions and universities in the country. In 1976, the Research Department, under the leadership of Chakravarty, organized a three-day national seminar at State Central Library hall, Shillong, on the occasion of Silver Jubilee of the Department, to evaluate research performance of the department during past twenty-five years. The seminar was attended by eminent persons like D.C. Sircar (Calcutta), B.K. Roy Burman (New Delhi), Ram Rahul (New Delhi), K. Suresh Singh (New Delhi), C.D. Tripathi (Lucknow), Lakshman Mahapatra (Bhuvaneswar), and M.C. Goswami (Guwahati) as resource persons. It was indeed an unusual way of celebrating silver jubilee and the last major work of Chakravarty before retirement. Chakravarty retired from service as Director of Research, Govt. of Arunachal Pradesh, in 1978.

Chakravarty was deeply involved in some critical issues related to the development of administration in NEFA as the historian played a historical role in some matters of national interest in that part of India. In 1953 he was deputed by the Govt. of India to the Tibetan capital to consult the records in erstwhile British Residency at Lhasa on the nature of Tibetan relations with the Tawang region. In this connection, Chakravarty had the privilege of an academic interaction with then Prime Ministers of India Sri Jawaharlal Nehru along with Dr. Verrier Elwin and Sri J. K. Ray ICS, then attached to the PMO. He cherished the memory of that meeting throughout his life, held great respect for Nehru's sense of history and shared it with many others in his old age. In 1953-54, when the services of the Indian Army became necessary to streamline civil administration in the larger Tawang region, including Bomdila and Sela, on which China began to voice a claim, Chakravarty was the first civilian officer who extensively toured the Tawang area and prepared geographical, historical and ethnographic reports for use of the Government of India. It was a common knowledge of the senior bureaucrats in the NEFA administration that the initial draft (based on records) for India's 'white paper' to China in 1961 was prepared by L.N. Chakravarty. During the Chinese invasion of 1962 Chakravarty was on a 'round-the-clock' duty in the control room in Shillong minutely recording the events and maintaining liaison with the concerned departments and organizations of the Government, including the All India Radio. He was awarded President of India's Gold Medal in 1972 for his meritorious services to the nation as a civil servant.[1]

An ardent devotee of the Ramakrishna Mission, L.N. Chakravarty lived almost thirty years after retirement concentrating only on reading religious books and scriptures, participating in social works inspired by the ideals of Ramakrishna-Vivekananda, and regularly visiting and participating in the discourses organized by the Shillong Centre of the Mission. Chakravarty passed away in his own house in Shillong on 10 September, 2006.[2] Institute of Northeast India Studies, Kolkata, has instituted the L.N. Chakravarty

Memorial Bennial Lectures in Arunachal Studies under an endowment made by Late Chakravaty's daughter Mrs. Sikha Bhattacharjee.[3]

Contributions to history

L.N. Chakravarty had begun his research activity by compiling a bibliography of the articles published in some journals and periodicals on hill tribes of Assam and the neighbouring areas. Published by Shillong Historical Society in 1950 as a booklet,[4] this bibliography contained a list of only about seventy articles which were mostly written by the British officers in Assam and NEFA and published in the *Asiatic Researches*, *Journal of the Asiatic Society of Bengal*, *Journal of Assam Research Society* and the *Assam Review*. As expected, content-wise those articles were related only to the hill tribes of Assam and erstwhile NEFA (Arunachal Pradesh). It was not a complete bibliography till date, and the compiler in his preface had said that he could list only those articles which were found in the available volumes of the relevant journals and periodicals in the Raj Bhavan Library and State Central Library in Shillong. However, this was the beginning of research interest for Chakravarty which eventually became the career for him once he joined as a Research Officer in the office of the Adviser to the Governor of Assam on NEFA administration in the NEFA Secretariat, Shillong.

The first major work of Chakravarty was his *Indo-Tibetan Relations, 1772-1951 (With special reference to the McMohan Line)*[5], which is a summary compilation of the records preserved in the old British Residency at Lhasa. The book is divided into seven chapters, viz. 'Early History', 'Mission of 1904', 'Simla Conference', 'Visiting Missions and Activities of Lhasa', 'Tawang', 'Lohit Valley' and 'Siang Valley'. The book contains seventeen appendices of invaluable documents, and there are three detailed maps of Se-La Sub-Agency, Lohit Valley and Siang Valley that are found in a folder bounded with the book. The author also referred to and quoted from the books like *India and Tibet* by H. Younghusband, *History of Relations of the Government with the Hill Tribes on the North-East Frontier of Bengal* by Alexander Mackenzie, *History of the Frontier Areas Bordering on Assam* by Robert Reid, *Tibetan Précis* by H. E. Richardson, and *A Collection of Treaties, Engagements and Sanands* by C. U. Aitchison. Printed at the Government Press, Shillong, this book was meant only for a limited circulation. Nonetheless, it revealed a lot of original facts and records on the subject and for the first time brought out the hidden facts behind the controversial McMohan Line. H. K. Barpujari[6] and P. L. Mehra[7] later on wrote scholarly books on McMohan Line, though they seem to have had no access to Chakravarty's work.

Chakravarty's *Glimpses of the Early History of Arunachal*[8] is indeed the first systematic work on the history of that border state of India, covering the period from prehistoric times to the constitution of the Union Territory in 1972. He called it 'early history' as it dealt with the period earlier than the time when then the area came to be known as Arunachal Pradesh. Divided into seven chapters, viz. 'Kameng Frontier Division', 'Subansiri Frontier Division', 'Siang Frontier Division'. 'Lohit Frontier Division', 'Tirap Frontier Division', 'Historical Ruins in Arunachal' and 'History of Posa', the book provides an outline history of Arunachal. The first five chapters are generally in the nature of ethnographic and historical accounts of the contemporary administrative divisions involving the land and the peoples, but those on historical ruins (or archaeology) and *'posa'* bear stamp of his serious scholarship. In discussing the historical ruins, the author provided details of the explorations and excavations; history of the sites gathered from myths and legends, descriptions and technical explanations of the artifacts and related those to the history and culture of the region. On the basis of archaeological evidences, most of which he himself explored and excavated, Chakravarty argued the fact of pan-Indian cultural influences in the Northeast since early times. Similarly, in case of *'posa'* he began with the meaning of the term, related it to the concept of taxes and tributes prevalent among the Arunachal tribes who considered it as a preemptive right to collect essential items from the plains and documented the presence of lowland slaves in the hill tribal villages ever since the British officials filed records of their tours in those villages. And to do all that, Chakravarty drew data from the Assamese chronicles, Persian accounts and Sanskrit texts for comparing with the oral traditions in the hills, besides ransacking the British records. The author provided at the end of the book a meticulously prepared very long list of raids by the people of Arunachal on the plains of Assam during the British period and the casualties and booties collected during those raids. For these, he painstakingly used the archival records maintained by the British officials. In the chapters on administrative divisions also the author made mention of the historical sites and ruins and discussed the religious and customary practices and beliefs of the various tribes in those divisions.

Chakravarty's contribution to the historical research in Arunachal Pradesh includes a booklet on Malinithan, the most publicized archaeological site in the state which Chakravarty had himself excavated in 1960s and which yielded a large number of icons and sculptures of popular Brahmanical deities that are similar to those found across the subcontinent. The booklet, entitled *Malinithan*, contains coloured photographs of selected sculptures recovered from the excavated site with descriptive and explanatory notes by L.N. Chakravarty.[9] The booklet was published and widely circulated by the Department of Information & Public Relations, Govt. of Arunachal Pradesh, and distributed to the visiting tourists in large number. In course of time, Manilithan became an identity for Arunachal Pradesh across the country, and even in abroad, because of the booklet entitled *Malinithan*.[10]

As a historian

L.N. Chakravaty was a historian by education and profession; he did his Masters in History & Archaeology, taught history in colleges for sometime and finally, served in a research department - beginning as Research Officer in History & Archaeology and ultimately elevated to the highest position of its Director - where research was his salaried duty. However, if the volume of publication is the criteria of becoming a historian, Chakravarty does not have much to his credit. He authored two books, namely, *Indo-Tibetan Relations* (1953) and *Glimpses of the Early History of Arunachal* (1973). He also authored a pictorial and annotated album of the artifacts revealed in one of his own excavated sites, namely, *Malinithan* (Shillong, 1972). Early in life, he had compiled and published a bibliography, albeit as an amateur exercise, namely, *Bibliography of Assam and Neighbouring Areas* (Shillong, 1950). He wrote some articles, but the number of such articles also seems to be not large. However, Chakravarty had his own explanation for not publishing much. The history of the NEFA area in 1950s and 60s had become sensitive and confusing due to claims and counter claims by India and China over the McMahan Line. What were published in those days by the researchers were mostly monographs in ethnography and philology on individual tribes. As a Research Officer, and later on as Deputy Director and Director, his job was not only to do research but also to administer research. His research was as an officer and the findings were the property of the government. He submitted his studies in the form of reports to the authorities and most of these might be still available in the files of the old NEFA Administration and the Home Ministry of the Govt. of India.[11] After retirement, his philosophy of life changed when he found joy in reading *Ramakrishna Kathamritra* and the related books. His favourite reads were the volumes in the series *Bharater Sadhak* and *Ramyani Biksha*, and he raised a large personal collection of such books of his choice. He discussed academics only when his old friends and colleagues or officers from his old department visited him or the research scholars in the universities came to him for his guidance.

Irrespective of the number or volume, the works of L.N. Chakravarty were indeed pioneering in the history and archaeology of Arunachal Pradesh. His *Indo-Tibetan Relations* (1953) and *Glimpses of the Early History of Arunachal Pradesh* (1973) are two major works, both of which he wrote in his official capacity. The pictorial booklet *Malinithan* is another such official publication of the Department of Information & Public Relations, Govt. of Arunachal Pradesh, which contains the coloured pictures of the sculptures of Brahmanical deities and other artifacts that were revealed in the excavation conducted by Chakravarty, with notes and annotations by the author. His *Glimpses of the Early History of Arunachal* is the first book in history of Arunachal Pradesh. Though titled as 'early', the book dealt with history of the area till the birth of Arunachal Pradesh as a Union Territory and provided an outline for further research in the subject. His real contribution was in field of archeology as he did the explorations of the archeological sites in Arunachal Pradesh like Bhismaknagar, Bhalukpung, Ita Fort, etc. and did a major excavation in Malinithan which revealed a large number of artifacts, including the sculptures of Brahmanical deities, establishing, according to the author, the fact of pan-Indian culture continuum in the region. The booklet on Malinithan, containing coloured photographs of some of the excavated sculptures and explanatory notes, is a guide to further research in the subject. As a historian, he was always careful about the authenticity of the data he used and his statements of facts are always documented. Although the absence of a bibliography in his *Glimpses of the Early History of Arunachal* is a seeming departure from the standard norm of history writing in the contemporary world, the footnotes served the purpose of documentation by the historian.

An objective estimate of L.N. Chakravarty as a historian of Arunachal Pradesh should involve an assessment of his explorations and excavations of the pre-historic and archaeological sites generating material evidence for the early periods as alternative or complimentary to literary source which is almost next to nothing in case of the preliterate societies like those in Arunachal Pradesh, the role Research Department played under his leadership in the promotion of historical research, and the impact of Chakravarty's pioneering *Glimpses of the Early History of Arunachal* (1973) on further research in history of Arunachal Pradesh. As a matter of fact, the foundation of Arunachal Studies was laid by the eminent anthropologist Verrier Elwin who contributed books and monographs, some of which highlighted the policy implications.[12] The Research Department and the Directorate of Information and Public Relations, NEFA Administration (later, Govt. of Arunachal Pradesh) sponsored and published a large number of books written by officers and research staff in NEFA Administration, including the senior officials like Advisors (later on, Chief Commissioner/Lieutenant Governor). Among the academic historians, S.K. Bhuyan had edited a large number of *Buranjis* which contained valuable information on the nature of relations of the Ahom rulers of Assam with the frontier tribes including those of Arunachal Pradesh and Lakshmi Devi used those *Buranjis* in her *Ahom-Tribal Relations* (1966).[13] H.K. Barpujari's *Problem of the Hill Tribes : North-East Frontier*, vol. I (1970)[14] dealt with early British policies towards those tribes. Barpujari also presented some seminal papers on the tribes of North-East Frontier (later on Arunachal Pradesh) in seminars and conferences at the national level.[15] D. Ering contributed a substantive paper on the tribes in NEFA in *The Tribal Situation in India* (1972).[16] There must have been few other papers on specific aspects of tribal life and culture. However, Chakravarty's book was the first full length work in history of Arunachal Pradesh. This was followed by two important works by J.N. Chowdhury,* namely, *Arunachal Panorama* (1973)[17] and *Arunachal through*

---

* Late Jyotirindranath (J.N.) Chowdhury, who served as Librarian of the erstwhile NEFA (later on, Arunachal Pradesh) Central Library at Shillong, was one of the pioneer researchers in history and culture of Arunachal Pradesh. A librarian by profession, Chowdhury was a prolific writer with an inimitable literary style and history was a great passion for him. His contributions in history and culture of the Khasis and that of Sylhet-Cachar are also immense. Late Chowdhury's major contributions on Arunachal Pradesh are *Hill Miris of Subansiri* (Shillong, 1970), *A Comparative Study of Adi Religion* (Shillong, 1971), *Arunachal Panorama* (Shillong, 1973) and *Arunachal through the Ages* (Research Department, Govt. of Arunachal Pradesh, Shillong, 1982). He also published some articles on Tibet, particularly in the historical and cultural context of Northeast Frontier of India, e.g. "Shamanism and Tibet", *Quest*, no. 50, 1966 and "British Contribution to the Confusion of Tibet's Status", *Quest*, no. 54, 1971. Chowdhury's *The Khasi Canvas* (Shillong, 1978) is indeed a significant contribution in studying history and culture of the Khasis of Meghalaya. He also published several articles on the subject. His contribution on Sylhet-Cachar area included Jyotirindranath Chowdhury et al (ed.), *Srihatta-Cacharer Itihas O Sanskritir Ruprekha* in Bengali (Shillong, 1995) which came out only about two years before his death. The bibliography of his publications shows that Chowdhury continued to write and publish with added vigour after his retirement from service. A tall personality in the social life of Shillong, he looked after Rabindra-Smriti Ganthagar, a voluntary public library and a heritage institution of Shillong, at the centre of the city, with great care and affection as a social service to the literati among the Shillongites. Chowdhury also had edited a collection in Bengali, entitled *Sangridi* (Shillong, 1993), containing contributions of some of the eminent scholars of Northeast on history, culture and cultural life in Shillong and Sylhet-Cachar. The collection is indeed a rich profiling of the cultural and urban growth of Shillong and the historical connections of the Khasi people with their southern neighbours. Lived for whole his life in Shillong, Chowdhury was at home in both Bengali and Khasi languages. His *Ki Khun Khasi Khara* (The Khasi People) in Khasi (Shillong, 1995) was among his last great works. [+ Editor's Addendum]

the Ages (1982).[18] Chowdhury also wrote few other books and articles on Arunachal Pradesh.[19] Chowdhury's *Arunachal Panorama*, which is a work in the olden 'land and people' tradition, devoted three chapters on history and archaeology, while his *Arunachal through the Ages* is a book entirely on the history of Arunachal from pre-history to 1982. In both the works Chowdhury repeatedly cited the work of L.N. Chakravarty and acknowledged the assistance he received from the latter. In the meantime, M.L. Bose* of Dibrugarh University wrote a book on British policy in NEFA, based on archival records and covering the entire period of British relations with the tribes.[20] This was followed by the work of Subid Chatterjee, entitled *A Comprehensive History of Arunachal Pradesh*.[21] M.L. Bose also later on wrote a book on history of Arunachal Pradesh.[22] The North East India History Association (NEIHA, founded in 1979) played a significant role in encouraging and promoting research in history of Arunachal Pradesh, like all other states in the Northeast, by its liberal approach in exploring the source-materials by opening its membership to all lovers of history, and the teachers in colleges and universities in the region, across the disciplines, including those in Arunachal Pradesh, involved themselves in the organization. The seventh annual session of NEIHA at J.N. College, Pasighat, in 1987, saw large participation of the scholars in Arunachal Pradesh.[23] S. Dutta, later on, brought out a collection of the papers published in Proceedings volumes of NEIHA, entitled *Studies in History, Economy and Culture of Arunachal Pradesh*.[24] In the meantime, the establishment of the Arunachal (now Rajiv Gandhi) University (1988), with a department of history as one of its first departments, was another milestone in the progress of research in history of Arunachal Pradesh. The works of the faculty and their research scholars and the seminars organized by the department from time to time have contributed immensely towards exploration of new information and upgradation of existing literature on the subject. The recent publication of a work on Buddhism by Sristidhar Dutta and Byomakesh Tripathi[25] bears an imprint of the qualitative improvement in historiography of Arunachal Pradesh. *Sources of History of Arunachal Pradesh*,[26] edited by Dutta and Tripathi, is a collection of papers presented in a seminar at the department of history, Arunachal University. The Research Department (now Directorate of Research), Govt. of Arunachal Pradesh, has also continued to work and bringing out publications according to its own charter. The full length studies are coming out on the pre-historic and archaeological sites

* Late Professor M.L. Bose of Dibrugarh University, who began his teaching career in Tura College, Garo hills, and served for some years D.H.S.K. College, Dibrugarh, was one of the main architects of the department of history of the Dibrugarh University and a distinguished historian of Northeast India. He regularly presented papers on Assam and the Northeast Frontier in Indian History Congress and various other seminars and published a large number of papers in various journals, including *Shodhak*, a quarterly research journal of history, published from Jaipur, Rajasthan, and the Journal published by department of history, Dibrugarh University. His major works include *British Policy in the North-East Frontier Agency* (Concept Publishing House, New Delhi, 1979), *Constitutional Development of North-East India* (Concept Publishing House, New Delhi, 1979), *Development of Administration in Assam* (Concept Publishing House, New Delhi, 1985), *Social History of Assam* (Concept Publishing House, New Delhi, 1989) and *History of Arunachal Pradesh* (Concept Publishing House, New Delhi, 1997). [*Editor's Addendum]

once explored by L.N. Chakravarty.[27] However, the scholars who now work on the history and archaeology of Arunachal Pradesh do refer to the pioneering works of Chakravarty and his book *Glimpses of the Early History of Arunachal* is considered relevant even today.

Notes & References

1. The Medal is in possession of the family.
2. This brief biographical-sketch of Late Lakshminarayan Chakravarty (*ne* L. N. Chakravarty) has been prepared by the author of this paper on the basis of a brief bio-data that seems to have been prepared by Chakravarty himself in his life-time, his pension related papers, and by consulting members of the family, and what Late Chakravarty in his old age had told this author by way of recollections. The 'Obituary' published in *The Shillong Times* dated 12th September 2006 has also been consulted. Incidentally, Late L. N. Chakravarty was the maternal grandfather of the author of this paper and she had the opportunity to hear from him many stories of his life. In deed, it was this grandfather who encouraged her to do MA in ancient history and undertake research in ancient Indian history and culture and to use his personal collection of books in that field. She had seen many distinguished historians, some of them his former colleagues, and even young research scholars, visiting Chakravarty in his retired life and discussing ancient Indian history and culture and historical research. Chakravarty passed away in his own house at Polo Hill, Shillong, on 10th September, 2006.
3. *INEIS Letter* 4, October 2009.
4. *Bibliography of Assam and Neighbouring Areas*, a booklet compiled by L. N. Chakravarty, Shillong Historical Society, Shillong, 1950.
5. L. N. Chakravarty, *Indo-Tibetan Relations, 1772-1951 (With special reference to the McMohan Line)*, The Assam Government Press, Shillong, 1953.
6. H. K. Barpujari, *Problem of the Hill Tribes : North East Frontier*, vol. III (Inner Line to McMohan Line), Spectrum Publications, Guwahati, 1980.
7. Parshotam Mehra, *Negotiating with the Chinese 1846-1987, Problems and Perspectives* (First H.K. Barpujari Endowment Lecture, Department of History, North-Eastern Hill University, Shillong), Reliance Publishing House, New Delhi, 1989. Mehra had earlier written his *McMohan Line and Beyond*, New Delhi, 1976.
8. L. N. Chakravarty, *Glimpses of the Early History of Arunachal*, Research Department, Arunachal Pradesh Administration, Shillong, 1973.
9. *Malinithan*, Department of Information and Public Relations, Government of Arunachal Pradesh, Shillong, n.d. [1972?].
10. This information was given by Shri H. Khound, formerly Director, DIPR, Arunachal Pradesh and a personal friend of L. N. Chakravarty.
11. Revealed by L.N. Chakravarty to this author in reply to a question.
12. Among Dr. Verrier Elwin's works mention should particularly be made of his *A Philosophy of NEFA* (Shillong, 1953), *Myths of the North-East Frontier of India* (Shillong, 1958), *The Art of the North-East Frontier of India* (Shillong, 1959), *India's North-East Frontier in the Nineteenth Century* (Shillong, 1959), *Democracy in NEFA* (Shillong, 1965), and *A New Book of Tribal Fiction* (Shillong, 1971).
13. Lakshmi Devi, *Ahom-Tribal Relations*, Assam Book Depot, Gauhati, 1966.

14. H. K. Barpujari, *Problem of Hill Tribes : North East Frontier*, vol. I, Lawyer's Book Stall, Gauhati, 1970.
15. H.K. Barpujari, "Early British Relations with Bhutan", *Proceedings of the Indian History Congress*, 1951; "British Policy Towards Hill Tribes in the North-East Frontier", *The Assam Tribune*, 11 April 1952; "The Early Phase of Resistance Movement in the North-East Frontier, 1828-31", *Proceedings of the Indian Historical Records Commission,* vol. XXXI, part II, 1955; "New Light on the Resistance Movement in North-East Frontier", *Proceedings of the Indian Historical Records Commission,* vol. XXXII, part II, 1956; "Tariff Walls in the North-North Frontier, 1826-58", *Journal of Indian History* (Trivandrum), vol. I, 1959; "The Genesis of NEFA", *Proceedings of the Indian Historical Records Commission,* vol. XXXV, part II, 1960; "The Attempted Traffic with the Chinese through the North-East Frontier", *Proceedings of the Indian History Congress*, 1961; "Pemberton's Mission to Bhutan : Immediate and Ultimate Objectives", *Proceedings of the Indian History Congress*, 1966; *Problems of the North-East Frontier*, Presidential Address, Section III, Modern India Section, Indian History Congress, Muzaffarpur, 1972; " Book Review – Karunakar Gupta's *The Hidden History of Sino-Indian Frontier*, Calcutta, 1974", *The Indian Historical Review*, vol. II, no. 1, 1975.
16. D. Ering, "The North-East Frontier Agency" in K. Suresh Singh (ed.), *The Tribal Situation in India*, Indian Institute of Advanced Study, Shimla, 1972.
17. J.N. Chowdhury, *Arunachal Panorama*, Shillong, 1973.
18. J.N. Chowdhury, *Arunachal through the Ages*, Research Department, Govt. of Arunachal Pradesh, Shillong, 1982.
19. J.N. Chowdhury's other books and articles on Arunachal Pradesh include *The Hill Miris of Subansiri*, Shillong, 1970; *A Comparative Study of Adi Religion*, Shillong, 1971; "Shamanism and Tibet", *Quest*, no. 50, 1966; "British Contribution to the Confusion of Tibet's Status", *Quest*, no. 54, 1971.
20. M.L. Bose, *British Policy in the North-East Frontier Agency*, Concept Publishing House, New Delhi, 1979.
21. Subid Chatterjee, *A Comprehensive History of Arunachal Pradesh*, Pub. by Rina Chatterjee, Calcutta, 1994.
22. M.L. Bose, *History of Arunachal Pradesh*, Concept Publishing House, New Delhi, 1997.
23. The seventh session of NEIHA at Pasighat (1986) is also memorable for the falicitation of Professor H.K. Barpujari. The H.K. Barpujari felicitation volume, entitled *Studies in History of North East India* (J.B. Bhattacharjee ed., NEHU Publications, Shillong, 1986) was presented to Professor Barpujari in that function.
24. S. Dutta (ed.),:*Studies in the History, Economy and Culture of Arunachal Pradesh*, Himalayan Publishing House, New Delhi, 1997.
25. Sristidhar Dutta & Byomakesh Tripathi, *Buddhism in Arunachal Pradesh*, Indus Publishing House, New Delhi, 2008. For a review of the book see *Northeast Researches*, vol. II, Institute of Northeast Studies, Kolkata, March, 2011, pp. 99-100.
26. Sristidhar Dutta & Byomakesh Tripathi (eds.), *Sources of History of Arunachal Pradesh*, Gyan Publishing House, New Delhi, 2008.
27. For example, D.K. Borah et al's recently published monographs on *Ita Fort* and *Naksaparvat*, namely, D.K. Bora, D.K. Duarah & B. Paul, *Impact of Urbanisation in Arunachal Preadesh*, Directorate of Research, Govt. of Arunachal Pradesh, Itanagar, 1997.and D.K. Bora, A.A. Ashraf & J.C. Dutta, *Medieval Life at Naksaparvat*, Directorate of Research, Govt. of Arunachal Pradesh, Itanagar, 1997.

21

Ningthoukhongjam Khelchandra Singh (1920-2011)

—*Ningombam Basanta*

Biographical Sketch

Ningthoukhongjam Khelchandra Singh, who is popularly known as Pandit Khelchandra, passed away on 30th January, 2011, after a brief illness. His death is tantamount to the closing of a living private library of Manipur on its culture and history. In fact, it may not be improper to describe him as a living encyclopaedia considering his vast knowledge on culture and history of Manipur. By his numerous writings in journals and books, the culture and history of Manipur, which was at one time in confinement of local scholars and custody of ancient literature (*Puyas*), became popular among general public, particularly the scholars working on history of Manipur. In recognition of his contribution the Sahitya Akademi conferred on him its highest honour 'Fellow of Sahitya Akademi' in 1999.

Born on 1 September, 1920 at Uripok Ningthoukhongjam Leikai, Imphal, N. Khelchandra had the opportunity to acquaint many noted personalities of the time through his father Late N. Angou Singh, a noted *Nat Sankritan* artist. His mother was Nongthombam Sangai Devi of Uripok Achom Leikai. Thus, he was born in a respected family of *Nat* artist who had large followers in Manipur. A matriculate, he was educated in Imphal. Khelchandra joined the Manipur Secretariat Service at a young age, in 1939, and retired as an Under Secretary in 1978. He was initiated into the study of archaic literature of Manipur at a tender age of fourteen. He visited many Gurus and Pandits of Manipuri literature and culture, including Late Pandit Dinachandra Singh, Pandit Parasuram, Pandit Madhop, Pandit Chandra and Pandit Deva Singh. For years he delved deep into the ancient manuscripts under the guidance of local Pandits learning about the legends, hymns, chronicles, folklore, romance and poetry of Manipur. His retirement from service provided him the opportunity to devote himself completely to serious study. In fact, his career in scholarship began after his retirement. He guided many research scholars and was for some time a visiting fellow in Manipuri Language and Literature at JNU Centre of Post Graduate Studies, Imphal. He also taught Manipuri Language and Literature in many institutions.

Pandit Khelchandra was associated with several literary and cultural institutions in Manipur and visited many such institutions all over India as an exponent of Manipuri culture. He was President, Manipuri Sahitya Parishad; Vice-Chairman, Jawaharlal Nehru Manipur Dance Academy; President, Manipur Historical Society; President, Manipur Martial Arts Association; President, Atombapu Research Centre, Manipur, etc. He was also a member of the expert committees for Manipur State Kala Akademi, Department of Arts and Culture, Govt. of Manipur, Manipur University and various other organisations and institutions. He represented Manipur in the Indian Historical Records Commission in its Kolkata, Patna, Trivandrum and Panaji sessions. He participated as a representative of Manipuri culture in Purba Bharat Sanskritik Sammelan held in Calcutta (1997) and Indian History Congress at Bombay (1980). His contributions in the promotion of culture and literature of Manipur got due recognition from different quarters. For the first time he was honoured by Manipuri Sahitya Parishad (1977) by presenting the title of '*Gaveshana Bhusan*'. His contribution was recognized by State Kala Akademi (1980) by awarding him a Fellowship. In 1987, the Government of India honoured him by awarding 'Padma Sree'.[1]

Progress of historical research in Manipur

Manipur has a rich *Puya* (chronicle) tradition. These *puyas* are basically literary works from which the elements of history can be extracted. Some of those can be enlisted as follows : (1) *Meitei Ningthourol Lambuba*, (2) *Moirang Ningthourol Lambuba*, (3) *Kangleiron*, (4) *Ahoupung Lalupan*, (5) *Kanglei Lamthou*, (6) *Khundarol*, (7) *Chekkhong*, (8) *Langthabal Lol* (9) *Shanggai Phamang*, (10) *Khagemba Yumbi*, (11) *Khagemba Yumlep*, (12) *Chakpa Khunthok Khunda*, (13) *Chengleiron*, (14) *Luwanglon*, (15) *Ningthouchalon*, (16) *Angom Khoira*, (17) *Angom Khonghou*, (18) *Poireiton Khunthokpa*, (19) *Khuman Lol*, (20) *Luwang Leikharol*, (21) *Naothingkhong Phambal Kaba*, (22) *Thawanthaba Hiran*, (23) *Takhen Ngamba*, (24) *Shamshok Ngamba*, (25) *Awa Ngamba*, (26) *Kha-e-Ngamba*, (27) *Urok-Ushai Lon*, (28) *Nongpok Haram, Nongchup Haram*, (29) *Kumphilon*, (30) *Nongkhrang*, (31) *Miyat*, (32) *Gambhir Singh Nonggaba*, (33) *Pakhangba Nonggaron*, and (34) *Cheitharol Kumbaba*. Among these, *Cheitharol Kumbaba* is the most celebrated royal chronicle of Manipur where a chronology of the reigning kings beginning from 33 A.D. down to the last monarch of Manipur is available.

The contacts with the British since the early part of the 19th Century saw the beginning of modern writings in history of Manipur. In fact, modern history writing is rightly seen as a contribution of the colonial ethnographers and administrators who were posted in Manipur. R.B. Pemberton's *Report on the Eastern Frontier of British India* (Calcutta, 1835) which devoted a large section on Manipur may be regarded as a pioneering work on the modern history in Manipur. W. McCulloch, who served twenty seven years in Manipur as Political Agent, published his *Account of the Valley of Manipur and surrounding hill tribes* in 1859. McCulloch was succeeded by R. Brown, a Sergeant, as Political Agent, who published his *statistical Account of Manipur* in 1874, which is an important study on history and culture of the people of Manipur. Alexander Mackenzie's *History of the Relations of the Government with Hill Tribes on the North-East Frontier of Bengal* (Calcutta, 1884) was an attempt in writing history on the basis of British official records. Manipur, though outside British India, occupied an important place in this work. This book represents the official view of historical events and is regarded as 'authentic history' based on official records. T.C. Hodson, who served as Assistant Political Agent, was the first scholar with anthropological knowledge to study the Meiteis, Nagas and Kukis. His *The Meiteis* (London, 1908) is a study specifically on the Meiteis; their society, polity, religion and culture based on the ethnological and historical evidence. Hodson's another work is *Naga Tribes of Manipur* (London, 1911). Robert Reid, a Governor of Assam, wrote *History of the Frontier Areas Bordering on Assam from 1883-1941* (Calcutta, 1942) in continuation of the work of Mackenzie, devoting a chapter on Manipur, the Anglo-Manipur War and colonial rule in Manipur.

The local scholars of Manipur, who were equipped with Sanskrit and English education, started writing history of Manipur in early decades of the 20th century. Some of them had the influence of Indian renaissance and were inspired to trace the origin of Manipur through interpretation of the Vedic sources. Among them Panditraj Atombapu Sharma and W. Yumjao Singh were the forerunners. The former represented the literary school and the latter represented the historical school. Pt. Atombapu (1889-1963) wrote more than one hundred books and papers. His first well known book was *Haree Mayee* (translated into English by Arambam Dorendro Singh), which was reviewed by J.C. Higgins of the Indian Civil Service. It deals with the Vedic interpretation of the origin and history of Manipur. His *Manipur Itihas* was published in 1940 and *Pakhangba* in 1952. W. Yumjao Singh was an archaeologist, and his *Report on the Archaeological Studies* (Bulletin No. 1. 1935) is a landmark in the historical studies in Manipur. Khumanthem Kaomacha's *Manipur Iteebrittee* (Imphal, 1938) is an improved account of history of Manipur. He made a list of the books alleged to have been burnt during the reign of King Garibniwaj under the instruction of a Hindu missionary. Mutum Jhulon's translation of *Vijoy Panchali* into English is another attempt on writing a history of Manipur. This book informs that the reign of Charairongba (1697–1709) saw the construction of a temple of Shri Krishna in Manipur and the translation work on *Ramayana* in Manipuri began in the reign of King Bheigyachandra (1759-1798). A reference in *Kumbaba* shows that *Bijoy Panchali* was being written in Bengali by Lairikyengbam Hanjaba, Tulsi Narayanan and Kritichandra in that period. It also mentions that five *skinda* of *Sibabagabat* had arrived in Manipur in November 1789. However, the translation work on *Ramayana* was continued by Ningombam Ibobi Singh of Singjamei Okram Leikai and Pandit N. Khelchandra in the 20th century, while the *Mahabharata* was translated by their elder contemporary Pandit Kalachand Shastri (Chingangbam).

Meanwhile, the historians from the neighbouring states began to take interest in history of Manipur in their works. A.C. Banerjee's *Eastern Frontier of British India* (Calcutta, 1943) and *British Annexation of Burma* (Calcutta, 1948), S.K. Bhuyan's *Anglo-Assamese Relations* (Gauhati, 1949), and R.M. Lahiri's, *Annexations of Assam* (Calcutta, 1954) covered Manipur in relevant contexts. Suniti Kumar Chatterji, who is always remembered as a friend of Manipur and Manipuri literature, devoted a sizable section of his *Kirata-Jana- Kriti* (Calcutta, 1950) on early history, language and culture of Manipur. However, a full-length engagement on history of Manipur began with Jyotirmay Roy's *History of Manipur* (Calcutta, 1958). Roy taught history at D.M. College, Imphal, for many years and had some accesses to local sources, besides the British official records. His book was the first of its kind in English. This work is factual and refreshing in comparison with the monotony of the earlier works. No wonder, Roy's work was followed by small but handy works of the local scholars. H. Bijoy Singh's *Meitrabaki Wari* (Imphal, 1960), Nandalal Sharma's *Meitrabak* (Imphal, 1960), and L. Iboongohal Singh's *Introduction to Manipur* (Imphal, 1960; 1963) are among those books. Nandalal Sharma's *Meitrabak* is still an important book for reference next to Hodson's *The Meitheis*. R.K. Jhalajit Singh's *A Short History of Manipur* (Imphal, 1965) is a history of the Ningthouja dynasty of Manipur based on indigenous sources which were not utilized earlier. Built upon the royal chronicle, *Cheitharol Kumbaba*, for the early period and other sources for the later periods, this book was an improvement on Roy's *History of Manipur* (1958).

In 1960's there was a strong awareness of the need for historical writings in Manipur. The publication of old chronicles and historical literature was taken up by research organisations and individual scholars who were given financial assistance by the state. The *Cheitharol Kumbaba*, the royal chronicle of Manipur, was edited by L. Iboongohal Singh and N. Khelchandra Singh and published by the Manipuri Sahitya Parishad in 1967. O. Bhogeswar Singh edited and published *Ningthourol Lambuba* (another chronicle, though without chronology) in 1968. Many other early historical works in Manipuri were also edited and published around the time. Y. Bheigya's *Leithak Leikharon*, N. Khelchandra's *Chada Laihui*, *Naothingkhong Phambal Kaba* and *Khumanlol* (genealogy of the Khuman clan), O. Bhogeswar's *Ningthourol Sheireng*, Khumanlambam Yaima's *Phakhangba Phambal* (coronation of Pakhangba) and *Poireiton Khunthokpa* (colonization of Poireiton) are among those historical literature and chronicles which were edited and published by the scholars in later part of 1960s. The *Vijoy Panchali*, in four volumes, written originally by one Kritichandra in Bengali, was translated into Manipuri by Mani Singh and Mangi Singh and published in parallel Bengali and Manipuri (Imphal, 1966). This was followed by modern historical works in Manipuri like L. Chandramani Singh's *Manipur Itihas* (1970), which deals with Anglo-Manipuri relations up to 1891, W. Gourchandra's *Manipurigi Aroiba lal* (war of 1891), R.K. Sanahal's *Chingthangkhomba Ganga Chatpa'* (Bheigyachandra's pilgrimage to Bengal), *Bir Tikendrajit Singha* and *Thangal General*, and N. Khelchandra's *Ariba Manipuri Shaityagi Itihas* (1969). Among the historical literary works edited and published by the scholars in early 1970s were O. Bhogeswar's *Sanamahi Laikan*, *Kangbalon* (Chronicle of Kangba) and *Shakok Lamlen* (a work on Meitei religious belief), Chandrasekhar's *Loiyamba Shilyen* (Royal Decree of Loiyamba), and N. Ibochouba's *Thiren Layat* (a text on Meitei philosophy). The institutions like Manipuri Sahitya Parishad, Manipur University (erstwhile J.N.U. Post Graduate Centre), Manipur State Kala Akademi, Manipur State Museum, Manipur State Archives, State Archaeology Department, and Mutua Museum contributed immensely to the growth of historical studies which began almost as a social movement in 1960s. The archaeological excavations carried out by O.K. Singh of the Archaeology Department, Govt. of Manipur, in Khangkhui Cave (Ukhrul), Tharon Cave (Tamenglong) and Napachik (Wangoo) revealed many new objects and artefacts. The collections and publications of inscriptions, sculptures, coins and other evidences are also being published. Mutua Museum's publications on inscriptions and coins have broken new grounds in epigraphic and numismatic studies. P. Gunindro's *Manipuri Numismatics* (Imphal, 1983) is a remarkable work by a local scholar.

On cultural and ethnographic studies there are works like *Ritual Dances of Manipur* by Lightfoot, *Aspects of Indian Culture* (1993) and *Manipuri Dance* (1997) by E. Nilakanta Singh, *Religion of Manipur* by S.N. Parratt, *An Introduction to Tribal Language and Culture* by K.B. Singh, *Naga Polity* and *Socio-Cultural life of the Nagas* by M. Horam, *Naga struggle against the British under Jadonang and Gaidinliu* by Asoso Yuno, *Anal – A Transborder Tribe of Manipur* by Gangmumei Kabui, *Feminism in a Traditional Society: Women of Manipur Valley* by M. Chaki-Sarkar and *A History of Manipur - Early Period* by W. Ibohal Singh. Sanajaoba Naoria's edited *Manipur: Past and Present* (3 vols.) is a compendium on various aspects of history, society, polity and culture of Manipur, which is considered a useful reference work because of the documents like chronicles, treaties and constitutional extracts. Gangmumei Kabui's *History of Manipur* (1991) is a definitive history of ancient and medieval Manipur based on standard historical methodology. Lal Dena's (ed.) *Modern History of Manipur (1826-1947)* is a collection of papers by G. Kabui, Lal Dena and N. Joykumar Singh on different aspects of modern history of Manipur. N. Joykumar Singh's *Social Movements in Manipur (1919-1950)* is also a pioneering work in the subject. Pandit N. Khelchandra Singh's *Documents of the Anglo-Manipur War of 1891* (in three vols.) is a very useful work both for scholars and the common people. Lal Dena's *British Policy Towards Manipur* (2008) is among the recent works on colonial history.[2] The contemporary historical research is, however, focused on the Merger of Manipur into India (1949) and the Revolt of Hijam Irabot Singh (1948-1951). A mention may be made of H. Bhuban Singh's *Merger of Manipur* and *Annexation of Manipur* which are collections of papers on the National Convention on Merger (1949). K. Manimohon Singh's *H. Irabot Singh and his political movement* is a full scale study on the great revolutionary leader of modern Manipur. There are a large number of books and papers written on this great leader.[3]

Contributions of Pandit Khelchandra

Pandit N. Khelchandra's familiarity with the archaic script and literature of Manipur since his tender age gained him the confidence of many people in lending their support in his academic persuasions. In fact, he was successful in collecting a sizeable amount of ancient literatures which were in the custody of many *Maichous* (local scholars) and are not easily handed over to anybody. Pandit Khelchandra possessed the techniques, talent, persistency and academic honesty which are essential qualities in collecting the *Puyas*. By his consistency, commitment and dedication to the culture of Manipur, he was able to maintain at home a library of rare manuscripts even at his advance age. He had collected around 300 archaic texts on various subjects like history, philosophy, art, religion, mythology, creation theory, etc. His activities were centred mostly in editing and translating archaic literature into modern Manipuri, which include (1) *Sharit Sharat* (art of unarmed combat), (2) *Cheitharol Kumbaba*, (3) *Thainagi Sheireng*, (4) *Chinggoirol*, (5) *Chada Laihui*, (6) *Chainarol*, (7) *Naothingkhong Phambal Kaba*, (8) *Famlol*, (9) *Langgol Shagol Thaba*, (10) *Chothe Thangwai Pakhangba*, (11) *Khunung Lichat Shajat*, (12) *Manipuri Lon-gei*, (13) *Thawanthaba Hiran*, (14) *Nongban Pombi Luwaoba*, and (15) *Rupaban*. In fact, Pandit Khelchandra was in the centre of the new awakening in Manipur in 1960s regarding the history and culture of the Manipuris. His translations and publications of the archaic Manipuri texts and chronicles in modern Manipuri gave a fillip to historical research in Manipur as the source materials were thus made available to the local scholars in the language and script they could use. The publication of *Cheitharol Kumbaba*, which he edited jointly with L. Iboongohal Singh, in particular, was indeed a turning point since this royal chronicle is considered as the most detailed and authenticated source for studying the early history of Manipur. Khelchandra wrote and published *Ariba Manipuri Sahityagi Itihas* tracing the origin and development of Manipuri literature from the earliest times. Besides some of the master pieces in early Manipuri literature, he also translated parts of *Ramayana* and *Mahabharata*, namely, *Aswamedha Parva Mahabharat* and *Utterkand Ramayan* which not only demonstrated his competence in Sanskrit but also his desire to introduce the great Indian epics to the Manipuri readers in their own language.

Khelchandra wrote some books in English also on history and language of Manipur, which include (1) *Manipuri to Manipuri and English Dictionary* (1964), (2) *Battle of Khongjom*, i.e. Manipur's last battle fought with the British (1963), (3) *Manipuri Language – Status and Importance* (1975), (4) *Documents of Anglo-Manipuri War 1891*, 3 volumes (1984), and (5) *Thangal General*, a Manipuri hero (1992). He contributed biographies of Pt. Raj Atombapu Sharma and Thangal General to the *Dictionary of National Biography* edited by S.P. Sen.[4] His writings in the form of articles are found in various journals, souvenir, anthology and collections which are published by various institutions and organizations, particularly the Department of Art and Culture and Department of Information and Public Relations, Govt. of Manipur.[5]

In Manipuri, Khelchandra contributed a large number of articles in the journal *Sahitya* which is published regularly by Manipuri Sahitya Parishad, an organisation he was actively involved and served once as its President. This journal has been playing a crucial role in the development of Manipuri language and literature for many years. He began contributing to the journal since 1965 with an article entitled "*Meiteilongi Banangi Maramda*" (4th issue, January, 1965). Among his other articles in the same journal mention may be made of (1) "*Nongban Pombi Luwaoba*", (2) "*Moirang Ningthourol Lambuba*", (3) "*Manipurda Pallamba Meitei Kanglupshinggi Maramda Neinaba*", (4) "*Laithem Eshei*", (5) "*Yumsharon*", (6) "*Thangal General*", (7) "*Manipuri Thajat*", (8) "*Lam*", (9) "*Mera Haochongba*", and (10) "*R.K.C.S. Ki Maramda Eina Khanghouba*" which are cited by many scholars in their writings.

Khelchandra played a historic role in retrieving and preserving the ancient Manipuri script. He was a proponent of the 35 alphabet Meitei script and strongly emphasised that the Manipuri language is a tonal language, because in this language a word with different tones, depending on the level of tone, may be high or low, bears different meanings. For example, the word *'Mi'* bears the meaning of both spider and shadow depending upon the tone and context of their use. Again, the word *'Mee'* means human being. The word *'Chaba'* when used in low tone is a matter of 'temporary show' or 'thin looking', but when it is used in high tone it may mean 'to eat' or 'well fitting of dress'. It so happens in other words like *'Muba' 'Taba'* and *'Lengba'* etc. He said that the vowel 'EE' is missing in the 27 alphabet Meitei script. He considered it a folly to opt for 27 alphabet structure as the word *'Mee'* cannot be written and it would not be possible to differentiate between *'Mi'* (spider) and *'Mee'* (human being). So, he concluded that the proponents of 27 alphabet are also little creatures like spider, and not human beings. His observation was that the 27 alphabet script suffers from many defects and as such it cannot help people to read all the Manipuri manuscripts which form a treasure of Manipuri knowledge and culture. It also cannot read the old stone inscriptions erected by different Manipuri kings. It would be a dishonour to the stone inscriptions of Konthoujam Lairembi, Ningel, Khoibu and Phayeng to vote for 27 alphabet. On the other side, the 35 alphabet script can read all the ancient manuscripts, stone inscriptions, etc. Tonal problem does not occur in the 35 alphabet structure. He was of the view that more number of alphabet means the richness of Manipuri script. He saw no harm keeping them, since our forefathers have already preserved them for a long time. It is not fare to cut them and throw them away. We can keep them as it is, even without using them. Reading of the alphabet as *Ka, Kha, Ga* etc. is not an isolated feature as the same reading is found in other southeast Asian countries like Malaysia, Laos, Kampuchea, Thailand, Myanmar, etc. On the book *Wakoklon Thilen Salai Amailon Pukok* written by Thokachanba, Khelchandra was of the view that the manuscript was his own creation without having the knowledge of linguistic science. He opined that the controversy of Meitei script can be resolved neither through gun point nor by voting on the issue, but only by adhering to the science of language. So, he made a call to the linguists to make a study of the problem so as to find out the appropriate script.[6]

As a historian

Among his voluminous contributions in various aspects of history, culture, literature and other disciplines, Pandit N. Khelchandra Singh's contribution in the reconstruction of history of Manipur has tremendously influenced the researchers in the subject. His books and articles which contained aspects of history of Manipur and opened up new areas of research may be listed as : (a) *Battle of Khongjom* (Manipur's last battle fought with the British), (b) *Thangal General* (A Manipuri Hero), (c) *Documents of Anglo-Manipuri War* (in three vlumes), (d) *Ariba Manipuri Sahityagi Itihas*, (e) *Chothe Thangwai Pakhangba*, (f) *Thawanthaba Hiran*, and (g) *Nongban Pombi Luwaoba* among the books, while the articles include (a) 'Lam' (b) 'Thangal General', (c) 'Nongban Pombi Luwaoba', (d) 'Moirang Ningthourol Lambuba', and many others. He did a great service to the cause of historical research in Manipur by editing and publishing a good number of *puyas* (chronicles) which are the most valued sources of history. The *puyas* edited by him include (i) *Chada Laihui*,[7] (ii) *Thainagi Seirang*,[8] (iii) *Naothingkhong Phambal Kaba*,[9] (iv) *Khuman Kangleirol*,[10] (v) *Chingoiron*,[11] (vi) *Chainarol*[12] and, of course, (vii) *Cheitharol Kumbaba*.[13] Among these, *Cheitharol Kumbaba*, the royal chronicle, beginning from 33 AD to 1891 AD, edited by L. Iboongohal and N. Khelchandra, is generally accepted as the most important source for reconstructing the history of Manipur. Khelchandra also edited and published a number of other chronicles. The publication of these source books acted as a fillip to historical research in Manipur and greatly helped the researchers in their work.

Pandit Khelchandra was not a trained researcher in history, but he possessed a strong sense of history and was driven by his instinctive commitment to unfold the cultural heritage of his people to the world. His works are mostly compilations and translations of the archaic literature into modern Manipuri. These works are in the nature of historical literature and contain information which legitimately belong to the domain of history. He built an archive of manuscripts in his own house which is a treasure for the researchers in history of Manipur. He wrote *Manipur Itihas*[14] (history of Manipur) in Manipuri for the general readers. His *Ariba Manipuri Sahityagi Itihas*[15] is a comprehensive history of Manipuri literature. His *Ariba Manipuri Lonjei*[16] is another major contribution in literary and cultural history of Manipur. His *A Catalogue of Manipuri Manuscripts*[17] and *Parishadki Ariba Manipuri Wareng Lairik*[18] are like ready reckoner for the researchers to locate unpublished sources. He also wrote books and articles on historical personalities and historical events in both Manipuri and English. His works depended mostly on literary sources, namely, the archaic Manipuri texts. He used references abundantly in most of his writings. In case of the modern period, he relied on the records of the British Government, *Darbar* proceedings, administration reports, tour diaries of Political Agents, and books written by the officials. What is most commendable about his publications in Manipuri language is his command in the language. A prolific writer in modern Manipuri, his translations and interpretations of the archaic literature into modern Manipuri are indispensable to the research scholars in history of Manipur.

Notes & References

1. Biographical Sketch of Pandit Khelchandra has been prepared with the help of N. Tombraj, second son of Pandit Khelchandra, Dr. N. Deven Singh, third son of Pandit Khelchandra, Ch. Khaba (Hemchandra), a close follower of Pandit Khelchandra, and by consulting some papers preserved in their family, including the citation conferring the honour of a Fellow by Sahitya Akademi, New Delhi and the text of Pandit Khelchandra's speech accepting the Fellowship, and relevant issues of *Sahitya*, a journal of Manipuri Sahitya Parishad, Imphal.

2. Lal Dena, *British Policy Towards Manipur*, Nongeen Publications, Impahl, 2008.

3. For more details on historical writings on Manipur see Gangumei Kamei, *Philosophy of History and Historiography of Manipur*, M.U. Research Club, Imphal, 1997 and bibliography and bibliotheca notes in Rena Laisram, *Early Meitei History : Religion, Society & the Manipur Puyas*, Akansha Publishing House, New Delhi, 2009 and J.B. Bhattacharjee (ed.), *State and Economy in Pre-Colonial Manipur*, Akansha Publishing House, New Delhi, 2010.

4. S.P. Sen (ed.), *Dictionary of National Biography*, Institute of Historical Studies, vols. III-IV, Calcutta, 1972-73.
5. The author is thankful to the family of Late Pandit N. Khelchandra Singh for allowing access to the personal collections of the Pandit for a survey of the books and articles written by him in this section.
6. See relevant issues of *Sahitya*, a journal of Manipuri Sahitya Parishad, Imphal, particularly his articles "*Meiteilongi Banangi Maramda*" (4th issue, January, 1965) and "*Manipurda Pallamba Meitei Kanglupshinggi Maramda Neinaba*" (22nd issue, August 1974) in that journal..
7. N. Khelchandra Singh (ed.), *Chada Laihui*, Imphal, 1966.
8. N. Khelchandra Singh (ed.), *Thainagi Seirang*, Imphal, 1966.
9. N. Khelchandra Singh (ed.), *Naothingkhong Phambal Kaba*, Imphal, 1979.
10. N. Khelchandra Singh (ed.), *Khuman Kangleirol*, Atombapu Research Centre, Imphal, 1979.
11. N. Khelchandra Singh (ed.), *Chingoiron*, Manipur State Kala Academy, Imphal, 1982.
12. N. Khelchandra Singh (ed.), *Chainarol*, Imphal, 2003.
13. L. Iboongohal Singh & N. Khelchandra Singh (ed.), *Chritharol Kumbaba*, Manipuri Sahitya Parishad, Imphal, 1967, reprint 1989.
14. N. Khelchandra Singh, *Manipur Itihas*, Imphal, 1970.
15. N. Khelchandra Singh, *Ariba Manipuri Sahityagi Itihas*, Imphal, 1969.
16. N. Khelchandra Singh, *Ariba Manipuri Lonjei*, Manipur State Kala Academy, Imphal, 1978.
17. N. Khelchandra Singh (ed.), *A Catalogue of Manipuri Manuscripts*, Manipuri Sahitya Parishad, Imphal, 1984.
18. N. Khelchandra Singh (ed.), *Parishadki Ariba Manipuri Wareng Lairik*, Manipuri Sahitya Parishad, Imphal, 1972.

22

Tajenyuba Ao (1926-1994)

—*I. Wati Imchen*

Biographical Sketch

Tajenyuba Ao,[1] who had a successful career as a lawyer, writer, politician and social worker, besides being an ardent nationalist, was born at Mangmetong, a village in the Mokokchung district of Nagaland, on 18 November 1926, in a family that enjoyed relative affluence through his father's gainful employment as one of the first village school masters. His father Manglalepden, who had studied up to class V at Golaghat, became a Pandit in 1909 receiving a monthly salary of Rs.10/-.[2] Tajenyuba showed early signs of intelligence as he began reading books from a notably young age with particular penchant for history, law and culture. In 1945, Tajenyuba passed the Middle English Examination securing first division, which earned him a merit scholarship from the government. After securing first division in the Matriculation Examination in 1950, he went to Guwahati to study Science at the Cotton College. In 1955, he graduated with distinction in Mathematics. He graduated in law from the Earle Law College in 1958 and soon joined as a Junior Advocate at Gauhati High Court, thus becoming the first lawyer among the Nagas.[3]

While a student in Gauhati, Tajenyuba became involved in various activities of the Naga students and often found himself arguing and defending the right to self-determination of the Nagas, though many were cynical towards the Naga demand for independence as baseless and lacking history of the Naga people.[4] He was also deeply concerned with the loss of own culture by the Nagas due to Western influence and Christianity and embarked upon writing essays and books on the history and culture of the Nagas. In 1957, his first book *Ao Naga Customary Laws* was published.[5] In the meantime, he joined politics and was elected as a Member of the first Nagaland Legislative Assembly in 1964 from Koridang constituency as a candidate of the Democratic Party.[6] He was not happy with the manner in which a cease-fire agreement was signed between the government of India and the secessionist Naga leaders, on 6 September 1964, which, according to him, ridiculed the election held early that year. He took this position in a booklet entitled *Nagas In the Cross*

Road in which he strongly urged for a honourable settlement between the Government of India and the Naga leaders, minimizing the question of secession and without altering the physical map of India.[7] He argued that the honourable settlement shall be one in which the government is not required to withdraw completely from the hills and the Nagas are not forced to go back to savagery.[8] As the situation remained volatile, Tajenyuba and 11 other members of the Democratic Party resigned from the Assembly, on 8 December 1964, to work for peace in Nagaland.[9] However, after some years of uneasy peace, when the next assembly election was held in 1969, Tajenyuba was re-elected from his old constituency as a nominee of the United Front of Nagaland (UFN). In 1974 elections also he was re-elected to the house, but this time as a candidate of the United Democratic Front (UDF) which formed the government and Tajenyuba became the Deputy leader of the legislature party.[10]

Meanwhile, on 26 January 1967, Tajenyuba married Ruth, daughter of Medemdangba Longkumer of Dibuia village, who was a trained Nurse from Assam Medical College, Dibrugarh, and served in various hospitals in Assam from 1957 to 1966. A woman with full of passion for learning, Ruth studied arts at evening colleges at Tezpur and Nowgong, besides her normal nursing duty, and graduated in 1967. She then briefly taught in a private school at Dimapur and finally, joined the government service in Nagaland as a school teacher and eventually served in various capacities, like District Adult Education Officer and Deputy Inspector of Schools, and retired as a Headmistress in 1996.[11] She was indeed a strong support to Tajenyuba in his works, particularly educational and literary.

In 1981, Mokokchung Law College was established at the initiative of the Ao Students' Conference,[12] and Tajenyuba, who was by then the senior-most advocate among the Nagas, became the first Principal of the college and held the post till his death in 1994.[13] He built the college with great affection and care, and wrote and published help books for the students of law.[14] He was actively involved in celebrations commemorating 100 years of Christianity in Nagaland in 1972 and that occasion inspired him to write the book *Christianity versus the Ao Nagas* (1984).[15] In the meantime, he had gradually withdrawn himself from politics and was relatively free to concentrate on the development of his college and write more on Naga history and culture. However, the book *Nagaism*,[16] compiled and edited by Tajenyuba in 1986, became his party's manifesto during 1989 elections.[17] Tajenyuba Ao died at Dimapur on 7 December 1994, but his mortal remain was taken to his native village Mangmetong where it was finally laid to rest. In recognition of his academic excellence the Mangmetong Students' Union constituted an award in his name in 1995.[18]

Studies on the Nagas

The Naga Hills became an area of interest for anthropological study from the time the British administrators had undertaken observing and recording the cultural life of the Nagas. The officials also created records for writing history in future through their reports, diaries and reminiscences. Thus, A. J. Moffat Mills' *Report on the Province of Assam*[19] and Major John Butler's *Travels and Adventures in the Province of Assam*[20] are two contemporary works that are important for studying the British annexation of the Naga Hills from beginning to the termination of tenth expedition in 1851. Sir Robert Reid's

History of the Frontier Areas Bordering On Assam from 1883-1941[21] is a continuation of the history of relations since 1882, where Alexander Mackenzie had left off his work *History of the Relations of Government with the Hill Tribes of the North-East Frontier of Bengal*.[22] The monographs written by the British administrators, missionaries and anthropologists in early 20th century are also important from historical point of view since some of those dealt with origin, migration, settlement, customs and practices, etc. of the various Naga tribes. These monographs include J. H. Hutton's *The Sema Nagas*[23] and *The Angami Nagas*[24], J. P. Mill's *The Ao Nagas*[25], *The Lotha Nagas*[26], and *The Rengma Nagas*[27], and W. C. Smith's *The Ao Naga Tribe of Assam*[28]. The *Naked Nagas*[29] by Von Fürer Haimendorf recorded personal experiences of the author among the Konyaks and several other tribes of the Naga Hills. As regards history of the British period, H.K. Barpujari's multivolume *Problem of the Hill Tribes : North-East Frontier* is a monumental work which critically examined the British policy towards the hill tribes, including the Nagas.[30] *The Comprehensive History of Assam*, edited by H.K. Barpujari in five volumes, also includes the relevant aspects of history of the Nagas, particularly of the modern period.[31] Similarly, the Anglo-Naga Relations found close treatment in a Ph. D. thesis (1970) of Gauhati University by S.K. Barpujari.[32] In fact, S.K. Barpujari* published a large number of research

---

* S.K. Barpujari (Surya Kanta Barpujari, younger brother of H.K. Barpujari) is generally known as a historian of the Nagas, because there was a time when he was the only one around to have done a Ph. D. on Naga history and available to contribute research papers on aspects of history of the Nagas in seminars and conferences. Born in Jorhat on 15 December 1919, S.K. Barpujari was educated in Jorhat, Guwahati and Dacca. After his M.A. in Modern History from the Dacca University, he began his career as a Lecturer in History in Handique Girls' College, Guwahati, served as Principal, Haflong College, and then joined Gauhati University as a Reader in History, where from he retired in early 1980s. He was awarded Ph.D. by the Gauhati University in 1970 for his thesis on 'Anglo-Naga Relations, 1835-1890', which he prepared under the supervision of famous historian Professor A.C. Banerjee of Calcutta University (author of *Eastern Frontier of British India*, Calcutta, 1943). On his retirement from Gauhati University, S. K. Barpujari was awarded a Senior Fellowship by the Indian Council of Historical Research (ICHR) to work on 'a documentary history of the Nagas'. He completed the project within the stipulated period of three years. For this project and earlier for his Ph. D., Barpujari worked in Assam Secretariat Records, Shillong (now Assam Archives, Dispur), West Bengal Archives, Calcutta and National Archives of India, New Delhi, consulting and collecting records on the Nagas. He contributed a large number of research papers in seminars and conferences and occasional collections, including *Proceedings of the Indian History Congress* and *Proceedings of North East India History Association*, on the modern history of the Nagas covering aspects of British policy, administration, resistance, economic change, frontier trade, education and Christianity. The book *The Nagas ; The Evolution of their History and Administration, 1832-1939 - A Documentary Study* (Spectrum Publications, Guwahati/ New Delhi, 2003) by S.K. Barpujari is indeed indispensable for further research in modern history of the Nagas. S.K.Barpujari (ed.), *Alexander Mackenzie and the Evolution of British Policy towards the Hills in North-East Frontier of India* (Spectrum Publications, New Delhi, 2003) is a significant contribution on the subject. *The History of the Dimasas* (N.C. Hills Autonomous District Council, Haflong, 1996) is a remarkable work which S.K. Barpujari edited and most its chapters he wrote himself. A founder member of the North East India History Association (NEIHA) and one of its main architects, he presided over the fourth annual session of NEIHA at Barpani in 1983. He is also intimately associated with the Indian History Congress, Institute of Historical Studies (Calcutta), Assam Research Society, and North-East India Council for Social Science Research. Although now-a-days he is unable to move out to attend seminars and conferences due to old-age, the nonagenarian historian is engaged in his Guwahati residence in reading and writing, and one of his latest papers is "Rai Bahadur Kanaklal Barua" in B. Sarma (ed.), *Kamarupa Anusandhana Samiti Through the Ages*, Kamarupa Anusandhana Samiti, Guwahati, 2012). [*Editor's Addendum]

papers on the Nagas in 19th and 20th centuries in various journals and proceedings, and one of his latest publications in the subject is *The Nagas : The Evolution of their History and Administration, 1832-1939 - A Documentary Study*.[33] However, the Nagas did not have their history presented in one book till M. Alemchiba published his *A Brief Historical Account of Nagaland* in 1970.[34] M. Horam's *Social and Cultural Life of Nagas*[35] is basically a study of the Thangkhuls in the State of Manipur, while Nirmal Nibedon's *Nagaland - The Night of the Guerrillas*[36] is an account by a journalist of the insurgency between 1968 and 1972. However, Horam's *Naga Polity*[37] is a study of traditional political systems of the Nagas of Nagaland. On the other hand, Milada Ganguli's *A Pilgrimage to the Nagas*[38] is based on her intimate knowledge of the land and its people, history and culture, its problems and progress. Hokishe Sema's *Emergence of Nagaland: Socio-Economic and Political Transformation and Future*[39] is limited to his personal observations on the socio-economic and political conditions of Nagaland. V. K. Nuh's *Nagaland Church and Politics*[40] summarizes the role of church in Naga politics. Among the historical works, Ashikho Daili Mao's *Nagas Problems and Politics*[41] deals with evolution of the Naga society during pre-colonial, colonial and post-colonial periods. *Ancient Ao Naga Religion and Culture*[42] by Panger Imchen is important for its account of socio-cultural beliefs and practices in traditional Ao Naga society and their responses to Christianity. Piketo Sema's *British Policy and Administration in Nagaland 1881-1947*[43] is a serious research work that studied the different facets of colonial policy and administration in Naga hills. Visier Sanyu's work, *History of Nagas and Nagaland (Dynamics of Oral Tradition in Village Formation)*,[44] attempted to reconstruct the history of the Nagas with the help of oral sources. Another historical work *The Angami Nagas and the British 1832-1947*[45] by L. Atola Changkiri, provides a comprehensive and critical analysis of the British relations and their consequences, besides geographical, ethnological and historical background of the Angami Nagas. In his book, *From Phizo to Muivah*[46] A. Lanunungsang Ao studied the Naga political theory and practice in making Naga history. Kaka D. Iralu's *The Naga Saga* [47] is a historical account of the 62 years of Indo-Naga conflict and the stories of those who were never allowed to tell it.

The history of Christianity among the Nagas has emerged over the years as an important area of research because of its impact on the history and culture. The work of M. M. Clark, *A Corner in India*[48], is the first book of its kind, which contains valuable historical information. In her book, Clark not only provided first hand account of the American Mission's work in the Naga Hills but also narrates the life and culture of the people with whom she was associated for many years. V. H. Sword's *Baptists in Assam: A Century of Missionary Service 1836-1936*[49] provides a general account of the history of American Baptist Mission in Northeast India. Narola Rivenburg's *The Star of the Naga Hills*[50], edited and published in 1941, is a collection of letters written between 1883 and 1936. These institutional histories were written by foreign missionaries providing historical accounts of their respective mission works. They also captured the life and culture of the people at the period of their writings. F. S. Downs' first detailed study *The Mighty Works of God: A Brief History of the Council of Baptist Churches in North East India: The*

Mission Period 1836-1950[51] was based on his sustained research on history of Christianity in Northeast India for many years. This was followed by his *Christianity in North East India in Historical Perspective*[52] and *History of Christianity in India,* Vol. V.[53] His most recent work *The Christian Impact on the Status of Women in North East India*,[54] covered in considerable details the changing status of women in Nagaland as a result of the impact of Christianity. P. T. Philip and Joseph Puthenpurakal in their works *The Growth of Baptist Churches in Nagaland*[55] and *Baptist Mission in Nagaland*[56] respectively, dealt exclusively with the advent and the growth of Baptist Mission in Nagaland. Vihuli Sema's unpublished Ph.D. thesis "The American Baptist Mission in Nagaland (1836-1950)"[57] studied the impact of Christianity in Nagaland, although the scope of her work was limited only to the American Baptist Mission. Angeline Lotsüro's *The Nagas A Missionary Challenge*[58] is a scholarly book which exposes the true face of Naga Christianity. The writings on the Catholic Mission in Nagaland became more numerous after 1947. Monsignor Marengo in his 'Memoirs'[59] narrated the activities of the Catholic Churches in Nagaland in general and his service towards the same in particular. C. Becker's *History of the Catholic Mission in North-East India*[60] is essentially a general history of the Catholic Missions in Northeast India. D. R. Syiemlieh's *A Brief History of the Catholic Church in Nagaland*[61] discusses the advent and the growth of Catholic Churches in the state, while S. Coelho's *Even to the North East: The Story of the Jesuits in Nagaland*[62] is another illuminating work in the subject. These contemporary writings are denominational histories.

Contributions to history

Tanjenyuba Ao was not a professional historian, but he was meritorious, highly educated and a lawyer by education and profession. The spirit of Naga nationalism drew him to study the history and culture of the Nagas and he immensely contributed to the subject as an insider, drawing his data from the traditions and studying them as a scholar and a writer. His first book *Ao Naga Customary Laws*, published in 1957, was essentially an attempt to bring forth a simple codification of the Ao Naga customs and customary rules. He said, "We the Aos have been experiencing various trials, standing on the threshold of changes and inter-changes ... indeed, Christianity has brought tremendous enlightenments in the country but, the resultant effect of conversion is a balanced ruin on the culture."[63] He carried on further field work in the subject and a revised and enlarged edition of the *Ao Naga Customary Laws* came out in 1980.[64] This was widely accepted, and became a prescribed text for the department of Anthropology at Gauhati University.[65] However, his *A History of Anglo-Naga Affairs 1832-1913*,[66] published in 1958, is a major contribution to the modern history of the Nagas, presented systematically and chronologically. In writing this book, Tajen heavily depended on official and non-official archival materials. Though the work was very sketchy, it proved to be of immense value to the researchers for historical reconstruction of the Anglo-Naga relations. His *Christianity versus the Ao Nagas*, published in 1984, is an important contribution in the Church history.[67] It is interspersed by a number of passages about the American Baptist Mission and the Naga response to Christianity. The author also gave a fairly integrated narrative about the traditional Ao Naga religious ceremonies and practices along with critical analysis.

Tajenyuba had, in the meantime, gradually withdrawn himself from active politics and concentrated on his work at the college and writing on history and culture of the Nagas. In 1986, he compiled and edited a book entitled *Nagaism* which is a brief historical account of Naga politics and nationalism.[68] In commemoration of the 25 years of cease-fire in Nagaland in 1989, he wrote a booklet entitled *The Genesis of Indo-Naga Cease-Fire* (1989) in Ao language.[69] These two books are very important for further research in contemporary political history of Nagaland since 1947. In *Genesis of Indo-Naga Cease-Fire*, he briefly narrated the earlier history, like the Ahom-Naga relations; British occupation of the Naga hills; genesis of the Naga nationalism and cease-fire and, more significantly, political development that were unfolding after the declaration of the cease-fire. Nonetheless, his main contribution to Naga history is *British Occupation of Naga Country*[70] (1993) in which, besides the annexation story, he recounted the internal conflicts in leadership and the genesis of subsequent splits within the NSCN. The book came out at a time when the Nagas were confused and vacillating between the two factions of NSCN, the one led by Isak and Muivah and the other by Khaplang. The publication of the book generated huge controversy and the author was threatened even to the extent of taking his life by one of the factions. However, the book is packed with facts and thought-provoking comments and it strikes a balance between compilation and interpretation as it is presented without distorting the original sources. In response to threats on his life, Tajenyuba Ao had said, "Even if I die now or I am killed, I will die happily because finally, the truth has been published."[71]

As a historian

Tajenyuba Ao had written more than seven books and several articles on history and culture of the Nagas. Once he said, "To be a good historian one should be very bold otherwise he can not write true history."[72] Th. Muivah, General Secretary of NSCN, during his visit to Mangmetong in April 2010, while paying tribute to Tajenyuba in presence of a large audience, said, "Tajenyuba was never neutral between rights and wrongs."[73] In deed, he was courageous, straightforward and indomitable in spirit, who not only wrote on Naga history and culture but also played a historic role in shaping the political destiny of the Nagas during his lifetime. He was a major player in contemporary Naga history and he wrote earlier history by using sources. His contributions to contemporary political history and church history or history of Christianity in Nagaland are immense. In case of church history, in particular, his research was largely based on primary sources; namely, records of the British administration and the Baptist Missions, their annual reports, and letters, and he presented his studies systematically in a chronological order. As it is understandable, not being a trained historian, there are some problems of conceptual or theoretical clarity in his writings. Nevertheless, his books, particularly *Ao Naga Customary Laws, History of Anglo-Naga Affairs 1832-1913* and *British Occupation of Naga Country*, opened up new vistas to the scholars who are interested in Naga history and culture. Most of all, Tajenyuba made Naga history accessible and enjoyable to a mass audience.

Notes & References

1. He was known in short as Tajen Ao. Hence, these two names are used interchangeably.
2. Repalemba Imchen, *Tesayur Manglalepden (1894-1970)*, published by Manglalepden chir aser semchirtem, Kohima, 2008, p. 54.
3. Rosemary Jamir, *Nagas in Nagaland - Who's Who 1990*, Etiben Printers & Publishers Association, Dimapur, 1991, p. 253.
4. As told by Mrs. Ruth, wife of Tajenyuba, dated Yimyu, March 23, 2011.
5. Tajen Ao, *Ao Naga Customary Laws*, Published by the author, Mokokchung, 1957.
6. *Results of the General Assembly Elections of Nagaland* (Third Edition), Directorate of Economics and Statistics, Government of Nagaland, 1993, p. 3.
7. Tajen Ao, *Nagas in the Cross Road*, Laksmi Printing Press, Gauhati, November 1964.
8. *Ibid.*, p. 17.
9. Interview: I. Bendangangshi, dated Ungma, March 26, 2011.
10. *Statistical Report on General Election, 1974 to the Legislative Assembly of Nagaland*, Election Commission of India , New Delhi 1974, pp. 41 & 71.
11. *Shisatongtep*, An official bulletin of Ongpangkong Baptist Church, Yimyu, Vol 3, May-August 2007, p. 3.
12. Temjenkaba, "Profile of Mokokchung Law College", *Mokokchung Law College Silver Jubilee Souvenir*, 2006, p. 6.
13. The Ao Students Conference, during its meeting held on 19-21 January 2011 at Ungma, resolved to take up to the Government of Nagaland to rename the Mokokchung Law College, as Tajenyuba Memorial Law College.
14. Tajen Ao, *Questions and Answers on Land Laws*, Published by author, Mokokchung, 1991; *Questions and Answers on Jurisprudence*, Published by author, Mokokchung, 1992; *Questions and Answers on Jurisprudence*, Published by author, Mokokchung, 1992.
15. Tajen Ao, *Christianity Versus the Ao Nagas*, Tribal Gospel Mission Publishers, Mokokchung, 1984.
16. Tajen Ao, *Nagaism*, Published by District Committee, Nagaland Peoples Party, Mokokchung, 1986.
17. *Ibid.*
18. This award carries a citation and cash award which is given annually to the best amongst the Mangmetong students in class 10.
19. A. J. Moffat Mills, *Report on the Province of Assam*, reprinted by Publication Board, Assam, Gauhati, 1984. First published in 1853.
20. Major John Butler, *Travel and Adventures in the Province of Assam*, Vivek Publishing Company, Delhi, 1978. First Published in 1855.
21. Sir Robert Reid, *History of the Frontier Areas Bordering on Assam from 1883-1941*, Shillong, 1942.

22. A. Mackenzie, *The North-East Frontier of India*, Mittal Publications, Delhi, 1995. This book was first published in 1884 entitled *History of the Relations of Government with the Hill Tribes of the North-East Frontier of Bengal* (Bengal Government Press, Calcutta).
23. J. H. Hutton, *The Sema Nagas,* Oxford University Press, Bombay 1968. First published by Macmillan & Co. Limited, London, 1921.
24. J. H. Hutton, *The Angami Nagas,* Oxford University Press, Bombay 1969. First published by Macmillan & Co. Limited, London, 1921.
25. J. P. Mills, *The Ao Nagas,* Macmillan & Co. Limited, London, 1926.
26. J. P. Mills, *The Lotha Nagas,* Second edition by Directorate of Art and Culture, Government of Nagaland, 1980. First published by Macmillan & Co. Limited, London, 1922.
27. J. P. Mills, *The Rengma Nagas,* Second edition by Directorate of Art and Culture, Government of Nagaland, 1982. First published by Macmillan & Co. Limited, London, 1937.
28. W. C. Smith, *The Ao Naga Tribe of Assam*, Macmillan & Co. Ltd., London, 1925.
29. Fürer Haimendorf, *Naked Nagas*, (First published in 1939), Reprinted Calcutta, 1968.
30. H.K. Barpujari, *Problem of the Hill Tribes : North-East Frontier*, Lawyer's Book Stall, Gauhati, 1970-81.
31. H.K. Barpujari (ed.), *The Comprehensive History of Assam*, 5 vols., Guwahati, 1990-93.
32. S.K.Barpujari, "Anglo-Naga Relations, 1835-1890", Unpublished Ph. D. thesis, Gauhati University, 1970.
33. S.K. Barpujari, *The Nagas : The Evolution of their History and Administration, 1832-1939- A Documentary Study*, Spectrum Publications, Guwahati/New Delhi, 2003.
34. M. Alemchiba, *A Brief Historical Account of Nagaland*, Kohima, 1970.
35. M. Horam, *Social and Cultural Life of Nagas,* B. R. Publishing Corporation, Delhi, 1992.
36. Nirmal Nibedon, *Nagaland, the Night of the Guerrillas*, Lancer Publishers, Delhi, 1978.
37. M. Horam. *Naga Polity*, B.R. Publishing Corporation, New Delhi, 1975.
38. Milada Ganguli, *A Pilgrimage to the Nagas*, Oxford & IBH Publishing Co., New Delhi, 1984.
39. Hokishe Sema, *Emergence of Nagaland: Socio-Economic and Political Transformation and Future*, New Delhi, 1984.
40. V. K. Nuh, *Nagaland Church and Politics*, Vision Press, Kohima, 1986.
41. Ashikho Daili Mao, *Nagas Problems and Politics*, Ashish Publishing House, New Delhi, 1992.
42. Panger Imchen, *Ancient Ao Naga Religion and Culture*, Har-Anand Publications, Delhi, 1993. Panger Imchen, a prolific and a budding Naga writer, had written seven books. He died at the age of 36 (March 1994).
43. Piketo Sema, *British Policy and Administration in Nagaland 1881-1947*, Scholar Publishing House, New Delhi, 1992.
44. Visier Sanyu, *History of Nagas and Nagaland (Dynamics of Oral Tradition in Village Formation*, Commonwealth Publishers, New Delhi, 1996.

45. L. Atola Changkiri, *The Angami Nagas and the British 1832-1947*, Spectrum Publications, New Delhi, 1999.
46. A. Lanunungsang, *From Phizo to Muivah*, Mittal Publication, New Delhi, 2002.
47. Kaka D. Iralu, *The Naga Saga*,(first published in 2000), Third Edition, Published by the author, Kohima, 2009.
48. M. M. Clark, *A Corner in India*, American Baptist Publication Society, Philadelphia 1907. Reprinted in India by Christian Literature Centre, Gauhati, 1978.
49. V. H. Sword, *Baptist in Assam: A Century of Missionary Service 1836-1936*, First published in USA by Conference Press in 1935. Reprinted in India by United Publishers, Gauhati, 1992.
50. Narola Rivenburg, (ed.), *The Star of the Naga Hills*, The American Baptist Publication Society, Philadelphia, 1941.
51. F. S. Downs, *The Mighty Works of God: A Brief History of the Council of Baptist Churches in North East India: The Mission Period 1836-1950*, Christian Literature Centre, Gauhati, 1971.
52. F. S. Downs, *Christianity in North East India in Historical Perspective,* Gauhati, 1983.
53. F.S. Downs, *History of Christianity in India*, Vol. V, Part - 5, The Church History Association of India (CHAI), Bangalore, 1992.
54. F.S. Downs, *The Christian Impact on the Status of Women in North East India* (Professor H.K. Barpujari Endowment Lectures), North Eastern Hills University Publications, Shillong, 1996.
55. P. T. Philip, *The Growth of Baptist Churches in Nagaland*, Christian Literature Centre, Gauhati, 1976.
56. Joseph Puthenpurakal, *Baptist Mission in Nagaland*, Vendrame Missiological Institute, Shillong, 1984.
57. Vihuli Sema, "The American Baptist Mission in Nagaland (1836-1950)", unpublished Ph.D. thesis, North-Eastern Hills University, Shillong, 1984.
58. Angeline Lotsüro's *The Nagas A Missionary Challenge*, Vendrame Missiological Institute Publications, Shillong, 2000.
59. Monsignor Marengo, "Memoirs" Vol I & II (typed script) available at the Documentation centre, Sacred Heart Theological Collage Library, Shillong.
60. C. Becker's *History of the Catholic Mission in North-East India*, translated & edited by C. Staddler and S. Karotemprel, Vendrame Institute, Shillong, 1980.
61. D. R. Syiemlieh, *A Brief History of the Catholic Church in Nagaland*, Vendrame Institute Publications, Shillong, 1990.
62. S. Coelho, *Even to the North East: The Story of the Jesuits in Nagaland*, Catholic Publication Centre, Kohima, 1984.
63. Tajen Ao, *Ao Naga Customary Laws*, Published by the author, Mokokchung, 1957.
64. Tajen Ao, *Ao Naga Customary Laws*, Ananda Printing House, Jorhat, 1980.

65. Rosemary Jamir, *op. cit.*, p.254
66. Tajen Ao, *A History of Anglo-Naga Affairs 1832-1913*, published by author and printed at the Tribune Press, Gauhati, 1958.
67. Tajen Ao, *Christianity Versus the Ao Nagas*, Tribal Gospel Mission Publishers, Mokokchung, 1984.
68. Tajen Ao, *Nagaism*, Published by District Committee, Nagaland Peoples Party, Mokokchung, 1986.
69. Tajen Ao, *The Genesis of Indo-Naga Cease-Fire*, Suyim Press, Mokokchung, 1989. Ao is one of the Naga languages, spoken by the Ao Nagas who predominantly inhabit the Mokokchung District of Nagaland.
70. Tajen Ao, *British Occupation of the Naga Country*, Naga Literature Society, Mokokchung, 1993.
71. As told to the author of this paper in 1993. The writer of this paper is the nephew of late Tajenyuba who had the opportunity to associate and share ideas during the time Tajenyuba was writing his last book, *British Occupation of the Naga Country*, during 1991-1993.
72. As told to the author of this paper in 1993.
73. Video clips of Th. Muivah's visit to Mangmetong village, June 30, 2010.

23

Elangbam Nilakanta Singh (1927-2000)

—Rena Laisram

Biographical Sketch

Born at Keisamthong Elangbam Leikai (Imphal, Manipur), Elangbam Nilakanta Singh (1927-2000) represents the intellectual tradition of Manipur's most creative and vibrant period in its history. His early years in school were spent at Churachandpur, where his father was posted as a school teacher. A district largely inhabited by the Kuki-Chin group of people; this was to have an impact on his perspectives in search for Manipur's cultural identity. After passing matriculation examination (1945) of Calcutta University from Johnston School, Imphal, he obtained I.A. from Murarichand College, Sylhet (now in Bangladesh) and B.A., M.A. (Philosophy), and LL.B. from Gauhati University. He was initiated into the teaching profession as a Lecturer in Philosophy in D.M. College, Imphal. He held the office of the Director of Social Welfare, Art and Culture, Govt. of Manipur (1978-86) and was actively engaged in different capacities such as Founder Secretary, Manipur State Kala Academy (1972-78), Consultant and Senior Research Associate, Manipur University (1989) and as Faculty Member of Department of Philosophy in Manipur University (1996-97). He was the General Secretary of *Manipuri Sahitya Parishad* (1958, 1964-68), served as its President (1993-94) and continued as an executive member of the *Parishad* till the last days of his life. Nilakanta Singh was actively associated with many literary, and social and cultural organisations such as *The Cultural Forum Manipur*, *Naharol Sahitya Premi Samity*, *Geeta Mandal*, *ISKCON*, *Mutua Museum*, *Divine Life Society*, *Sri Aurobindo Society*, *J.N. Dance Academy*, etc. He travelled widely and contributed research papers in many seminars and conferences within the country and outside. He was honoured with the *Sahitya Academy Award* (1987) for his poem *'Tirtha Yatra'* and was conferred the *Padmashree* by the Govt. of India in the year 1999. He passed away on 11 February 2000 in Imphal.

Boundaries of Manipuri Literature

All disciplines require periodic thinking, none more so perhaps than history.[1] In the 1970's and early 1980's philosophers of history began to see all writings as *'texts'*- all products of particular social conditions.[2] New Historicism as a critical theory attempts simultaneously to understand cultural and intellectual history through literature, which documents the discipline of the History of Ideas. This assumption can be seen in the light of Hayden White's[3] support of the 'the value of narrativity,' as an essential constituent of historical experience and method. In his seminal work titled *Metahistory: The Historical Imagination in Nineteenth-Century Europe*,[4] he argues that historical writings are structured on literary principles, and that "the techniques or strategies that historians and imaginative writers use in the composition of their discourses can be shown to be substantially the same, however different they may appear on a purely surface, or dictional, level." Without going into the debate on the impact of post-modernism on historiography, it is however crucial to mention that the theorists "promoted good writing as a normal historical practice."[5]

20th century Manipur, both in its history and historiography, appears as a striking era of productive intellectual activity, the unique political experiences and cultural developments acting as fertile ground for stimulation of the literary practice. The raid of Imphal by Japan in the Second World War (1939-45)[6] and merger of the erstwhile kingdom with the Indian Union (1949)[7] were landmarks in Manipur's history which opened the gates of the society to the outside world. In the political developments following the Anglo-Manipuri War (1891), Maharaja Churachand[8] (1891-1941) initiated the revitalization of the traditional religio-cultural institutions and strict measures were taken to systematically Sanskritize virtually every aspect of Meitei culture and tradition.[9] Consequently values and attitudes to life and social and political question of the time acquired a new dimension. The century also witnessed the spread of education, beginning of print journalism (1929) with establishment of the first private press (Churachand Printing Press), followed by the State Press and the founding of the Aryan Theatre (1935) to encourage performing arts. The contemporary environment of profound changes experienced in nearly every aspect of the people's lives kindled a new consciousness which brought forth a 'renaissance'[10] in Manipuri literature.

Contributions to history

The life and works[11] of Elangbam Nilakanta Singh, a prolific writer of Manipur, is better known as a poet, philosopher and a crusader for cultural integration, but rarely as a historian. On the other hand, Nilakanta's life exemplifies a profile of struggle to put Manipur on the cultural map of India and in this mission he combined in himself the qualities of a historian and a thinker. The focus of this study is his contribution to historiography and historical literature in the context of Manipur as also within the larger framework of India. The literature review and content analysis, therefore, are limited only to the works necessary in assessing Nilakanta Singh as a historian. In fact, history writing, as an important form of narrative in a society, constructs, organizes and shares knowledge through a particular form of representation i.e. speech, writing, language, and understanding - or what is called discourse. The methodology of history is linked with two aspects of historical writing viz; the relationship between source and narrative, and theoretical underpinnings of interpretation.[12] While each generation of scholars in Manipur re-thought the way in which history was conceived and written, the process acquired a new dimension against the backdrop of the rapid historical developments in 20th century Manipur. Nilakanta Singh was a college student when he published his first poem *Manipur*[13] in a vernacular journal (1949) which was eulogized as representative of the contemporary atmosphere of uncertainty, in the aftermath of the *Battle of Imphal* (1944) in the Second World War. A few lines freely translated from the poem echoes the sentiment of the scholar:[14]

On this late afternoon of Rath Jatra
All directions of Manipur are filled with
the chanting of
Jaya Jaganath, Jaya Jaganath,
But the firmament is tinged with darkness,
hatred and unending recriminations.
***
Whither is the way
When there is discrepancy between principle and practice?
Now the tandav dance of Rudra,
Manifesting the devastating posture of Nataraja,
In broad daylight, predators are roaming
Freely in parts of Asia and Africa
***
O Mother Manipur, one day your children
will trace you
like Dushyanta with eyes bathed in tears,
But by that time where shall they find you?
Where shall they find you?

Manipur did mark a turning point in the course of Manipuri poetry when he makes an appeal beyond his own time in the context of the changing world of 'mechanical civilization' and disintegrating values. A productive poet, thinker and critic, he has about twenty books to his credit and the works reveal his extensive reading and sharp response to the literary trends of the time. This had a deep and lasting impact on the literary sensibility of Manipuri literature. In an attempt to create awareness about the rich heritage of the people, he wrote extensively both in Manipuri and in English. His major works in Manipuri include *Achaiba Lei* (poetry 1957), *Manipuri Kavitagi Chhanda* (1968), *Chatlaseene Kadaidano Ebani* (poetry 1971), *Matamgi Wakhal* (poetry 1973), *Tirtha Yatra* (poetry 1985) and *Sanskrit Ki Salon* (prose 1991). Some of the works in English are *Aspects of Indian Culture* (1997), *Manipuri Dance* (1997), and Monograph on *Pandit Atombapu Sharma* (1998). *Pukning Liekolgi Athuppada* (poetry, 2000), a travelogue *Americaga Unaba* and a collection of poems titled '*America Gi Esei*' were published posthumously. *Americaga Unaba* discovers various aspects of American literature, culture, politics, film, music and theatre. Nilakanta Singh's experiences in America provoked him to address the question of identity of the Manipuri diaspora and he asks: are they American, Manipuri-American or simply Manipuri?

Nilakanta Singh's monograph on *Pandit Atombapu Sharma* (1998) is indicative of the socio-political milieu of the time which gives a sense of the historiographic attempts at claiming an Aryan ancestry for the Meiteis. The Sanskrit tradition exemplified by the works of Phurailatpam Atombapu Sharma (1889-1963)[15] reflects the historical contextualism - 'fields' of cultural production influenced by the ideological assumptions current in 20th century Manipur which had an impact on historical thinking. The writings included literal translations, adaptations or transliteration of various Sanskrit and Bengali works along with creative works based on local themes but inspired by Hindu myths[16]. The depth of his scholarship lies in the fact that it was for the first time that any attempt was made at approximation of the Meitei pantheon with Hindu *Puranic* deities[17]. This being the objective the Sanskrit scholar often made references to the Vaisnava texts in Sanskrit in order to explore the link between the Meitei and Vedic rituals while interpreting *mantras*. He touched almost all aspects of Sanskrit learning-the *Vedas*, the *Upanishads* and the *Puranas*, *Mahabharata*, *Ramayana*, astronomy, astrology, Sanskrit grammar and metrics - indeed the entire spectrum of Sanskrit learning.[18] His interpretation of the deities and clans (*salais*) of the society, days of the week, months and seasons in the context of evolution of the Brahmanical culture in India became a matter of fascinating interest. The *Puyas* now came to be known as *Manipur Puranas* which came to represent a new form and extension of the Vedic tradition. Appointed *Raj Pandit* in the royal court during the reign of Maharaja Churachand, the king relied heavily on the scholarship of Atombapu Sharma, for all matters related to religion and dissemination of the *brahmanical* ideology to the populace at large. For Atombapu, Manipur was the *Pratnauka* or the ancient homeland of the Aryan people in Northeast India.[19] His contention was that ancient Manipuri culture was 'contemporaneous with Vedic culture and might even be possibly earlier.' Nilakanta Singh indulges in the debate on the identification of *Manipura* in the *Mahabharata* when he refers to *Pandita-Raj Atombapu Memorial Lecture*[20] delivered by the historian R.C. Majumdar and the critical edition of the *Mahabharata* published by the Bhandarkar Oriental Research Institute.[21]

Nilakanta Singh comments that the Vedic-centric approach in Manipur historiography constructed through publications and performing arts by the Sanskrit scholars gave birth to a new cultural identity of the Meiteis. Through print journalism and performing arts Atombapu was able to reach out to the wider audience and was also instrumental in arousing political consciousness among the people.[22] An exponent of Manipuri dance and music, he explored in depth aspects of *kirtana* and the *rasleela* which were the vehicles of Vaisnava *ethos*. Through translations of the *Bhagavata Purana* and Bharata Muni's *Natyasastra* he popularised the cultural heritage of the Manipuri dance and drama not just in Manipur but also beyond the boundaries of the state. Appreciating Atombapu's contribution to the Sanskrit tradition in Manipur, and referring to him as a "much misunderstood scholar", Nilakanta Singh quotes the remark of the Indologist, Suniti Kumar Chatterji[23]: "From what the *Pandita-raj* did for the integration of Hinduism and the harmonisation of Manipuri life with Hindu thought and culture, it will be easily conceded that he too was a *rishi* of the modern age." Chatterji argued that the Mongoloid peoples of the Northeast - the 'Kirata' - had a unique and important contribution to make to Indian culture, and could not be regarded as simply an appendage to the Aryan mainstream[24].

Atombapu's assertion that brahmanical ideology existed from the beginning of Manipur's history proved to be beneficial for the burgeoning political movement for integration with mainstream India. It became the political agenda of the Manipur Congress Party which portrayed Manipur as part of 'Hindu' India; the ideology exploited to reconstruct the 'official' history of Manipur. Thus, religious ideology as a powerful symbol of group identity became instrumental in the nationalist construction of a Meitei identity. The 'texts' reflect the literary side of the struggle for 'power' and by the 20th century the rich Sanskrit tradition could no longer be ignored in the dynamic narrative discourse. The Aryan imprint was made concrete through historiographic construction in the form of specific myths and symbols thereby creating the ground for assertion of a distinct Meitei identity. The identification of Nongpok Ningthou and Panthoibi with Siva and his spouse, parallels between *lai* (deity) and *linga* are notions derived from the Hindu world view. Some myths were obviously based on Hindu mythology such as the myth of the dead cow, and of Pakhangba and Sanamahi circumambulating the throne of their father. The reign of Churachand had witnessed an increase in the power of the *brahmanas* to a degree never before known in Manipur. Through historiographic constructions attempts were made to establish the primacy, both in terms of time and of authority, of the brahmanical ideology as the supposed upholders of the original Vedic tradition of Manipur, which in turn sought to give a literary and religious basis for socio-political claims to power.

Nilakanta Singh had a keen interest in world literature particularly the works of Rabindranath Tagore, S. Radhakrishnan, Bankimchandra, Sankaradeva, Swami Vivekananda, Vinoba Bhave, Aurobindo and Karl Marx imbibing thoughts from the philosophers, thinkers and poets which he assimilated into his own sensibility. Aurobindo's spirituality had a deep influence on him and he quotes: "religion is that instinct, idea, activity, discipline in man which aims directly at the Divine, while all the rest seem to aim at it only indirectly and reach it with difficulty after much wandering and stumbling in the pursuit of the outward and imperfect appearance of things. The answer lies not in accepting one of the alternatives (either science or religion) but in a creative synthesis of both." The author says that there is no point lamenting for old religions which have to necessarily go, but the spiritual essence is bound to survive in the views of the people, consciously or unconsciously. The old religion survives in a new form and gets metamorphosed into a new style of life. The march of human cycle, according to him, indicates that one must adopt a futuristic outlook for- "We can go back to the Vedas but cannot live the Vedic symbolism". He opines that the future belongs to a creative synthesis of science and spirituality as: "One must not confuse a religious teaching and a spiritual teaching. Religious teaching belongs to the past and stops all progress. Spiritual teaching is the teaching of the future. It enlightens the consciousness and prepares it for the future realization. A spiritual teaching is above religions and strives towards a total truth. It teaches us to come into direct contact with the Divine." Thus as Aurobindo says, "we can wait for the advent and the progress of the spiritual age". The history of human civilization, as Nilakanta Singh believes, has now come to a point "when man starts expressing religion in depth in terms of spirituality when even approximates to the latest findings of modern science". Further, there is a basic identity of human religious urge, the sameness of the religious urge all over the world and the inherent desire to be at peace with one's surroundings.

Nilakanta Singh made serious efforts to bring to focus the history and culture of the Meiteis in the national context through sustained research, voluminous writings in the form of books, research articles, presidential addresses and by training and encouraging young researchers. For him, Manipur is synonymous with dance, martial arts and sports. He believed that "Manipur is a unique confluence of cultures, one South Asian represented by Hindu culture and the other South East Asian represented by Meitei culture." According to him, the cultural heritage[25] of the Meiteis may be understood in two phases viz;– the pre-Vaishnavite ("not pre-Hindu") phase of the early period dominated by Tantric cult (at least from about 10th Century A.D.) with the *Lai-Haraoba* festivals, *Maibas* and *Maibis* (priests and priestesses), and the Vaishnavite phase since 15th Century A.D. There is also the Shiva-Devi worship associated with *Tantrism*. He dwelt at length on the Vaisnavite tradition in Manipur and the influence of Bengali on Manipuri culture and literature.[26] He thus opines: "....perhaps it is true to say that even Bengal Vaishnavism has been perfected and enriched with artistic expression in the form of Manipuri *sankirtana* and *Rasleela*"[27]. The relevance of the two epics viz; *Ramayana* and *Mahabharata* in historical and contemporary times were themes he focused within the broader framework of Bhakti tradition in Manipur. The festivals such as *Holi* (*Yaosang*), *Ratha Yatra, Jhoolan Yatra, Janmashthami, Radhastami* and *Durga Puja* and even *dhop* and *Manoharsai* singing of Bengali *Kirtana*, have been reborn in the Vaisnavite Manipur. In the book titled *Manipuri Dance* (1997)[28] he explored both the oral and textual sources to study the origin, history and development of the classical dance including its movements and communication. He analysed at length aspects of authenticity and distortion in the *Raasleela* dance since its introduction by Maharaja Bhagyachandra (1779 A.D), in which the king himself played *mridanga* in the *Nat-Sankirtana* performance preceding the dance. "The soul of Manipuri dance lies in its traditional restrains, subdued movement and eloquent silence."[29] In an attempt to understand the Manipuri dance from a wider perspective, he studied dances in ancient India and said that during the period, "drama was inseparable from dance."[30] He says that the artistic vision finds expression in the exquisite textiles, colour sense, handicrafts and above all, the Manipuri style of living. The ethical dimension of the culture of the valley, Manipuris as evident in their martial arts; viz. sword and spear fights, wrestling, foot-hockey and polo has now been universally recognised.

Nilakanta Singh was equally conscious of the rich traditions of the tribes inhabiting the hill districts of Manipur particularly their "distinct forms of dance, music and festivals along with the exquisite textiles, colour sense and beautiful handicrafts". Highlighting the rich cultural heritage of the Tangkhuls, Mao-Nagas, Kabuis, Kuki-Chin-Mizo group of people inhabiting the South of Manipur, Hmars, Thadous, Kom, Chiras and Taraos, he opines that each community with their own festivals are "expressive of the joy of life and beauty of human existence." He laments that "it is a fashion to call their religions animistic with a belief in spirits and deities, which does not mean much and even amounts to a distortion of the proper perspective, depriving us of the meaning of symbolism associated with such religions. All these religions have their distinctive perception of the nature of the soul (or sometimes multiple souls), and of the Dead, doctrine of *Karma*, Supreme Deity and Gods and spirits including ancestor spirits and tutelary deities of the village etc. It is extremely difficult to understand these primitive religions in their authenticity as modern practical mentality shall undoubtedly colour the interpretation. At the most we can have a superficial understanding of it." He believes that it is possible that the hill people have forgotten the symbolism of the ancient and stuck to conventional forms of religion, having lost the sense of communion with the various deities - "Only a few priests and priestesses preserve this tradition with some occult powers which are often utilized for non-spiritual and egoistic purposes."

Dealing with the religious philosophy of some of the tribes, he explains that the Kabuis believe in a multiple of gods and goddesses, local deities and spirits and also in a Supreme God, *Ra-Gang* (King of Gods) whose abode is in Heaven and who is immortal and eternal. The Mao Nagas conceive of Soul as "the minute replica of the individual", a notion also shared by the Thadou Kukis and many other Naga tribes. Blood sacrifice is the main means of propitiation and exorcism in the case of the PaiteIs who believe in spirits- both good and evil. The Koms believe in spirits and other natural forces and also in ancestor worship. The Hmars also believe in a supreme Deity called *Pathien* (creator of all beings). The belief in a Supreme God is also shared by the Thadous and Vaipheis besides the various spirits who are equally worshipped and feared. Nilakanta Singh observes: "The core primitive religion as reflected in the life-style of the people of the hills of Manipur is the belief in magic and ancestor-cum-deities and other spirits pervading the village. It represents the manifestation of religion in various phases of culture and civilization, indicating the origin of the magico-religious cults of the later *Tantrikas* associated the *tantrik* belts of North-East India which extends from Tibet, Nepal, Bhutan to Assam and other parts of North-East India and Bengal."

He discussed in his writings about the changes taking place in the tribal societies on account of the coming of institutionalized religions such as Hinduism and Christianity[31] and the impact it had on the age-old customs and religions of various communities. Writing on the *Status of Religion in Tribal Areas of Manipur*,[32] the author voices his concerns when he asks: "Are the tribal religions of Northeast India going to be swept off from the face of Earth?" Stating that more than seventy percent of the entire population in the hills have adopted Christianity, he goes on to say that "the British system of education along with the modernization processes have now opened the eye of the educated old and young men to the world of science and the spirit of inquiry and investigation." The Kabuis were among the few tribes who did not embrace Christianity and they reacted also to the coming of Brahmanical faith in the erstwhile kingdom.

Nilakanta Singh observes that "the tribals have now become proud of their cultural heritage, even though they cannot go back to the primitive religions. The educated people of the hills being conscious of their proud heritage in human values have to assimilate other modernist traits of the culture from a wide spectrum and are marching forward." Christianity represents modernization among the tribes which brought about changes in various facets of their life. "The participation of the tribes in their political development along with other modernizing forces generated by mass media, the application of science and technology to their style of life is also responsible for their neglect of the primitive faiths." The sense of cultural identity - "a 20th century phenomenon, has affected the elites among them and they have become much more aware of their cultural roots which finds expression in organizing such major festivals like *Kut* for the Kukis and 'seed sowing' for the Nagas organized annually on a state level." In the article on '*Regional and National Content in Post-independence Manipuri Literature*', he addresses the issue of the search for self-identity and revivalism among the Meiteis inhabiting the Manipur valley terming it as "a welcome spirit of enquiry."[33] According to him there is an increasing awareness about the "non-Aryan elements racial affinities among the people of the valley and the hills of Manipur which religions, for historical reasons, tried to conceal."[34]

Nilakanta Singh was concerned with the deeper issues of life and philosophized with intense expression and scholarly erudition. In an article titled '*Unity in Indian Literature*',[35] he talked about universal literature and contemporaneity of all great writings in all languages of the world through extracts of poems written in the same mood though in different languages across India in the post-partition period. Invited by the Asom Sahitya Sabha to inaugurate the *Lecture-series in Memory of Late Tirtha Ram Bordoloi*, he attempted to investigate the cultural expressions of the seven states of Northeast India particularly its arts and folk traditions. On modern Manipuri theatre he said that it saw its birth in the early part of the 20th century, with *Nara Singh* (1925), the first historical play directed by L.Iboongohal Singh. Nilakanta Singh compares the *Shumang-leela* (traditional theatre performed in the courtyard) of Manipur with the *Bhaona* performing art in Assam and explored the connection between the Vaisnavite traditions of Assam and Manipur. Describing himself as a 'Manipuri seriously engaged in a search for identity', the publication of the book titled *Aspects of Indian Culture*[36](1982) was, in his own words, "an attempt to provide a perspective of a Manipuri looking with pride at his own culture and people struggling to understand them." Opening the discussion with a chapter on '*The Glory that is Manipur*', the collection of essays discuss not just the culture of the Meiteis but also varied subjects such as dances in ancient India, aspects of Indian culture represented by the Bhakti movement, Saratchandra of Bengali literature, Aurobindo and the Mother "at whose feet I have decided to fathom the meaning of life."

Looking for answers to social and cultural issues requires a study of social and cultural history and the circumstances in the life of Nilakanta Singh were naturally intertwined with the nature of the work he produced. The voluminous works of the scholar reveals that he considered history to be crucial for social development and attempted to find answers to the problems which confronted contemporary Manipur society. His enriched modern Manipuri literature and his involvement in keeping the literary movement vibrant cannot be denied. Nilakanta Singh secured his position as the pioneer of modern Manipur poetry, revolutionizing the literary taste of the post-world war period. He considered it a social responsibility to enlighten the people outside the state about the rich cultural heritage of Manipur and its linkages with the other parts of India. Therefore, at times he even indulged in writing on burning and controversial issues such as that related to a manuscript *Govinda Sangeet Leela Vilas*.[37] He comes across as an original thinker, with an approach which was direct and pragmatic. He had independent views on a wide range of subjects which covered Philosophy, Metaphysics, Theology and History. He enjoyed regional and national repute for his contributions to the study of the Meiteis in particular and in his efforts at understanding cultural linkages between Manipur and the Indian mainstream.

As a historian

Nilakanta Singh's works reveal his interest in a wide-range of diverse subjects such as spiritualism, science and spirituality, Netaji and religion, Marxian aesthetics, Vaisnavism, Tantricism, Christianity, cultural links between Manipur, Assam, Bengal and Southeast Asia, art and culture of Northeast India, Manipuri dance and contemporary issues such as questions of identity, regionalism and national integration. His writings even sought to correct certain contemporary injustices, which provide a particularly useful insight into his character. A multi-faceted personality, he engaged himself in philosophical as well as non-philosophical activities, because those are the activities to which his reason, which is to say his philosophy, would recommend him. He was motivated by a desire to bring about 'integration of humanity'[38] being deeply committed to Aurobindo's philosophy and he was as much interested in changing society as in describing it. Nilakanta Singh's idea of Manipuri 'renaissance' may be said to have represented a rebirth of ideals and a sense of humanism which he expressed through varied forms; viz. poetry, prose and anthology.

History is not simply a neutral discipline founded upon an immutable body of facts.[39] A great deal of historical writing ranks as literature, particularly the genre known as creative nonfiction. A historical perspective involves the capacity to view the present in relation to the past and to discern what in the present is only of passing interest and what are the more significant currents affecting the present day of life. Making a strong case for 'literary history'[40] George Macaulay Trevelyan argued that only history of high literary quality could convey facts and opinions about the past 'in their full emotional and intellectual value.'[41] Apart from the scientific and speculative functions of history, he stressed on the 'planning and writing of a powerful narrative of historical events.'[42] Nilakanta Singh's contribution to history lies in his consciously connecting the intellectual dimensions of the past, present and future of Manipur's history. He integrated into his works contemporary developments in interpreting past events through a distinct moral lens containing as it was, a mine of historical information particularly on Manipur. The range of subjects is immense allowing the compression of a great deal of historical information and working the disparities of historical subjects into a coherent narrative. He pursued History as a narrative that went beyond kings and battles, to act as an explanation of the present, with moral and philosophical meanings. In this he relied not just on particularities of what happened but also upon intuition, imagination, empathy and wisdom to reconstruct a meaningful account. His place as a historian of Manipur derives not from evaluating his contributions as works of history but reading Manipuri literature as a form of historical narrative. Indeed, Nilakanta Singh's abundant literary output offers a deep insight into the history and culture of Manipur and is indispensable for those engaged in an enquiry into the cultural history of the state and region. In fact, studying the works of Elangbam Nilakanta Singh is assessing the boundaries of Manipuri Literature and appreciating his contributions as those of a historian.

Notes & References

1. Anthony Pagden, "Rethinking the Linguistic Turn: Current Anxieties in Intellectual History", *Journal of the History of Ideas*, Vol. 49, No. 3 (Jul. - Sept.), University of Pennsylvania Press, 1988, p. 519

2. New Historicism as a school of literary theory developed in the 1980s, primarily through the work of the critic Stephen Greenbalt, and gained widespread influence in the 1990s. It shares many of the assumptions with what is often called Cultural Materialism. See H. Aram Veeser, *The New Historicism*, Routledge, 1989

3. Hayden White, *Content of the Form*, 1987; Hayden White is a post-modernist philosopher and historian in the tradition of literary criticism, perhaps most famous for his work *Metahistory: The Historical Imagination in Nineteenth-Century Europe*, The John Hopkins University Press, Baltimore, 1973; *Metahistory* in White's formula belongs to the emergent vein of academic discourse called "historicism."

4. See Hayden White, *Metahistory: The Historical Imagination in Nineteenth-Century Europe, op.cit*.

5. J. Richard Evans, *In Defence of History*, Granta Books, London, 1977, pp.244-246

6. The Japanese raided and bombed Imphal on May 10, 1942

7. After the *Instrument of the Merger of Manipur Act* was signed in 1949, Manipur was put under Central administration for 23 years.

8. N. Basanta, *Socio-Economic Change in Manipur*, Imphal, 1998, p.46. The *Maharaja* was given the responsibility to take charge of religious and customary practices and in this he was assisted by religious institutions such as the *Brahma Sabha* and *Pandit Loisang*.

9. Before the 19th century, Manipuri was written in a script called the Meitei *mayek* which was replaced by Bengali script in the wake of Vaisnavite influence as late as the 18th century A.D.

10. With lack of patronage of the indigenous script and language in the wake of introduction of Vaisnavism, the spirit of exclusivism was carried out to the extent of condemning the local script and its usage which had to wait till the western educated pioneers of Manipur brought a 'renaissance' of the rich literature from the early part of the 20th century. See Thoithoi O'Cottage, The New Faces of Manipuri Literature during Renaissance and After, *Cottage Reader:Journal of Philosophy, Art and Culture*, Issue 1.1, Library of Springbell Cottage, 9 Sept, 2009. http//www.cottagereader. wordpress. com, accessed on 2.3.11

11. The published works both in Manipuri and English include *Achaiba lei* (poetry 1957), *Manipuri Kabitagi Chhanda Neinaba* (1968), *Chatlaseene Kadaidano Ebani* (poetry 1971), *Matamgi Wakhal* (poetry 1973), *Tirtha Yatra* (poetry 1985), *Sanskrit Ki Salon* (prose 1991), *Houjiki Sahitya Amasung Sanskriti* (prose 1998), *Fragments of Manipuri Culture* (1993), *Aspects of Indian Culture* (1997), *Manipur Dance* (1997), *Monograph on Bhadra*, *Monograph on Pandit Atombapu Sharma* (1998), *Pukning Liekolgi Athuppada*(2000) (posthumous publication), *Americaga Unaba* (2001) (posthumous publication), *Americagi Esei.* Select papers, articles and chapters include: "The Cultural Heritage of Manipur", *Dialogue: A Quarterly Journal of Astha Bharati-AIR, Volume 1 No. 1,* Delhi, July- September, 1999, and "Status of Religion in Tribal Areas of Manipur" The Manipur Page, www.epao.net accessed on 3.3.11.

12. K.N. Panikkar, "Intellectual History: Conceptual and Methodological Issues," *Keynote Address*: *National Seminar on: Towards an Intellectual History of Northeast India - Pre to Post Colonial Periods,* Department of History, NEHU, Shillong, 23-24 Nov. 2010.

13. Elangbam Nilakanta Singh, *Chatlaseene Kadaidano Ebani* , City Press, Imphal, 1971, pp. 7-8

14. Ch. Manihar Singh, *A History of Manipuri Literature*, Sahitya Akademi, New Delhi, 2003 (2nd Edition), p.255.

15. Atombapu was taught Sanskrit by his father, Nikunjabihari, and at the age of 20 became a teacher in a local Sanskrit school. A few years later he persuaded the Durbar to enforce Sanskrit as part of the curriculum of the Johnstone School and had got himself appointed to teach there. Consequently he was able to influence a whole generation of elite educated Manipuris with his theories with little opposition.

16. The Atombapu Research Centre, Imphal has preserved both the published and unpublished works of the scholar. For a select list of the works see E. Nilakanta Singh, *Pandit Atombapu Sharma*, Sahitya Academi, Calcutta, 1998, pp.39-42.

17. In *Meitei Kirtana*, Atombapu gives a list of as many as 168 names of the traditional deity Sanamahi which include Vishnu, claiming that Sanamahi is worhipped in the form of the divine bird=-Garuda, the vehicle of Visnu.

18. Atombapu Sharma had fifty original works to his credit. His scholarly publications include *Ras-Panchadhyaya*, *Chaitanya-Chantamrita* and translated Jayadeva's *Geet Govinda* and *Bhagavata Gita*. He also interpreted performing arts of *Rasleela* and *Nat Sankirtana* from Bharat Muni's *Natya Shastra* (100 AD).

19. E. Nilakanta Singh, *Pandit Atombapu Sharma*, Sahitya Academi, Calcutta, 1998, p.19.

20 . The lecture was published in the form of a book titled *Expansion of Aryan Culture in Eastern India*.

21. See "*Manipur and the Mahabharata*" in E. Nilakanta Singh, *Aspects of Indian Culture*, Jawaharlal Nehru Manipur Dance Academy, Imphal, 1982, pp.84-85

22. The first daily published in Manipuri was titled *Dainik Manipur Patrika* (1933), followed by a literary and cultural journal called *Lalit Manjari Patrika* (1934) and another daily titled *Bhagyavati Patrika* (1946).

23. S. K. Chatterji, "Religious and Cultural Integration of India : Atombapu of Manipur", *Atombapu Memorial Lecture*, Atombapu Research Centre, Imphal, 1967.

24. S.K. Chatterji, *Kirata-Jana-Krti : The Indo-Mongoloids and their Contribution to the History and Culture of India,* The Asiatic Society, Calcutta, 1974.

25. Elangbam Nilakanta Singh, "The Cultural Heritage of Manipur", *Dialogue: A Quarterly Journal of Astha Bharati-AIR*, Volume 1 No. 1, Delhi, July- September, 1999.

26. E. Nilakanta Singh, *Fragments of Manipuri Culture*, Omsons Publications, New Delhi, 1993.

27. E. Nilakanta Singh, *Aspects of Indian Culture*, *op.cit.*, 1982, pp. 133-34.

28. E. Nilakanta Singh, *Manipuri Dance*, Omsons Publications, New Delhi, 1997.

29. *Ibid.*, p.15.

30. E. Nilakanta Singh, *op.cit.*, p. 81.

31. Christianity came to Manipur in the early part of the 20th century. The American Baptist Mission Society was allowed to work among the Tangkhuls of Ukhrul district as early as 1896. Twelve young men were first baptized in 1901 by Rev. W. Pettigrew. It was followed by the opening of other centres and arrival of other missionary groups in various areas of the hills of Manipur. Roman Catholic Mission also joined the movement a little later and is now associated with the starting of various schools all over the valley and the hills.

32. E. Nilakanta Singh," *Status of Religion in Tribal Areas of Manipur*", *op.cit.*

33. E. Nilakanta Singh, *Aspects of Indian Culture*, *op.cit.*, p.134

34. *Ibid.*

35. *Ibid.*, pp. 36-38.

36. *Ibid.*

37. Sumit Mukherjee, "Mystery of a Manuscript," *The Telegraph*, Calcutta, February 28, 1992, http://www.telegraphindia.com/

38. E. Nilakanta Singh, *Manipuri Dance*, *op.cit.*, p. 36.

39. John C.B. Webster, *Studying History*, Macmillan, Delhi, 1997, p. 6.

40. *Ibid.*, pp. 14-15.

41. George Macaulay Trevelyan, "Clio, A Muse," in *Clio, A Muse and Other Essays*, Books for Library Press, Freeport, 1968, p. 143.

42. *Ibid.*, p. 160.

24

Jalad Baran Ganguly (1928-2010)

—Jayati Bhattacharjee

Biographical Sketch

An economist by education and profession but more distinguished as a social scientist, Jalad Baran Ganguly was among few scholars who contributed immensely to popularize inter-disciplinary approach in historical research in Northeast India. Born to Raimohan Ganguly and Dinamoni Devi on 1 April 1928 in Dacca, where his father was an employee in a shipping company, Jalad Baran obtained his M.A. and Ph.D. in Economics from Calcutta University and began his career in 1962 as a Lecturer in Economics at Maharaja Bir Bikram College (MBB College), Agartala. He served as Principal, Jawaharlal Nehru College, Pasighat (1965-71), Reader in Economics, P. G. Wing, MBB College, Agartala (1972-76), Principal, Govt. Women's College, Agartala (1976-79), Professor of Economics, Calcutta University P. G. Centre, Agartala (1980-83), Director, C.U.P.G. Centre (1983-87) and finally, as the first Vice-Chancellor of Tripura University (1987-93), Agartala. After retirement, he was associated for sometimes as Visiting Fellow with Omeo Kumar Das Institute of Social Change and Development, Guwahati. A distinguished educationist and social scientist, Ganguly served in many committees constituted by the Central and State Governments, University Grants Commission and Indian Council of Social Science Research, attended a large number of seminars and conferences, delivered endowment lectures, and published extensively in journals, proceedings and collections. He was associated for life with the organizations like North-East India Council for Social Science Research, North East India History Association, Indian Anthropological Society, and Institute of Northeast India Studies. He presided over the seventh annual session of the North East India History Association (NEIHA) at Pasighat (Arunachal Pradesh) in 1986 and delivered the H.K. Barpujari Endowment Lectures at the Department of History, Dibrugarh University, in 1994. Ganguly passed way in Calcutta on 4 April 2010 after a brief spell of old-age ailments.[1]

Contributions to history

J.B. Ganguly wrote at least four books and a large number of papers on Northeast India over a period of forty years covering a very wide range of research areas, like economic history, transition from shifting to settled cultivation, economic changes in tribal areas, state and social formations, higher education, and development and working of the self-governing institutions in the region. His major contributions for which he shall be remembered as a historian of the Northeast are his books which include (i) *Economic Problems of the Jhumias of Tripura*;[2] (ii) *The Benign Hills*;[3] (iii) *Sustainable Human Development in the North-Eastern Region of India*;[4] and (iv) *An Economic History of North East India (1826-1947)*.[5] A good number of his research papers in journals, proceedings and collections are also basically contributions to history.[6] His Presidential Address to North East India History Association at Pasighat Session in 1986, in particular, is a remarkable contribution in which he made a strong case for understanding the historical processes in the Northeast through trans-frontier and cross-border trades.[7] The papers on transition and changes in the tribal societies of Tripura are essentially in the field of history.[8] Two papers on Tripuri state formation in Tripura are also important contributions to history.[9] The historic role of tea industry in British colonialism in Assam and the oppressions and exploitations of the immigrant labour community by the tea-planters are recaptured in some of his seminal papers.[10] As a historian, he found that the economic backwardness of the region over a long period of time was an important factor for the growth of insurgency in the Northeast.[11] He began his enquiries into the historical causes of economic backwardness of the Northeast as early as in 1974 and eventually developed it in the political economy perspective in which Ganguly was always at home.[12] He also attempted at developing an alternative framework for studying the economic history of the tribes in the region.[13] Finally, *An Economic History of North East India (1826-1947)* is the *magnum opus* for which J.B. Ganguly shall be remembered for a long time as a historian of Northeast India.

An economist-turned-social scientist, history was the key to all social analyses in the format that J.B. Ganguly developed and followed. That he was at home in social theories and that the Marxian philosophy and method had some influence on him become evident while closely following his works. However, he never allowed himself to be dominated by theories unless his position is vindicated by empirical evidence. In whatever theme he worked, the approach he followed naturally drove him to find out historical roots of the problem he was studying and in doing that he always searched for facts from history. While writing history, he was seemingly very clear of the importance of primary sources. He used the archival documents and official reports as well as indigenous chronicles of the Northeast, wherever available, alongside the secondary sources. All his works in history are well documented. Readability is another hallmark of Ganguly's writings. He always wrote in lucid language, using simple sentences.

Assessing the research contributions of J.B. Ganguly to the Northeast, S.B. Chakrabarti observes:

> "Ganguly's discernible intellectual concern was to understand the politico-historical as well as emerging socio-economic aspects of social formation and social transformation of Northeast India in general and the states of Assam, Tripura, Arunachal Pradesh and Manipur in particular. He virtually dedicated himself in this stupendous task like an insider travelling back and forth in the far flung hilly terrain. Being an economist by training, his usual emphasis was on the economic content for such studies, but he was equally aware of the need to place a problem in its historical context along with the concomitant socio-cultural inputs. Though multi-disciplinary treatments, his studies are free from unnecessary technical jargons and easily understandable even to the general readers. Whether it is border trade of undivided Assam with the neighbouring countries

like Bhutan, Tibet or Burma, or the process of peasantization in Tripura and other parts of the Northeast, his lucid presentation of the facts and interpretations are smoothly readable and absorbing to all readers. This holds equally good when one reads his articles on ethnic conflicts or insurgency, or problems and prospects of autonomous management over traditional and community resource-base. If one carefully tries to narrow down the primacy of his explorations into the studies on Northeast India it is immediately prioritized on the problem of land and production and the evolution of political governance. This is precisely the reason which perhaps prompted him to complete a monumental work, namely, *An Economic History of North East India (1826-1947)*, when he was already seventy-eight years old."[14]

Ganguly's most significant contribution to historiography of Northeast India is undoubtedly his *An Economic History of North East India (1826-1947)* which filled in a critical vacuum in the historical literature on the region. The students of economic history are greatly benefited by its publication and the book is likely to continue as a prescribed text book for economic history courses on the Northeast for many years. Before publication of this book, there was no such work in economic history that would cover the whole of Northeast for the period since the advent of the British in one book. Ganguly filled in that vacuum by his work. As regards the objective of the work, he said in his 'Preface' : "It was felt that in the field of historical studies relating to the causes of economic change and growth in this region in the colonial period there existed some gaps which need to be addressed." He further said, "Economic changes and growth in North East India from 1826 to 1947 under colonial rule reflect the processes of structural changes in political, social, cultural and economic organizations of production impacting on the region's economic growth and distribution of goods and services among different classes of people." and "This work is an endeavour to capture the forces of these changes and evaluating their consequences on the wellbeing of the people in the colonial period."[15] These statements of the author are enough indications not only of the objective but also his approach in writing the book.

A huge book of more than five hundred pages in twenty-six chapters with six appendices, Ganguly's *An Economic History of North East India (1826-1947* deals with almost all aspects of economic history of the region from the beginning of British annexation to the end of their rule. The organization of the contents is a splendid pronouncement of the competence of the author in handling the materials he had painstakingly gathered and presenting those in a perspective that he had developed on the basis of the data. In four chapters in part one, the author engaged himself in defining the regional perspective (of economic history) in approach towards writing an economic history of Northeast India, geographical and historical backgrounds of the region, political economy of imperial intervention, pre-colonial systems of land distribution and labour utilization, and tribal economic formations in Northeast India in the pre-colonial period. In explaining the approach in writing the economic history he discussed the hard issues like Northeast as an economic entity, an analytical framework for economic history, historical perspective of the north-eastern economy, capital accumulation process, modes of resource use, women's role in economy, periodization of history, and source materials (for writing economic history of the Northeast). Similarly, the treatment of historical background bears the stamp of his understanding of the historical processes in the region in earlier periods, as he picked up the themes like slavery and status of women as critical in case of the areas that had gone through the process of locally developed state formations, like Assam, Manipur and Tripura. He also examined the variables of economic formations in the tribal areas outside the pre-colonial state system through models of cultivation, typical *jhum* model, manufactures, trade and exchange, and technology.

Part two of the book (containing twenty-two chapters) is dedicated to the 'economy of the states' (Assam, Manipur and Tripura) in the colonial period. In this part, the changes are discussed through a variety of contents that include polity, economy and people in the colonial period, population profile, material life of the people, post-annexation reorganization of revenue systems, cash crunch and hardships of the peasants, land revenue assessments, revenue regulations and revenue maximization, wasteland settlement, origin and growth of tea industry, social cost, exploitation of labour, collective bargaining, and role of tea in economy, population growth and agricultural progress, changes in population density, immigration of East Bengal peasants, tea garden workers and Nepali graziers, impact of immigration on economy and society, changing rulral economy, rural markets, rural indebtedness, and cooperative movement, forest wealth and its management, forest in economy, and British forest policy, development of infrastructure, roads, waterways and railways, post and telecommunication, industries, cottage and rural industries, impact of great depression (1929), urbanization, occupational distribution of population, impact of world wars on economy, war-time inflation, public health, commercial and co-operative banking, Bengal famine (1943) and its impact, constitutional evolution of polity and economic measures of popular ministries in Assam; material life, daily bread, varieties and mode of cultivation, importance of rice in subsistence, salt manufacturing, stimulants and drugs, dwellings, dresses, hill economy, energy, transport, manufactures, professional skills, money and exchange, *lallup* (manorial) system, land-holdings, women in economy, capital accumulation, princely state and economic recovery, revenue education and skill formation, urbanization, industry, trade and commerce, economic changes during world wars, fiscal arrangements, etc. in Manipur; structural changes in socio-economic formations, education, medical and postal services, communications, land revenue, distributive aspects of growth, immigration and population change, war-time scarcities and inflation, social unrests, etc. in Tripura.

The change and continuity in the tribal areas of Northeast India during the colonial period has been discussed in as many as six appendices, viz. 'demographic change', 'impact of the rise of population', 'growth of literacy and education', 'livelihood pattern', 'North Eastern Frontier Tracts', and 'elements of continuity in the tribal areas', and those too with adequate notes and references. An economist by training, the author inserted seventy-nine tables (worked out by him) in the text, which not only economized the space but also spectacularly weighed in favour of the presentation becoming more effective. The bibliography is so exhaustive that it does not leave any room for questioning the genuineness and quality of the sources. The book is rigorously documented; the statements of facts and supportive views are appropriately authenticated by citations in the endnotes (notes & references). The lucidity of language, spontaneity in presentation and continuity of narrations that are indeed so common in all other works of Ganguly has been zealously maintained in the book.

Reviewing J.B. Ganguly's *An Economic History of North East India (1826-1947)* in *Northeast Researches* (Journal of the Institute of Northeast India Studies), Mahadev Chakravarti, a distinguished historian of Northeast India, says,

> "The time-frame of the present book (1826-1947) begins with the Treaty of Yandaboo in 1826, when Assam became an integral part of Bengal Presidency of the colonial rulers. At the outset we should also point out that due to different perspectives, sharp differences have always existed, and continue to persist even today, among the Indian and the Western scholars in their evaluation of the impact of British colonial rule over the economy, society and polity of India. Whatever be the arguments of the Western scholars, it is difficult to deny that the chief motive of the British to establish political control in India was mainly economic and commercial and the institutions and the infrastructure in India were mainly developed to serve colonial economic interests. The present perceptive and thoughtful study of Northeastern region covers the period of colonial rule especially in Assam as also to a lesser degree in Manipur and Tripura, witnessing far-reaching changes in political and socio-economic spheres of the area. The concept in the present book is of 'seven sisters', not 'eight' and Sikkim is excluded. Like his predecessors in this field of study, the Three Phases of Economic Exploitation of the Indian economy under the British rule, e.g. *the Mercantilist Phase* (which *marked the beginning of the 'Drain of Wealth' from India to England)*, *the Period of Industrial Capital,* and *finally, Finance Capitalism* have been analyzed by Ganguly in this book." [16]

As a historian

J.B. Ganguly, a well known scholar in Northeast India Studies, made significant research contributions in social sciences, including economics and history. Though an economist by education and profession, some of his books and papers are directly in the field of history. He wrote a large number of papers on important themes of history like the roots of economic backwardness and insurgency, frontier trade, demographic change, agricultural development, changes in patterns of landholdings, state formation, etc. in the region and finally, wrote a book on the economic history of Northeast India covering the whole region during the entire period of British colonial rule. And in doing so, he followed the historical method and the standard norms and practices in history writing and used both primary and secondary sources like any professional historian. In fact, no historian in Northeast India has so far contributed so much in economic history of the region as did J.B. Ganguly. His last seminal work, *An Economic History of North East India (1826-1947)*, will remain a standard work on the subject for a long time.

Ganguly's *An Economic History of North East India (1826-1947)* by its title is pronouncedly a work in history (i.e. economic history) of a demarcated geographical space (namely, Northeast India) and of a period (viz. 1826 to 1947). Both the dates are historically accepted landmarks, i.e. 'beginning' and 'end' of the British rule in the region, taking care of the requirement of delimiting 'time and space' in historical writings. The source materials used are those conventional for the historians and the treatment is systematically chronological. His background in economics was an advantage for the author to analyze and interpret the sources and to explain the changes over time and space. In his three other major works, viz. *Economic Problems of the Jhummias of Tripura* (1969), *The Benign Hill* (1983) and *Sustainable Human Development in the North-Eastern Region of India* (1996), and in most of his research papers, chronological treatment and use of conventional historical data are indeed explicit. The literary style and formatting are exceedingly committed to time and space, and the experience of past dominate the analyses of present and directions for the future. No wonder, his works in economics also sometimes look like presenting economic contents in the platter of history. The example is his "Economic Backwardness and Economic Growth of the North-Eastern Region", published in a journal of economics in 1974.[17] While attempting to develop a methodology for studying regional economic development also he insisted on a historical approach and the use of historical data.[18] It may not, therefore, be wrong to say that J.B. Ganguly was more a historian than an economist.

The use of the term 'political economy' in Ganguly's works and his method of organization of the materials, formatting the presentations and, above all, attempts to identify classes and class analyses are some of the indications of the author's fascination for the doctrine of 'historical materialism', or his inclination for a 'left of the centre' approach. This might also suggest his affiliation to the Marxian method, though he had no pretensions either way. In this respect J.B. Ganguly's position is comparable to that of Amalendu Guha,* another economist-turned-historian, who is well known for his significant contributions to the historiography of Northeast India and for his commitment to the

---

*A distinguished historian of national and international fame, Amalendu Guha is a trend-setter in historiography of Northeast India. Known in his young days more as a poet and a left activist in Assam, Guha was born in Imphal in 1924 where his father Jamini Sundar Guha was a serving teacher in a high school He did his M. A. in Economics from Calcutta University in 1947, began his career as a Lecturer in Economics in Darrang College, Tezpur, in 1948, and was awarded Ph. D by Indian School of International Studies, New Delhi, in 1962, for his thesis 'Economic Transition in Afghanistan, 1929-61'. He worked as a Reader in Gokhale Institute of Politics and Economics, Pune, and thereafter, in Delhi School of Economics, Delhi, and finally, as Professor of Economic History at the Centre for Studies in Social Sciences (CSSS), Calcutta. While in CSSS, he contributed some occasional papers outlining new research areas in Northeast India and those papers were widely circulated to the scholars in the region. A popular poet and essayist in Assamese, his collection of poems (*Tomaloi*, Calcutta, 1960) and two tavellogues – one of Soviet Union (*Soviet Deshat Ebhumuki*, Calcutta, 1958) and the other of Afghanistan (*Afghanistanat Ebhumuki*, Calcutta, 1961) had already made a place for him in the literary circles in Assam, while the publication of his *Central Asia : Movement of Peoples and Ideas from Times Pre-historic to Modern* (Peoples Publishing House, New Delhi, 1970) established him as a historian of great height. He presided over history session of the Asam Sahitya Sabha at Golaghat in 1978, second annual session of the Northeast India History Association at Dibrugarh in 1981, and Modern India Section of the Indian History Congress at Burdwan in 1983. His presidential addresses are often quoted by scholars for his secular, scientific and theoretical interpretations. On his retirement from active service, he returned to stay permanently at Guwahati and to concentrate on research on the Northeast. He was associated for sometimes as a Visiting Fellow with Omeo Kumar Das Institute of Social Change and Development, Guwahati, where J.B. Ganguly was also then a Visiting Fellow. *Planter-Raj to Swaraj – Freedom Struggle and Electoral Politics in Assam, 1826-1947* (ICHR, New, 1977; reprint Peoples Publishing House, New Delhi, 1988) and *Medieval and Early Colonial Assam – Society, Polity and Economy* (K.P. Bagchi & Co., Calcutta, 1991) are among Guha's major works on the Northeast. His *Zamidarkalin Goalpara Jilar Artha-Samajik Obastha – Eti aitihasik dristipat* (B.N. College, Dhubri, 1988), in Assamese, is another seminal work. He also contributed two chapters (one each in vol. I & II respectively) on Northeast India in Tapan Roy Choudhury, Irfan Habib and Dharam Kumar (ed.), *The Cambridge Economic History of India* (Cambridge University Press, Cambridge, 1982; Indian reprint Orient Longman, New Delhi, 1988) and a paper entitled "Neo-Vaishnavism to Insurgency : a study of the peasants uprising in eighteenth century Assam" in *Oppression and Resistance : Essays in Honour of Samar Sen* (K.P. Bagchi & Co., Calcutta, 1984). He published a large number of papers in research journals, proceedings, periodicals and occasional collections on topics covering economic change, social and state formations, emergence and role of middle class, working class formations, peasant and labour movements, revolts, resistance and protest movements, etc. in the Northeast. Some of his articles published in *Economic and Political Weekly* and some Assamese periodicals had generated prolonged intellectual debates on theoretical issues. Guha is still engrossed in exploring new areas in Northeast India Studies and he is frequently visited by scholars at his Guwahati residence. [*Editor's Addendum]

Marxian method of historical analysis. Nonetheless, the Marxist School is one of the recognized schools in the science of historiography and its relevance, particularly in explaining the economic change over time and space, is also well established. Moreover, it is clearly evident from his works that Ganguly was never dogmatic in his approach and he had no agenda to prove or disprove a point beyond the available empirical evidence. His works are always source-based and rigorously documented, his sources are by and large conventional and his bibliographies are exhaustive to the possible.

Notes & References

1. S.B. Chakrabarti, "An Economist Among Social Scientists ; Some Reflections", *Northeast Researches*, Journal of Institute of Northeast India Studies, Kolkata, vol. I, March 2010, pp. 1-6.
2. J.B. Ganguly, *Economic Problems of the Jhummias of Tripura*, Bookland House Pvt. Ltd., Calcutta, 1969.
3. J.B. Ganguly, *The Benign Hill*, Tripura Darpan Prakashan, Agartala, 1983.
4. J.B. Ganguly, *Sustainable Human Development in the North-Eastern Region of India*, Regency Publications, New Delhi, 1996.
5. J.B. Ganguly, *An Economic History of North East India (1826-1947)*, Akansha Publishing House, New Delhi, 2006.
6. For example, "Economic Backwardness and Economic Growth of the North-Eastern Region", *The Indian Economic Journal*, vol. XXII, 1974; "Tea Industry in the Economic Development of North-Eastern Region", *Problems of Tea Industry in N. E. India*, NEICSSR, Shillong, 1981; "Economic Development and Social Tension in the Northeastern Region" in B. L. Abbi (ed.), *North East Region : Problems and Prospects of Development*, Centre For Research in Rural and Industrial Development, Chandigarh, 1984; "The Economic Content of the State Formation in Medieval Tripura", *Proceedings of North East India History Association*, Sixth Session, Agartala, 1985, reprinted in J.B. Bhattacharjee (ed.), *Studies in Economic History of North East India*, Har-Anand Publications, New Delhi, 1994; "Role of the Autonomous District Council in Fulfilling the Tribal Aspirations for Development in Tripura" in S.B. Chakrabarti (ed.), *Social Science and Social Concern*, Mittal Publications, Delhi, 1988; "The Plight of the Tea Garden Workers in Assam in the Pre-Independence Days" in Sebastian Karotemprel & B. Datta Ray (eds.), *Tea Garden Labourers of North-East India*, Vendrame Institute, Shillong, 1990; "The Process of Transition from Communal to Individual Land Tenure System in Tripura" in Buddhadeb Chowdhury (ed.), *Tribal Transformation in India*, vol. I, Inter-India Publications, New Delhi, 1992; "Structural Changes in Assam's Economy 1826-1947", H.K. Barpujari Endowment Lecture, Dibrugarh University, 1994; "Political Economy of Development and the Agrarian Transition in North East India", *Professor P. C. Goswami Memorial Lecture*, Department of Commerce, Gauhati University, 1997; "Insurgency in Northeast India : An Assessment" in B. Pakem (ed.), *Insurgency in North East India*, Omson Publications, New Delhi, 1997; "Human Development in Assam" in P. Baishya et. al. (ed.), *Development Issues of North-East India*, Lawyer's Book Stall, Guwahati, 1997; "Tripura Tribes in Transition : A Study in the Conceptual Formulations of the Process of Change" in Manish Kumar Raha & Aloke Kumar Ghosh (eds.), *North-East India : The Human Interface*, Gyan Publishing House, New Delhi, 1997; "Tribes into Castes and Peasants : The Tripura Tribes", Publication of IIAS, Shimla, 1997; "Structural Changes in Jhum-Based Economy and Growing Inequalities in North-Eastern Tribal Society" in M.C. Behera & N.C. Roy (eds.), *Trends in Agrarian Structure in the Hills*

of North East India, Commonwealth Publishers, New Delhi, 1997; "Evolution of Tribal-Non-Tribal Relations in Tripura" in Ajit K. Danda (ed.), *Ethnicity, Nationalism and Integration*, The Asiatic Society, Calcutta, 1999; "Producing Economic History of the Tribes of North-East India (An Exercise in Methodology)" in P. M. Passah (ed.), *In Defence of Regional Economic Development in India*, Akansha Publishing House, New Delhi, 2006; "Economic Aspect of the State Formation in Medieval Tripura" in F.A. Qadri (ed.), *Society and Economy in North-East India*, Volume 2, Regency Publications, New Delhi, 2006; "Terrorism in North East India" in Ashok Kumar Roy & S.K. Agnihotri (eds.), *Terrorism and Peace Initiatives in North East India*, Om Publications, New Delhi, 2007.

7. J.B. Ganguly, "Presidential Address", *Proceedings of North East India History Association*, Seventh Session, Pasighat, 1986, pp. 1-16.

8. J.B. Ganguly, "The Process of Transition from Communal to Individual Land Tenure System in Tripura" in Buddhadeb Chowdhury (ed.), *Tribal Transformation in India*, vol. I, Inter-India Publications, New Delhi, 1992; "Tripura Tribes in Transition : A Study in the Conceptual Formulations of the Process of Change" in Manish Kumar Raha & Aloke Kumar Ghosh (eds.), *North-East India : The Human Interface*, Gyan Publishing House, New Delhi, 1997; "Tribes into Castes and Peasants : The Tripura Tribes", Publication of IIAS, Shimla, 1997; "Structural Changes in Jhum-Based Economy and Growing Inequalities in North-Eastern Tribal Society" in M.C. Behera & N.C. Roy (eds.), *Trends in Agrarian Structure in the Hills of North East India*, Commonwealth Publishers, New Delhi, 1997.

9. J.B. Ganguly, "The Economic Content of the State Formation in Medieval Tripura", *Proceedings of North East India History Association*, Sixth Session, Agartala, 1985; "Economic Aspect of the State Formation in Medieval Tripura" in F.A. Qadri (ed.), *Society and Economy in North-East India*, Volume 2, Regency Publications, New Delhi, 2006.

10. J.B. Ganguly, "Tea Industry in the Economic Development of North-Eastern Region", *Problems of Tea Industry in N. E. India*, NEICSSR, Shillong, 1981; "The Plight of the Tea Garden Workers in Assam in the Pre-Independence Days" in Sebastian Karotemprel & B. Datta Ray (eds.), *Tea Garden Labourers of North-East India*, Vendrame Institute, Shillong, 1990.

11. J.B. Ganguly, "Economic Development and Social Tension in the Northeastern Region" in B. L. Abbi (ed.), *North East Region : Problems and Prospects of Development*, Centre For Research in Rural and Industrial Development, Chandigarh, 1984; "Insurgency in Northeast India : An Assessment" in B. Pakem (ed.), *Insurgency in North East India*, Omson Publications, New Delhi, 1997; "Terrorism in North East India" in Ashok Kumar Roy & S.K. Agnihotri (eds.), *Terrorism and Peace Initiatives in North East India*, Om Publications, New Delhi, 2007.

12. J. B. Ganguly, "Economic Backwardness and Economic Growth of the North-Eastern Region", *The Indian Economic Journal*, vol. XXII, 1974; "Political Economy of Development and the Agrarian Transition in North East India", *Professor P. C. Goswami Memorial Lecture*, Department of Commerce, Gauhati University, 1997.

13. J.B. Ganguly, "Producing Economic History of the Tribes of North-East India (An Exercise in Methodology)" in P. M. Passah (ed.), *In Defence of Regional Economic Development in India*, Akansha Publishing House, New Delhi, 2006.

14. S.B. Chakrabarti, "An Economist Among Social Scientists ; Some Reflections", *Northeast Researches*, Journal of Institute of Northeast India Studies, Kolkata, vol. I, March 2010, p. 2.

15. J.B. Ganguly, *An Economic History of North East India (1826-1947)*, *op. cit.*, please see 'Preface'.
16. Mahadev Chakravarti, "Book Review – Jalad Baran Ganguly, An Economic History of North East India (1826-1947)", *Northeast Researches*, Journal of the Institute of Northeast India Studies, Kolkata, Vol. I, March 2010, p. 110.
17. J.B. Ganguly, "Economic Backwardness and Economic Growth of the North-Eastern Region", *The Indian Economic Journal*, vol. XXII, 1974.
18. J.B. Ganguly, "Producing Economic History of the Tribes of North-East India (An Exercise in Methodology)" in P. M. Passah (ed.), *In Defence of Regional Economic Development in India*, Akansha Publishing House, New Delhi, 2006.

25

Lakshmi Devi (1931-1989)

—Priyam Goswami

Biographical Sketch

Lakshmi Devi was born on 19 June 1931 at Guwahati to Haramohan Goswami and Kanaklata Devi. Having passed her Matriculation examination from Panbazar Higher Secondary School, Guwahati, she enrolled at Handique Girls' College, Guwahati, from where she graduated in 1948 with Honours in History. Two years later, she got her Masters degree in History from Gauhati University. Being motivated by Professor Sachidananda Bhattacharya, Head of the Department of History, Gauhati University, to undertake research work, Lakshmi Devi enrolled in the Ph.D. programme of Gauhati University under his supervision. Professor Bhattacharya took keen interest in her work and throughout her life he remained a constant source of inspiration to her. Lakshmi Devi's years of hard labour finally bore fruit in 1960 when she was awarded the degree of Ph.D. by the Gauhati University for her thesis entitled "The Relations of the Ahom Kings with the Tribal Peoples of Assam". In fact, Lakshmi Devi was the first lady to be awarded the Ph.D. degree of Gauhati University.

Lakshmi Devi started her teaching career in 1959 as a Lecturer in History at Arya Vidyapeeth College, Guwahati. Four years later she married Dharanidhar Sarma, a lawyer, and subsequently, she joined Cotton College where she served till she retired in 1988 as Head of the Department of History. A conscientious teacher, she devoted almost all her time to academic pursuits. In 1978, she presided over the History session of the Asam Sahitya Sabha held at Golaghat. She had several post-retirement plans among which one was to write the history of Assam for students in English. Unfortunately, failing health prevented her from pursuing her dreams. The project remained incomplete as she passed away on 3 March 1989, at the age of 58.

Contributions to history

Lakshmi Devi is remembered primarily for her contribution to the study of the history of the Ahom period in Assam. Apart from her main work, *Ahom-Tribal Relations,* her important contributions to the historical writings include *Asom Buranji/Asom Desar Buranji* (in Assamese), and the portion on history in *Samaj Vidya* (Assamese) co-authored with Dandeshwar Gogoi and Joychandra Das. Apart from these, she wrote articles of popular interest in magazines and newspapers and stories from history for children in a book called *Asom Desor Sadhu* (Assamese). The presidential address (1978) to the History session of the Asam Sahitya Sabha was another important contribution.

Lakshmi Devi's major work, *Ahom-Tribal Relations* was the modified version of her doctoral dissertation of Gauhati University, and it was first published in 1968.[1] Incorporating suggestions made by S.K. Bhuyan, who by then had taken over as the Director of the Department of Historical and Antiquarian Studies (DHAS), Govt. of Assam, Guwahati, and B.K. Barua, Dean, Faculty of Arts, Gauhati University, the author attempted to present a critical and unbiased history of the relations of the Ahom kings with the tribal people of Assam, both plains and hills. Till then, Edward Gait's *A History of Assam* had been the only authoritative book which discussed Ahom-tribal relations by making use of indigenous sources, such as the *Buranjis*.[2] However, in Gait's broad treatment of the entire Ahom period certain aspects, like the Ahom–tribal relations, for instance, were touched upon in a very sketchy manner. S. K. Bhuyan's *Anglo Assamese Relations (1776-1826)* also dealt with the reigns of only the last five Ahom rulers.[3] Hence, Lakshmi Devi's work was the first research work covering a very important aspect of the history of Assam in the entire Ahom period. Her detailed study of the relations of the Ahom kings with the tribal people of Assam, which is based mainly on primary sources and supplemented by secondary sources, was thus a pioneering effort in the field. And herein lies the historiographic importance of the work.

Ahom-Tribal Relations (1968) is a source-based work by Lakshmi Devi. Apart from the published *Buranjis,* she consulted many unpublished *Buranjis* and rare books preserved in the DHAS, Guwahati. Published works in Assamese included, among others, *Asam Buranji, Deodhai Assam Buranji, Asamar Padya Buranji, Tungkhungia Buranji, Kachari Buranji, Jayantia Buranji, Tripura Buranji, Darrang Raj Vamsavali, Asam Deshar Itihas, Ahomar Sesh Yugar Buranji* and *Purani Asam Buranji.* Unpublished primary sources in Assamese included transcripts of letters between kings and officers of Assam and the courts of Delhi, Dacca, Koch Behar, Jayantia, Cachar and Sylhet; transcripts of descriptions of miscellaneous events like revolt of Miris, romance of Ramdhvaj Singha's daughter etc.; transcripts of accounts of the different phases of Ahom rule; transcript of Maniram Dewan's *Buranji Vivek Ratna*, Part II and transcript of *Asam Buranji* by Padmeswar Naobaicha Phukan. Apart from the secondary sources available in English,[4] she also consulted several works in Assamese and Bengali.[5]

The organization of the book reveals another interesting area the author did with extreme care. Lakshmi Devi classified the relations of the Ahom kings with the tribal population under two heads, *viz.,* relations with the plains tribes and relations with the hill tribes, on the basis of the policies adopted by the Ahom rulers towards them. She points out that with regard to the plains tribes, namely, the Morans, Barahis, Chutiyas,

Kacharis and Koches, the Ahom rulers generally penetrated into their territories using force only if diplomatic strategies failed. Sukapha, the first Ahom king, had in fact brought the Moran and Barahi tribes under his control soon after he established his kingdom in Assam through matrimonial alliances and by affording them equal treatment. Thus from the very beginning, the Ahoms were guided by principles of political expediency in their social dealings with the divergent groups that dwelt in the Brahmaputra Valley. In the case of those tribes who refused to submit voluntarily, military force was used to coerce them into submission. The Chutiya kingdom, for instance, was annexed by Suhungmung (1497-1539 AD) in 1523 AD. However, in order to integrate the Chutiyas, who possessed a distinct socio-cultural heritage, into Ahom society, the path was paved for the creation of a new sub-tribe among the Chutiyas, known as the Ahom-Chutiyas. The Kacharis were allowed to retain their hill tracts on condition of acknowledging the suzerainty of the Ahom ruler, but the plains areas were incorporated into the Ahom dominion. Relations with the Koches were far more turbulent, primarily because of the division of Koch kingdom into two parts (Koch Behar and Koch Hajo) in 1581 and the consequent entry of the Moghuls in Koch politics. Despite the adverse circumstances, attempts were made to maintain friendly relations and exchange regular diplomatic correspondences with the kings of Koch Behar.

Lakshmi Devi points out that the Ahom method of maintaining relations with the hill tribes was developed to suit the exigency of the time and situation. The existence of numerous economically fragile hill tribes on her northern, eastern and western boundaries created problems of security for the Ahom government. Raids into the fertile plains below through the *duars* (mountain passes) were common occurrences. But the Ahom government intended neither to completely subjugate the hill people and include their territories in the Ahom kingdom nor meddle in their internal administration. Their policy was one of conciliation backed by a display of force when the occasion demanded. In order to maintain peace and stability in the frontier areas, the Ahom rulers adopted the *posa* system which regularized the claims of the hill people to a share of the produce of the fertile *duar* areas. In certain cases, revenue-free lands and *beels*, along with *paiks,* were also granted. In return for these privileges, the hill people were expected to accept the suzerainty of the Ahom ruler. As long as the agreements were not violated, their autonomy was respected.

Lakshmi Devi gives an interesting account of the genesis of the shared control of the Buriguma, Kulling and Kariapar *duars* between the Bhutias and Ahoms during the reign of Jayadhwaj Singha. She mentions that the Bhutias exploited the chaotic situation following the Ahom-Mughal conflicts by occupying the territories between the hills and the Gohain Kamal Ali. Chandra Narayan, the Darrangi Raja, was instructed to clear the tract up to the Brahmakunda. The Bhutias requested that they be allowed to retain at least half of the occupied territory. Jayadhwaj Singha had acceded to the request; but when the actual arrangement was made, the local Ahom officials who had been bribed by the Bhutias, granted the entire tract up to the Gohain Kamal Ali to the Bhutias. Lakshmi Devi surmises that since this arrangement pricked the conscience of the corrupt Ahom officials, they also made arrangements for the transfer of control of the above- mentioned *duars* by the Bhutias to the Ahoms for four months every year.[6] Another interesting finding of Lakshmi Devi, which has far reaching implications, is that the Bhutias of Kariapar *duar* owed allegiance to Tibet and not to Punakha.[7]

The author emphasized upon the realistic and judicious manner in which Ahom-tribal relations were conducted. Relying heavily on primary sources for her information, she has discussed at length relations with all the major tribes, both hills and plains, inhabiting the region. Substantiating her arguments with facts, she has refuted statements made by earlier scholars like Edward Gait and S.K. Bhuyan on several occasions.[8] Nonetheless, she admitted that her work is indeed a pioneering effort and that her own conclusions may be questioned in the face of new evidence. But the very fact that she treaded on new grounds, raised new questions and opened up new avenues for other researchers to work upon is in itself very commendable of a historian.

Although *Ahom-Tribal Relations* was the most important contribution of Lakshmi Devi to the historical writings on Northeast India, her another important work was *Asom Buranji*,[9] a text book in Assamese prescribed by the Board of Secondary Education, Assam, for the Higher Secondary level. The book was also prescribed by the Dibrugarh University for the pre-degree level. In order to suit the requirements of the syllabus of that University, she edited her *Asom Buranji* in a new format and the work was published as *Asom Desar Buranji*, in 1975, with the chapters on colonial and post-colonial developments being omitted. It is indeed creditable that Lakshmi Devi was able to incorporate all the major developments in the history of Assam from the earliest times to the end of British rule in a comprehensive manner in this book. Till the publication of this book, the second edition of Gait's *History of Assam* (1926), was practically the only comprehensive work on the period. Padmanath Gohain Barua's *Asomar Buranji*, which covered the developments until the early 20th century, was more in the nature of eulogy of the Raj than history as it should be. Lakshmi Devi's work, therefore, helped in filling a large vacuum, although she was constricted by the requirements of a text book. On the basis of available material she successfully summarized the major developments in the pre-Ahom period in a convenient and very readable format. She depended heavily on the works of K.L. Barua, P.C. Choudhury, B.K. Barua, Padmanath Bhattacharyya, Banikanta Kakati and Nakul Chandra Bhuyan for information, and this was, perhaps, inevitable. However, the selection of topics, the presentation and the conclusion were her own.

Although writing a text book for the students, Lakshmi Devi made use of the latest evidence available at that time to arrive at certain conclusions. For instance, on the basis of the Ambari Stone Inscription (1232 AD), she concluded that although Jayapala had been hitherto regarded as the last ruler of the Pala dynasty on the basis of the Silimpur Stone Inscription, the mention of Samudrapala "as powerful as the Sun God" showed that the Pala dynasty did not end in 1138 AD. She assumes, on the basis of the Ambari Stone Inscription, that the Pala dynasty continued to rule over Kamrupa until the middle of the 13th century. The history of the Barabhuyans was also reconstructed by Lakshmi Devi although her dependence on already published secondary sources is apparent. She depended heavily on the works of Nakul Chandra Bhuyan and Sarbananda Rajkumar and accepted their views in the absence of other dependable sources. She believed that since Nakul Chandra Bhuyan was a descendent of the Barabhuyans he was likely to have "stated the truth".

While depending on oral sources to trace the genesis of many developments, Lakshmi Devi critically examined those sources with logic and arguments. In reconstructing the history of the Khen Dynasty, for instance, she has relied both on published and oral traditions. However, she has not entered into the debates regarding the reliability or otherwise of the antecedents of Nilambar (Kanteswar, according to legends) and has merely made a reference to it in a footnote. The book also provides interesting information regarding Brahmin and Muslim migrations into Kamarupa. Relying on Minhaz's *Tabaquat-i-Nasiri* and Ram Charan Thakur's *Gurucharit Katha,* she relates an interesting account of the settlement of Brahmins from Kanauj in Kamarupa during the reign of Durlabh Narayan (1330-1350 AD). She also mentions that sectarian differences between the descendents of Queen Lakshmi led one section of the Barabhuyans to migrate from the north bank to the south bank of the Brahmaputra. The Barabhuyans who stayed back on the north bank named their capital Lakhimpur, after their erstwhile queen, Lakshmi. She also mentions that Dharmanarayan, ruler of Gauda, gifted seven Brahmin and seven Kayastha families to the Kamata ruler, Durlabh Narayan, and that Sankaradeva's ancestor, Chandibor, belonged to one of these families. Lakshmi Devi's source of information on this Brahmin-Kayastha settlement was obviously the *Gurucharit.*

For the information on Ahom relations with the frontier tribes in *Asom Buranji* or *Asom Desar Buranji*, Lakshmi Devi relied on her own thesis for which she had already consulted most of the available material. In fact, as mentioned earlier, the subject reflects her original contribution to the historiography of the region. She is of the opinion that the Assamese origin of the nomenclature of many tribes is a reflection of the close ties between the hills and the plains, e.g., *Panibatia, Hatigharia, Tablungia, Paniduaria, Barduaria, Kapahcor Aka, Namsangia* etc. and that close interaction between the different groups resulted in the emergence of Assamese language as the *lingua franca* amongst themselves. On the basis of the *Darrang Raj Vamsavali,* she mentions the assistance lent by Naranarayan to Emperor Akbar during the latter's invasion of Gauda in 1576 to avenge his defeat at the hands of the Gauda ruler. She concedes that there is no specific mention of this assistance in Muslim chronicles, but in order to strengthen her argument she cites the reference of Naranarayan's gift of 54 elephants along with other presents in the *Akbarnamah.*

Although the *Asom Buranji* / *Asom Desar Buranji* is basically a political history of the region, the author has not confined herself to polity alone but has dwelt on aspects of society and culture as well. Lakshmi Devi has also referred to some ecological changes that occurred during the reign of Jayadhwaj Singha, thus providing the cue that such studies could be taken up by scholars in future. She mentions that owing to a natural calamity during the time of Jayadhwaj Singha, the course of the Brahmaputra had shifted southward thereby upsetting the river system south of the mighty river. She mentions that prior to the coming of the Ahoms, the Brahmaputra had flowed further north. The Dihing, flowing through the southern bank of the Brahmaputra, had converged with that river further west touching the present Kaziranga forest lands. The change in course, however, had resulted in the Dihing converging with the Brahmaputra at present-day Dihingmukh. Assuming the name Barnadi, the river bisected the Dikhow, another tributary of the Brahmaputra, downstream and formed the present river island of Majuli. The portion of the Dikhow river that formed the Majuli island came to be known as the Tuni. This information is apparently accessed from the *Buranjis*.

Lakshmi Devi's work is indeed commendable considering the fact that she was able to present a brief but comprehensive account of the history of Assam. On occasions, however, she has uncritically accepted prevailing opinions of other writers as axiomatic truth. She has accepted the view that Suhungmung's reign may be considered as the 'Golden Age' in the history of Assam.[10] The statement is obviously very subjective and in order to arrive at such a conclusion more in-depth analysis and comparisons are called for. Further, attributes of an 'age' to be described as 'golden' requires definition. Three other examples may be cited : (i) Lachit Barphukan had killed his maternal uncle for his dereliction of duty stating that that "an uncle is not greater than the motherland";[11] (ii) the Burmese had used new born babies in catapults to bring down fruit from tree;[12] (iii) the account of the punishments inflicted on Jaymati, wife of the Ahom prince, Gadapani.[13] Keeping in mind that the book was written as text book, these statements should perhaps have been subjected to some critical evaluation. However, despite these minor shortcomings, *Asom Buranji* succeeded in filling a big vacuum in the existing literature and serving as an appropriate textbook for the undergraduate students.

Another text book which Lakshmi Devi contributed was *Samaj Vidya,*[14] co-authored by Dandeswar Gogoi, Secretary, Board of Secondary Education and Joychandra Das, Assistant Principal Teacher, Oil India High School, Duliajan. The book, which was published in 1960, was approved by the Director of Public Instructions, Assam, as a text book for Higher Secondary and Multipurpose Schools for classes VIII, IX, X and XI. It comprised of sections on Civics, History, Geography, Political Science and Economics. While keeping in mind the nature of the book and its target readership, the authors attempted to present a fairly comprehensive insight into numerous aspects of the social sciences. The portion on history was written by Lakshmi Devi in which starting with pre-historic and ancient societies, the author has provided an outline of all the major ancient civilizations of the world, *viz.* the Indus Valley, Assyrian, Sumerian, Babylonian, Egyptian, Chinese, Greek and Roman civilizations and has also written on the impact of Christianity on the world. The section on Indian history spans the entire period from the earliest times till the years after independence. The general idea is no doubt to provide an overview of the major developments in Indian history in a chronological manner. Major developments in the world like the renaissance in Europe, geographical discoveries, rise of democracy in Great

Britain, American War of Independence, French Revolution, Industrial Revolution and the advent of mercantilism and colonialism have also been discussed, albeit briefly. Given the limitations of writing for just one section under the banner of 'Social Studies', Lakshmi Devi had to restrict herself to presenting a mere overview of the topics that she discussed. The integration of history with other subjects in humanities, had reduced its role in the curriculum. However, it is important to note that at that time social studies was a compulsory subject for students of all streams, Humanities, Science and Commerce, up to Class X. It is essential for young minds to understand the background to the present so that values, beliefs and practices are understood and not taken for granted. Apart from encouraging social understanding and cohesion, the lesson of history enables one to act rationally based on knowledge. In order to be relevant, therefore, history ought to be taught as a separate subject and not merely as part of another subject. The book *Samaj Vidya* reflects the constraints in which Lakshmi Devi had to write the portion on history thereby preventing her from doing full justice to the study.

As a historian

Lakshmi Devi worked on the Ahom period in Assam history at a time when no systematic study was available on that period, particularly the relations of the Ahom kings with the neighbouring hill tribes. She was a pioneer researcher in that field, who explored the area, identified the sources and conceptualized the nature and method of relationship. It is only during the last few decades that considerable work has been done by historians on several aspects of the history of pre-colonial Assam. Nonetheless, Lakshmi Devi's study of Ahom relations with the neighbouring tribes has not been followed up in further detail by any other scholar. Hence, her contribution in this field still remains the only authoritative work on the subject. It was based primarily on primary sources, and supplemented by secondary sources. She not only used all the published indigenous sources, namely, *Buranji*, in Ahom and Assamese, but also a large number of such unpublished *Buranjis* in various collections. The writing of pre-degree and degree level standard text books in regional language is another area in which Lakshmi Devi had excelled in Assam. Her *Asom Buranji / Asom Desar Buranji* appropriately served the purpose of a text book for which it was planned and authored. While doing so, she not only drew material from the published chronicles of Assam (*Buranjis*) and secondary works in English but also integrated in the content original material from unpublished *Buranjis*, ancient and medieval inscriptions, translations of Persian chronicles and reports on newly explored and excavated archaeological sites. Besides serving the purpose of a text book for the students, it indeed became an original work in Assamese for the general readers interested in history of Assam. The need for such a book was felt by the lovers of history in Assam for a long time. Lakshmi Devi's work filled in that vacuum and served a twin purpose.

Notes & References

1. Lakshmi Devi, *Ahom-Tribal Relations,* Assam Book Depot, Guwahati, 1968.
2. Edward Gait, *A History of Assam*, first published 1906; second revised edition Thacker Sprink & Co., Calcutta, 1926, reprint EBH Publishers (India), Guwahati, 2008.

3. S.K.Bhuyan, *Anglo-Assamese Relations, 1776-1826*, DHAS, Gauhati, 1949.
4. Lakshmi Devi consulted the works of S.K. Bhuyan, Edward Gait, S. Endle, J.P. Mills, L.W. Shakespear, J.H. Hutton, B.K. Kakati and P.R.T. Gurdon, among others, while writing her thesis.
5. Works in Assamese and Bengali included Gunabhiram Barooah, *Assam Buranji*, 1st edn, Calcutta 1876; S.K. Bhuyan, "Rajeswar Singha", published as a serial in *Banhi*, Vols. XV and XVI, Guwahati 1925-26; Khan Choudhury Amanatulla Ahmed, *Koch Beharer Itihash*, Part I, 1936; Surendranath Sen, *Prachin Bangala Patra Sankalan*, Vol. I, Calcutta University, 1942; Maheswar Neog, *Sree Sree Sankardev*, 2nd edn., Guwahati, 1952; P.C. Bhattacharyya (ed), *Asomar Janajati*, Asam Sahitya Sabha, Guwahati, 1962; Sarbananda Rajkumar, *Chutiya, Bhuyan Aru Matak Rajya*, 1st edn., Guwahati , 1965.
6. *Ibid*. pp. 61-63.
7. *Ibid*. p. 50.
8. For instance, Lakshmi Devi, *op.cit*. pp. 134, 318.
9. First published in 1960.
10. L. Devi, *Asom Desar Buranji*, Guwahati, 1975, p. 208.
11. *Ibid*., p. 260.
12. *Ibid*, p. 336.
13. *Ibid*, p.275
14. Dandeswar Gogoi et al, *Samaj Vidya*, Guwahati , 1960.

26

Sujit Choudhury (1937-2009)

—Sanjib Deblaskar

Biographical Sketch

A historian, an intellectual and a social activist, Sujit Choudhury was born on 14 December 1937 in Pailgaon, Sylhet, Assam. His father Bidhu Bhushan Choudhury was a freedom fighter, who participated in the Civil Disobedience Movement and Quit India Movement, courted arrest and suffered police atrocities during imprisonment which took a heavy toll on his health. The Bengali weekly he started independently, *Jugasakti*, is still current in Karimganj, Assam. This patriotic and idealist father left an indelible impression on the young mind of Sujit. Following the partition, the family settled in Karimganj in 1948. Sujit was then only eleven years old. He studied in Govt. High School, Karimganj, had his graduation from Karimganj College, and M.A. in History from Gauhati University. He did his Ph.D on 'Folk Cults of the Barak Valley' at the Folklore Research Department, Gauhati University. He taught history in Rabindrasadan College, Karimganj, Assam (1964 to 1997), had been a Resident Fellow at Indian Institute of Advance Studies, Simla (1993-95) and a Visiting Fellow at Netaji Subhash Centre for Research in National Movement and National Integration, Assam University, Silchar (1998-2000). He breathed his last on 9 March 2009 in Bangalore, far away from his utopia - the valley of Barak.[1]

History was his core discipline, but Sujit Choudhury treaded at ease the varied branches of literature, folklore, anthropology, mythology, politics, journalism, and even film and art appreciation. An inter-disciplinary researcher, his main field was ancient history in the light of folklore, mythology, theology and comparative religion. As it would be evident from his publications he subscribed to the ideology of the left school of Indian historians, like D.D. Kosambi, R. S. Sharma, Romila Thapar, Bipan Chandra and Irfan Habib, and his scholarship is manifest in scores of his articles in the journals, magazines and newspapers, including *Journal of the Folklore Society*, Kolkata, *Journal of the Ananda Ram Baruah Institute of Language, Art and Culture*, Guwahati, *Journal of Indian Institute of Advanced Study*, Shimla, *Journal of the Department of Bengali*, University of Gauhati, *Parichay*,

The Economic and Political Weekly, *The Statesman*, *Mainstream*, *Point Counterpoint*, etc. His work on matripotestal authority in ancient India, entitled *Prachin Bharate Matri Pradhanya: Kimbodontir Punarbichar* (1990), in Bengali, won him the much coveted Narsingha Das Award of the University of Delhi in 2000. His most remarkable work is on the ancient history of Sylhet-Cachar in Bengali, entitled *Srihatta-Cacharer Prachin Itihas* (1992, 2003 and 2006). He was an acclaimed expert on Bibhutibhusan Bandopadhyaya, the great 20th century Bengali novelist. One of his scholarly papers has been included in Sahitya Akademy's collection of essays on Bibhutibhusan, which was originally presented by him as Bibhutibhushan Centenary Lecture (2003) at Jadavpur University under the aegis of Sahitya Akademi, New Delhi. He lectured and wrote extensively on literature, folklore, language and culture. In 2004 he received the Sahitya Akademy Award for his translation of the Assamese short stories of Nirmalprabha Bardoloi (National Book Trust, New Delhi). In 2007, Choudhury published a Bengali rendering of the famous 'Introduction` to Tagore's *Gitanjali*' (1913) by the Irish poet and critic, W.B.Yeats, along with the text of the lecture of Rabindranath Tagore before the Nobel Foundation at Budapest in 1926.[2]

As an intellectual, Sujit Choudhury was a keen observer of the post-independence political scenario in Northeast India and was concerned with the predicaments of the Bengalis and other ethic and linguistic minorities in Assam. He wrote extensively on the problems of those groups in the context of Assam Official Language Act of 1960, the Assam agitation in 1979 and ethnic, linguistic and communal tension and violence that surfaced in the region from time to time. Notwithstanding his total involvement in research on ancient history of Barak-Surma valley, Choudhury continued to write on the political, economic, social and ethnic issues with serious academic overtone. The deprivations and repressions of the linguistic minorities and other displaced groups had prompted him to turn into an intellectual activist. He became an ideologue of the linguistic and cultural umbrella organization, *Barak Upatyaka Banga Sahitya O Sanskriti Sammelan*, an apolitical organization, which stands for the democratic rights of the linguistic and ethnic minorities and the multi-cultural identity of Assam. The *Sammelan* had awarded him the prestigious Rajmohan Nath Centenary Award and the Achyutcharan Tatvanidhi Award for life time achievements in historical and social research. His two-volume memoir *Harano Din Harano Manush*' (2005, 2010) in Bengali constitute an academically serious narrative of the ill-fated partition in an aesthetically tested prose.[3]

Research Field

Sujit Choudhury's research field in history was undivided Barak-Surma valley or Sylhet-Cachar of British Assam. He emerged as a historian of the valley at a critical juncture when different linguistic groups in Northeast India had begun to assert their identity at the stress of political processes and as a result of which the linguistic minorities or peripheral communities suffered a sense of cultural insecurity. For the people of Barak valley, the root of all problems was the fateful partition of India which had divided the erstwhile Surma valley division of Assam between East Pakistan and Assam (India) and the people in the Assam part (i.e. the present-day Barak valley districts) were cast within one of the Indian states that did not represent their hopes and aspirations. In fact, the districts of Cachar and Sylhet in the north-eastern corner of traditional Bengal were transferred to Assam from the Dacca Division of Bengal in 1874 and this area was not covered by the mainstream historiography either of Bengal or of Assam. Achyutcharan Choudhury Tattvanidhi's *Srihatter Itibritta*, (1910/1919)[4] was the only worthwhile work on the area. Although a voluminous work, Cachar had found a place only in its appendix. Upendra Chandra Guha's *Kacharer Itibritta* (1910)[5] had to a limited extent filled in that vacuum. However, neither of the two works had adequately covered the ancient history of the area. On the other hand, the ancient period was more important for an understanding of the ethnic and cultural identity of the indigenous people of Barak-Surma valley since the Indo-Aryan settlements in the valley had taken place in that period. Sujit Choudhury, as a historian, made a beginning at that point of time as he attempted to study a left-out portion of the mainstream Indian historiography. In fact, the task before the post-independence historians in the region was to reconstruct its history under the changed circumstances and eke out a place for the region in the historiography of the Northeast vis-à-vis the mainstream historiography of the country. Choudhury felt that regional history should be looked upon as a part of national history by situating it in a national perspective and the national history would be baseless if not cast on the regional background. He is indeed one of those historians in the Northeast who had sought to open a new vista in the regional historiography by situating the local or regional annals within the ambit of national historiography. Choudhury's work was facilitated to a great extent by two major publications on the history of Barak-Surma valley, viz. *Copper-plates of Sylhet* (1967) by Kamalakanta Gupta[6] and *Cachar Under British Rule in North East India* (1977) by J.B. Bhattacharjee.[7] Gupta's work is a collection of the ancient inscriptions of the Sylhet region (with original texts, translations and analyses), while Bhattacharjee in his documented study brought out the Bengal dimension of the Barak-Surma valley as an insight for further research in the history of the valley. Sujit Choudhury[8] established the Bengal dimension by his sustained research in the subject in which Gupta's work probed handy for a bunch of unassailable conventional evidence.

Contributions to history

Sujit Choudhury traversed from folklore to literature, social science to prose narratives, partition politics to communalism, Gandhism to Marxism, subaltern issues to sub-nationalism, tribal studies to the roots of linguistic chauvinism, and he has left behind a wide range of writings in the form of books, pamphlets, articles, research papers presented in seminars, lectures, keynote addresses, etc. The notable feature of his writings is that in most of them his historian entity is prominently manifested. If we start with his folklore study, it was indeed the making of the historian. With a view to developing a 'better understanding of the people and society' Choudhury travelled extensively in the rural Barak valley and collected data on folk religious rites and rituals, along with different lore or tell-tale connected with such rituals, and with the help of these he undertook a serious project to have a glimpse of the early historical social structure encompassing a geographical area covering the entire Surma-Barak or Sylhet-Cachar region. This is the first time that the folklores of Sylhet-Cachar have been studied in the same line that the western social anthropologist James Frazer had followed.[9] Choudhury combined with Frazer's method the perceptions of D.D. Kosambi.[10] His essays on *Savitri- Satyavan* episode, *Kartikeyo* myth, cult of the eunuchs and the mother cult in ancient India, which were published in Bengali periodicals in the late 1970s and early 80s, were later on compiled as *Prachin Bharate Matripradhanya: Kimbadantir Punarbichar,* (1990)[11] and *Folklore and History: A Study of the Hindu Folkcults of the Barak Valley of Northeast India* (1996).[12] Between the collections, he focused on the prevalence of matriarchy in early India, including the Northeast, and also discussed the cult-sites and folkcults of Barak valley, like *Bhuvan*, *Siddheswar*, *Badsah*, *Ranachandi*, *Nimata*, *Nouka Puja* and some of the agricultural and female rites. In studying *Savitri vrata,* a particular penance practiced by high caste married women in Sylhet-Cachar, he found linkage with the fertility cult prevalent in ancient Greece and Egypt and placed the origins of the ritual practice at a juncture of social transition when the introduction of plough-based agriculture resulted in the transfer of social power from womenfolk to the menfolk. Thus, plough became a symbol of male dominance. In establishing the pan-Indian continuity of material culture in early Sylhet-Cachar, Choudhury extensively used the works of D.D. Kosambi[13] and D.P. Chattopadhyaya.[14] While reviewing Choudhury's first book *Prachin Bharate Matripradhanya: Kimbadantir Punarbichar* (1990), J.B. Bhattacharjee had commented, "Written in an elegant literary style, the book opens up a new vista of research in social sciences by introducing the regional context of some of the widely popular legends and a new element in measuring the pan-Indian culture continuum in the Northeast."[15] Choudhury's another contribution is a compilation of documents on what happened in Barak valley during the Sepoy Mutiny, entitled *Mutiny Period in Cachar*.[16] As a Visiting Fellow at the Institute of Advance Study, Shimla, Choudhury worked on the Bodoland Movement as an assertion of the ethnic identity within the state of Assam and produced a scholarly work entitled *The Bodos: Emergence and Assertion of an ethnic minority* (2007).[17]

In writing the early history of Sylhet-Cachar, Sujit Choudhury was aware of the limitations of the works of the historians like A.C. Choudhury (*Srihatter Itibritta*) and U.C. Guha (*Kacharer Itibritta*) as the paucity of source materials had stood on their way of elaborations. The region had figured in the works of the British civilians like R.B. Pamberton (*Report on the North East Frontier of British India*, Calcutta, 1835) W.W. Hunter (*A Statistical Account of Assam*, Vol. II, London, 1879), B.C. Allen (*Assam District Gazetteers*, Cachar & Sylhet, Calcutta, 1906), and E.A. Gait (*A History of Assam*, London, 1906). Among the Indian scholars, Padmanath Bhattacharyya Vidyavinode (*Kamrupa Sasanavali*, Rangpur, 1931), Radhagovinda Basak (*History of North-Eastern India*, Calcutta, 1934), Rajmohan Nath (*The Background of Assamese Culture*, Gauhati, 1948) had covered some aspects of history of the region. There were also scholarly essays on ancient history of Sylhet-Cachar by Indologists of national fame like Rajendralal Mitra, Srinivasa Shastri, Nalinikanta Bhattasali, D.R. Bhandarkar, J.C. Ghose, R.C. Majumdar, D.C. Sircar and many others in learned journals which had established the facts of political and cultural integration of the Barak-Surma valley in the mainstream society of the subcontinent during 7th to 12th century AD. Padmanath Bhattacharyya had published the penal codes of the kings of Cachar with a scholarly introduction in Bengali (*Herambarajyer Dandavidhi*, Gauhati, 1912). The publication of the *Copper-plates of Sylhet* by Kamalakanta Gupta (Sylhet, 1967), however, prepared the ground for further research in ancient history of the valley by putting together all the ancient inscriptions in a single collection. Throughout 1970s and 80s, J.B. Bhattacharjee had published a large number of research papers in national and international journals and proceedings and eventually brought out a collection of some of those papers which were relevant to the early history of Barak valley, entitled *Social and Polity Formation in Pre-Colonial North East India - The Barak Valley Experience* (New Delhi, 1991).[18] Bhattacharjee continued to work on state and social formations in Northeast India in the 1990s and thus came out his *Bhauma-Naraka Legend and State Formations in Pragjotisha-Kamarupa* (2004)[19] and *State and Wealth : Early States in Northeast India* (2010) which also included the Barak-Surma valley.[20] Sujit Choudhury approvingly referred to the works of J.B. Bhattacharjee in his writings, though Choudhury was of the view that the conventional sources speak more about the people in upper strata of the society and cannot be used as only source for understanding the life and condition of common people of the time. He, therefore, combined the non-conventional folklore materials with the scantily available conventional sources. In this respect he was impressed by the works of Nihar Ranjan Ray,[21] Suniti Kumar Chatterji[22] and Banikanta Kakati[23] who had interpreted the Brahmanical, Buddhist, Jaina and Tantric texts in light of the sources they gathered from the people.

In studying the early history of Sylhet-Cachar Sujit Choudhury began with early settlers in the valley, who according to him were Indo-Monoloids of Austric and Tibeto-Burman origins. In this respect, he relied primarily on the findings of Nihar Ranjan Ray who had observed in his *Bangalir Itihas* (1949) that the people of Bengal are a mixture of three races—the old Austroloid or *Kolik* with a tall head and a large nose; the Egypto-Asian or Melanid with tall head and not too big a nose; and the large nosed Alpine or East Brakid. The existence of Negroid blood is also apparent among the people of lower strata, and there is impact of Mongoloid blood within eastern, north-eastern and northern boundary of Bengal.[24] Choudhury subscribed to the view of Ray that the Mongoloid influence on the Bengalis of eastern, northern and north-eastern parts of Bengal was evident in their physical features and cultural traits; and as the Sylhet-Cachar region is situated on the north-eastern extremity of Bengal it is but natural that this influence would be more pronounced. He had also studied the works of the authorities like Sydney Endle[25] and Suniti Kumar Chatterji[26] and he wondered where the Indo-Mongoloid Bodos, who once formed majority among the settlers in the Barak-Barak valley, had ultimately gone. However, he eventually opined that the Bodo ethnic groups, including the Dimasas, were not initially acquainted with the plough based system of cultivation and with the advent of Arya-Brahminic groups, following the land grants in forested areas, some of these tribes, hitherto engaged in *jhum* cultivation, were initiated to the plough based agriculture and in this way the Indo-Mongoloid ethnic groups were integrated into the Brahminical fold at the dawn of agricultural revolution in the region. D.D. Kosambi had observed the process of admixture of the Brahminical groups in western and eastern parts of India, and Choudhury believed that the same process was operative in the north-eastern part of Bengal.[27] The state formation process in the region had been studied by J.B. Bhattacharjee (1991),[28] while Sujit Cohudhury threw interesting light on the working of the social forces touching upon the historicity of an intricate nature. With that aim in view Choudhury studied the cult-sites of *Siddeswer-Kapilasram* and *Bhuvan* shrine wherein he delved deep into the myths and cults which bear testimony to the admixture of tribalism with Aryanism.

The presiding deity of Siddheshwar-Kapilasram is Lord Shiva, and it is said that the author of *Samkhya* philosophy, sage Kapila, had worshipped this deity. No one can be sure as to who exactly was that sage, *Kapil muni*, but it is a fact that this illustrious philosopher has been credited with the establishment of another riverside shrine near Gangasagar at Sagardvip in West Bengal, like one on the bank of Barak, and both the places are agog with numerous legends about him. History is silent about it, but the practice of holy bath, the cult of *Varuni*, and the pre-Aryan cult of river goddess, which has some association with the two holy shrines, offered a hint towards the historicity behind the practices and cults. Choudhury analyzed the processes hitherto addressed by none. Analyzing the traditional practices and cults, he sought to study it from a different perspective. He took recourse to the Khasi-Jaintia practice of worshipping a water-deity, Goddess *Kupli*, and studied the entire matter from their perspective. In fact, there is a river - Kupili - originating from the Jaintia Hills, which was a sacred river to the Hinduised Jaintia kings, and the practice of human sacrifice was once associated with worship of the river. All these added a new dimension to the study of Northeast, which also has a historical continuity with mainstream of the country. He discussed the legend of *Puraraja* and his magic stone and of a snake deity which are also closely linked with the shrine. In fine, Kapilasram became a unique case-study of the fusion of pre-Aryan or non-Aryan cult with the Brahminical cult. What made the study of Sujit Choudhury unique is his way of viewing at the Austric Khasis and their interaction with the people in the semi-plain tracks of Sylhet-Cachar, their possession of the portions of Karimganj and northern Sylhet until 16th century and their adaptation of Hinduised cult retaining their own rites and customs. In this, he observed that, 'the bulk of the lower caste population of Surma valley were in fact Hinduised descendents of the Khasis and other Austric people who were early dwellers of the region'.[29] He drew the inference from the cult of *Baruni snan*, (holy bath practiced by the people of lower castes in Barak valley, including the *Baruis* or traders of betel leaves, a trade equally shared by the Khasis) and found its validity since, like Hindus of Barak-Surma valley, the Khasis also worshipped the river Kupli (having a close affinity with Kapilasram, the sacred bathing spot in Barak valley). The Hindu myths and rituals, according to him, were assimilated in folk religious practices. To touch upon the myth of Kapila of *Samkhya* philosophy, Choudhury observed that in view of the familiarity of Kapila with the aboriginal Kupli deity and the plausibility of 'conversion of a female deity into a male divinity', he preferred to give a patient hearing to those who ascribed a non-Aryan origin to the *Samkhya* philosophy, and among whom there were scholars like Haraprasad Shastri and D.P. Chattopadhyay.[30]

Choudhury studied a cult-spot on a hill top, i.e. Bhuvan in Cachar, which is a Shaivite shrine in a cave with numerous archeological relics, sculptures, and murals carved on walls, and some legends and myths associated with it. There is a statue of Bhubanesvari, a coarse form of primitive craftsmanship, an image resembling a tribal woman; and an image of Shiva, which, according to Choudhury, 'does not conform to any accepted concept of Shiva`.[31] Two sets of sculptural relics in the site represent two cultural phases, one reminding the 'crude primitive antiquity', and the other of 'a skilled sculptor'. Referring to Kosambi, Choudhury observed that the cult-spots on hill tops are generally of 'late highland origin' and commented that 'the primitive pastorals were nomadic people and Bhuvan hill was perhaps one of their seasonal camping sites'. He further stated, "Normally nomadism and cattle rearing were associated with a patriarchal society and as such people usually had a male guardian deity. The Shiva of Bhuvan hill might have his origin in such a male deity worshipped by the nomadic pastoralists who had once settled on this hill top."[32] He examined the probability of emergence of the shrine in early periods and opined that it might have originally developed as a camping centre for the traders operating in the region. He accepted the possibility of settlement of the Kirata or Indo-Monogaloids who, as opined by Banikanta Kakati, had arrived in the region following the Aryan invasion of Kamarupa in 2ndcentury AD. In words of Choudhury,

> It is likely that a group of these exiled Kiratas took shelter in the Bhuvan hill and laid the foundation of a *Saivite* cult spot there. The image of the deity with Indo-Mongoloid features and other crude images might be the handiwork of these Kiratas. The tradition that asserts that the tunnel of the Bhuvan hill has an underground link with the Kamakshya hill of Gauhati may be regarded as a popular version of the material and cultural connection which the early settlers of Bhuvan pahar had with Kamrupa.[33]

He also considered the Tripuri connection with Bhuvan, as he said,

> ...the Tripuris, before finally settling in modern Tripura, had a long sojourn in the vicinity of the Bhuvan hill. That the Tripuris had a zeal for undertaking large-scale sculptural projects is manifested in the sculpture of the Unokoti hill of Tripura, where hundreds of images are carved under the open sky.[34]

Choudhury found in the image of Bhubanesvera an 'affinity with the Buddhist deity' and recounted the findings of some historians that the Buddhism had once spread to Burma via Cachar and Manipur, and felt that Bhuvan might have played a role in the process. As some of the sculptural relics in the Bhuvan shrine are identifiable with the later Pala period of Bengal, the Buddhist tradition in Sylhet-Cachar found a separate treatment in Choudhury's work. He traced the existence of Buddhism in the area by his study of folk rites and found the mention of a Buddhist monastery in *Chandrapuri Visaya* (Sylhet) in a tenth century epigraphic record discovered in Paschimbhag (Sylhet). Therefore, the cave temple in Bhuvan, according to him, might have been converted into a Buddhist monastery, and the tradesmen, adventurers and missionaries, who carried Buddhism to Burma, might have 'contributed to the development of the cult-spot into a Buddhist centre.'[35] This shows the method of Choudhury as a historian who critically examined all the possibilities before arriving at a conclusion.

Sujit Choudhury's work is like an extension of the work of Nihar Ranjan Ray as regards the theoretical framework, in which the author made extensive use of non-conventional sources along with literature and inscriptions. Ray sought to extend his study by encompassing the myth and reality of ancient *Vanga*, including *Gauda, Pundra, Barendra, Kamarupa* and *Samatata*, and touching upon the peripheral areas of Cachar, Tripura and the bordering areas of Manipur. He mainly traced the process of ethno-cultural admixture in the region. Choudhury picked from where Ray had left and situated the history of Sylhet-Cachar in the mainstream historiography. Ray had observed,

> The Barak-Surma valley is nothing but the northern section of the Meghna valley (Dacca-Mymensin-Comilla). There is nothing like a natural boundary between these two valleys and that is why, the tradition and culture of these districts of East Bengal so easily spread into Sylhet-Cachar in ancient and medieval periods. Even now the society and culture of the Hindus and Muslims of Sylhet-Cachar is bound with the eastern districts of Bengal in one thread.[36]

Choudhury's study of the syncretic cults in Barak valley offers a new insight into history of the region. The advent of Islam with the Sufi *pir* from Yemen, Shahjalal, and his 360 warrior-saints as retinue brought a significant change in socio-political structure of the valley. The legend of Shahjalal and his encounter with Gaur Govinda, the last king of Sylhet, the supernatural power of the *pir* in controlling the cruel forces of nature, his offer of protection to the people against the onslaughts of nature, especially in tiger-infested region, and his leadership to the new converts in clearing the forests to extend cultivation, thus effecting a second agricultural revolution in the region, have been subjected to a broad analysis, in Choudhury's works, to understand the contemporary society in the region with all its religio-cultural and economic ramifications. He observed that the advent of Arya-Brahminic immigrants following the land grants in the ancient period had initiated the first agricultural revolution, and the same process was repeated in the second agricultural revolution with the advent of Islam in medieval period. His study of *Badsah* cult brought out that there was an economic regeneration of the peripheral folk at the patronage of the propagators of new religion and that some of the Muslim saints were transformed into Hindu deities, venerated by Hindus and Muslims alike.[37] He also studied the transformation of the deities of the Dimasa tribes - *Ranachandi* and *Nimata* - and their admission to local Hindu pantheon.[38] His "Eunuch Priesthood and Deity Darai"[39] and the study of *Manasa* cult in Cachar[40] brought out explanations for some of the unique religious practices in Barak-Surma valley. In the former, he traced the transformation of a water deity into a deity of fertility, which extended the domain of aquatic life to a broader land area. The same study was extended to *Manasa* cult to show how the female eunuch priests were later on replaced by male *Ojhas*, without any pretence to priesthood but wearing female attire. He believed that the epical *Brihannala* (disguised Arjuna in the court of Virata in the *Mahabharata*) probably had some linkage with these folk religious practices in the region. Similarly, his "*Swarna Godhikar Utsha Sandhane*" ('In search of Golden Iguana'),[41] made an intensive study of the animal motifs prevalent among the different ethnic groups, like the Khen, Tibeto-Burmese, Austro-Mongoloids, and the Bengalis.

The transformation of reptiles into divine figures in the trans-Himalayan region, according to him, is a legacy of the Mongoloid and Indo-Chinese traditions which assumed different forms in the hilly region of Assam and Arunachal Pradesh, and in riverine Bengal, where snake deity occupied an important position. The contention of the author is that the practice of endowing divinity to the reptile figures is a Mongolian practice, as exemplified in the concept of Dragon, which transformed into crocodile, *Makara*, the bearer of Goddess *Ganga*, in Eastern India. In Bengal's *Chandimangal* (17th century) the Goddess *Chandi* assumed the form of *Godhika* (reptile). In *Gosanimangal Kavya* (of North Bengal) a cowherd turned into a king by the blessing of *Chandi*, who appeared in his dream as a reptile and transformed into a sword at the touch of the boy. This king is not an imaginary figure but a historical person who reigned in the 15th century. A similar legend is current among the Dimasas where a king had obtained a golden sword (*Ranachandi*) by touching the tail of a fearsome snake. Choudhury referred to another legend current in Indo-China or Viet-Nam where Le Loı (a historical prince and founder of the Le dynasty in 1418 AD), having been ousted from the throne took to fishing and in course of his fishing, he came by a sword in a lake and had succeeded in regaining his lost kingdom with that weapon. When the king went to the lake to offer ovation, the sword sleeked out of the sheath and with a thunder roar assumed the form of a dragon, and finally, vanished in the water. Choudhury found a common pattern in all these legends, i.e. the transformation of the animal figures into deities, which, according to him, suggest the migration, acculturation and admixture of different ethnic groups prior to the era of documentary history.[42]

Choudhury studied literary works to recover historical contents and to find philosophical explanations for belief systems, social behaviours and practices. In a discourse on *Charyapada*, *Krishna katha* and *Mangalkavya*, he offered meaningful hints towards a social history that could be reconstructed from the literary works of ancient and medieval Bengal. He believed that some elements of social history intertwined with literature have remained unanswered. The ancient Bengali poetic compositions of 10th century, *Charyapada*, which were obtained from some notes as commentaries in Sanskrit written by Munidutta, impelled him to ask - for whom was the Sanskrit commentary anyhow? He argued that the folk variation of Buddhist cult, the obscure language of *charya*, the rudiments of folk philosophy later on manifested in the *bawl* and *sahajia* cults, are some of the missing points yet to be addressed by the historians. Thus, Choudhury found a new perspective for the study of *Radha-Krishna* cult and *Mangal kavya*. He observed that the Radha of Bengal in the *Vrindavan lila* (dalliance) of *Radha-Krishna* had given birth to a vast treasure of literature in Bengal, which is unparalleled in any literature. The *Vrindavan* came to be situated in every cottage of Bengal, including its peripheries like Barak-Surma valley, where the lowest of the low could view the bank of Yamuna, peacock's tail, pastoral tune, and the love tryst of *Raikishori*, as a reality around own environment.[43] He then argued that the process how Vrindavan could spread throughout Bengal can be traced by an in-depth study of the *Vaishnava* literature. Given the fact that the *Radha-Krishna Lila* had its origin in *Bramhabaibarta purana*, which is said to have been composed in Bengal in the 10th century, it was further glorified by the bards like Jaydev, Bidyapati and Chandidas, and Radha was conceptualized as an epitome of divine tryst by Rupsanatan Goswami, the myth had its origin exclusively in Bengal and its close vicinity. However, in Choudhury's view, the folk version of Radha-Krishna affair is not supported by the concept propounded by Rupsanatan. The illicit love affair between nephew and aunt throws some light on the social life of the period of its origin and the entire matter may be looked upon as a case of 'appropriation of a folk heroine' by the compiler of the *Purana*. Choudhury referred to an article by Sumanta Banerjee - "Radha: Appropriation of a folk heroine" - and desired that the historians would trace the process of evolution of the concept of Radha in the Vaishnavite cult. His own hypothesis is that the way Krishna, the Lord of the *Vaishnavas*, had alighted to Bengal from Vrindaban, in same way Rupsanatan had carried Radha to Vrindavan from Bengal, and this exchange has resulted in a unique union. If this hypothesis be addressed properly, the contribution of Bengal to Indian theology and culture would be more appreciated.[44]

Choudhury delved into the historicity of *Mangal kavya*, composed in the 16th-17th century, to throw new light on history of the trading communities in Bengal dating back from pre-Christian era to the early centuries of the Christian era. The *kavyas* no doubt refer to a golden era of trade in Bengal, but the question that remained unanswered is : when did the trading community emerge as the controlling force of society in Bengal? The unresolved questions also include : why the males among the trading communities had to give sanction to the worship of female deities, practiced secretly by the women as was found in *Chandimangal* and *Manasamangal*? Was it a tussle between matriarchal and patriarchal systems, or was it an outcome of the changed economic condition of the society, or was it a conflict between the immigrant Aryans and the indigenous non-Aryan populace? Choudhury noted that the period under consideration was a period of the expansion of Buddhism at the behest of the traders known as *banik* or *sresti,* who had carried Buddhism across the sea. It was probable that these missionary traders had married in the local families, which is the reason why they differed in practicing religion. He made a hint towards a conflict between Buddhism and the local religious practices as reflected in the *mangal kavyas*. He also referred to a stone inscription of Asoka where a cult termed as '*mangal*' was virtually forbidden, which makes it implicit that the cult represented in the *mangal kavya* did not receive social sanction when the trader-missionaries gained power. The conflict between the male-deity-worshipping traders and their female-deity-worshipping house-wives has in it the rudiments of history of social conflict which, according to Choudhury, if explored properly would throw new light on the earlier processes of social evolution and transition in greater Bengal, including Barak-Surma valley.[45]

Choudhury moved from medieval to modern Bengali literature to critique the works of well known novelists, Bibhutibhushan Bandopadhyay and Tarashankar Bandopadhyay, and the poet, Jibanananda Das, to explain the interface of literature and society over time and space. One of his papers entitled "*Bangaja Adhunikatar dvaita rup O Bibhuti-sahitya*" discarded the dominant view that the author of *Pather Panchali* was a romantic immersed in idyllic Bengal where characters 'exist in an eternal childhood' and interpreted this tendency of viewing the novelist to be a 'typical dichotomy of the Bengal intelligentsia, the limitation of Bengal version of modernity`. His reading of the same text touched upon the social realities of Bengal and found clue for interpretation of the concept of modernity in Bengal as represented by the literary luminaries like Pramathanath Bishi, Humayun Kabir and Buddhadev Basu.[46]

Sujit Choudhury might have worked more on mainstream Bengali literature and society, but the intellectual in him was pressed to the role of a social activist by the situation in Barak valley in the decades following the partition of India and to write numerous pamphlets and populist features and to deliver talks to refute the arguments of the forces who offered distorted interpretations of the socio-political reality of the valley. Six of his selected articles were compiled in a book, entitled *Barak Upatyakar Samaj O Rajniti* (2007), in which he addressed the problem of 'Bengalis' in the valley where the historical continuity of cultural and linguistic traditions had been sadly threatened. He traced the demographic evolution since 7th century AD to show that the valley was historically tied with Bengal and the Bengali community constituted more than 80% of the total population of the valley in all official censuses in 19th-20th century. The original Kirata settlers were spontaneously assimilated into the Hinduized society represented by the Bengalis and a part of the same society embraced Islam in the medieval period, whereas the other ethnic groups found in modern times are settlers on later dates. The Bengali identity came at a stake with the reorganization of Assam in 1874 when Cachar and Sylhet were transferred to Assam from the Dacca division of Bengal and the situation worsened after the partition in 1947 when only a small portion of the erstwhile Surma valley remained in India as part of Assam. He cited volumes of historical literature to probe his point. Choudhury also redefined the Bengali nationality in Barak valley perspective arguing that a person is a Bengali not by virtue of birth in Bengal but by inheriting the Bengali tongue, tradition and culture. He referred to Bangladeshi nationalism propounded by President Ershad and Begum Jia in Bangladesh, as distinct from Bengali nationality, to argue that the Bengalis in Barak valley had been fighting for identity as they were cast away from the boundary of Bengal by the 'cruel force of time'. He studied the rural-urban and Hindu-Muslim divide in the valley with a futuristic outlook. He was particularly confronted by the views of those who miss-represented linguistic identity and demography of the valley under the behest of chauvinistic literary cultural forums wielding influence on the ruling elites of Assam with an objective to project the valley of Barak as 'an immigrant-dominant land'. An ideologue of the *Barak Upatyaka Banga Sahitya O Sanskriti Sammelan*, Choudhury looked for a composite society in Barak valley with provision for cultural advancement of all ethno-linguistic communities. In the pamphlet *Barak Upatyaka Prasenge: Satya O Tathya* (1989), he cited examples from medieval texts of Barak valley to prove that the language current in the valley is Bengali - orthographically, semantically, and of course, grammatically, and the dialectical variation cannot be a point to abnegate its *bona fides*.[47]

Finally, Sujit Choudhury wrote an autobiographical work in two parts in Bengali, *Harano Din Harano Manush* (2005, 2010).[48] Part one recorded his childhood experience in

Sylhet, a buffer district in Assam, which earned a place of distinction for its bounty, rich natural resources and intellectual and cultural heritage. Cast in an autobiographical mode, it recounts the process of transition of an idyllic land towards a complex future. Viewed from the perspective of an adolescent, the book is a narrative of preparation for the historian who had imbibed the bearings of tradition that were to transform the boy into a keen observer of the society and the flora and fauna of the land along with folklore, folk rites and folk religion. The tradition of synthesis and religious harmony that were to be the major passion for the historian were his natural acquisitions. This part, which may be looked upon as a 'song of innocence', is an excellent literary piece with a soft and tender touch of nostalgia written in a romantic vein. The second part may be termed as the 'song of experience', where a sudden change in the socio-political life of Sylhet was a shocker. The feelings of wonder of childhood days turned out to be one of harrowing bewilderment; the religious intolerance and political intrigues threatening the foundation of existence, the process reaching its culmination in 1947 with division of the land on communal basis, resulting in cruel displacement of the people within their traditional homeland. The author himself was a victim of that partition. This pang of displacement and the nostalgic yarning for lost utopia, coupled with the distressing experience in a remote corner of India under a state that represented a different tradition and heritage, different culture and history, language and values, prompted Choudhury to unfold the history of his land with a view to seek a new foothold in the midst of abject uncertainties in post-independence scenario. To accomplish this he had to wander from ancient to medieval and to contemporary, from ethnic study to folklore and social anthropology, and from contemporary political history to study of ethnic, linguistic and religious communalism and cultural hegemony in Northeast India.

As a historian

A historian by education and profession, history was the first love of Sujit Choudhury, though as an intellectual of a high order he traversed through a large number of disciplines and was a voracious reader of books, especially in art, literature and philosophy. He looked for history in any piece he read. In writing history, he used both conventional and non-conventional sources. He interpreted myths and legends as well as ritual practices for reconstructing history from below. To him, history was essentially history of the people, and could not be confined to the ruling elites. He followed the same line of enquiry as did D.D. Kosambi, Nihar Ranjan Ray and several other historians in gathering source materials for writing history from the people themselves and while analyzing those information he compared them with the information provided by conventional archaeological, epigraphic and literary sources, wherever possible. In the words of J.B. Bhattacharjee, as he said while reviewing Choudhury's *Prachin Bharate Matri Pradhanya: Kimbodontir Punarbichar* (1990) :

> The slim but trim book of Dr. Sujit Choudhury is a compressed presentation of the analysis of a vast mass of data on a voluminous theme. The work is in the established tradition of content analysis in scientific social enquiry in a regional language, the

approach and hypothesis emerging spontaneously from the assimilation of facts. The author has used all possible data – the legends quoted in the epics and *puranas*, the relevant beliefs and practices in various parts of the country, the secular texts like *arthashastra*, *vikramovarsi*, *kathasaritsagar* and *ain-i-akbari*, and the archaeological and ethnographic material. He has compared the Indian legends with those of the Egyptians, Babylonians, Sumerians, Greeks, Romans, and the Chinese, used the standard works in folklore and history and cited the views of the authorities like Dinesh Chandra Sen, Nihar Ranjan Ray, Dharmanand Damodar Kosambi, Romila Thapar, Ram Sharan Sharma and many others in interpreting the legends and practices.[49]

The treatment of facts for Choudhury has been always critical and analytical. By and large, he subscribed to the materialist interpretation of history and historical method of class analysis. However, 'how the people view their own past' was one of his important concerns. His contribution in retrieving the history of the people of Barak-Surma valley is indeed phenomenal. *Srihatta-Kacharer Prachin Itihas* by Choudhury is a path-breaking work written strictly in historical methods to write back to history the people of a large area who were almost forgotten in history because of the colonial dispensation of artificially redrawing the provincial boundaries. One problem that seems inherent in his works is the absence of documentation. He did not use footnotes or endnotes in his writings; nor did he, in most cases, even append a bibliography. Nonetheless, he always discussed at length the sources, and also acknowledged the works he used, in the main text itself, as did Nihar Ranjan Ray in his celebrated *Bangalir Itihas*. Like Ray, Choudhury also had great command over language and his literary style is exceptionally pleasant.

Notes & References

1. For life-sketch see obituary in *Dainik Samayik Prasanga*, March 11, 2009.
2. Sujit Choudhury, *Gitanjali, Nobel Puraskar, Bitarka o Anyanya Prasanga*, Karimganj, 2007.
3. The biographical sketch of Sujit Choudhury has been compiled by this author with the help of the members of the family of Late Choudhury and his former colleagues and by going through the relevant issues of some of the newspapers published from Barak valley, like *Dainik Samayik Prasanga*, *Dainik Yugoshanka* and the weekly *Yugoshakti*.
4. Achyutcharan Choudhury Tattvanidhi, *Srihatter Itibritta*, Published by author, vol. I, Calcutta, 1910 (1317 BS), vol. II, Silchar, 1917 (1324 BS).
5. Upendra Chandra Guha, *Kacharer Itibritta*, Published by author, Dhaka, 1910.
6. Kamalakanta Gupta, *Copper-plates of Sylhet*, Published by author, Sylhet, 1967.
7. J.B. Bhattacharjee, *Cachar Under British Rule in North East India*, Radiant Publishers, New Deli, 1977.
8. Sujit Choudhury, *Srihatta-Kacharer Prachin Itihas*, Papyrus, Calcutta, 1992; 3rd revised & enlarged edition Dinkal Press Ltd., Silchar, 2006.
9. James Frazer, *Golden Bough*, London, 1963.
10. D.D. Kosambi, *Myth and Reality – Studies in the Formation of Indian Cultture*, 1st edn. 1962, reprint Popular Prakashan, Bombay, 1983.

11. Sujit Choudhury, *Prachin Bharate Matripradhanya: Kimbadantir Punarbichar*, Papyrus, Calcutta, 1990.
12. Sujit Choudhury, *Folklore and History: A Study of the Hindu Folkcults of the Barak Valley of Northeast India*, K.K. Publishers, New Delhi, 1996.
13. D.D. Kosambi, *An Introduction to the Study of Indian History*, 1st edn. 1956; reprint Popular Prakashan, Bombay, 2002.
14. D.P. Chattopadhyaya, *Lokayata – A Study in Ancient Indian Materialism*, People's Publishing House, New Delhi, 1959.
15. J.B. Bhattacharjee, "Book Review - *Prachin Bharate Matripradhanya: Kimbadantir Punarbichar* by Sujit Choudhury (Bengali) ", *The North-Eastern Hill University Journal of Social Sciences and Humanities*, Vol. IX, No. I, January-March 1991, p. 57.
16. Sujit Choudhury, *Mutiny Period in Cachar,* Tagore Society, Silchar, 1981.
17. Sujit Choudhury, *The Bodos: Emergence and Assertion of an ethnic minority*, Indian Institute of Advanced Studies, Shimla, 2007.
18. J.B. Bhattacharjee, *Social and Polity Formations in Pre-Colonial North East India*, Har-Anand/Vikas Publishing House, New Delhi, 1991; "The Ancient Political Structure of the Barak Valley", *The North-Eastern Hill University Journal of Social Sciences and Humanities*, vol x, no. 1, Shillong, 1922, pp. 1-36.
19. J.B. Bhattacharjee, *Bhauma-Naraka Legend and State Formations in Pragjotisha-Kamarupa*, NEIHA, Shillong, 2004.
20. J.B. Bhattacharjee, *State and Wealth : Early States in Northeast India*, DVS Publishers, Guwahati, 2010.
21. Nihar Ranjan Ray, *Bângâlir Itihâs* (Bengali), Book Emporium, Calcutta, 1356 BS (1949), reprint Deys' Publishing House, Calcutta, 1993.
22. Suniti Kumar Chatterji, *Kirâta-Jana-Kriti : The Indo-Mongoloids, Their Contributions to History and Culture of India*, The Asiatic Society, Calcutta, 1951.
23. Bani Kanta Kakati, *The Mother Goddess Kamakhya*, Lawyers Book Stall, Gauhati, 1948.
24. Nihar Ranjan Ray, *Bângâlir Itihâs* (Bengali), *op.cit*, p. 17.
25. Sydney Endle, *The Kacharis*, London, 1909.
26. Suniti Kumar Chatterji, *Kirâta-Jana-Kriti : The Indo-Mongoloids, Their Contributions to History and Culture of India*, *op.cit*.
27. Sujit Choudhury, *Srihatta-Kacharer Prachin Itihas*, *op.cit*, pp. 17-22.
28. J.B. Bhattacharjee, *Social and Polity Formations in Pre-Colonial North East India*, *op.cit*.
29. Sujit Choudhury, *Folklore and History: A Study of the Hindu Folkcults of the Barak Valley of Northeast India*, *op.cit.*, p. 38.
30. *Ibid*, pp. 31-46.
31. *Ibid*, p. 48.
32. *Ibid*, p. 49.

33. *Ibid.*

34. *Ibid*, p. 50.

35. *Ibid*, pp. 47-52.

36. Nihar Ranjan Ray, *Bângâlir Itihâs* (Bengali), *op.cit*, p. 17, portion translated in J.B. Bhattacharjee, "The Ancient Political Structure of the Barak Valley", *The North-Eastern Hill University Journal of Social Sciences and Humanities*, vol. X, no. 1, Shillong, 1922, p. 3.

37. Sujit Choudhury, *Folklore and History: A Study of the Hindu Folkcults of the Barak Valley of Northeast India*, *op.cit.*, pp. 53-62.

38. *Ibid*, pp. 63-71.

39. Sujit Choudhury, "The Eunuch Priesthood and Deity Darai: A Case Study" in Soumen Sen (ed.), *Folklore in North East India*, Omsons Publishers, New Delhi, 1985, pp. 137-45.

40. Sujit Choudhury, *Folklore and History: A Study of the Hindu Folkcults of the Barak Valley of Northeast India*, *op.cit.*, pp. 72-79.

41. Sujit Choudhhury, "*Swarna Godhikar Utsha Sandhane*" ('In search of Golden Iguana'), *The Journal of Bangla Akademi*, Calcutta, 2002.

42. *Ibid.*

43. Sujit Choudhury, *Chinna Chinta, Bhinna Mat*, Jugoshakti Prashan, Karimganj, 2009, p. 131.

44. *Ibid*, p. 139.

45. Sujit Choudhury, *Nirbachita Prabandha*, Poulami Prakashan, Agartala, 2003.

46. Sujit Choudhury, *Chinna Chinta, Bhinna Mat*, Jugoshakti Prakashan, Karimganj, 2009.

47. Sujit Choudhury, *Barak Upatyakar Samaj O Rajniti*, Jugoshakti Prakashan, Karimganj, 2007; *Barak Upatyaka Prasenge: Satya O Tathya*, Barak Upatyaka Banga Sahitya O Samskriti Sanmelon, Silchar, 1989;

48. Sujit Choudhury, *Harana Din Harano Manush*, Pt. I, Jugoshakti Prakashan, Karimganj, 2006 and Pt. II, Dinkal Press Ltd, Silchar, 2010.

49. J.B. Bhattacharjee, "Book Review - *Prachin Bharate Matripradhanya: Kimbadantir Punarbichar* by Sujit Choudhury (Bengali) ", *The North-Eastern Hill University Journal of Social Sciences and Humanities*, Vol. IX, No. I, January-March 1991, pp. 56-57.

27

Dipankar Banerjee (1954-2011)

—*Sarbani Bhattacharjee*

Biographical Sketch

Dipankar Banerjee, Head, Department of History, Gauhati University, at the time of his passing away on 19 March 2011, was a promising historian who had already made a mark as a historian by making substantive contributions in new areas and his untimely death is an irreparable loss to the historiography of Northeast India. Born in Guwahati (Assam) on 11 January 1954, Banerjee was educated in Guwahati, Dhubri and New Delhi. An M.A. in Modern History of Gauhati University, M. Phil of Jawaharlal Nehru University, New Delhi and Ph.D. of Gauhati University, he began his teaching career, first, temporarily in Biswanath College, Chariali and Darrang Cullege, Tezpur and, then, in Pandu College, Guwahati. He joined the department of History, Gauhati University, in December 1984 and was the Head of that Department since 2010. He was associated with several research organizations, including North East India History Association (NEIHA) to which he was a Life Member almost from the beginning and played an active role in organizing its two sessions at Guwahati (1988 & 2003), and published a large number of research papers in various journals and proceedings, including the *Proceedings* of NEIHA. The series of articles he wrote in *Samay Prabaha*, a Bengali daily published from Guwahati, in early 1990s, on the heritage institutions, buildings and memorials in greater Guwahati were absolutely based on his painstaking field work. A very popular teacher at Gauhati University, he also successfully guided doctoral research in women and labour histories of Assam.

As a researcher, Banerjee did his doctoral work on working class movement in colonial Assam and made a mark in that field by contributing papers in seminars and conferences on labour strikes in industries like Digboi Refinery and the Dhubri Match Factory. His major publications include *Heritage Guwahati* (2004), *Labour Movement in Assam* (2005), and *Brahmo Samaj and North East India* (2006). He also edited a volume on the history of Gauhati High Court (2007) and co-edited with Ranju Bezbaruah and Priyam Goswami *Sources of Studies in History of North East India* (2007). *Jyotiprasad Agarwala* (2010), a biographical study of the first Assamese film-maker and one of the greatest playwrights, poets and lyricists of Assam, who was also a freedom fighter, journalist and an essayist, under the series Legends of Culture from India's Northeast, was his last major work.

A social activist in many ways, Banerjee was associated with Rotary Club, INTACH, Vivekananda Kendra, Gauhati Brahmo Samaj, NE Sound Archive, JRMDGPC Trust, Association of British Scholars in India and Heritage Recording Inc., UK, and many other regional, national and international organizations. He was instrumental in establishing the Amalendu Banerjee Foundation at Guwahati in memory of his father who was once a legend as a successful teacher of history at B.N. College, Dhubri, and the Foundation, among other activities in the fields of education, literature and culture, has been publishing a journal *Phoenix* recapturing pages of the cultural history of modern Assam. For Vivekananda Kendra, Guwahati, Banerjee worked in an innovative way for preserving history of the Northeast by preparing live cassettes on cultural events and personalities. The CDs he made on 'Vivekananda in Northeast' and 'Sculptures of Assam' in that series earned him immense praise and popularity. He visited USA under International Visitors' Program, led the Rotary GSE Team from RI Dist 3240 to UK, and served as the International RYLA Counsellor at IWU, Texas, USA. He was honoured with an award at the Assam Convention at Calgary, Canada, in 2006. Indeed like Vivekananda Kendra, his association with the rotary movement was also phenomenal. In August 2010, Banerjee attended an international conference of the present, past and future Rotary Governors at Bangkok. In fact, he was already unanimously elected to take over as a District Governor of the Rotarians in Guwahati, but this too did not actually happen due to the sudden call from the world beyond.

A prolific writer and fluent speaker in Assamese, Bengali and English, Dipankar Benerjee always won the heart of every one who came in contact with him by his pleasing personality and his devotion to work. He was a proud son of Guwahati and Assam and always wanted to do something for his city and his state by way of protecting, preserving and studying the heritage and sharing the glory of that heritage with the world. The untimely passing away of this talented and devoted historian is indeed upsetting for many academic programmes that were on his cards for the Northeast and for which he worked till he breathed his last. He was invited as a resource person to a workshop on social science research in Northeast India at the Asiatic Society, Calcutta, in March 2010, and Banerjee utilized his participation in persuading the Asiatic Society to sponsor a national seminar on Northeast at Gauhati University and to hold the inaugural K.K. Handiqui Memorial Lecture on that occasion. Banerjee made all the preparations for the twin event, but when the seminar and the lecture were being held at the Gauhati University, on 11-13 March 2011, he was undergoing treatment at the Tata Cancer Hospital in Mumbai. He was not only a Life Member of the Institute of Northeast India Studies but also deeply involved in conceptualizing the Institute as an instrument to bring Northeast India Studies into national and global focus. He was working towards starting a Local Centre of the Institute at Guwahati and it was only then that the death took him away. The historian who was due to contribute a biographical essay for the H.K. Barpujari centenary volume is also among the historians who are in the great beyond.[1]

Contributions to history

Dipankar Banerjee did his doctoral work on working class movement in colonial Assam and he made a mark in that field by contributing papers in seminars and conferences on labour strikes in the industries like Digboi Refinery and the Dhubri Match Factory and the plantation labour movements in tea gardens. The study of the plantation (i.e. tea) labour movements seems to have drawn his attention to the Brahmo Samaj which was the first organization to raise voice against the exploitation of the helpless immigrant labour in the tea gardens. Eventually, he produced a full length study on the Brahmo Samaj in Northeast India. In fact, Banerjee presented at least seven papers on plantation and non-plantation labour movements in Assam in various sessions of the North East India History Association.[2] His two major research publications in modern history are *Labour Movement in Assam* (2005),[3] and *Brahmo Samaj and North East India* (2006).[4] The *Labour Movement in Assam* is basically a study with special reference to the workers' strike in the Assam Oil Company at Digboi and most of the chapters are on that historic strike which assumed a nationalist dimension due to the intervention of the leaders of the on-going national movement in the country. However, the book began with the beginning of labour movements and the growing consciousness among the working class in Assam and covered a number of other movements. His *Brahmo Samaj and North East India* mainly covered the activities of the Samaj in Brahmaputra Valley, Khasi hills and the tea gardens of Assam and assessed its role in socio-economic, educational and intellectual spheres. The sound methodology – balanced use of archival and non-archival primary and secondary sources and meticulous documentation – is a very strong point in Banerjee's both the works. The 'forewords' are contributed by eminent historians J.B. Bhattacharjee and Amalendu De respectively.

As said already, Banerjee was involved in preparing the layout and editing a volume on the Gauhati High Court on the occasion of its golden jubilee (1998), *Gauhati High Court in Pictures*, which contains some rare photographs, important documents and statistical information that are useful for research in legal history of modern Northeast and the Guwahati city.[5] He also edited *The Book of Assam Tea* and *S.K. Bhuyan in Parliament*, and completed his *Heritage Shillong* (in the format of *Heritage Guwahati*) which is likely to be published shortly.[6] Dipankar Banerjee and Priyam Goswami are associate editors of the volume entitled *Sources of Studies in History of North East India* (2007),[7] edited by Ranju Bezbaruah, that contains the papers presented in a national seminar organized by the North-Eastern Regional Centre of the Indian Council of Historical Research at Guwahati in March 2002 and it serves as a major reference on the Northeast.

Banerjee is also well known for popular writings on historical themes, which is certainly important not only for creating historical awareness among the masses but also in involving the people in protecting and preserving their own heritage, something that is seldom attempted by the institutional historians at the highest rung of the academia. The '*aitihya*' (heritage) series of articles he wrote in *Samay Prabaha* on the heritage sites and buildings of Guwahati was indeed a pioneering effort that made Banerjee popular as a historian in Assam. He also wrote an excellent article in *Ninth Column* on some of the institutions in Guwahati that were more than hundred years old.[8] These articles formed the nucleus of his more popular *Heritage Guwahati* (2004), published by the Govt. of Assam with a foreword by the Prime Minister of India, Dr. Manmohan Singh.[9] Similarly, his *Jyotiprasad Agarwala* (2010)[10] is an excellent biographical study of the first Assamese film-maker and one of the greatest playwrights, poets and lyricists, who was also a freedom fighter, journalist and an essayist, which the literati in any part of the world would love to read to know about a great legend of culture from India's Northeast. Resourceful in content, pleasant in literary flavour of an analytical language, annotated with rare topical photo illustrations and innovative graphics, and skillfully designed by the imaginative author himself, Jyotiprasad has indeed been served in a new platter by Dipankar Banerjee.

As a historian

Dipankar Banerjee was a student of Professor H.K. Barpujari at his M.A. in Modern History at Gauhati University. He also did his M. Phil at the Jawaharlal Nehru University (JNU), New Delhi, at a time when the Centre of Historical Studies in that University had on its faculty some of the great historians in the country, like Sarvepalli Gopal, Romila Thapar, Bipan Chandra, Sabyasachi Bhattacharya, K.N. Panikar and Harbans Mukhia, who are well known for their contributions in promoting secular, scientific and analytical history writing in India, and historiography formed a compulsory component of the curriculum in that Centre. This background in research methods and philosophy of history was a strong point in Banerjee's research works as it is evident in his publications. His two books, namely, *Labour Movement in Assam* and *Brahmo Samaj and North East India* and some research papers in those two fields in various journals and proceedings are indeed his major contributions to historiography of Northeast India. He wrote those books and papers strictly according to historical methods and introduced new areas that were not taken up by other historians for full length studies. In an important area of modern history like the labour movement, his *Labour Movement in Assam* is so far the only book in the Northeast. He also supervised research in new areas, like labour history and women study. His one student completed doctoral work on trade union movement in Assam and another on women participation in freedom movement in the Barak valley of Assam.

Banerjee was also a historian with a difference, and this is in the sense that he wrote both for (i) the general readers and (ii) those who are disciplined in history. When he wrote for the general readers he did not burden them with the technicality of notes and references that are required in works of the historians, but he always took care to ensure that the facts are correctly presented. The objective in those writings was to create awareness about history and a sense of pride among the people about their common heritage and to ensure protection and preservation of the relics of the past that are usually landmarks in social development. His series of articles in newspapers and the CDs he made for the Vivekananda Kendra, like 'Vivekananda in Northeast' and 'Sculptures of Assam', were primarily intended to tell history to the common people. His *Jyotiprasad Agarwala* introduces an icon of culture from the Northeast to the boundless world. Similarly, the *Heritage Guwahati* is an innovative effort to draw attention of the readers in rest of the country and abroad to some of the treasures that make the region special and what others also would like to experience. It is understood that he had completed a similar monograph on Shillong and that is now awaiting publication. He might have followed the same format and methodological approach for studying the heritage of Shillong which he developed for his work on Guwahati. On the other hand, his *Labour Movements in Assam* and *Brahmo Samaj and North East India* and the research papers he contributed in academic journals and proceedings are strictly within the parameters of the works of a historian. What is important to appreciate here is that it is never easy for an institutional historian to address the readers at two very different levels, namely, (i) the generality among the readers to whom the dilly dally of methodology is not only unnecessary but also a wizard that detracts the readability, and (ii) the mainstream professionals in the discipline of history and allied disciplines within social sciences for whom the hardcore technicality of research methodology is always important for scientific analyses. The professionally trained historians are bound by the norms and ethics of the discipline and, therefore, generally averse to popular writings. Banerjee attempted both, and he did it with considerable ease.

Dipankar Banerjee was a student of the legend called H.K. Barpujari and that he was a deter-mined follower of that hard taskmaster in historiography is evident from his tribute to the legend, which is also a reflection of Banerjee's own view of history. To quote Banerjee,

> This uncompromising and committed historian (H.K. Barpujari) had a relentless quest for truth. On several occasions he boldly proclaimed that the duty of a historian is to unearth the truth fearlessly and that he should not submit to political or any other pressure, internal or external. He did not submit to any 'ism' and urged upon the historians to 'explore truth, the whole truth and nothing but the truth'. The commitment, ideal of steadfastness and devotion he has left behind in the field of historical research in the region is exemplary.[11]

Notes & References

1. The biographical sketch of Dipankar Banerjee has been compiled by this author on the basis of information gathered from some of his colleagues in the department of history, Gauhati University and the Chairman and some members of Board of Trustees, Institute of Northeast India Studies, who knew Banerjee closely. The assistance has also been taken from the obituaries published in some of the newspapers and periodical in Guwahati, including *Sambad Lahari* dated 29 March 2011 and *Ninth Column* (11th Year), Maligaon, Guwahati, 2011. We are indeed thankful to Dr. Prasun Barman of Cotton College, Guwahati, for sending copies of those publications to the Institute.

2. Dipankar Banerjee, "Non-Plantation Labour Movement in Assam : A Study of Assam Oil Company Workers' Strike (1939)", *Proceedings of North East India History Association* (hereafter *PNEIHA*), 2nd session, 1981, pp. 226-235; "A brief note on the role of Congress in the Labour Struggle in Assam during 1919-1939", *PNEIHA*, 3rd session, 1982, pp. 162-190; "Historic Assam-Bengal Railway Workers' Strike (1921) : A Survey", *PNEIHA*, 4th session, 1983, pp. 176-183; "Genesis of Labour Movement among the Non-Plantation Workers and

Wage Earners in Assam", *PNEIHA*, 6th session, 1985, pp. 383-392; "Match Factory Workers of Assam : Some Reflections on their Early Movements (1928-37)", *PNEIHA*, 9th session, 1988, pp. 458-469; "Tea Garden Labour and Cotton-Curzon Controversy", *PNEIHA*, 12th session, 1992, pp. 194-198; "Impact of Brahmo Samaj in the Brahmaputra Valley and its concern for Tea Garden Labour", *PNEIHA*, 22nd session, 2001, pp. 246-255.

3. Dipankar Banerjee, *Labour Movement in Assam*, Anamika Publishing House, New Delhi, 2005,

4. Dipankar Banerjee, *Brahmo Samaj and North East India*, Anamika Publishing House, New Delhi, 2006.

5. *The Gauhati High Court in Pictures*, Guwahati, 2006.

6. Shantanu Roychoudhury, "*Dr. Dipankar Bandopadhyay – Ek Byaktigata Anubhav* " (in Bengali), in Prasun Barman (ed.), *Ninth Column* (11th Year), Maligaon, Guwahati, 2011, pp. 272-75.

7. Ranju Bezbaruah (ed.), *Sources of Studies in History of North East India*, ICHR, New Delhi, 2007.

8. Dipankar Bandopadhyay, "*Guwahatir Katipay Shatavarsa Prachin Pratistan*" (Bengali), in Prasun Barman (ed.), *Ninth Column* (8th Year), Maligaon, Guwahati, 2008, pp. 63-72.

9. Dipankar Banerjee, *Heritage Guwahati*, Govt. of Assam, Guwahati, 2004.

10. Dipankar Banerjee, *Jyotiprasad Agarwala*, Jeewan Ram Mungi Devi Goenka Public Charitable Trust, Guwahati/Shillong, 2010.

11. Dipankar Banerjee, "In Memorium" in Reeta Baruah (ed.), *Prof. H.K. Barpuari : Tributes*, Guwahati, 2003, p. 102.

Our Contributors

Dr. Mahadev Chakravarti, formerly Mahatma Gandhi Professor of History, Tripura University, Agartala

Dr. Subir Kar, formerly Professor of Bengali, Assam University, Silchar

Dr. Nishipad Dev Choudhury, formerly Deputy Director, Department of Archeology, Govt. of Assam, Guwahati

Dr. Milton S. Sangma, formerly Professor of History, North-Eastern Hill University, Shillong & Pro-Vice Chancellor, NEHU, Tura Campus, Meghalaya

Dr. Gajendra Adhikary, Principal, D. K. Girls' College, Mirza, Assam

Dr. Ananda Gopal Ghosh, Professor of History, North Bengal University, Siliguri, West Bengal

Dr. D. R. Syiemlieh, Vice-Chancellor, Rajiv Gandhi University, Itanagar

Dr. (Mrs) Shiela Bora, formerly Professor of History, Dibrugarh University, Dibrugarh, Assam

Dr. J. B. Bhattacharjee, Chairman, Institute of Northeast India Studies, Kolkata

Dr. H. Sudhir, Assistant Professor, Department of History, Manipur University, Imphal

Dr. Anowar Hussain, Professor of History, Dibrugarh University, Dibrugarh, Assam

Dr. (Ms) Jayati Bhattacharjee, Lecturer in History, Women's College, Shillong

Dr. Sekhar Brahma, Registrar, Bodoland University, Kokrajhar, Assam

Dr. Romesh Buragohain, formerly Principal, City College, Guwahati

Dr. Sagar Boruah, Principal, Khagarijan College, Nagaon, Assam

Dr. Shrutidev Goswami, formerly Professor of History, Dibrugarh University, Dibrugarh, Assam

Dr. Rajen Saikia, formerly Head, Department of History, Nagaon Girls' College, Nagaon, Assam

Dr. Sangkima, Principal, Government Aizawl College, Aizawl

Dr. Amalendu Bhattacharjee, Head, Department of Bengali, G. C. College, Silchar, Assam

Dr. Jahar Kanti Sen, Principal, Gurukul Junior College, Silchar, Assam

Ms. Sarbani Bhattacharjee, Research Scholar, Department of History, North-Eastern Hill University, Shillong

Dr. Ningombam Basanta, Sr. Lecturer in History, Thambal Marik College, Oinam, Manipur

Dr. I. Wati Imchen, Department of History, Fazl Ali College, Mokokchung, Nagaland

Dr. (Mrs) Rena Laisram, Associate Professor, Department of History, Gauhati University, Guwahati

Dr. (Mrs) Priyam Goswami, Professor of History, Gauhati University, Guwahati

Mr. Sanjib Deblaskar, Editor, *Sambhar*, and a freelance researcher, Silchar, Assam.

Index

■■■